THE RELIGION OF NATURE DELINEATED

WILLIAM WOLLASTON

© 2022 Culturea Editions
Editions : Culturea (Hérault, 34)
ISBN : 9782382743393
Date de parution : avril 2022
Tous droits réservés pour tous pays

I
Of Moral Good and Evil

The foundation of religion lies in that difference between the acts of men, which distinguishes them into *good, evil, indifferent*. For if there is such a difference, there must be religion; and contra. Upon this account it is that such a long and laborious inquiry has been made after some general *idea*,[1] or some *rule*,[2] by comparing the foresaid acts with which, it might appear to which kind they respectively belong.[3] And though men have not yet agreed upon any one, yet one certainly there must be.[4] That, which I am going to propose, has always seemed to me not only evidently true, but withal so obvious and plain, that perhaps for this very reason it has not merited the notice of authors. And the use and application of it is so easy, that if things are but fairly permitted to speak for themselves their own natural language, they will, with a moderate attention, be found *themselves* to proclaim their own rectitude or obliquity; that is, whether they are disagreeable to it or not. I shall endeavor by degrees to explain my meaning.

I. *That act which may be denominated morally good or evil, must be the act of a being capable of distinguishing, choosing, and acting for himself*:[5] or more briefly, *of an intelligent and free agent*. (Because, in proper speaking, no act at all can be ascribed to that which is not endowed with these capacities. For that which cannot distinguish, cannot choose: and that which has not the opportunity, or liberty, of choosing for itself and acting accordingly from an internal principle, acts, if it acts at all, under a necessity incumbent *ab extra*. But that which acts thus, is in reality only *an instrument* in the hand of something which imposes the necessity; and cannot properly be said *to act*, but *to be acted*. The act must be the act of an agent, therefore not of his instrument.

A being under the abovementioned inabilities is, as to the morality of its acts, in the state of inert and passive matter, and can be but a *machine*: to which no language or philosophy ever ascribed ἤθη or *mores*.

II. *Those propositions are true, which express things as they are*: or, *truth is the conformity of those words or signs, by which things are expressed, to the things themselves*. Definition.

III. *A true proposition may be denied, or things may be denied to be what they are, by deeds, as well as by express words or another proposition*. It is certain there is a meaning in many acts and gestures. Everybody understands weeping,[6] laughing, shrugs, frowns, etc.; these are a sort of universal language. Applications are many times made, and a kind of dialogue maintained, only by casts of the eye and motions of the adjacent muscles.[7] And we read of feet that speak;[8] of a philosopher who answered an argument by only getting up and walking;[9] and of one who pretended to express the same sentence as many ways by gesticulation, as even Cicero himself could by all his *copia* of words and eloquence.[10] But these instances do not come up to my meaning. There are many acts of other kinds, such as constitute the character of a man's conduct in life, which have *in nature*, and would be taken by any indifferent judge, *to have a signification* and *to imply some proposition*, as plainly to be understood as if it was declared in words: and therefore if what such acts declare to be, is not, they must contradict truth, as much as any false proposition or assertion can.

If a body of soldiers, seeing another body approach, should fire upon them, would not this action declare that they were enemies? And if they were not enemies, would not this military language declare what was false? No, perhaps it may be said: this can only be called a mistake, like that which happened to the Athenians in the attack of Epipolæ,[11] or to the Carthaginians in their last encampment against Agathocles in Africa.[12] Suppose then, instead of this firing, some officer to have *said* they were enemies, when indeed they were friends: would not that sentence affirming them to be enemies be false, notwithstanding he who spoke it was mistaken? The truth or falsehood of this affirmation does not depend upon the affirmer's knowledge or ignorance, because there is a certain sense affixed to the words, which must either agree or disagree to that concerning which the affirmation is made. The thing is the very same still, if into the place of *words* be substituted *actions*. The salute here was in nature the salute of an enemy, but should have been the salute of a friend: therefore it implied a falsity. Any spectator would have understood this action as I do: for a declaration that the other were enemies. Now, what is to be understood has a meaning, and what has a meaning may be either true or false, which is as much as can be said of any verbal sentence.

When Popilius Lænas solicited to have Cicero proscribed, and that he might find him out and be his executioner,[13] would not his carriage have sufficiently signified, to anyone who was ignorant of the case, that Tully[14] either was some very bad man and deserved capital punishment, or had some way grievously injured this man (or at least had not saved his life, nor had as much reason to expect his service and good offices upon occasion, as he ever had to expect Tully's)? And all these things being false, were not his behavior and actions expressive of that which was false, or contradictions to truth? It is certain he *acted as if* those things had been true which were not true, and as if those had not been true which were true (in this consisted the fault of his ingratitude); and if he in words had *said* they were true or not true, he had done no more than *talk as if* they were so. Why then should not to *act* as if they were true or not true, when they were otherwise, contradict truth as much as to *say* they were so, when they were not so?[15]

A pertinacious objector may perhaps still say: it is the business of soldiers to defend themselves and their country from enemies, and to annoy them as opportunity permits; and self-preservation requires all men not only barely to defend themselves against aggressors, but many times also to prosecute such, and only such, as are wicked and dangerous: therefore it is natural to conclude that they are enemies against whom we see soldiers defending themselves, and those men wicked and dangerous whom we see prosecuted with zeal and ardor. Not that those acts of defending and prosecuting *speak* or *signify* so much, but conjectures are raised upon the common sense which mankind has of such proceedings. Answer: If it be natural to conclude anything from them, do they not naturally convey the notice of something to be concluded? And what is conveying the notice of anything, but notifying or signifying that thing? And then again, if this signification is natural and founded in the *common* principles and sense of mankind, is not this more than to have a meaning which results only from the use of some *particular* place or country, as that of language does?

If A should enter into a compact with B, by which he promises and engages never to do some certain thing, and after this he does that thing: in this case, it must be granted that his act interferes with his promise, and is contrary to it. Now it cannot interfere with his promise, but it must also interfere with the truth of that *proposition* which says there was such a promise made, or that there is such a compact subsisting. If this proposition be true, "A made such a certain agreement with B," it would be denied by this, "A never made any agreement with B." Why? Because the truth of this latter is inconsistent with the agreement asserted in the former. The formality of the denial, or that which makes it to be a denial, is this inconsistency. If, then, the behavior of A be inconsistent with the agreement mentioned in the former proposition, that proposition is as much denied by A's *behavior*, as it can be by the latter, or any other, proposition. Or thus: If one proposition imports or contains that which is contrary to what is contained in another, it is said to contradict this other, and denies the existence of what is contained in it. Just so if one act imports that which is contrary to the import of another, it contradicts this other, and denies its existence. In a word: if A by his actions denies the engagements to which he has subjected himself, his actions deny them; just as we say, Ptolemy by his writings denies the motion of the earth, or his writings deny it.[16]

When the question was asked, "Whose sheep are these?" the answer was, "Ægon's: for he committed them to my care"[17] (he uses and disposes of them as his). By this act Damœtas understood them to be his; and if they had not been his, but Alphondas's or Melibœus's, Ægon, by an act very intelligible to Damœtas, had expressed what was not true. What is said here is the stronger, because he who has the use and disposal of anything, has all that he can have of it; and, vice versa, he who has the all (or property) of anything, must have all the use and disposal of it. So that a man cannot more fully proclaim anything to be his than by using it, etc. But of this something more hereafter.

In the Jewish history, we read that when Abimelech saw Isaac sporting[18] with Rebecca, and taking conjugal liberties,[19] he presently knew her to be Isaac's wife; and if she had not been his wife, the case had been as in the preceding instance. If it be objected that she might have been his mistress or a harlot, I answer that so she might have been though Isaac had told him by *words* that she was his wife. And it is sufficient for my purpose, and to make acts capable of contradicting truth, if they may be allowed *to express things as plainly and determinately as words can.* Certainly Abimelech gave greater credit to that information which passed through his eye, than to that which he received by the ear;[20] and to what Isaac did, than to what he said. For Isaac had told him that she was not his wife, but his sister.[21]

A certain author[22] writes to this purpose: "If a soldier, who had taken the oath to Cæsar, should run over to the enemy, and serve him against Cæsar, and after that be taken; would he not be punished as a deserter, and a perjured villain? And if he should plead for himself that he never denied Cæsar, would it not be answered that with his tongue he did not deny him, but with his actions (or by facts) he did?" And in another place, "Let us (says he) suppose some tyrant command a Christian to burn incense to Jupiter, without adding anything of a verbal abnegation of Christ: if the Christian should do this, would it not be manifest to all that *by that by that very act he denied him*;" (and I may add: consequently denied those propositions which affirm him to be the Christ, a teacher of true religion, and the like)?[23]

When a man lives as if he had the estate which he has not, or was in other regards (all fairly cast up) what he is not, what judgment is to be passed upon him? Does not his whole conduct breathe untruth? May we not say (if the propriety of language permits), that he *lives a lie*?[24]

In common speech we say some actions are insignificant, which would not be sense if there were not some that are *significant*, that have a tendency and meaning. And this is as much as can be said of articulate sounds: that they are either significant or insignificant.[25]

It may not be improperly observed, by the way, that the significance here attributed to men's acts, proceeds not always from nature, but sometimes from custom and agreement among people,[26] as that of words and sounds mostly does. Acts of the latter kind may, in different times and places, have different or even contrary significations. The generality of Christians, when they pray, take off their hats; the Jews, when they pray[27] or say any of their Berakhot, put them on. The same thing which among Christians denotes reverence, imports irreverence among the Jews. The reason is because covering the head with a hat (if it has no influence upon one's health) is in itself an indifferent thing, and people by usage or consent may *make* it interpretable either way. Such acts seem to be adopted into their language, and may be reckoned part of it. But acts of the former kind, such as I chiefly here intend, have an unalterable signification, and can by no agreement or force ever be made to express the contrary to it. Ægon's treating the flock, and disposing of it as if it was his, can by no torture be brought to signify that it was not his. From whence it appears that *facts* express, more strongly even than words themselves;[28] or, to contradict any proposition by facts is a fuller and more effectual contradiction than can possibly be made by words only.[29] Words are but arbitrary signs[30] of our ideas, or indications of our thoughts (that word, which in one language denotes "poverty,"[31] in another denotes "riches"[32]): but *facts* may be taken as the *effects* of them, or rather as the *thoughts themselves produced into act*; as the very conceptions of the mind, brought forth and grown to maturity; and therefore as the most natural and express representations of them. And, besides this, they bear certain respects to things which are not arbitrary, but as determinate and immutable as any ratios are in mathematics. For the facts, and the things they respect, are *just what they are*, as much as any two given quantities are; and therefore the respects interceding between those must be as fixed as the ratio is, which one of these bears to the other: that is, they must remain the same, and always speak the same language, till things cease to be what they are.

I lay this down then as a fundamental maxim, *That whoever acts as if things were so, or not so, does by his acts declare, that they are so, or not so* as plainly as he could by words, and with more reality. And if the things are otherwise, his acts contradict those propositions which assert them to be as they are.[33]

IV. *No act (whether word[34] or deed) of any being to whom moral good and evil are imputable, that interferes with any true proposition or denies anything to be as it is, can be right.* For,

1. If that proposition, which is false, be wrong,[35] that act which *implies* such a proposition, or is founded in it, cannot be right, because it is the very proposition itself in practice.
2. Those propositions which are true, and express things as they are, express the *relation* between the subject and the attribute as it is; that is, this is either affirmed or denied of that according to the nature of *that relation*. And further, this relation (or, if you will, the nature of this relation) is determined and fixed by the natures of the things themselves. Therefore nothing can interfere with any proposition that is true, but it must likewise interfere with nature (the nature of the relation, and the natures of the things themselves, too), and consequently be *unnatural*, or *wrong in nature*. So very much are those gentlemen mistaken, who by *following nature* mean only complying with their bodily inclinations, though in opposition to truth or at least without any regard to it. Truth is but a conformity to nature, and to follow nature cannot be to combat truth.[36]
3. If there is a supreme being, upon whom the existence of the world depends, and nothing can be in it but what He either causes or permits to be, then to own things *to be as they are* is to own what He causes, or at least permits, *to be thus caused or permitted*: and this is to take things as He gives them, to go into His constitution of the world, and to submit to His will, revealed in the books of nature.[37] To do this, therefore, must be agreeable to His will. And if so, the contrary must be disagreeable to it, and, since (as we shall find in due time) there is a perfect rectitude in His will, certainly *wrong*.

    I desire that I may not be misunderstood in respect to the actings of wicked men. I do not say: it is agreeable to the will of God that what is *ill* done by them, should be *so* done, i.e. that they should use their liberty ill; but I say: when they have done this and committed some evil, it is agreeable to His will, that we should allow it to *have been* committed, or, it would be disagreeable to His will, that we should *deny* it to have been committed.

As the owning of things, in all our conduct, to be as they are, is direct obedience:[38] so the contrary, not to own things to be or to have been, that are or have been, or not to be what they are, is direct rebellion against Him who is the Author of nature. For it is as much as to say, "God indeed causes such a thing to be, or at least permits it, and it is; or the relation that lies between this and that, is of such a nature, that one may be affirmed of the other, etc.—this is true, but yet to me it shall not be so: I will not endure it, or act as if it were so; the laws of nature are ill-framed, nor will I mind them or what follows from them; even existence shall be nonexistence when my pleasures require." Such an impious declaration as this attends every voluntary infraction of truth.

4. Things cannot be denied to be what they are, in any instance or manner whatsoever, without contradicting axioms and truths eternal. For such are these: *everything is what it is*; *that which is done, cannot be undone*; and the like. And then if those truths be considered as having always subsisted in the Divine mind, to which they have always been true, and which differs not from the Deity himself, to do this is to act not only in opposition to His government or sovereignty, but to His nature,[39] also: which, if He be perfect, and there be nothing in Him but what is most right, must also upon this account be most wrong.

   Pardon these inadequate ways of speaking of God. You will apprehend my meaning, which perhaps may be better represented thus: If there are such things as axioms, which are and always have been immutably true, and consequently have been always known to God to be so,[40] the truth of them cannot be denied any way, either directly or indirectly, but the truth of the Divine knowledge must be denied too.

5. Designedly to treat things as being what they are not is the greatest possible absurdity. It is to put bitter for sweet, darkness for light, crooked for straight, etc. It is to subvert all science, to renounce all sense of truth, and flatly to deny the existence of anything. For nothing can be true, nothing does exist, if things are not what they are.

   To talk to a post, or otherwise treat it as if it was a man, would surely be reckoned an absurdity, if not distraction.[41] Why? because this is to treat it as being what it is not. And why should not the converse be reckoned as bad; that is, to treat a man as a post,[42] as if he had no sense, and felt not injuries which he does feel; as if to him pain and sorrow were not pain; happiness not happiness. This is what the cruel and unjust often do.

6. Lastly: To deny things to be as they are is a transgression of the great law of our nature, the law of reason. For truth cannot be opposed, but reason must be violated. But of this more in the proper place.

Much might be added here concerning the amiable nature[43] and great force[44] of truth. If I may judge by what I feel within myself, the least truth cannot be contradicted without much reluctance: even to see other men disregard it does something more than displease; it is *shocking*.

V. *What has been said of acts inconsistent with truth, may also be said of many omissions or neglects to act: that is, by these also true propositions may be denied to be true; and then those omissions, by which this is done, must be wrong for the same reasons with those assigned under the former proposition.*

Nothing can be asserted or denied by any act with regard to those things to which it bears no relation: and here no truth can be affected. And when acts *do* bear such relations to other things, as to be declaratory of something concerning them, this commonly is visible, and it is not difficult to determine whether truth suffers by them or not. Some things cannot possibly be done, but truth must be directly and positively denied; and the thing will be clear. But the cases arising from omissions are not always so well determined and plain: it is not always easy to know when, or how far, truth is violated by omitting. Here, therefore, more latitude must be allowed, and much must be left to everyone's own judgment and ingenuity.

This may be said in general: that when any truth would be denied by acting, the omitting to act can deny no truth. For no truth can be contrary to truth.[45] And there may be omissions, in other cases, that are silent as to truth. But yet there are *some* neglects, or refusals to act, which are manifestly inconsistent with it (or, with some true propositions).

We before supposed A to have engaged *not to do* some certain thing, etc.; if now, on the other side, he should by some solemn promise, oath, or other act undertake *to do* some certain thing before such a time, and he voluntarily[46] omits to do it, he would behave himself as if there had been no such promise or engagement, which is equal to denying there was any: and truth is as much contradicted in this as in the former instance.

Again, there are some ends which the nature of things and truth require us to aim at, and at which therefore if we do not aim, nature and truth are denied. If a man does not desire to prevent evils, and to be happy, he denies both his own nature and the nature and definition of happiness to be what they are. And then further, willingly to neglect the *means* leading to any such end is the same as not to propose that end, and must fall under the same censure. As retreating from any end commonly attends the not advancing towards it, and that may be considered as an act, many omissions of this kind may be turned over to the other side,[47] and brought under the foregoing proposition.

It must be confessed there is a difficulty as to the means by which we are to consult our own preservation and happiness: to know what those are, and what they are with respect to us. For our abilities and opportunities are not equal; some labor under disadvantages invincible: and our ignorance of the true natures of things, of their operations and effects in such an irregular distempered world, and of those many incidents that may happen either to further or break our measures, deprive us of certainty in these matters. But still we may judge as well as we can, and do what we can,[48] and the neglect to do this will be an omission within the reach of the proposition.

There are omissions of other kinds, which will deserve to be annumerated to these by being either total, or notorious, or upon the score of some other circumstance. It is certain I should not deny the *Phœnissæ* of Euripides to be an excellent drama by not reading it; nor do I deny Chihil-menâr to be a rare piece of antiquity by not going to see it. But, should I, having leisure, health, and proper opportunities, read nothing, nor make any inquiries in order to improve my mind and attain such knowledge as may be useful to me, I should then deny my mind to be what it is, and that knowledge to be what it is. And, if it does not appear precisely into what kind of studies this respect to truth will carry a man, preferably to all others, how far it will oblige him to continue his pursuit after knowledge, and where the discontinuance begins to be no offence against truth, he must consult his own opportunities and genius, and judge for himself as well as he can.[49] This is one of those cases which, I said before, were not so well determined.

If I give nothing to this or that poor body, to whom I am under no particular obligation, I do not by this deny them to be poor, any more than I should deny a man to have a squalid beard by not shaving him, to be nasty by not washing him, or to be lame by not taking him on my back.

Many things are here to be taken into consideration (according to the next proposition): perhaps I might encroach upon truth by *doing* this; and then I cannot by *not doing* it.[50] But if I, being of ability to afford now and then something in charity to the poor, should yet never give them anything at all, I should then certainly deny the condition of the poor to be what it is, and my own to be what it is: and thus truth would be injured. So, again,

If I should not say my prayers at such a certain hour, or in such a certain place and manner, this would not imply a denial of the existence of God, His providence, or my dependence upon Him: nay, there may be reasons, perhaps, against that particular time, place, manner. But if I should *never* pray to Him, or worship Him at all, such a total omission would be equivalent to this assertion: "There is no God who governs the world, to be adored," which, if there is such a being, must be contrary to truth. Also generally and notoriously to neglect this duty (permit me to call it so), though not quite always, will favor, if not directly proclaim, the same untruth. For certainly to worship God after this manner is only to worship him accidentally, which is to declare it a great accident that he is worshipped at all, and this approaches as near as it is possible to a total neglect. Besides, such a sparing and infrequent worshipper of the Deity betrays such a habitual disregard of Him, as will render every religious act insignificant and null.

Should I, in the last place, find a man grievously hurt by some accident, fallen down, alone, and without present help like to perish; or see his house on fire, nobody being near to help or call out: in this extremity if I do not give him my assistance immediately, I do not do it at all: and by this refusing to do it according to my ability, I deny his case to be what it is; human nature to be what it is; and even those desires and expectations, which I am conscious to myself I should have under the like misfortune, to be what they are.

VI. *In order to judge rightly what anything is, it must be considered not only what it is in itself or in one respect, but also what it may be in any other respect which is capable of being denied by facts or practice: and the whole description of the thing ought to be taken in.*

If a man steals a horse and rides away upon him, he may be said indeed, by riding him, to use him as a *horse*, but not as *the horse of another man* who gave him no licence to do this. He does not therefore consider him as being what he is, unless he takes in the respect he bears to his true owner. But it is not necessary, perhaps, to consider what he is in respect to his color, shape, or age: because the thief's riding away with him may neither affirm nor deny him to be of any particular color, etc. I say therefore, that those, and all those properties, respects, and circumstances, which may be contradicted by practice, are to be taken into consideration. For otherwise the thing to be considered is but imperfectly surveyed, and the whole compass of it being not taken in, it is taken not as being what it is, but as what it is *in part* only, and in other respects perhaps as being what it is not.

If a rich man, being upon a journey, should be robbed and stripped, it would be a second robbery and injustice committed upon him to take from him part of his then character, and to consider him only as a rich man. His character completed is *a rich man robbed and abused*, and indeed, at that time, a *poor man*[51] and distressed, though able to repay afterwards the assistance lent him.

Moreover, a man, in giving assistance of any kind to another, should consider what his own circumstances are, as well as what the other's are.[52] If they do not permit him to give it, he does not by his forbearance deny the other to want it: but if he should give it, and, by that, deny his own or his family's circumstances to be what they are, he would actually contradict truth. And since (as I have observed already) all truths are consistent, nor can anything be true any further than it is compatible with other things that are true, when both parties are placed in a right light, and the case properly stated for a judgment, the latter may indeed be truly said to want assistance, but not the assistance of the former: any more than a man who wants a guide, may be said to want a blind or a lame guide. By putting things thus may be truly known what the latter is with respect to the former.

The case becomes more difficult when a man (A) is under some promise or compact to assist another (B), and at the same time bound to consult his own happiness, provide for his family, etc., and he cannot do these if he does that, effectually. For what must A do? Here are not indeed opposite *truths*, but there are truths on opposite *sides*. I answer: though there cannot be two incompatible duties, or though two inconsistent acts cannot be both A's duty at the same time (for then his duty would be an impossibility); yet an obligation, which I will call mixed, may arise out of those differing considerations. A should assist B, but so as not to neglect himself and family, etc.; and *so* to take care of himself and family, *as* not to forget the other engagement, as well and honestly as he can. Here the importance of the truths on the one and the other side should be diligently compared, and there must in such cases be always some exception or limitation understood. It is not in man's power to promise absolutely. He can only promise as one who may be disabled by the weight and incumbency of truths not then existing.

I could here insert many instances of partial thinking which occur in authors, but I shall choose only to set down one in the margin.[53]

In short, when things are truly estimated, persons concerned, times, places,[54] ends intended,[55] and effects that naturally follow, must be added to them.

VII. *When any act would be wrong, the forbearing that act must be right; likewise when the omission of anything would be wrong, the doing of it (i.e. not omitting it) must be right.* Because *contrariorum contraria est ratio.*

VIII. *Moral good and evil are coincident with right and wrong.* For that cannot be good, which is wrong; nor that evil, which is right.

IX. *Every act therefore, of such a being as is before described, and all those omissions which interfere with truth (i.e. deny any proposition to be true, which is true; or suppose anything not to be what it is, in any regard)*[56] *are morally evil, in some degree or other; the forbearing such acts, and the acting in opposition to such omissions are morally good; and when anything may be either done, or not done, equally without the violation of truth, that thing is indifferent.*

I would have it to be minded well, that when I speak of acts inconsistent with truth, I mean *any* truth: any true proposition whatsoever, whether containing matter of speculation, or plain fact. I would have everything taken to be what in fact and truth it is.[57]

It may be of use, also, to remember that I have added those words *in some degree or other.* For neither all evil nor all good actions are equal.[58] Those truths which they respect, though they are equally true, may comprise matters of very different importance;[59] or more truths may be violated one way than another:[60] and then the crimes committed by the violation of them may be equally (one as well as the other) said to be crimes, but not *equal crimes.*[61] If A steals a book from B which was pleasing and useful to him, it is true A is guilty of a crime in not treating the book as being what it is: the book of B, who is the proprietor of it, and one whose happiness partly depends upon it; but still if A should deprive B of a good *estate*, of which he was the true owner, he would be guilty of a much greater crime. For if we suppose the book to be worth to him one pound, and the estate £10,000, that truth which is violated by depriving B of his book, is in effect violated 10,000 times by robbing him of his estate. It is the same as to repeat the theft of one pound 10,000 times over; and therefore if 10,000 thefts (or crimes) are more and all together greater than one, one equal to 10,000 must be greater too: greater than that which is but the 10,000th part of it, sure. Then, though the convenience and innocent pleasure that B found in the use of the book was a degree of happiness, yet the happiness accruing to him from the estate, by which he was supplied not only with necessaries but also with many other comforts and harmless enjoyments, vastly exceeded it. And therefore the truth violated in the former case was, "B had a property in that, which gave him such a degree of happiness:" that violated in the latter, "B had a property in that, which gave him a happiness vastly superior to the other." The violation therefore in the latter case is upon this account a vastly greater violation than in the former. Lastly, the truths violated in the former case might end in B, those in the latter may perhaps be repeated in them of his family, who subsist also by the estate and are to be provided for out of it. And these truths are very many in respect of every one of them, and all their descendents. Thus the degrees of evil or guilt are as the importance and number of truth violated.[62] I shall only add, on the other side, that the value of good actions will rise at least in proportion to the degrees of evil in the omission of them: and that therefore *they* cannot be equal, any more than the opposite evil omissions.

But let us return to that which is our main subject: the distinction between moral good and evil. Some have been so wild as to deny there is any such thing: but from what has been said here, it is manifest that there is as certainly moral good and evil as there is true and false; and that there is as natural and immutable a difference between those as between these, the difference at the bottom being indeed the same.[63] Others acknowledge that there is indeed moral good and evil, but they want some criterion, or mark, by the help of which they might know them apart. And others there are who pretend to have found that rule, by which our actions ought to be squared and may be discriminated, or that ultimate end, to which they ought all to be referred:[64] but what they have advanced is either false, or not sufficiently guarded, or not comprehensive enough, or not clear and firm,[65] or (so far as it is just) reducible to *my* rule. For

They, who reckon nothing to be good but what they call *honestum*,[66] may denominate actions according as that is, or is not, the cause[67] or end[68] of them: but then what is *honestum*?[69] Something is still wanting to measure things by, and to separate the *honesta* from the *inhonesta*.

They who place all in "following nature,"[70] if they mean by that phrase acting according to the natures of things (that is, treating things as being what they in nature are, or according to truth) say what is right. But this does not seem to be their meaning. And if it is only that a man must follow his own nature,[71] since his nature is not purely rational, but there is a part of him which he has in common with brutes, they appoint him a guide which I fear will mislead him, this being commonly more likely to prevail than the rational part. At best this talk is loose.

They who make *right reason*[72] to be the law by which our acts are to be judged, and according to their conformity to this, or deflection from it, call them lawful or unlawful, good or bad, say something more particular and precise. And, indeed, it is true that whatever will bear to be tried by right reason, is right; and that which is condemned by it, wrong. And moreover, if by "right reason" is meant that which is found by the right use of our rational faculties, this is the same with truth; and what is said by them will be comprehended in what I have said. But the manner in which they have delivered themselves is not yet explicit *enough*.[73] It leaves room for so many disputes, and opposite right-reasons, that nothing can be settled, while everyone pretends that *his* reason is right. And besides, what I have said extends farther: for we are not only to respect those truths which we discover by reasoning, but even such matiers of fact as are fairly discovered to us by our senses. We ought to regard things as being what they are, which way soever we come to the knowledge of them.

They, who, contenting themselves with superficial and transient views, deduce the difference between good and evil from the *common sense* of mankind,[74] and certain *principles*[75] that are born with us,[76] put the matter upon a very infirm foot. For it is much to be suspected there are no such innate maxims as they pretend, but that the impressions of education are mistaken for them; and besides that, the sentiments of mankind are not uniform and constant, as that we may safely trust such an important distinction upon them.[77]

They, who own nothing to be good but *pleasure*, or what they call *jucundum*, nothing evil but pain,[78] and distinguish things by their tendencies to this or that,[79] do not agree in what this pleasure is to be placed,[80] or by what methods and actings the most of it may be obtained. These are left to be questions still. As men have different tastes, different degrees of sense and philosophy, the same thing cannot be pleasant to all; and if particular actions are to be proved by this test, the morality of them will be very uncertain: the same act may be of one nature to one man, and of another to another. Besides, unless there be some strong limitation added as a fence for virtue, men will be apt to sink into gross voluptuousness, as in fact the generality of Epicurus's herd have done[81] (notwithstanding all his talk of temperance, virtue, tranquility of mind, etc.); and the bridle will be usurped by those appetites which it is a principal part of all religion, natural as well as any other, to curb and restrain. So these men say what is intelligible indeed, but what they say is false. For not all pleasures, but only such pleasure as is *true*, or happiness (of which afterwards), may be reckoned among the *fines*, or *ultima bonorum*.

He,[82] who, having considered the two extremes in men's practice, in condemning both which the world generally agrees, places virtue in the *middle*, and seems to raise an idea of it from its situation at an equal distance from the opposite extremes,[83] could only design to be understood of such virtues as *have* extremes. It must be granted indeed, that whatever declines in any degree toward either extreme, must be so far wrong or evil; and therefore that which equally (or nearly) divides the distance, and declines neither way, must be right; also, that his notion supplies us with a good direction for common use in many cases. But then, there are several obligations that can by no means be derived from it: scarce more than such as respect the virtues couched under the word "moderation." And even as to these, it is many times difficult to discern which is the middle point.[84] This the author himself was sensible of.[85]

And when his master, Plato, makes virtue to consist in such a likeness to God[86] as we are capable of (and God to be the great exemplar), he says what I shall not dispute. But since he tells us not how or by what means we may attain this likeness, we are little the wiser in point of practice: unless by it, we understand the practice of truth, God being truth, and doing nothing contrary to it.[87]

Whether any of those other foundations upon which morality has been built will hold better than these mentioned, I much question. But if the formal ratio of moral good and evil be made to consist in a conformity of men's acts to the truth of the case or the contrary, as I have here explained it, the distinction seems to be settled in a manner undeniable, intelligible, practicable. For as what is meant by *a true proposition* and *matter of fact* is perfectly understood by everybody; so will it be easy for anyone, so far as he knows any such propositions and facts, to compare not only *words*, but also *actions* with them. A very little skill and attention will serve to interpret even these, and discover whether they speak truth or not.[88]

X. *If there be moral good and evil, distinguished as before, there is religion, and such as may most properly be styled natural.* By "religion" I mean nothing else but an obligation to do (under which word I comprehend acts both of body and mind. I say, *to do*) what ought not to be omitted, and to forbear what ought not to be done. So that there must be religion if there are things of which some ought not to be done, some not to be omitted. But, that there are such, appears from what has been said concerning moral good and evil: because that which to omit would be evil, and which therefore being done would be good or well done, ought certainly by the terms to be done; and so that which being done would be evil, and implies such absurdities and rebellion against the supreme being as are mentioned under proposition IV, ought most undoubtedly not to be done. And then, since there is religion, which follows from the distinction between moral good and evil; since this distinction is founded in the respect which men's acts bear to truth; and since no proposition can be true which expresses things otherwise than as they are in nature: since things are so, there must be religion, which is founded in nature, and may upon that account be most properly and truly called the "religion of nature" or "natural religion;" the great law of which religion, the law of nature, or rather (as we shall afterwards find reason to call it) of the Author of nature is,

XI. *That every intelligent, active, and free being should so behave himself as by no act to contradict truth; or, that he should treat everything as being what it is.*[89]

Objections, I am sensible, may be made to almost anything;[90] but, I believe, none to what has been here advanced, but such as may be answered. For to consider a thing as being something else than what it is, or (which is the same) not to consider it as being what it is, is an absurdity indefensible. However, for a specimen, I will set down a few. Let us suppose some gentleman who has not sufficiently considered these matters, amidst his freedoms, and in the gaiety of humor, to talk after some such manner as this: "If everything must be treated as being what it is, what rare work will follow? For,

1. "To treat my enemy as such is to kill him, or revenge myself soundly upon him.
2. "To use a creditor who is a spendthrift, or one that knows not the use of money, or has no occasion for it, as such, is not to pay him. Nay further,

3. "If I want money, don't I act according to truth if I take it from somebody else, to supply my own wants? And more, do not I act contrary to truth if I do not?
4. "If one, who plainly appears to have a design of killing another, or doing him some great mischief, if he can find him, should ask me where he is, and I know where he is; may not I, to save life, say I do not know, though that be false?
5. "At this rate I may not, in a frolic, break a glass, or burn a book, because forsooth to use these things, as being what they are, is to drink out of the one, not to break it; and to read the other, not burn it.
6. "Lastly, how shall a man *know* what is true: and if he can find out truth, may he not want the power of acting agreeably to it?"

To the first objection it is easy to reply from what has been already said. For if the objector's enemy, whom we will call E, was *nothing more* than his enemy, there might be some force in the objection; but since he may be considered as something else besides that, he must be used according to what he is in other respects, as well as in that from which he is denominated the objector's (or O's) enemy. For E, in the first place, is a *man*; and as such may claim the benefit of common humanity, whatever that is: and if O denies it to him, he wounds truth in a very sensible part. And then, if O and E are fellow-citizens, living under the same government and subject to laws, which are so many common covenants, limiting the behavior of one man to another, and by which E is exempt from all private violence in his body, estate, etc., O cannot treat E as being what he is, unless he treats him also as one who, by common consent, is under such a protection. If he does otherwise, he denies the existence of the foresaid laws and public compacts, contrary to truth. And besides, O should act with respect to *himself* as being what he is: a man himself, in such or such circumstances, and one who has given up all right to private revenge (for that is the thing meant here). If truth, therefore, be observed, the result will be this: O must treat E as *something compounded* of a man, a fellow-citizen, and an enemy, all three; that is, he must only prosecute him in such a way as is agreeable to the statutes and methods which the society have obliged themselves to observe. And even as to legal prosecutions, there may be many things still to be considered. For E may show himself an enemy to O in things that fall under the cognizance of law, which yet may be of moment and importance to him or not. If they are such things as really affect the safety or happiness of O or his family, then he will find himself obliged, in duty and submission to truth, to take refuge in the laws, and to punish E, or obtain satisfaction, and at least security for the future, by the means there prescribed. Because if he does not, he denies the nature and sense of happiness to be what they are; the obligations, which, perhaps we shall show hereafter, he is under to his family,[91] to be what they are; a dangerous and wicked enemy to be dangerous and wicked; the end of laws, and society itself, to be the safety and good of its members, by preventing injuries, punishing offenders, etc., which it will appear to be when that matter comes before us. But if the enmity of E rises not beyond trifling or more tolerable instances, then O might act against truth if he should be at more charge or hazard in prosecuting E than he can afford, or the thing lost or in danger is worth; should treat one that is an enemy in little things, or a little enemy, as a great one; or should deny to make some allowances, and forgive such peccadillos, as the common frailty of human nature makes it necessary for us mutually to forgive, if we will live together. Lastly, in cases of which the laws of the place take no notice, truth and nature would be sufficiently observed if O should keep a vigilant eye upon the steps of his adversary, and take the most prudent measures that are compatible with the character of a private person, either to assuage the malice of E, or prevent the effects of it; or perhaps, if he should only not use him as a friend.[92] For this if he should do, notwithstanding the rants of some men, he would cancel the natural differences of things, and confound truth with untruth.

The debtor in the second objection, if he acts as he says there, does, in the first place, make himself the *judge* of his creditor, which is what he is not. For he lays him under a heavy sentence, an incapacity in effect of having any estate, or any more estate. In the next place, he arrogates to himself more than can be true: that he perfectly knows not only what his creditor and his circumstances are, but also what they ever will be hereafter. He that is now weak, or extravagant, or very rich, may for ought he knows become otherwise. And, which is to be considered above all, he directly denies the money, which is the creditor's, to be the creditor's. For it is supposed to be owing or due to him (otherwise he is no creditor); and if it be due to him, he has a right to it; and if he has a right to it, *of right* it is his (or, it is *his*). But the debtor, by detaining it, uses it as if it was his own, and therefore not the other's: contrary to truth. To pay a man what is due to him does not deny that he who pays may think him extravagant, etc., or any other truth; that act has no such signification. It only signifies that he who pays thinks it due to the other, or that it is his: and *this* it naturally does signify. For he might pay the creditor without having any other thought relating to him, but would not without this.

Answer to objection the 3rd: Acting according to truth, as that phrase is used in the objection, is not the thing required by my rule; but, so to act that *no truth* may be *denied* by any act. Not taking from another man his money by violence is a forbearance, which does not signify that I do not want money, or which denies any truth. But taking it denies that to be his, which (by the supposition) is his. The former is only, as it were, silence, which denies nothing: the latter, a direct and loud assertion of a falsity; the former, what can contradict no truth, because the latter does. If a man wants money through his own extravagance and vice, there can be no pretence for making another man to pay for his wickedness or folly. We will suppose, therefore, the man who wants money to want it for necessaries, and to have incurred this want through some misfortune, which he could not prevent. In this case, which is put as strong as can be for the objector, there are ways of expressing this want, or acting according to it, without trespassing upon truth. The man may by honest labor and industry seek to supply his wants; or he may apply as a supplicant,[93] not as an enemy or robber, to such as can afford to relieve him; or if his want is very pressing, to the first persons he meets, whom truth will oblige to assist him according to their abilities; or he may do *anything but* violate truth,[94] which is a privilege of a vast scope, and leaves him many resources. And such a behavior as this is not only agreeable to his case, and expressive of it in a way that is natural, but he would deny it to be what it is if he did not act thus. If there is no way in the world by which he may help himself without the violation of truth (which can scarce be supposed. If there is no other way) he must even take it as his fate.[95] Truth will be truth, and must retain its character and force, let his case be what it will. Many things might be added. The man, from whom this money is to be taken, will be proved (section VI) to have a right to defend himself and his, and not suffer it to be taken from him; perhaps he may stand as much in need of it, as the other, etc.

Answer to objection the 4th: It is certain, in the first place, that nothing may willingly be done which in any manner promotes murder: whoever is accessory to that, offends against many truths of great weight. 2. You are not obliged to answer the *furioso*'s question. Silence here would contradict no truth. 3. No one can tell, in strict speaking, where another is, if he is not within his view. Therefore, you may *truly* deny that you know where the man is. Lastly, if by not discovering him you should endanger your life (and this is the hardest circumstance that can be taken into the objection), the case then would be the same as if the inquirer should say, "If you do not murder such a one, I will murder you." And then be sure, you must not commit murder, but must defend yourself against this, as against other dangers, against Banditti, etc., as well as you can. Though merely to deny truth by words (I mean, when they are not productive of facts to follow, as in judicial transactions, bearing witness, or passing sentence) is not equal to a denial by facts; though an abuse of language is allowable in this case, if ever in any; though all sins against truth are not equal, and certainly a little trespassing upon it in the present case, for the good of all parties,[96] as little a one as any; and though one might look on a man in such a fit of rage as mad, and therefore talk to him not as a man but a madman; yet truth is sacred,[97] and there are other ways of coming off with innocence: by giving timely notice to the man in danger, calling in assistance, or taking the advantage of some seasonable incident.[98]

The 5th objection seems to respect inanimate things, which, if we must treat according to what they are, it is insinuated we shall become obnoxious to many trifling obligations, such as are there mentioned. To this I answer thus: If the glass be nothing else but an useful drinking-glass, and these words fully express what it is, to treat it accordingly is indeed to drink out of it, when there is occasion and it is truly useful, and to break it designedly is to do what is wrong.[99] For that is to handle it as if it neither was useful to the objector himself, nor could be so to anyone else, contrary to the description of it. But if there be any *reason* for breaking the glass, then something is wanting to declare fully what it is. As, if the glass be poisoned: for then it becomes a "poisoned drinking-glass," and to break or destroy it is to use it according to this true description of it. Or, if by breaking it anything is to be obtained which more than countervails the loss of it, it becomes a glass with that circumstance: and then for the objector to break it, if it be his own, is to use it according to what it is. And, if it should become, by some circumstance, useless only, though there should be no reason for breaking it, yet if there be none against it, the thing will be indifferent and matter of liberty. This answer, *mutatis mutandis*, may be adapted to other things of this kind, books, or anything else. As the usefulness or excellence of some books renders them worthy of immortality, and of all our care to secure them to posterity,[100] so some may be used, more like what they are, by tearing or burning them than by preserving or reading them: the number of which, large enough already, I wish you may not think to be increased by this which I here send you.

Here two things ought to be regarded:

1. That though to act against truth in any case is wrong, yet, the degrees of guilt varying with the importance of things, in some cases the importance one way or the other may be so little as to render the crime evanescent or almost nothing.[101] And,
2. that inanimate beings cannot be considered as capable of wrong treatment, if the respect they bear to living beings is separated from them. The drinking-glass before-mentioned could not be considered as such, or be what it now is, if there was no drinking animal to own and use it. Nothing can be of any importance to that thing itself, which is void of all life and perception. So that when we compute what such things are, we must take them as being what they are in reference to things that have life.

The last and most material objection, or question rather, shall be answered by and by. In the meantime, I shall only say that if in any particular case truth is inaccessible, and after due inquiry it does not appear what, or how, things are, then this will be true: that the case or thing under consideration is doubtful; and to act agreeably unto this truth is to be not opinionative nor obstinate, but modest, cautious, docile, and to endeavor to be on the safer side. Such behavior shows the case to be as it is. And as to the want of power to act agreeably to truth, that cannot be known till trials are made: and if anyone does try, and do his endeavor, he may take to himself the satisfaction, which he will find in section IV.

II
OF HAPPINESS

That which demands to be next considered, is *happiness*: as being in itself most considerable; as abetting the cause of truth; and as being indeed so nearly allied to it, that they cannot well be parted. We cannot pay the respects due to one, unless we regard the other. Happiness must not be denied to be what it is, and it is by the practice of truth that we aim at that happiness which is true.

In the few following propositions I shall not only give you my idea of it, but also subjoin some observations which, though perhaps not necessary here, we may sometime hereafter think no loss of time or labor to have made *en passant*: such as men of science would call some of them *porismata*, or corollaries, and some *scholia*, I shall take them as they fall in my way promiscuously.

I. *Pleasure is a consciousness of something agreeable; pain of the contrary: and vice versa, the consciousness of anything agreeable is pleasure; of the contrary pain.* For as nothing that is agreeable to us can be painful at the same time, and as such; nor anything disagreeable pleasant, by the terms; so neither can anything agreeable be for that reason (because it is agreeable) not pleasant, nor anything disagreeable not painful, in some measure or other.

Observation 1: Pleasures and pains are proportionable to the perceptions and sense of their subjects, or the persons affected with them. For consciousness and perception cannot be separated: because as I do not perceive what I am not conscious to myself I do perceive, so neither can I be conscious of what I do not perceive, or of more or less than what I do perceive. And therefore, since the degrees of pleasure or pain must be answerable to the consciousness which the party affected has of them, they must likewise be as the degrees of perception are.

Observation 2: Whatever increases the power of perceiving, renders the percipient more susceptive of pleasure or pain. This is an immediate consequence, and to add more is needless, unless, that among the means by which perceptions and the inward sense of things may in many cases be heightend and increased, the principal are reflection and the practice of thinking. As I cannot be conscious of what I do not perceive, so I do not perceive that which I do not advert upon. That which makes me feel, makes me advert. Every instance therefore of consciousness and perception is attended with an act of advertence, and as the more the perceptions are, the more are the advertences or reflections; so, vice versa, the more frequent or intense the acts of advertence and reflection are, the more consciousness there is, and the stronger is the perception. Further, all perceptions are produced in time; time passes by moments; there can be but one moment present at once; and therefore all present perception, considered without any relation to what is past, or future, may be looked upon as momentaneous only. In this kind of perception, the percipient perceives as if he had not perceived anything before, nor had anything perceptible to follow. But in reflection there is a repetition of what is past, and an anticipation of that which is apprehended as yet to come: there is a connection of past and future, which by this are brought into the sum, and superadded to the present or momentaneous perceptions. Again, by reflecting we practice our capacity of apprehending; and this practicing will increase and, as it were, extend that capacity to a certain degree. Lastly, reflection does not only accumulate moments past and future to those that are present, but even in their passage it seems to multiply them. For time, as well as space, is capable of indeterminate division, and the finer or nicer the advertence or reflection is, into the more parts is the time divided, which, while the mind considers those parts as so many several moments, is in effect rendered by this so much the longer. And to this experience agrees.

Observation 3: The causes of pleasure and pain are relative things, and, in order to estimate truly their effect upon any particular subject, they ought to be drawn into the degrees of perception in that subject. When the cause is of the same kind, and acts with an equal force, if the perception of one person be equal to that of another, what they perceive must needs be equal. And so it will be likewise, when the forces in the producing causes and the degrees of perception in the sentients are reciprocal. For (which does not seem to be considered by the world, and therefore ought the more particularly to be noted) if the cause of pleasure or pain should act but half as much upon A as it does upon B, yet if the perceptivity of A be double to that of B, the sum of their pleasures or pains will be equal. In other cases they will be unequal. As, if the *causa dolorifica* should act with the same impetus on C with which it acts upon D, yet if C had only two degrees of perception and D had three, the pain sustained by D would be half as much more as that of C, because he would perceive, or feel, the acts and impressions of the cause more by so much. If it should act with twice the force upon D which it acts with upon C, then the pain of C would be to that of D as 2 to 6: i.e. as one degree of force multiplied by two degrees of perception to two degrees of force multiplied by three of perception. And so on.

Observation 4: Men's respective happinesses or pleasures ought to be valued as they are to the *persons themselves* whose they are, or according to the thoughts and sense which *they* have of them: not according to the estimate put upon them by other people, who have no authority to judge of them nor can know what they are, may compute by different rules, have less sense, be in different circumstances,[102] or such as guilt has rendered partial to themselves. If that prince who, having plenty and flocks many, yet ravished the poor man's single ewe-lamb out of his bosom, reckoned the poor man's loss to be not greater than the loss of one of his lambs would have been to him, he must be very defective in moral arithmetic, and little understood the doctrine of proportion. Every man's happiness is *his* happiness, what it is to him; and the loss of it is answerable to the degrees of his perception, to his manner of taking things, to his wants and circumstances.[103]

Observation 5: How judicious and wary ought princes, lawgivers, judges, juries, and even masters to be! They ought not to consider so much what a stout, resolute, obstinate, hardened criminal may bear, as what the weaker sort, or at least (if that can be known) the persons immediately concerned can bear: that is, what any punishment would be to them. For it is certain: all criminals are not of the former kind, and therefore should not be used as if they were. Some are drawn into crimes which may render them obnoxious to public justice, they scarce know how themselves; some fall into them through necessity, strength of temptation, despair, elasticity of spirits and a sudden eruption of passion, ignorance of laws, want of good education, or some natural infirmity or propension; and some who are really innocent are oppressed by the iniquity or mistakes of judges, witnesses, juries, or perhaps by the power and zeal of a faction with which their sense or their honesty has not permitted them to join. What a difference must there be between the sufferings of a poor wretch—sensible of his crime or misfortune, who would give a world for his deliverance if he had it—and those of a sturdy veteran in roguery; between the apprehensions, tears, faintings of the one, and the brandy and oaths of the other; in short, between a tender nature and a brickbat!

Observation 6: In general, all persons ought to be very careful and tender where any other is concerned. Otherwise they may do they know not what. For no man can tell, by himself, or any other way, how another may be affected.

Observation 7: There cannot be an equal distribution of rewards and punishments by any stated human laws.[104] Because (among other reasons) the same thing is rarely either the same gratification or the same punishment to different persons.

Observation 8: The sufferings of brutes are not like the sufferings of men.[105] They perceive by moments, without reflection upon past or future, upon causes, circumstances, etc.

Time and life without thinking are next neighbors to *nothing*: to no-time and no-life.[106] And therefore, to kill a brute is to deprive him of a life, or a remainder of time, that is equal to little more than nothing: though this may perhaps be more applicable to some animals than to others. That which is chiefly to be taken care of, in this matter, is that the brute may not be killed unnecessarily; when it is killed, that it may have as few moments of pain as may be;[107] and that no young be left to languish. So much by the way here.

II. *Pain considered in itself is a real evil, pleasure a real good.* I take this as a *postulatum* that will, without difficulty, be granted. Therefore,

III. *By the general idea of good and evil the one (pleasure) is in itself desirable, the other (pain) to be avoided.* What is here said, respects mere pleasure and pain, abstracted from all circumstances, consequences, etc. But, because there are some of these generally adhering to them, and such as enter so deep into their nature that, unless these be taken in, the full and true character of the other cannot be had, nor can it therefore be known what happiness is, I must proceed to some other propositions relating to this subject.

IV. *Pleasure compared with pain may either be equal, or more, or less: also pleasures may be compared with other pleasures,*[108] *and pains with pains.* Because all the moments of the pleasure must bear some respect, or be in some ratio, to all the moments of pain—as also all the degrees of one to all the degrees of the other—and so must those of one pleasure, or one pain, be to those of another. And if the degrees of intenseness be multiplied by the moments of duration, there must still be some ratio of the one product to the other.

That this proposition is true, appears from the general conduct of mankind; though in some particulars they may err and wrong themselves, some more, some less. For what does all this hurry of business, what do all the labors and travels of men tend to, but to gain such advantages as they think do exceed all their trouble? What are all their abstinences and self-denials for, if they do not think some pleasures less than the pain that would succeed them? Do not the various methods of life show that men prefer one sort of pleasure to another, and submit to one sort of pain rather than to have another? And within ourselves we cannot but find an indifference as to many things, not caring whether we have the pain with the pleasure obtained by it, or miss the pleasure, being excused from the pain.

V. *When pleasures and pains are equal, they mutually destroy each other; when the one exceeds, the excess gives the true quantity of pleasure or pain.* For nine degrees of pleasure, less by nine degrees of pain, are equal to nothing; but nine degrees of one, less by three degrees of the other, give six of the former net and true.

VI. *As, therefore, there may be true pleasure and pain: so there may be some pleasures which, compared with what attends or follows them, not only may vanish into nothing, but may even degenerate into pain, and ought to be reckoned as pains;*[109] *and, vice versa, some pains that may be annumerated to pleasures.* For the *true quantity of pleasure* differs not from that *quantity of true pleasure*; or, it is so much of that kind of pleasure which is *true* (clear of all discounts and future payments); nor can the true quantity of pain not be the same with that quantity of true or mere pain. Then the man who enjoys three degrees of such pleasure as will bring upon him nine degrees of pain, when three degrees of pain are set off to balance and sink the three of pleasure, can have remaining to him only six degrees of pain: and into these therefore is his pleasure finally resolved. And so the three degrees of pain which anyone endures to obtain nine of pleasure, end in six of the latter. By the same manner of computing, some pleasures will be found to be the loss of pleasure, compared with greater; and some pains, the alleviation of pain, because by undergoing them greater are evaded.[110] Thus the natures of pleasures and pains are varied, and sometimes transmuted—which ought never to be forgot.

Nor this neither: As, in the sense of most men, I believe, a little pain will weigh against a great deal of pleasure,[111] so perhaps there may be some pains which exceed all pleasures; that is, such pains as no man would choose to suffer for any pleasure whatever, or at least any that we know of in this world. So that it is possible the difference, or excess of pain, may rise so high as to become immense, and then the pleasure to be set against that pain will be but a point, or cypher: a quantity of no value.

VII. *Happiness differs not from the true quantity of pleasure; unhappiness of pain. Or: any being may be said to be so far happy, as his pleasures are true, etc.* That cannot be the happiness of any being, which is bad for him; nor can happiness be disagreeable. It must be something, therefore, that is both agreeable and *good* for the possessor. Now, present pleasure is for the present indeed agreeable; but if it be not true, and he who enjoys it must pay more for it than it is worth, it cannot be for his good, or good for him. This therefore cannot be his *happiness*. Nor, again, can that pleasure be reckoned happiness, for which one pays the full price in pain: because these are quantities which mutually destroy each other. But yet since happiness is something which, by the general idea of it, must be desirable, and therefore agreeable, it must be some kind of pleasure:[112] and this, from what has been said, can only be such pleasure as is true. That only can be both agreeable and good for him. And thus everyone's happiness will be as his true quantity of pleasure.

One that loves to make objections may demand here whether there may not be happiness without pleasure: whether a man may not be said to be happy in respect to those evils which he escapes, and yet knows nothing of; and whether there may not be such a thing as *negative* happiness. I answer: an exemption from misfortunes and pains is a high privilege, though we should not be sensible what those misfortunes or dangers are from which we are delivered, and in the larger use of the word may be styled a happiness. Also, the absence of pain or unhappiness may perhaps be called negative happiness, since the meaning of that phrase is known. But, in proper speaking, happiness always includes something positive. For *mere* indolence resulting from insensibility, or joined with it, if it be happiness, is a happiness infinitely diminished: that is, it is no more a happiness than it is an unhappiness; upon the confine of both, but neither. At best, it is but the happiness of stocks and stones:[113] and to these I think happiness can hardly be, in strictness, allowed. 'Tis the privilege of a stock to be what it is, rather than to be a miserable being: this we are sensible of, and therefore, joining this privilege with our own sense of it, we call it happiness; but this is what it is in our manner of apprehending it, not what it is in the stock itself. A sense, indeed, of being free from pains and troubles is attended with happiness: but then the happiness flows from the sense of the case, and is a *positive* happiness. While a man reflects upon his negative happiness, as it is called, and enjoys it, he makes it positive: and perhaps a sense of immunity from the afflictions and miseries, everywhere so obvious to our observation, is one of the greatest pleasures in this world.

VIII. *That being may be said to be ultimately happy, in some degree or other, the sum total of whose pleasures exceeds the sum of all his pains:* or, ultimate happiness is the sum of happiness, or true pleasure, at the foot of the account. And so, on the other side, *that being may be said to be ultimately unhappy, the sum of all whose pains exceeds that of all his pleasures.*

IX. *To make itself happy is a duty, which every being, in proportion to its capacity, owes to itself; and that which every intelligent being may be supposed to aim at, in general.*[114] For happiness is some quantity of true pleasure: and that pleasure which I call "true," may be considered by itself, and so will be justly desirable (according to propositions II, and III). On the contrary, unhappiness is certainly to be avoided, because being a quantity of mere pain, it may be considered by itself as a real, mere evil, etc., and because if I am obliged to pursue happiness, I am at the same time obliged to recede, as far as I can, from its contrary. All this is self-evident. And hence it follows, that,

X. *We cannot act, with respect to either ourselves or other men, as being what we and they are, unless both are considered as beings susceptive of happiness and unhappiness, and naturally desirous of the one and averse to the other.* Other animals may be considered after the same manner in proportion to their several degrees of apprehension.

But, that the nature of happiness and the road to it, which is so very apt to be mistaken, may be better understood—and true pleasures more certainly distinguished from false—the following propositions must still be added:

XI. *As the true and ultimate happiness of no being can be produced by anything that interferes with truth and denies the natures of things, so neither can the practice of truth make any being ultimately unhappy.* For that which contradicts nature and truth, opposes the will of the Author of nature (whose existence, etc., I shall prove afterwards); and to suppose that an inferior being may, in opposition to His will, *break through* the constitution of things, and by so doing make himself happy, is to suppose that being more potent than the Author of nature, and consequently more potent than the author of the nature and power of that very being himself, which is absurd. And as to the other part of the proposition, it is also absurd to think that, by the constitution of nature and will of its author, any being should be finally miserable only for conforming himself to truth, and owning things and the relations lying between them to be what they are. It is much the same as to say God has made it natural to contradict nature, or unnatural, and therefore punishable, to act according to nature and reality. If such a blunder (excuse the boldness of the word) could be, it must come either through a defect of power in Him to cause a better and more equitable scheme, or from some delight which he finds in the misery of his dependents. The former cannot be ascribed to the First cause, who is the fountain of power; nor the latter to Him who gives so many proofs of his goodness and beneficience. Many beings may be said to be happy, and there are none of us all who have not many enjoyments;[115] whereas, did he delight in the infelicity of those beings which depend upon Him, it must be natural to Him to make them unhappy, and then not one of them would be otherwise in any respect. The world in that case, instead of being such a beautiful, admirable system, in which there is only a mixture of evils, could have been only a scene of mere misery, horror, and torment.

That either the enemies of truth (wicked men) should be ultimately happy, or the religious observers of it (good men) ultimately unhappy, is such injustice, and an evil so great, that sure no Manichean will allow such a superiority of his evil principle over the good, as is requisite to produce and maintain it.

XII. *The genuine happiness of every being must be something that is not incompatible with, or destructive of, its nature,*[116] *or the superior or better part of it, if it be mixed.* For instance, nothing can be the true happiness of a *rational* being, that is inconsistent with *reason*. For all pleasure, and therefore be sure all clear pleasure and true happiness, must be something agreeable (proposition I): and nothing can be agreeable to a reasoning nature, or (which is the same) to the reason of that nature, which is repugnant and disagreeable to reason. If anything becomes agreeable, to a rational being, which is not agreeable to reason, it is plain his reason is lost, his nature depressed, and that he now lists himself among irrationals, at least as to that particular. If a being finds pleasure in anything unreasonable, he has an unreasonable pleasure; but a rational nature can like nothing of that kind without a contradiction to itself. For to do this would be to act as if it was the contrary to what it is. Lastly, if we find hereafter that whatever interferes with reason, interferes with truth, and to contradict either of them is the same thing, then what has been said under the former proposition does also confirm this: as what has been said in proof of this, does also confirm the former.

XIII. *Those pleasures are true, and to be reckoned into our happiness, against which there lies no reason.* For when there is no reason against any pleasure, there is always one for it,[117] included in the term. So when there is no reason for undergoing pain (or venturing it), there is one against it.

Observation: There is therefore no necessity for men to torture their inventions in finding out arguments to justify themselves in the pursuits after worldly advantages and enjoyments, provided that neither these enjoyments, nor the means by which they are attained, contain the violation of any truth, by being unjust, immoderate, or the like.[118] For in this case there is no reason why we should not desire them, and a direct one why we should, viz. because they are enjoyments.

XIV. To conclude this section: *The way to happiness and the practice of truth incur the one into the other.*[119] For no being can be styled happy, that is not ultimately so: because if all his pains exceed all his pleasures, he is so far from being happy that he is a being unhappy or miserable, in proportion to that excess. Now, by proposition XI, nothing can produce the ultimate happiness of any being, which interferes with truth; and therefore, whatever does produce that, must be something which is consistent and coincident with this.

Two things then (but such as are met together, and embrace each other), which are to be religiously regarded in all our conduct, are *truth* (of which in the preceding section) and *happiness* (that is, such pleasures as accompany or follow the practice of truth, or are not inconsistent with it, of which I have been treating in this). And as that religion, which arises from the distinction between moral good and evil, was called *natural*, because grounded upon truth and the natures of things; so perhaps may that too, which proposes happiness for its end, inasmuch as it proceeds upon that difference which there is between true pleasure and pain, which are physical (or *natural*) good and evil. And since both these unite so amicably, and are at last the same, here is *one* religion which may be called natural upon *two* accounts.

III
OF REASON, AND THE WAYS OF DISCOVERING TRUTH

My manner of thinking, and an objection formerly made, oblige me in the next place to say something concerning the means of knowing what is true: whether there are any that are sure, and which one may safely rely upon. For if there be not, all that I have written is an amusement to no purpose. Besides, as this will lead me to speak of reason, etc., some truths may here (as some did in the former section) fall in our way, which may be profitable upon many occasions; and what has been already asserted, will also be further confirmed.

I. *An intelligent being, such as is mentioned before, must have some immediate objects of his understanding, or at least a capacity of having such.* For if there be no object of his intellect, he is intelligent of nothing, or not intelligent. And if there are no immediate objects, there can be none at all: because every object must be such (an object) either in itself immediately, or by the intervention of another which is immediate, or of several, one of which must at least be immediate.

II. *An intelligent being, among the immediate objects of his mind, may have some that are abstract and general.* I shall not at present inquire how he comes by them (it matters not how), since this must be true if there is any such thing as a rational being. For, that reason is something different from the knowledge of particulars may appear from hence: because it is not confined to particular things or cases. What is reason in one instance, is so in another. What is reasonable with respect to Quinctius, is so in respect of Nævius.[120] Reason is performed in *species*. A rational being, therefore, must have some of these *species* (I mean specific and abstract *ideas*) to work with, or some superior method, such as perhaps some higher order of reasoners may have but we have not.

The knowledge of a particular *idea* is only the particular knowledge of that idea or thing: there it ends. But *reason* is something universal, a kind of general instrument, applicable to particular things and cases as they occur. We reason about particulars, or from them; but not *by* them.

In fact we find within ourselves many logical, metaphysical, mathematical ideas, no one of which is limited to any particular or individual thing—but they comprehend whole classes and kinds. And it is by the help of these that we reason and demonstrate. So that we know, from within ourselves, that intelligent beings not only may have such abstract ideas as are mentioned in the proposition, but that some actually have them: which is enough for my purpose.

III. *Those ideas or objects that are immediate, will be adequately and truly known to that mind whose ideas they are.* For ideas can be no further the ideas of any mind, than that mind has (or may have) a perception of them: and therefore that mind must perceive the whole of them, which is to know them adequately.

Again: these ideas being immediate, nothing (by the term) can intervene to increase, diminish, or any way alter them. And to say the mind does not know them truly, implies a contradiction, because it is the same as to say that they are misrepresented: that is, that there are intervening and misrepresenting ideas.

And lastly: there cannot be an immediate perception of that which is not; nor therefore of any immediate object otherwise than as it is. We have indeed many times wrong notions, and misperceptions of things: but then these things are not the immediate objects. They are things, which are notified to us by the help of organs and media, which may be vitiated, or perhaps are defective at best, and incapable of transmitting things as they are in themselves, and therefore occasion imperfect and false images. But then, even in this case, those images and ideas that are immediate to the percipient are perceived as they are: and that is the very reason why the originals, which they should exhibit truly, but do not, are not perceived as they are. In short, I only say the mind must know its own *immediate ideas*.

IV. *What has been said of these ideas which are immediate, may be said also of those relations or respects which any of those ideas bear immediately each to other: they must be known immediately and truly.* For if the relation be immediate, the ideas cannot subsist without it; it is of their nature: and therefore they cannot be known adequately, but this must be known too. They are in this respect like the *ideas* of whole and part. The one cannot be without the other: nor either of them not discover that relation by which the one must be always bigger and the other less.

To say no more, we may satisfy ourselves of the truth of this, as well as of the foregoing propositions, from the experiences of our own minds, where we find many relations that are immediately seen, and of which it is not in our power to doubt.[121] We are conscious of a knowledge that consists in the intuition of these relations. Such is the evidence of those truths, which are usually called axioms, and perhaps of some short demonstrations.

V. *Those relations or respects which are not immediate, or apparent at the first view, may many times be discovered by intermediate relations, and with equal certainty.* If the ratio of B to D does not instantly show itself, yet if the ratio of B to C[122] does, and that of C to D,[123] from hence the ratio of B to D[124] is known also. And if the mean quantities were ever so many, the same thing would follow; provided the reason of every quantity to that which follows next in the series be known. For the truth of this I vouch the mathematicians:[125] as I might all, that know any science, for the truth of the proposition in general. For thus theorems and derivative truths are obtained.

VI. *If a proposition be true, it is always so, in all the instances and uses to which it is applicable.* For otherwise it must be both true and false. Therefore

VII. *By the help of truths already known, more may be discovered.* For

1. Those inferences, which arise presently from the application of general truths to the particular things and cases contained under them, must be just. E.g. "The whole is

bigger than a part": therefore A (some particular thing) is more than half A. For it is plain that A is contained in the *idea* of whole, as half A is in that of part. So that if the antecedent proposition be true, the consequent, which is included in it, follows immediately, and must also be true. The former cannot be true unless the other be so too. What agrees to the genus, species, definition, whole, must agree to the species, individuals, thing defined, the part. The existence of an effect infers directly that of a cause; of one correlate that of the other; and so on. And what is said here holds true (by the preceding proposition) not only in respect of axioms and first truths, but also and equally of theorems and other general truths, when they are once known. These may be capable of the like applications; and the truth of such consequences as are made by virtue of them, will always be as evident as that of those theorems themselves.

2. All those conclusions which are derived through mean propositions that are true, and by just inferences, will be as true as those from which they are derived. My meaning is this: every just consequence is founded in some known truth, by virtue of which one thing follows from another, after the manner of steps in an algebraic operation; and if inferences are so founded, and just, the things inferred must be true, if they are made from true premises.

Let this be the form of an argument. M = P: S = M: *ergo* S = P. Here if S = M be false, nothing is concluded at all: because the middle proposition is in truth not S = M, but perhaps S = M*a*, which is foreign to the purpose. If S = M be true, but M = P false, then the conclusion will indeed be a right conclusion from those premises: but they cannot show that S = P, because the first proposition, if it was expressed according to truth, would be M*e* = P, which is another thing, and has no place in the argument. But if these two propositions are both true, M = P, S = M, then it will not only be rightly concluded, but also true, that S = P. For the second or middle proposition does so connect the other two, by taking in due manner a term from each of them, (or to speak with the logicians, by separately comparing the predicate or *major* term of the conclusion with the *medium* in the first proposition, and the subject or *minor* term with it in the second), that if the first and second are true, the third must be so likewise, all being indeed no more than this: P = M = S. For here the inference is just, by what goes before, being founded in some such truth as this, and resulting immediately from the application of it, *Quæ eidem æqualia sunt, et inter se sunt æqualia*; or *Quæ conveniunt in eodem tertio, etiam inter se conveniunt*; or the like.[126] Now if an inference thus made is justifiable, another, made after the same manner, when the truth discovered by it is made one of the premises, must be so too; and so must another after that; and so on. And if the last, and all the intermediate inferences, be as right as the first is supposed to be, it is no matter to what length the process is carried. All the parts of it being locked together by truth, the last result is derived through such a succession of mean propositions as render its title to our assent not worse by being long.

Since all the forms of true syllogisms may be proved to conclude rightly, all the advances made in the syllogistic method, toward the discovery or confirmation of truth, are so many instances and proofs of what is here asserted. So also are the performances of the mathematicians. From some self-evident truths and a few easy theorems, which they set out with at first, to what immense lengths, and through what a train of propositions, have they propagated knowledge! How numerous are their theorems and discoveries now, so far once out of human ken!

I do not enter so far into the province of the logician as to take notice of the difference there is between the analytic and synthetic methods of coming at truth or proving it; whether it is better to begin the disquisition from the subject, or from the attribute. If, by the use of proper media, anything can be shown to be or not to be, I care not from what term the demonstration or argument takes its rise. Either way, propositions may beget their like, and more truth be brought into the world.

VIII. *That power which any intelligent being has—of surveying his own ideas and comparing them; of forming to himself, out of those that are immediate and abstract, such general and fundamental truths as he he can be sure of;*[127] *and of making such inferences and conclusions as are agreeable to them, or to any other truth, after it comes to he known; in order to find out more truth, prove or disprove some assertion, resolve some question, determine what is fit to be done upon occasion, etc., the case or thing under consideration being first fairly stated and prepared—is what I mean by the faculty of reason, or what entitles him to the epithet "rational."* Or in short, *Reason is a faculty of making such inferences and conclusions as are mentioned under the preceding proposition, from anything known or given.*

The Supreme being has no doubt a direct and perfect intuition of things, with their natures and relations, lying as it were all before Him, and pervious to His eye; or at least we may safely say that He is not obliged to make use of our operose methods by ideas and inferences, but knows things in a manner infinitely above all our conceptions. And as to superior finite natures, what other means of attaining to the knowledge of things they may have is a thing not to be told by me, or how far they may excel us in this way of finding truth. I have an eye here chiefly to our own circumstances. Reason must be understood, when it is ascribed to God, to be the *Divine* reason; when to other beings above us, to be *their* reason; and in all of them, to transcend ours as much as their natures respectively do our nature.[128]

It cannot be amiss to note further, that though a man who truly uses his rational powers—has abstract and universal ideas obtained by reflection; out of these frames to himself general truths, or apprehends the strength of such, and admits them, when they occur to him; by these, as by so many standards, measures and judges of things; and takes care to have the materials which he makes use of in reasoning, to be rivetted and compacted together by them—yet by a *habit* of reasoning he may come to serve himself of them, and apply them so quick, that he himself shall scarce observe it. Nay, most men seem to reason by virtue of a habit acquired by conversation, practice in business, and examples of others, without knowing what it is that gives the solidity even to their own just reasonings: just as men usually learn rules in arithmetic, govern their accounts by them all their days, and grow very ready and topping in the use of them, without ever knowing or troubling their heads about the demonstration of any one of them. But still though this be so, and men reason without adverting upon general ideas and abstract truths, or even being aware that there are any such—as it were by rule or a kind of rote—yet such there are, and upon them rests the weight of reason as its foundation.

This, by the way, helps us to detect the cause why the generality of people are so little under the dominion of reason: why they sacrifice it to their interests and passions so easily; are so obnoxious to prejudices, the influence of their company, and din of a party; so apt to change, though the case remains the very same; so unable to judge of things that are ever so little out of the way; and so conceited and positive in matters that are doubtful, or perhaps to discerning persons manifestly false. Their reasoning proceeds in that track which they happen to be got into, and out of which they know not one step, but all is to them *Terra incognita*; being ignorant of the scientific part, and those universal, unalterable principles, upon which true reasoning depends, and to find which and the true use of them are required cool hours and an honest application, beside many preparatives.

In the next place, it must be noted that one may reason truly from that which is only probable, or even false.[129] Because just inferences may be made from propositions of these kinds: that is, such inferences may be made as are founded in certain truths, though those propositions themselves are not certainly true. But then what follows or is concluded from thence, will be only probable, or false, according to the quality of that proposition, or those propositions, from which the inference is made.

Again, it should be observed that what I have said of reasoning, chiefly belongs to it as it is an *internal* operation. When we are to present our reasonings to others, we must transfer our thoughts to them by such ways as we can. The case is to be stated in a manner suitable to their capacities; a fair narration of matters of fact, and their circumstances, to be made; many times persons and things to be described by proper *diatyposes* and the like: all which are additional labor, and take up much room in discourses and books, and are performed by different authors upon different subjects, and in different kinds of writing, with an infinite variety of methods and forms, according to men's different views and capacities; and many times not without a necessity of some condescensions, ascititious advantages, and even applications to the passions. But notwithstanding this, in strict reasoning nothing is required but to lay steps in a due order, firmly connected, and expressed properly, without flourish;[130] and to arrive at truth by the shortest and clearest gradation we are able.

Once more: perhaps disputacious men may say I ascribe the investigation of truth to one faculty, when it is in reality the joint business of several. For when we go about this work, we are forced to make use of subordinate powers, and even external helps; to draw diagrams and put cases in our own imagination; to correct the images there, compound them, divide them, abstract from them; to turn over our memory, and see what has been entered and remains in that register; even to consult books, and use pen and ink. In short, we assemble all such axioms, theorems, experiments, and observations, as are already known, and appear capable of serving us, or present themselves upon the opening and analysis of the question or case before us. And when the mind has thus made its tour, fetched in materials from every quarter, and set them in its own view, then it contemplates, compares, and methodizes them; gives the first place to this, the second to that, and so on; and when trials do not succeed rightly, rejects some, adopts others, shifts their order, etc., till at last the series is so disposed that the thing required comes up resolved, proved, or disproved, by a just conclusion from proper premises. Now, in this process there seem to be many faculties concerned in these acts of circumspection, recollection, invention, reflection, comparing, methodizing, judging. But what if all this be so? I do not exclude the use of such subservient powers, or other helps as are necessary to the exerting this faculty of reason; nor deny the mind matter to work upon. I may allow all the intellectual faculties their proper offices, and yet make reason to be what I have described it to be.

IX. *There is such a thing as right reason,* or, *Truth may be discovered by reasoning.*[131] The word "reason" has several acceptations. *Sometimes* it is used for that power mentioned in the last proposition, as when we say: "Man is a being endowed with reason." And then the sense of *this* proposition must be this: that there is such a use to be made of this power, as is right, and will manifest truth. *Sometimes* it seems to be taken for those general truths, of which the mind possesses itself from the intimate knowledge of its own ideas, and by which it is governed in its inferences and conclusions, as when we say: "Such a thing is agreeable to reason:" for that is as much as to say it is agreeable to the said general truths, and that authentic way of making deductions which is founded in them. And then the sense of this proposition is that there *are* such general truths, and such a right way of inferring. Again: *sometimes* it seems to stand only for some particular truth, as it is apprehended by the mind with the causes of it, or the manner of its derivation from other truth: that is, it differs not from truth execept in this one respect, that it is considered not barely in itself, but as the effect and result of a process of reasoning; or it is truth with the arguments for our assent, and its evidences, about it; as when it is said: "that such or such an assertion is reason." And then the sense of the proposition is that there are truths so to be apprehended by the mind. So all comes to this at last: truth (or there are truths, which) may be discovered, or found to be such, *by reasoning.*

If it were not so, our rational faculties, the noblest we have, would be vain.

Beside, that it is so appears from the foregoing propositions and what we know within ourselves. 'Tis certain we have immediate and abstract ideas: the relations of these are adequately known to the mind, whose ideas they are; the propositions expressing these relations are evidently known to be true; and these truths must have the common privilege and property of all truths: to be true in all the particulars and uses to which they are applicable. If, then, any things are notified to us by the help of our senses, or present themselves by any other way or means, to which these truths may be immediately applied, or from whence deductions may be made after the forementioned manner, new truths may be thus collected. And since these new truths, and the numerous descendents that may spring from their loins, may be used still in the same manner, and be as it were the seed of more truth, who can tell at what undescried fields of knowledge even men may at length arrive? At least, nobody can doubt but that much truth, and particularly of that kind which is most useful to us in our conduct here, is discoverable by this method.

They, who oppugn the force and certainty of reason, and treat right reason as a chimera, must argue against reason either with reason, or without reason. In the latter way they do nothing; and in the former they betray their own cause, and establish that which they labor to dethrone. To prove there is no such thing as right reason, by any good argument, is indeed impossible: because that would be to show there is such a thing, by the manner of proving that there is not.

And further, if this proposition be not true, there is no right reasoning in Euclid; nor can we be sure that what is there demonstrated is true. But to say this, I am sure, is absurd. Nor do I desire that this proposition, which I here maintain, should be esteemed more certain than those demonstrated by him: and so certain it must be, because there can be no certainty in them, if this be not true.

The great objection against all this is taken from the many instances of false reasoning and ignorance, with which the practices, discourses, writings of mankind are too justly taxed. But, in answer to it, I would have it minded that I do not say men may not, by virtue of their freedom, break off their meditations and inquiries prematurely, before they have taken a sufficient survey of things; that they may not be prepossessed with inveterate errors, biased by interest, or carried violently down with the stream of a sect or fashion, or dazzled by some darling notion or bright name;[132] that they may not be unprovided of a competent flock of *præcognita* and preparative knowledge; that (among other things) they may not be ignorant of the very nature of reasoning, and what it is that gives sinews to an inference, and makes it just; that they may not want philosophy, history, or other learning, requisite to the understanding and stating of the question truly; that they may not have the confidence to pretend to abilities which they have not, and boldly to judge of things as if they were qualified, when they are not; that they may not be impotent in their elocution, and misrepresent their own thoughts, by expressing themselves ill, even when within themselves they reason well; that many understandings may not be naturally gross, good heads often indisposed, and the ablest judges sometimes overseen, through inadvertence or haste—I say none of these things. The contrary, I confess, is manifest: and it is in opposition to those errors, which appear in these cases under the name of reason, that we are forced to add the epithet *right*, and to say *right reason* instead of reason only, to distinguish it from that which wrongfully assumes that appellation. Nor, moreover, do I say that by reasoning the truth is to be discovered in *every* case: that would imply an extent of knowledge which we cannot pretend to. I only say that there is such a thing as right reason, and truth discoverable by it.

I might add that he whose faculties are entire and sound, and who by a proper exercise of his mind in scientific studies first opens and enlarges its capacity, and renders his intellectuals active and penetrating; takes care to furnish himself with such leading truths as may be useful to him, and of which he is assured in his own breast; and in treating any subject keeps them still in his eye, so that his discourse may be agreeable to them: I say, such a one is not in much danger of concluding falsely. He must either determine rightly, or soon find that the subject lies out of his reach. However he will be sensible that there are many things, within his sphere, concerning which he may reason; and that there are truths to be found, by this use of his faculties, in which he may securely acquiesce.

Thus, that question supposed to be asked, "How shall a man know what is true?" is in part answered. More shall be added by and by: only a proposition or two, which ought not to be omitted, must be first inserted.

X. *To act according to right reason, and to act according to truth, are in effect the same thing.* For in which sense soever the word "reason" is taken, it will stand either for truth itself, or for that which is instrumental in discovering and proving it to be such: and then, with respect to this latter sense, whoever is guided by that faculty, whose office consists in distinguishing and pointing out truth, must be a follower of truth, and act agreeably to it. For to be governed by any faculty or power is to act according to the genuine decisions and dictates of it.

That reason which is *right* (by the meaning of the words) must conclude rightly: but this it cannot do if the conclusion is not true, or truth.

That is (for so I would be understood), if the principles and premises from whence it results are true,[133] and certainly known to be so, the conclusion may be taken as certain and absolute truth; but otherwise the truth obtained at the end of the argument is but hypothetical, or only this: that such a thing is so, *if* such another, or such others are so or so.

XI. *To be governed by reason is the general law imposed by the Author of nature*[134] *upon them whose uppermost faculty is reason; as the dictates of it, in particular cases, are the particular laws to which they are subject.* As there are beings which have not so much as sense, and others that have no faculty above it; so there may be some who are endowed with reason, but have nothing higher than that. It is sufficient, at present, to suppose there may be such. And then if reason be the uppermost faculty, it has a right to control the rest by being such. As, in sensitive animals, sense commands gravitation and mechanical motions in those instances for which their senses are given, and carries them out into spontaneous acts: so, in rational animals, the gradation requires that reason should command sense.

It is plain that reason is of a commanding nature:[135] it enjoins this, condemns that, only allows some other things, and will be paramount (in an old word, τὸ ἡγεμόνικὸν[136]) if it is at all. Now, a being who has such a determining and governing power, so placed in his nature as to be essential to him, is a being certainly framed to be governed by that power. It seems to be as much designed by nature, or rather the Author of nature, that rational animals should use their reason, and steer by it, as it is by the shipwright that the pilot should direct the vessel by the use of the rudder he has fitted to it. The rudder would not be there if it was not to be used; nor would reason be implanted in any nature only to be not cultivated and neglected. And it is certain it cannot be used, but it must command: such is its nature.

It is not in one's power deliberately to resolve not to be governed by reason. For (here, the same way of arguing may be used that was lately) "if he could do this, he must either have some reason for making that resolution, or none. If he has none, it is a resolution that stands upon no foundation, and therefore in course falls: and if he has some reason for it, he is governed by reason. This demonstrates that reason must govern."

XII. *If a rational being, as such, is under an obligation to obey reason, and this obedience, or practice of reason, coincides with the observation of truth, these things plainly follow:*

1. That what is said in section I, proposition IV must be true with respect to such a being for this further cause: because, to him, nothing can be right that interferes with reason, and nothing can interfere with truth but it must interfere with reason. Such a harmony there is between them. For whatever is known to be true, reason either finds it, or allows it, to be such. Nothing can be taken for true by a rational being, if he has a reason to the contrary.
2. That there is to a rational being such a thing as *religion*, which may also, upon this further account, properly be called *natural*. For certainly to obey the law which the Author of his being has given him, is religion; and to obey the law which He has given, or revealed to him by making it to result from the right use of his own natural faculties, must be to him his *natural religion*.
3. A careful observation of truth, the way to happiness, and the practice of reason are in the issue the same thing. For, of the two last, each falls in with the first, and therefore each with other. And so, at last, natural religion is grounded upon this triple and strict alliance, or union, of *truth*, *happiness*, and *reason*, all in the same interest, and conspiring by the same methods, to advance and perfect human nature; and its truest definition is: "The pursuit of happiness by the practice of reason and truth."

Permit me here again to insert an observation *obiter*.

Observation: The κριτήριον[137] of right reason and truth, or that which is to be regarded in judging of right and truth, is *private*; that is: everyone must judge for himself. For since all reasoning is founded originally in the knowledge of one's own private ideas, by virtue of which he becomes conscious of some first truths that are undeniable; by which he governs his steps in his pursuits after more truths, etc.; the criterion, or that by which he tries his own reasonings and knows them to be right, must be the *internal* evidence he has already of certain truths, and the agreeableness of his inferences to them. One man can no more discern the objects of his own understanding, and their relations, by the faculties of another, than he can see with another man's eyes, or one ship can be guided by the helm of another. They must be his *own* faculties and conscience that must determine him. Therefore, to demand another man's assent to anything, without conveying into his mind such reasons as may produce a sense of the truth of it, is to erect a tyranny over his understanding and to demand a tribute which it is *not possible* for him to pay.[138] It is true, indeed, though I cannot see with another man's eyes, yet I may be assisted by another who has better eyes, in finding an object and the circumstances of it; and so men may be *assisted* in making their judgments of things. They may be informed of things which they did not know before, and which yet require a place among those that are to be considered; and they may be directed what to advert principally upon, how to state the question, how to methodize their thoughts, and in general how to reason: especially if they want learning, or have only that part of it which is little conversant in close reflections, and does not teach them to reason, or (as the case too often is) teaches them not to reason. But still this is all in order to produce such a light in them, that by it *they* may see and judge for themselves. An opinion, though ever so true and certain to one man, canot be transfused into another as true and certain by any other way but by opening his understanding, and assisting him so to order his conception that he may find the reasonableness of it *within himself*.

To prevent mistakes, I pray take notice here that, though I say men must judge for themselves, I do not say they must in all cases *act* according to their private and single judgments. In respect of such things as are private, and concern themselves *only*, or such as are left open and subject to every man's own sense, they may and ought, only preserving a due deference to them who differ from them, and are known upon other occasions to have more knowledge and literature than themselves; but when a society is concerned, and has determined anything, it may be considered as one person of which he, who dissents from the rest, is only perhaps a small particle; and then his judgment will be in a manner absorbed and drowned in that of the majority, or of them to whom the power of judging is entrusted. But I must not digress too far from the main business, the ways of coming at *truth*.

XIII. *The reports of sense are not of equal authority with the clear demonstrations of reason, when they happen to differ.* It is true, the *ideas* caused by the impression of sensible objects are real ideas, and truly known to the mind as they are in themselves; and the mind may use them, and reason truly upon them: that is, the mind may make a right use of the ideas which it finds in itself. But then, whether these are the true ectypes of their originals, and drawn to the life, is many times a question—and many times it is evident they are not. For that which has been anticipated under proposition III, but properly belongs to this, must be acknowledged. They are conveyed through media and by instruments susceptive of different dispositions and alterations, and may consequently produce different representations; and these cannot all be right. But suppose those instruments and media to be as entire and pure as when entirest and purest; yet still there may be, in many respects, an incapacity in the faculty to notify things just as they are. How mightily are the shape and size of a visible object varied upon us according to its distance, and the situation of the place from whence the prospect is taken? Now, these things cannot be said of the reports, or rather determinations, of reason. For in pure reasoning we use our own ideas for *themselves*, and such as the mind knows them to be, not as representatives of things that may be falsely exhibited. This *internal* reasoning may indeed be wrongly applied to *external* things, if we reason about them as being what they are not; but then this is the fault not of reason, but of sense, which reports the case wrong, or perhaps of the person, who has not been sufficiently industrious to inform himself.

The same familiar instance of vision proves further, that reason may be applied to *overrule* and *correct* sense. For when the pictures of objects are pricked out by the pencils of rays upon the retina of the eye, and do not give the true figure of those objects (as they not always do, being diversely projected, as the lines proceeding from the several points happen to fall upon that concave surface); this, though it might impose upon a being that has no faculty superior to sense, does not impose upon our reason, which knows *how* the appearance is altered, and *why*. To think the sun[139] is not bigger than it appears to the eye to be,[140] seems to be the last degree of stupidity. He must be a brute (so far from being a philosopher), who does not know that the same line (e.g. the diameter of the sun) at different distances subtends different angles at the eye. A small matter of reason may serve to confute sense in this and the like cases.

Objection: How can reason be more certain than sense, since reason is founded in abstractions which are originally taken from sensible objects? Answer: Perhaps the mind may, by being exercised at first about particular objects, by degrees find in itself this capacity of considering things by their species, making abstractions, etc. which it would not have done, had it never known any of these particulars. But then, after it has found this capacity in itself, and attained to the knowledge of abstract and general ideas, I do not see why this capacity of reasoning by the help of them may not be tried, upon this proficience, to censure and correct the advices of sense concerning even such particulars as first gave occasion to the mind to exert this capacity and raise itself. Is it a new thing for a scholar, to make such a progress in learning as to be able afterward to teach the master, from whom he received his first rudiments? May not the modern philosophers correct the ancients, because these first showed them the way, and led them into the study of nature? If we look impartially into the history of learning, and even of religion, we shall find that truth has generally advanced by degrees, and many times (very many; as if that was the method of introducing knowledge among men) risen out of fable and error, which gave occasion to those inquiries by which themselves were detected. Thus, blind ignorance was succeeded by a twilight of sense; this brightend by degrees; at last the sun, as it were, rose upon some parts of the commonwealth of learning, and cleared up many things; and I believe many more will in time be cleared, which, whatever men think, are yet in their dark and uncultivated state. The understanding, though it starts from particulars, in time makes a further progress, taking in generals, and such notions logical, metaphysical, etc., as never could possibly come in by the senses.[141] Besides, further, the capacity itself, of admitting and considering general ideas, was originally in the mind, and is not derived from without. The intelligences communicated by sense are only an occasion of using what it had before.[142] Just as a master may, by the exercises he sets, excite the superior capacity of his scholar.

In a word: no man does, or can pretend to, believe his senses when he has a reason against it, which is an irrefragable proof that reason is above sense and controls it. But,

XIV. *The reports of sense may be taken for true, when there is no reason against it.*[143] Because when there is no reason not to believe, that alone is a reason for believing them. And therefore,

XV. *In this case, to act according to them* (i.e. as taking the informations of sense to be true) *is to act according to reason and the great law of our nature.*

Thus, it appears that there are two ways by which we may assure ourselves of the truth of many things,[144] or at least may attain such a degree of certainty as will be sufficient to determine our practice: by *reason,* and by *sense under the government of reason,* that is, when reason supports it, or at least does not oppose it. By the former, we discover speculative truths; by the latter, or both together, matters of fact.

XVI. *Where certainty is not to be had,*[145] *probability must be substituted into the place of it*: that is, *it must be considered, which side of the question is the more probable.*

Probability, or that which in this case may incline one to believe any proposition to be true rather than false, or anything to be rather than not to be, or the contrary, will generally show itself upon the application of these and suchlike rules:

1. That may be reckoned probable, which, in the estimation of reason, appears to be more agreeable to the constitution of nature. Nobody can certainly foretell that sice-ace will come up upon two dies fairly thrown before ambs-ace: yet anyone would choose to lay the former, because in nature there are twice as many chances for that as for the other. If a strolling wolf should light upon a lamb, it is not evidently known that he will tear the lamb, but there is such a natural propension in that kind to do it, that nobody would much question the event. (This instance might have been taken from amongst men, who are generally, as far as they can be, wolves one to another.) If a parent causes his child to be instructed in the foundations of useful learning, educates him virtuously, and gives him his first impulse and direction in the way to true happiness, he will be more likely to proceed and continue in it, than he would be to hit upon it, and continue in it too, if he was left to himself to be carried away by his own passions, or the influence of those people into whose hands he might fall, the bias of the former lying towards vice, and misery in the end, and the plurality of the latter being either wicked or ignorant or both. So that the advantage, in point of probability, is on the side of good education.[146] When Herodotus writes that the Egyptian priests reported the sun had, within the compass of 11,340 years, twice risen where it now sets and set where it rises,[147] what is fit to be believed concerning the truth of this relation (as of many others) is easily discernable by this rule. Herodotus, possibly delighting in teratical stories, might tell what he never heard; or the passage may be an interpolation; or it may be altered in transcribing; or the priests, who pretended much to a knowledge of great antiquities, might, out of mere vanity, to show what children the Greeks were in respect of them, invent such a monstrous relation, and impose it upon them whom they thought to have not much science among them; or it might be got into their memoirs before their time, who related it to Herodotus, and so pass upon posterity, as many other fictions and legends have done. These are such things as are well known to have happened often. But, that the diurnal rotation of the earth about her axis should be inverted is a phenomenon that has never been known to happen by anybody else, either

before or since; that is favored by no observation; and that cannot be without great alteration in the mundane system, or those laws by which the motions of the planets, and of our earth among the rest, are governed. That this account, then, may be false is very consistent with the humor and circumstances of mankind: but that it should be true is very inconsistent with those laws by which the motions of the celestial bodies seem to be regulated, and tend to persevere in their present courses and directions. It is therefore in nature much more probable that this account is false. The odds are on that side.

2. When any observation has hitherto constantly held true, or most commonly proved to be so, it has by this acquired an established credit; the cause may be presumed to retain its former force, and the effect may be taken as probable, if in the case before us there does not appear something particular: some reason for exception. No man can demonstrate that the sun will rise again, yet everyone does, and must, act as if that was certain:[148] because we apprehend no decay in the causes which bring about this appearance, nor have any other reason to mistrust the event, or think it will be otherwise a few hours hence than it has been hitherto. There is no apodictical argument to prove that any particular man will die: but yet, he must be more than mad who can presume upon immortality here, when he finds so many generations all gone, to a man, and the same enemies that have laid them prostrate still pursuing their victories. These, and suchlike, though in strictness perhaps not certainties, are justly current for such: so great is their probability. There are other observations which, though not so infallible as those, deserve yet to be thought of, and to have a share in the direction of our judgments. E.g. There have been men in the world, and no doubt still are, who, having had opportunities of imposing falsities upon mankind, of cheating, or committing other wickedness, have yet in spite of temptation preserved their integrity and virtue: but, since opportunity has so seldom failed to corrupt them who have been in possession of her, and men's interests and passions continue in general the same, it is more probable her charms will still have the same power and effect which they used to have; which whoever does not mind, will be woefully obnoxious to be abused by frauds pious and impious.[149] Briefly: when there is no particular reason for the contrary, what has oftenest happened may, from experience, most reasonably be expected to happen again.

3. When neither nature nor other observations point out the probable conjecture to us, we must be determined (if it be necessary for us to be determined at all) by the reports, and sense of them, whom we apprehend, judging with the best skill we have,[150] to to be most knowing[151] and honest.[152] Of all these rules, the first is that which deserves the principal regard; the other two are of use, when nature so utterly excludes us from her bosom that no opportunity is allowed of making a judgment.

4. Lastly: when nature, the frequent repetition of the same event, and the opinion of the best judges concur to make anything probable, it is so in the highest degree.

It appears, from what has been said concerning the nature and foundations of probability, that the force of it results from observation and reason together. For here, the one is not sufficient without the other. Reason without observation wants matter to work upon; and observations are neither to be made justly by ourselves, nor to be rightly chosen out of those made by others, nor to be aptly applied, without the assistance of reason. Both together may support opinion and practice in the absence of knowledge and certainty. For, those observations upon the nature of men and things which we have made ourselves, we know; and our own reasoning concerning them, and deductions from them, we know; and from hence, there cannot but arise in many cases an internal obligation to give our assent to this rather than that, or to act one way rather than another. And, as to the observations of others, they may be so cautiously and skillfully selected, as to become almost our own; since our own reason and experience may direct us in the choice and use of them. The remarks and advice of old men,[153] who have gone through variety of scenes, lived long enough to see the consequences of their own and other people's actings, and can now with freedom[154] look back and tell where they erred, are ordinarily sure to be preferred to those of young and raw actors. The *gnomæ*, apologues, etc. of wise men, and such as have made it their business to be useful spies upon nature and mankind, national proverbs, and the like,[155] may be taken as maxims commonly true. Men in their several professions and arts, in which they have been educated, and exercised themselves all their days, must be supposed to have greater knowledge and experience than others can usually have; and therefore, if through want of capacity or honesty they do not either lose or belie their opportunities and experience, they are, in respect of those things to which they have been bred and inured, more to be relied upon. And, lastly, histories written by credible and industrious authors, and read with judgment, may supply us with examples, parallel cases, and general remarks, profitable in forming our manners and opinions too. And by the frequent perusal of them, and meditation upon them, a dexterity in judging of dubious cases is acquired. Much of the temper of mankind, much of the nature and drift of their counsels, much of the course of Divine providence, is visible in them.

To conclude: that we ought to follow probability, when certainty leaves us, is plain, because then it becomes the only light and guide we have. For unless it is better to wander, and fluctuate in absolute uncertainty, than to follow such a guide—unless it be reasonable to put out our candle because we have not the light of the sun—it must be reasonable to direct our steps by probability, when we have nothing clearer to walk by. And if it be reasonable, we are obliged to do it by proposition XI. When there is nothing above probability, it does govern; when there is nothing in the opposite scale, or nothing of equal weight, this, in the course of nature, must turn the beam. Though a man, to resume the instance before, cannot demonstrate that sice-ace will come up before ambs-ace, he would find himself obliged (if he could be obliged to lay at all) to lay on that side; nor could he not choose to do it. Though he would not be certain of the chance, he would be certain of his own obligation, and on which side it lay.

Here, then, is another way of discovering, if not *truth*, yet what in practice may be supposed to be truth. That is, we may by this way discover whether such propositions as these be true: "I ought to do this, rather than that" or, "to think so, rather than the contrary."

Observation: I have done, now, what I chiefly intended here. But, over and above that, we may almost from the premises collect,

First, the principal causes of error, which I take to be such as these:

1. Want of faculties; when men pretend to judge of things above them. As some (straying out of their proper element and falling into the dark, where they find no ideas but their own dreams, come to) assert what they have no reason to assert, so others deny what there is the highest reason to believe, only because they cannot comprehend it.
2. Want of due reflection upon those ideas we have, or may have: by which it comes to pass that men are destitute of that knowledge which is gained by the contemplation of them, and their relations; misapply names, confusedly; and sometimes deal in a set of words and phrases to which no ideas at all belong, and which have indeed no meaning. Of kin to this is,
3. Want of proper qualifications and προπαιδεύματα.[156] As when illiterate people invade the provinces of scholars; the half-lettered are forward, and arrogate to themselves what a modest, studious man dares not,[157] though he knows more; and scholars that have confined themselves to one sort of literature, launch out into another: unsuccessfully all.
4. Not understanding in what the nature and force of a just consequence consists. Nothing more common than to hear people assert that such a thing follows from such a thing, when it does not follow: i.e., when such a consequence is founded in no axiom, no theorem, no truth that we know of.
5. Defects of memory and imagination. For men, in reasoning, make much use of these: memory is upon many occasions consulted, and sometimes drafts made upon the fantasy. If, then, they depend upon these, and these happen to be weak, clouded, perverted any way, things may be misrepresented, and men led out of the way by misshapen apparitions. There ought to be, therefore, a little distrust of these faculties, and such proper helps ought to be used, as perhaps the best judgments want the most.
6. Attributing too much to sense. For, as necessary as our senses are to us, there are certainly many things which fall not within their notice; many which cannot be exhibited after the manner of sensible objects, and to which no images belong. Everyone who has but just saluted the mathematics and philosophy, must be convinced that there are many things in nature which seem absurd to sense, and yet must be admitted.
7. Want of refinement, and the practice of thinking and reasoning by ourselves.[158] A rambling and irregular life must be attended with a loose and irregular head, ill-connected notions, and fortuitous conclusions. Truth is the offspring of silence, unbroken meditations, and thoughts often revised and corrected.
8. The strength of appetites, passions, prejudices. For by these the understanding may be corrupted, or overborne; or at least the operations of the mind must be much obstructed

by the intrusion of such solicitors as are no retainers to the rational powers, and yet strong, and turbulent. Among other prejudices, there is one of a particular nature which you must have observed to be one of the greatest causes of modern irreligion. While some opinions and rites are carried to such an immoderate height as exposes the absurdity of them to the view of almost everybody, but them who raise them, not only gentlemen of the *belles lettres*, but even men of common sense many times see through them; and then out of indignation and an excessive renitence, not separating that which is true from that which is false, they come to deny both, and fall back into the contrary extreme, a contempt of all religion in general.[159]

9. Ill stating of a question; when men either put it wrong themselves, or accept it so put from others. A small addition or falsity, slipped into the case, will ferment, and spread itself; an artificial color may deceive one; an encumbered manner may perplex one. The question ought to be presented before its judge clean, and in its natural state, without disguise or distortion. To this last may be subjoined another cause, nearly allied to it: not fixing the sense of terms, and (which must often follow) not rightly understanding what it is that is to be examined and resolved.

Secondly, the reason why the many are commonly in the wrong and so wretchedly misjudge things: The generality of people are not sufficiently prepared, by a proper education, to find truth by reasoning. And, of them who have liberal education, some are soon immersed and lost in pleasures, or at least in fashionable methods of living, rolling from one visit or company to another,[160] and flying from nothing so much as from themselves and the quiet retreats proper for meditation and reasoning; others become involved in business and the intricate affairs of life, which demand their attention and engross their time; others fall into a slothful neglect of their studies and disuse of what they have learnt, or want help and means to proceed, or only design to deceive life and gratify themselves with the amusements and sensual parts of learning; and others there are, whose misfortune it is to begin wrong, to begin with the conclusion, taking their opinions from places where they have been bred, or accommodating them to their situation in the world, and the conditions of that employment by which they are to get their bread, before they have ever considered them, and then making the subsequent business of their lives to dispute for them and maintain them, right or wrong. If such men happen to be in the right, it is luck, and part of their portion, not the effect of their improvements; and if they happen to be in the wrong, the more they study, and the more learning they get, the more they are confirmed in their errors, and having set out with their backs upon truth, the further they go, the more they recede from it. Their knowledge is a kind of negative quantity, so much worse or less than no knowledge. Of this sort there are many, and very few indeed (with respect to the bulk of mankind) whose determinations and tenets were ever in the form of questions; there could not otherwise be so many sects and different denominations of men as there are upon the face of the earth. The sum of all, in a few words, is this: many qualifications are requisite in order to judge of some truths, and particularly those which are of greatest importance: proper learning and penetration, vacancy from business, a detachment from the interest of all parties, much sincerity and a perfect resignation to the government of reason and force of truth; which are things not to be reconciled with the usual ignorance, passions, tumultuary lives, and other circumstances which carry most men transverse.

IV
OF THE OBLIGATIONS OF IMPERFECT BEINGS WITH RESPECT TO THEIR POWER OF ACTING

There remains yet another question—supposed also to be proposed by an objector—which must not be forgot, and upon which I shall bestow this very short section. The question was this: "If a man can find out truth, may he not want the power of acting agreeably to it?"

I. *Nothing is capable of no obligation.* For to oblige *nothing* is the same as *not* to oblige.

II. *So far as any being has no power or opportunity of doing anything, so far is that being incapable of any obligation to do it:* or, *no being is capable of any obligation to do that which it has not power or opportunity to do.* For that being, which has not the faculties or opportunity necessary to the doing of anything, is, in respect of that thing, a being utterly inactive—no agent at all—and therefore, as to that act, nothing at all.

To require, or command, one to do anything is to require him to apply a power superior to the resistence to be met with in doing it. To require him to apply such a power is the same as to require that his power, of such a kind and degree, be applied. But if he has no such power, then his power of that kind and degree is *nothing*: and it is nothing that is required to be applied. Therefore, nothing is required to be done. It is just the same as if a man was commanded to do something with his third hand, when he has but two: which would be the same as to bid him to do it with *no* hand, or *not* bid him do it.

Without more ado, it is a truth confessed by everybody, that nobody is obliged to impossibilities.

From hence will follow, after the manner of corollaries, the two following propositions:

III. *Inanimate and inactive beings are capable of no obligation: nor merely sensitive of any obligation to act upon principles, or motives above sense.*

IV. *The obligations of beings intelligent and active must be proportionable to their faculties, powers, opportunities; and not more.*

V. *To endeavor may fitly express the use of all the opportunities and powers that any intelligent and active, but imperfect, being has to act.* For to endeavor is to do what one can, and this as every such being may do, wherever he stands in the scale of imperfects; so none can do more. One may exert his endeavors with greater advantage or success than another, yet still they are but *endeavors.*

VI. *The imputations of moral good and evil to beings capable of understanding and acting must be in proportion to their endeavors:* or, *their obligations reach as far as their endeavors may.* This follows again from what has been said; and so does this:

VII. and lastly, *They who are capable of discerning truth, though not all truths, and of acting conformably to it, though not always or in all cases, are nevertheless obliged to do these, as far as they are able:* or, *it it is the duty of such a being sincerely to endeavor to practice reason; not to contradict any truth, by word or deed; and in short, to treat everything as being what it is.*

Thus the general duties of rational beings, mentioned in or resulting from the preceding sections, are brought together and finally fixed under the correction or limitation in this last proposition. This is the sum of their religion, from which no exemption or excuse lies. Everyone can endeavor; everyone can do what he can. But in order to that, everyone ought to be in *earnest*, and to exert himself *heartily*: not stifling his own conscience, not dissembling, suppressing, or neglecting his own powers.

And now, needless to me seem those disputes about human liberty, with which men have tired themselves and the world. The case is much the same as if a man should have some great reward or advantage offered to him, if he would get up and go to such a place to accept it, or do some certain thing for it, and he, instead of going or doing anything, falls into a tedious disquisition about his own freedom: whether he has the power to stir, or whether he is not chained to his seat and necessitated to sit still. The short way of knowing this, certainly, is to try. If he can do nothing, no labor can be lost; but if he is capable of acting, and does not act, the consequences and blame must be justly chargeable upon himself. And, I am persuaded, if men would be serious, and put forth themselves,[161] that their wills are not so universally and peremptorily determined by what occurs, nor predestination and fate so rigid,[162] but that much is left to their own conduct.[163] Up and try.[164]

Sure it is in a man's power to keep his hand from his mouth; if it is, it is also in his power to forbear excess in eating and drinking. If he has the command of his own feet, so as to go either this way or that or no whither, as sure he has, it is in his power to abstain from ill company and vicious places. And so on.[165]

This suggests a very material thought: that *forbearances*, at least in all ordinary cases, are within our power;[166] so that a man may, if he will, forbear to do that which contradicts truth; but where acting is required, that very often is not in his power. He may want abilities, or opportunities, and so may seem to contradict truth by his omission, which, if his infirmities and disadvantages were taken into the account, and the case was rightly stated, he would be found not to do.

V
Truths Relating to the Deity: Of His Existence, Perfection, Providence, etc.

I have shown in what the nature of moral good and evil consists: viz. a conformity or disagreement to truth, and those things that are coincident with it, reason and happiness; also, how truth is discovered: by sense, or reason, or both. I shall now specify some of those truths which are of greatest importance and influence, and require more reasoning to discover them; leaving the rest (common matters of fact) to the common ways of finding them. They respect principally either the Deity, or ourselves, or the rest of mankind. The first sort are the subject of this section.

I. *Where there is a subordination of causes and effects, there must necessarily be a cause in nature prior to the rest, uncaused.* Or thus, *Where there is a series, in which the existence of one thing depends upon another, the existence of this again upon same other, and so upwards, as the case shall be, there must be some independent being, upon whom it does originally depend.*

If Z (some body) be put into motion by Y, Y by X, and X by W, it is plain that X moves Y, and Y moves Z only as they are first moved, X by W, and Y by X: that Z, Y, X are *moveds*, or rather Z more Y more X, taken together,[167] are *one moved*; that W stands here as the first mover, or author of the motion, unmoved by any other; that therefore without W there would be a *moved* without a *mover*, which is absurd;[168] and lastly, that of what length soever the series may be, the case will be ever the same: i.e. if there be no First mover,[169] unmoved, there must be a moved without a mover.

Further, if W, whom we will suppose to be an intelligent being, and to have a power of beginning motion, has this power originally in himself and independently of all others, then, here, not only the first mover in this series, but a *First being* and original cause is found. Because that, which has a power of beginning motion independent of any other, is a *mover independent*, and therefore is independent, or has an independent existence, since nothing can be a mover without *being*. But if W has not this power independently in himself, then he must receive it from some other, upon whom he depends, and whom we will call V. If then V has a power of conferring a faculty of producing motion, originally and independently in himself, here will be a First, independent cause. And if it can be supposed that he has it not thus, and that the series should rise too high for us to follow it, yet however we cannot but conclude that there is *some* such cause, upon whom this train of beings and powers must depend, if we reason as in the former paragraph. For,

Universally, if Z be any effect whatsoever, proceeding from or depending upon Y as the cause of its existence, Y upon X, X upon W, it is manifest that the existence of all—Z, Y, X—does originally come from W, which stands here as the Supreme cause, depending upon nothing: and that, without it, X could not be, and consequently neither Y, nor Z. Z, Y, X, being all effects (or dependents), or rather Z more Y more X *one effect*, without W there would be an effect without a cause. Lastly, let this retrogression from effects to their causes be continued ever so far, the same thing will still recur, and without such a cause as is before mentioned the whole will be an effect without an efficient, or a dependent without anything to depend upon: i.e. dependent, and not dependent.

Objection: The series may ascend *infinitely*,[170] and for that reason have no first mover or cause. Answer: If a series of bodies moved can be supposed to be infinite, then, taken together, it will be equal to an *infinite body* moved, and this moved will not less require a mover than a finite body, but infinitely more. If I may not be permitted to place a first mover at the top of the series, because it is supposed to be infinite and to have no beginning, yet still there must of necessity be *some* cause or author of the motion,[171] different from all these bodies, because their being (by the supposition) no one body in the series that moves the next, but only in consequence of its being moved first itself, there is no one of them that is not *moved*, and the whole can be considered together but as an infinite body moved, and which must therefore be moved by *something*.

The same kind of answer holds good in respect of all effects and their causes in general. An infinite succession of effects will require an infinite efficient, or a cause infinitely effective: so far is it from requiring none.

Suppose a chain[172] hung down out of the heavens from an unknown height, and though every link of it gravitated toward the earth, and what it hung upon was not visible, yet it did not descend, but kept its situation, and upon this a question should arise: "What supported or kept up this chain?" Would it be a sufficient answer to say that the first (or lowest) link hung upon the second (or that next above it), the second, or rather the first and second together, upon the third, and so on *ad infinitum*? For what holds up the *whole*? A chain of ten links would fall down, unless something able to bear it hindered; one of twenty, if not stayed by something of a yet greater strength, in proportion to the increase of weight; and therefore one of *infinite* links certainly, if not sustained by something *infinitely* strong, and capable to bear up an infinite weight. And thus it is in a chain of causes and effects[173] tending, or, as it were, gravitating, towards some end. The last (or lowest) depends, or (as one may say) is suspended upon, the cause above it; this again, if it be not the first cause, is suspended as an effect upon something above it, etc.[174] And if they should be infinite, unless (agreeably to what has been said) there is some cause upon which all hang or depend, they would be but an infinite effect without an efficient: and to assert there is any such thing, would be as great an absurdity as to say that a finite or little weight wants something to sustain it, but an infinite one or the greatest does not.

II. *A Cause or Being, that has in nature no superior cause, and therefore* (by the terms) *is also unproduced, and independent, must be self-existent; i.e. existence must be essential to him; or, such is his nature, that he cannot but be.*[175] For every being must either either exist of itself, or not of itself; that which exists not of itself must derive its existence from some other, and so be dependent; but the Being mentioned in the proposition is supposed to be independent, and uncaused. Therefore He must exist, not this way, but the other. The root of His existence can be sought for nowhere but in His own nature; to place it anywhere else is to make a cause superior to the Supreme.

III. *There must be such a Being.* For (besides what has been said already) if there was not at least one such Being, nothing could be at all.[176] For the universe could not produce itself,[177] nor could any part of it produce itself and then produce the rest, because this is supposing a thing to *act* before it *is*.

IV. *Such a Being as is before described, must not only be eternal, but infinite.* Eternal He must be, because there is no way by which such a Being can either begin or cease to be, existence being of His essence. And infinite He must be, because He can be limited by no other as to his existence. For if there was any being able to limit Him, He must be inferior to that being. He must also in that case be dependent, because he must be beholden to that being for his being what He is, and that He is not confined within narrower limits. Besides, if His presence (whatever the manner of it is) was anywhere excluded, He would not be there; and if not there, He might be supposed to be not elsewhere; and thus he might be supposed not to be at all. But such a Being, as is described in proposition II cannot so much as be *supposed* not to be.

V. *Such a Being is above all things that fall under our cognizance, and therefore his manner of existence is above all our conceptions.* For He is a necessary existent, but nothing within our comprehension is of this kind. We know no being, but what we can *imagine not to be* without any contradiction or repugnance to nature; nor do we know of any besides this Supreme being himself. For with respect to Him, indeed we know, by reasoning, that there must be One being who cannot be supposed not to be, just as certainly as we know there is anything at all; though we cannot know Him, and how he exists. Adequate ideas of eternity[178] and infinity are above us, us finites.[179]

In inquiring after the causes of things, when we find (or suppose) this to be the cause of that, another thing to be the cause of this again, and so on, if we can proceed, it may always be demanded with respect to the last cause that we can comprehend, "What is the cause of that?" So that it is not possible for us to terminate our inquiries of this kind but in something which is to us incomprehensible. And therefore the Supreme cause must certainly be such.[180] But though it is impossible for us to have an adequate notion of his manner of existence, yet we may be sure that,

VI. *He exists in a manner which is perfect.* For He, who exists of himself, depends in no regard upon any other, and (as being a Supreme cause) is the fountain of existence to other beings, must exist in the *uppermost* and *best* manner of existing. And not only so, but (since He is infinite and illimited) He must exist in the best manner *illimitedly* and *infinitely*. Now to exist thus is infinite goodness of existence, and to exist in a manner infinitely good is to be *perfect*.

VII. *There can be but One such Being.*[181] That is, as it appears by proposition III that there must be at least *one* independent Being, such as is mentioned in proposition I, so now that in reality there is *but One*.[182] Because his manner of existence being perfect and illimited, that manner of being (if I may speak so) is *exhausted* by Him, or belongs solely to Him.[183] If any other could partake with Him in it, He must want what that other had; be deficient and limited. Infinite and illimited enclose all.[184]

If there could be two Beings, each by himself absolutely perfect, they must be either of the same or of different natures. Of the same they cannot be, because thus, both being infinite, their existences would be concident: that is, they would be but the same or one. Nor can they be of different natures, because if their natures were opposite or contrary the one to the other, being equal (infinite both and everywhere meeting the one with the other), the one would just destroy or be the negation of the other;[185] and if they are supposed to be only different, not opposite, then if they differ as disparates, there must be some genus above them, which cannot be; and however they differ, they can only be said, at most, to be beings perfect in their respective kinds. But this is not to be absolutely perfect; it is only to be perfect in this or that respect: and to be only thus implies imperfection in other respects.

What has been here said is, methinks, sufficient to ruin the Manichean cause and exclude the independent principle of evil. For if we cannot account for the existence of that evil which we find, by experience, to be in the world, it is but one instance out of many of our ignorance. There may be reasons for it, though we do not know them. And certainly no such experience must make us deny axioms or truths equally certain.[186] There are, besides, some things relating to this subject which deserve our attention. For as to *moral* good and evil, they seem to depend upon ourselves.[187] If we do but endeavor, the most we can, to do what we ought, we shall not be guilty of not doing it (section IV), and therefore it is our fault, and not to be charged upon any other being,[188] if guilt and evil be introduced by our neglect or abuse of our own liberty and powers.[189] Then as to *physical* evil: without it much physical *good* would be lost, the one necessarily inferring the other.[190] Some things *seem* to be evil, which would not appear to be such if we could see through the whole contexture of things.[191] There are not more evil than good things in the world, but surely more of the latter.[192] Many evils of this kind, as well as of the former, come by our own fault; some perhaps by way of punishment, some of physic,[193] and some as the means to happiness not otherwise to be obtained. And if there is a future state, that which seems to be wrong *now* may be rectified *hereafter*. To all which more may yet be added. As: that matter is not capable of perfection, and therefore where that is concerned, there must be imperfections, and consequently evils.[194] So that to ask why God permits evil, is to ask why he permits a material world, or such a being as man is:[195] endowed indeed with some noble faculties, but encumbered at the same time with bodily passions and propensions. Nay, I know not whether it be not to ask why He permits any imperfect being, and that is, any being at all—which is a bold demand, and the answer to it lies perhaps too deep for us. If this world be designed for a *palæstra*, where men[196] are to exercise their faculties and their virtues, and by that prepare themselves for a superior state[197] (and who can say it is not?), there must be difficulties and temptations, occasions and opportunities for this exercise. Lastly, if there are evils of which men know not the true origin, yet if they would but seriously reflect upon the many marks of reason, wisdom, and goodness everywhere to be observed, in instances which they *do* or *may* understand, they could scarce doubt but the same things prevailed in those which they do *not* understand. If I should meet with a book, the author of which I found had disposed his matter in beautiful order, and treated his subjects with reason and exactness, but at last, as I read on, came to a few leaves written in a language which I did not know: in this case I should close the book with a full persuasion that the same vein of good sense which showed itself in the former and much greater part of it, ran through the other also, especially having arguments *a priori* which obliged me to believe that the author of it all was the same person. This I should certainly do, rather than deny the force of those arguments in order to assert two authors of the same book. But the evil principle has led me too far out of my way, therefore to return:

VIII. *All other beings depend upon that Being mentioned in the foregoing propositions for their existence.* For since there can be but one perfect and independent being, the rest must be imperfect and dependent; and since there is nothing else upon which they can ultimately depend, besides Him, upon Him they must and do depend.

IX. *He is therefore the Author of nature; nor can anything be, or be done, but what He either causes (immediately or mediately) or permits.* All beings (by the last) depend upon Him for their existence; upon whom depends their existence, upon him also must depend the intrinsic manner of their existence, or the *natures* of these beings; and again, upon whom depend their being and nature, upon Him depend the *necessary effects* and *consequences* of their being, and being such as they are in themselves. Then, as to the acts of such of them as may be free agents, and the effects of them, He is indeed *not* the Author of those, because, by the terms and supposition, they proceed from agents who have no necessity imposed upon them by Him to act either this or that way. But yet however these *free agents* must depend upon Him *as such*: from Him they derive their power of acting, and it is He who permits them to use their liberty, though many times, through their own fault, they use it amiss. And, lastly, as to the nature of those relations which lie between ideas or things really existing, or which arise from facts already done and past, these result from the natures of the things themselves—all which the Supreme being either causes or permits (as before). For since things can be but in one manner at once, and their mutual relations, ratios, agreements, disagreements, etc. are nothing but their manners of being with respect to each other, the natures of these relations will be determined by the natures of the things.

From hence, now it appears that whatever expresses the existences or nonexistences of things, and their mutual relations as they are, is true by the constitution of nature; and if so, it must also be agreeable to His perfect *comprehension* of all truth, and to His *will*, who is at the head of it. Though the act of A (some free agent) is the effect of his liberty, and can only be said to be *permitted* by the Supreme being; yet when it is once done, the relation between the doer and the deed, the agreement there is between A and the idea of one who has committed such a fact, is a fixed relation. From thenceforward it will always be predicable of him, that he was the doer of it: and if anyone should deny this, he would go counter to nature and that great Author of it, whole existence is now proved. And thus those arguments in section I, proposition IV which turned only upon a *supposition* that there was such a Being, are here confirmed and made absolute.

X. *The one supreme and perfect Being, upon whom the existence of all other beings and their powers originally depend, is that Being whom I mean by the word "God."*

There are other truths still remaining in relation to the Deity, which we may know, and which are necessary to be known by us, if we would endeavor to demean ourselves toward Him according to truth and what He is. And, they are such as not only tend to rectify our opinions concerning His nature and attributes, but also may serve at the same time as further proof of His existence, and an amplification of some things touched perhaps too lightly. As,

XI. *God cannot be corporeal:* or, *there can be no corporeity in God.* There are many things in matter utterly inconsistent with the nature of such a Being as it has been demonstrated God must be.

Matter exists in parts, every one of which, by the term, is imperfect;[198] but in a Being absolutely perfect, there can be nothing that is imperfect.

These parts, though they are many times kept closely united by some occult influence, are in truth so many distinct bodies, which may, at least in our imagination, be disjoined or placed otherwise; nor can we have any idea of matter, which does not imply a natural discerpibility and susceptivity of various shapes and modifications: i.e. mutability seems to be essential to it. But God, existing in a manner that is perfect, exists in a manner that must be uniform, always one and the same, and in nature unchangeable.

Matter is incapable of acting, passive only, and stupid: which are defects that can never be ascribed to him who is the First cause or Prime agent, the Supreme intellect, and altogether perfect.

Then, if He is corporeal, wherever there is a vacuum, He must be excluded, and so becomes a being bounded, finite, and, as it were, full of chasms.

Lastly, there is no matter or body which may not be *supposed not to be*; whereas the idea of God, or that Being upon whom all others depend, involves in it existence.

XII. *Neither infinite space, nor infinite duration, nor matter infinitely extended or eternally existing, nor any, nor all of these taken together, can be God.*[199] For,

Space, taken separately from the things which possess and fill it, is but an empty scene or vacuum; and to say that infinite space is God, or that God is infinite space, is to say that He is an infinite vacuum, than which nothing can be more absurd or blasphemous. How can space, which is but a vast void, rather the negation of all things than positively anything, a kind of diffused nothing; how can this, I say, be the First cause, etc. or indeed any cause? What attributes besides penetrability and extension, what excellencies, what perfections is it capable of?[200]

As infinite space cannot be God, though He be excluded from no place or space; so, though He is eternal, yet eternity or infinite duration itself is not God.[201] For duration, abstracted from all durables, is nothing actually existing by itself: it is the duration of a being, not a being.

Infinite space and duration, taken together, cannot be God: because an interminable space of infinite duration is still nothing but eternal space, and that is at most but an eternal vacuum.

Since it has been already proved that corporeity is inconsistent with Divine perfection, though matter should be infinitely extended or there should be an infinite quantity of it, yet still, wherever it is, it carries this inconsistence along with it.

If to matter be added infinite duration, neither does this alter the nature of it. This only supposes it to be eternally what it is, i.e. eternally incapable of Divine perfection.

And if to it you add the ideas of both infinite extension (or space) and duration too, yet still, so long as matter is matter, it must always and everywhere be incapable of Divinity.

Lastly, not the universe, or sum total of finite beings, can be God. For if it is, then everything is divine, everything God, or of God; and so all things together must make but one being.[202] But the contrary to this we see: there being evidently many beings distinct, and separable one from another, and independent each of other. Nay, this distinction and separation of existence, besides what we see without us, we may even feel within ourselves. We are severally conscious to ourselves of the individuation and distinction of our own minds from all other: nor is there anything of which we can be more certain. Were we all the same being, and had one mind, as in that case we must have, thoughts could not be private, or the peculiar thoughts of any one person, but they must be common acts of the whole mind, and there could be but one conscience common to us all.[203] Besides, if all things conjunctly are God or the Perfect being (I dread the mention of such things, though it be in order to refute them), how comes this remarkable instance of imperfection, among many others, to cleave to us: that we should not know even ourselves, and what we are?[204] In short, no collection of beings can be one being; and therefore not God. And the universe itself is but a collection of distinct beings.[205]

XIII. *It is so far from being true that God is corporeal, that there could be no such thing as either matter or motion, if there was not some Superior being upon whom they depended. Or, God is such a being, that without Him there could be neither matter nor motion.* This must be true of matter, because it has been proved already that there can be but one independent being, that he is incorporeal, and that the existence of all other beings must depend upon Him. But the same thing may be proved otherwise: If matter (I mean the existence of it) does not depend upon something above it, it must be an independent being; and if an independent being, a necessary being; and then there could be no such thing as a vacuum, but all bodies must be perfectly solid; and, more than that, the whole world could be but one such body, five times as firm as brass, and incapable of all motion. For that being which exists necessarily does necessarily exist: that is, it cannot *not* exist. But in a vacuum matter does not exist.

Moreover, if matter be an independent, necessary being, and exists of itself, this must be true of every particle of it; and if so, there could not only be no vacuum, but every particle must be everywhere. For it could not be limited to occupy only a place of such certain dimensions by its own nature, since this confinement of existence within certain bounds implies nonexistence in other places, beyond those bounds, and is equal to a negation of existence; and when existence is essential to any being, a negation of existence cannot be so. Nor, in the next place, could its existence be limited by anything else, because it is supposed to have its existence only of itself: i.e. to have a principle of existence in itself, or to have an existence that is not dependent upon or obnoxious to any other.

And, I may add still, if matter be self-existent, I do not see, not only how it comes to be restrained to a place of some certain capacity, but also how it comes to be limited in other respects, or why it should not exist in a manner that is in all respects perfect. So that thus it appears, matter must derive its existence from some other being, who causes it to be just what it is. And the being who can do this must be God.

It is to no purpose to object here that one cannot conceive how the existence of matter can be derived from another being. For God, being above our conceptions, the manner in which He operates, and in which things depend upon him, must also be inconceivable. Reason discovers that this visible world must owe its existence to some invisible Almighty being: i.e. it discovers this to be fact, and we must not deny facts because we know not *how* they are effected. It is far from being new, that our faculties should disclose to us the existence of things, and then drop us in our inquiry *how* they are. Thus much for matter.

As for *motion*: without a First cause, such as has been described, there could be none; and much less such motions as we see in the world. This may be immediately deduced from the foregoing paragraphs. For if matter itself could not be without such a cause, it is certain motion, which is an affection of matter, could never be.

But further, there could be no motion, unless either there be in matter itself a power of beginning it; or it is communicated from body to body in an infinite succession, or in a circle, and so has no beginning; or else is produced by some incorporeal being, or beings. Now as hardy as men are in advancing opinions that favor their vices, though never so repugnant to reason, I can hardly believe anyone will assert that a parcel of mere matter (let it be great or small, of any figure whatsoever, etc.) left altogether to itself, could ever of itself begin to move. If there is any such bold assertor, let him fix his eyes upon some lump of matter, e.g. a stone, piece of timber, or a clod (cleared of all animals), and peruse it well; and then, ask himself seriously whether it is possible for him in earnest to believe that that stone, log, or clod, though nothing corporeal or incorporeal should excite or meddle with it, might some time or other of itself begin to creep. However, to be short, a power of beginning motion is not in the idea of matter. It is passive, as we see, to the impressions of motion, and susceptive of it, but cannot produce it. On the contrary, it will always persist uniformly in its present state, either of rest or motion, if nothing stirs, diverts, accelerates, or stops it. Nor is there anything in all physics better settled than that which is called *vis inertiæ* or the inertia of matter.

The propagation of motion from body to body, without any First mover, or immaterial cause of motion, has been proved impossible, proposition I.

The supposition of a perpetual motion in a circle is begging the question. For if A moves B, B moves C, and so on to Z, and then Z moves A; this is the same as to say that A moves A, by the intervention of B, C, D,... Z: that is, A moves itself, or can begin motion.[206]

It remains then, that all corporeal motions come originally from some mover incorporeal, which must be either that Supreme and self-existing spirit himself, who is God, or such as will put us into the way how to find that there is such a Being (turn back to proposition I).

If we consider ourselves, and the voluntary motions begun by us, we may there see the thing exemplified. We move our bodies, or some members of them, and by these move other things, as they again do others, and know these motions to spring from the operations of our minds; but then we know also, that we have not an independent power of creating motion. If we had, it could not be so limited as our locomotive faculties are, nor confined to small quantities and certain circumstances only: we should have had it from eternity, nor could we ever be deprived of it. So that we are necessitated to look up and acknowledge some Higher being, who is able not only to produce motion, but to impart a faculty of producing it.

And if the petty motions of us mortals afford arguments for the being of a God, much more may those greater motions we see in the world, and the phenomena attending them: I mean the motions of the planets and heavenly bodies. For these must be put into motion, either by one common mighty Mover, acting upon them immediately, or by causes and laws of His appointment, or by their respective movers, who, for reasons to which you can by this time be no stranger, must depend upon some Superior, that furnish them with the power of doing this. And granting it to be done either of these ways, we can be at no great distance from a demonstration of the existence of a Deity.

It may perhaps be said that though matter has not the power of moving itself, yet it has an attractive force by which it can move other parts of matter, so that all matter equally moves and is moved. But, allowing those things which are now usually ascribed to attraction, we shall still be necessitated to own some Superior being whose influence mixes itself with matter, and operates upon it, or at least who, some way or other, imparts this force. For attraction, according to the true sense of the word, supposes one body to act upon another at a distance, or where it is not; but nothing can be an agent, where it is not at all. Matter can act only by contact, impelling contiguous bodies, when it is put into motion by something else, or resisting those which strike against it, when it is at rest. And this it does as matter: i.e. by being impenetrable to other matter; but attraction is not of the nature or idea of matter. So that what is called "attraction," is so called only because the same things happen as if the parts of matter did mutually attract; but in truth this can only be an effect of something which acts upon or by matter according to a certain law. The parts of matter seem not only to gravitate towards each other, but many of them to fly each other. Now these two contrary motions and seeming qualities cannot both proceed from matter *quà* matter; cannot both be of the nature of it: and therefore they must be owing to some external cause, or to some other being, which excites in them this as it were love and discord.[207]

Besides, as to the revolution of a planet about the sun, mere gravitation is not sufficient to produce that effect. It must be compounded with a motion of projection, to keep the planet from falling directly into the sun, and bring it about; and from what hand, I desire to know, comes this other motion (or direction)? Who impressed it?

What a vast field for contemplation is here opened! Such regions of matter about us, in which there is not the least particle that does not carry with it an argument of God's existence; not the least stick or straw, or other trifle that falls to the ground, but shows it; not the slightest motion produced, the least whisper of the air, but tells it.

XIV. *The frame and constitution of the world, the magnificence of it, the various phenomena and kinds of beings, the uniformity observed in the productions of things, the uses and ends for which they serve, etc., do all show that there is some Almighty designer, an infinite wisdom and power at the top of all these things: such marks there are of both.*[208] *or, God is that Being, without whom such a frame or constitution of the world, such a magnificence in it, etc., could not be.* In order to prove to anyone the grandness of this fabric of the world, one needs only to bid him consider the sun, with that insupportable glory and lustre that surrounds it; to demonstrate the vast distance, magnitude, and heat of it; to represent to him the chorus of planets moving periodically, by uniform laws, in their several orbits about it, affording a regular variety of aspects, guarded some of them by secondary planets, and, as it were, emulating the state of the sun, and probably all possessed by proper inhabitants; to remind him of those surprising visits the comets make us, the large trains, or uncommon splendor, which attends them, the far country they come from, and the curiosity and horror they excite not only among us, but in the inhabitants of other planets, who also may be up to see the entry and progress of these ministers of fate;[209] to direct his eye and contemplation through those azure fields and vast regions above him, up to the fixed stars, that radiant numberless host of heaven, and to make him understand how unlikely a thing it is that they should be placed there only to adorn and bespangle a canopy over our heads (though that would be a great piece of magnificence too), and much less to supply the places of so many glowworms, by affording a feeble light to our earth, or even to all our fellow-planets; to convince him, that they are rather so many other suns, with their several regions and sets of planets about them; to show him, by the help of glasses, still more and more of these fixed lights, and to beget in him an apprehension of their unaccountable numbers, and of those immense spaces that lie retired beyond our utmost reach and even imagination—I say, one needs but to do this, and explain to him such things as are now known almost to everybody, and by it to show that if the world be not infinite, it is *infinito similis,*[210] and therefore sure a magnificent structure, and the work of an infinite Architect. But if we could take a view of all the particulars contained within that astonishing compass, which we have thus hastily run over, how would wonders multiply upon us? Every corner, every part of the world is as it were made up of other worlds. If we look upon this, our seat (I mean this earth), what scope is here for admiration? The great variety of mountains, hills, valleys, plains, rivers, seas, trees, plants! The many tribes of different animals with which it is flocked! The multifarious inventions and works of one of these; that is, of us men, etc. And yet when all these (heaven and earth) are surveyed as nicely as they can be by the help of our unassisted senses, and even of telescopical glasses, by the assistance of good microscopes in very small parts of matter as many new wonders[211] may perhaps be discovered, as those already observed: new kingdoms of animals, new architecture and curiosity of work. So that, as before our senses and even conception fainted in those vast journeys we were obliged to take in considering the expanse of the universe, so here again they fail us in our researches into the principles and consistuent parts of it. Both the beginnings and the ends of things, the least and the greatest, all conspire to baffle us, and, which way ever we prosecute our inquiries, we still fall in with fresh subjects of amazement, and fresh reasons to believe that there are indefinitely still more, and more behind, that will forever escape our eagerest pursuits and deepest penetration.

This mighty building is not only thus grand, and the appearances stupendous in it, but the *manner* in which things are effected is commonly unintelligible, and their causes too profound for us. There are indeed many things in nature which we know, and some of which we seem to know the causes, but, alas! how few are these with respect to the whole sum? And the causes which we assign, what are they? Commonly such, as can only be expressed in general terms, while the bottoms of things remain unfathomable. Such as have been collected from experience, but could scarcely be known beforehand, by any arguments *a priori*, to be capable of rendering such effects; and yet till causes are known after that manner, they are not thoroughly understood. Such, as seem disproportionate and too little, and are so insufficient and unsatisfactory, that one cannot but be inclined to think that something immaterial and invisible must be immediately concerned. In short, we know many times that such a thing will have such an effect, or perhaps that such an effect is produced by such a cause, but the manner *how* we know not, or but grossly, and if such an hypothesis be true. It is impossible for us to come at the true principles of things, or to see into the economy of the finest part of nature and workings of the first springs. The causes that appear to us, are but effects of other causes; the vessels of which the bodies of plants and animals consist, are made up of other, smaller vessels; the subtlest parts of matter which we have any notion of (as animal spirits, or particles of light), have *their* parts, and may for ought we know be compound bodies; and, as to the substances themselves of all these things, and their internal constitution, they are hid from our eyes. Our philosophy dwells in the surface of nature.

However, in the next place, we ourselves cannot but be witnesses that there are stated methods, as so many set forms of proceeding, which things punctually and religiously keep to. The same causes, circumstanced in the same manner, have always the same success; all the species of animals among us, are made according to one general idea; and so are those of plants also, and even minerals: no new ones are brought forth or arisen anywhere, and the old are preserved and continued by the old ways.

Lastly, it appears, I think plainly enough, in the parts and model of the world, that there is a *contrivance* and a respect to certain reasons and *ends*. How the sun is posited near the middle of our system for the more convenient dispensing of his benign influences to the planets moving about him; how the plain of the earth's equator intersects that of her orbit, and makes a proper angle with it, in order to diversify the year and create a useful variety of seasons, and many other things of this kind, though a thousand times repeated, will always be pleasing meditations to good men and true scholars. Who can observe the vapors to ascend, especially from the sea, meet above in clouds, and fall again after condensation, and not understand this to be a kind of distillation in order to clear the water of its grosser salts, and then by rains and dews to supply the fountains and rivers with fresh and wholesome liquor, to nourish the vegetables below by showers which descend in drops as from a watering-pot upon a garden, etc.; who can view the structure of a plant or animal, the indefinite number of their fibers and fine vessels, the formation of larger vessels and the several members out of them, and the apt disposition of all these, the way laid out for the reception and distribution of nutriment, the effect this nutriment has in extending the vessels, bringing the vegetable or animal to its full growth and expansion, continuing the motion of the several fluids, repairing the decays of the body, and preserving life; who can take notice of the several faculties of animals, their arts of saving and providing for themselves, or the ways in which they are provided for, the uses of plants to animals, and of some animals to others, particularly to mankind, the care taken that the several species should be propagated out of their proper seeds (without confusion),[212] the strong inclinations implanted in animals for that purpose, their love of their young, and the like; I say, who can do this, and not see a *design*, in such regular pieces, so nicely wrought, and so preserved? If there was but *one* animal, and in that case it could not be doubted but that his eyes were made that he might see with them, his ears that he might hear with them, and so on, through at least the most considerable parts of him; if it can much less be doubted, when the same things are repeated in the individuals of all the tribes of animals; if the like observations may be made with respect to vegetables, and other things; and if all these kinds of things, and therefore much more their particulars, upon and in the earth, waters, air, are inconceivably numerous (as most evidently they are), one cannot but be convinced from that, which is so very obvious to every understanding, and plainly runs through the nobler parts of the visible world, that not only they, but other things, even those that seem to be less noble, have their ends too, though not so well understood.

And now, since we cannot suppose the parts of matter to have contrived this wonderful form of a world among themselves, and then by agreement to have taken their respective posts, and pursued constant ends by certain methods and measures concerted (because these are acts of which they are not capable), there must be some other Being, whose wisdom and power are equal to such a mighty work as is the structure and preservation of the world. There must be some almighty Mind, who models and adorns it, lays the causes of things so deep, prescribes them such uniform and steady laws, destines and adapts them to certain purposes, and makes one thing to fit and answer to another.[213]

That such a beautiful scheme, such a just and geometrical arrangement of things, composed of innumerable parts, and placed as the offices and uses and wants of the several beings require, through such an immense extent, should be the effect of *chance* only, is a conceit so prodigiously absurd that certainly no one can espouse it heartily, who understands the meaning of that word. "Chance" seems to be only a term by which we express our ignorance of the cause of anything. For when we say anything comes "by chance," we do not mean that it had no other cause, but only that we do not know the true cause which produced it, or interposed in such a manner as to make that fall out which was not expected. Nor can I think that anybody has such an idea of chance, as to make it an *agent* or really existing and acting cause of anything, and much less sure of *all* things. Whatever events or effects there are, they must proceed from some agent or cause, which is either free or not free (that is, necessary). If it be free, it wills what it produces, and therefore that which is produced is produced with design, not by chance. If it acts necessarily, the event must necessarily be, and therefore it is not by accident. For that which is by accident or chance only, might not have been; or, it is an accident only that it is. There can be therefore no such cause as chance. And to omit a great deal that might yet be said, matter is indefinitely divisible, and the first particles (or atoms) of which it consists must be small beyond all our apprehension; and the chances that must all hit to produce *one* individual of any species of material beings (if only chance was concerned), must consequently be indefinitely many; and if space be also indefinitely extended, and the number of those individuals (not to say of the species themselves) which lie dispersed in it indefinite, the chances required to the production of them all, or of the universe, will be the rectangle of one indefinite quantity drawn into another. We may well call them infinite. And then, to say that anything cannot happen unless infinite chances coincide, is the same as to say there are infinite chances against the happening of it, or odds that it will not happen; and this, again, is the same as to say it is impossible to happen, since if there be a possibility that it may happen, the hazard is not infinite. The world therefore cannot be the child of chance.[214] He must be little acquainted with the works of nature, who is not sensible how delicate and fine they are; and the finer they are, the grosser were those of Epicurus.[215]

If it should be objected that many things seem to be useless, many births are monstrous, or the like, such answers as these may be made: The uses of some things are known to some men, and not to others; the uses of some are known now, that were not known to anybody formerly; the uses of many may be discovered hereafter; and those of some other things may forever remain unknown to all men, and yet be in nature, as much as those discovered were before their discovery, or are now in respect of them who know them not. Things have not, therefore, no uses, because they are concealed from us. Nor is nature irregular, or without method, because there are some seeming deviations from the common rule. These are generally the effects of that influence which free agents and various circumstances have upon natural productions, which may be deformed or hurt by external impressions, heterogeneous matter introduced, or disagreeable and unnatural motions excited; and if the case could be truly put, it would no doubt appear that nature proceeds as regularly (or the laws of nature have as regular an effect), when a monster is produced, as when the usual issue in common cases. Under these circumstances the monster is the *genuine* issue: that is, in the same circumstances there would always be the same kind of production. And, therefore, if things are now and then misshaped, this infers no unsteadiness or mistake in nature. Besides, the magnificence of the world admits of some *perturbations*; not to say, requires some *variety*. The question is: Could all those things, which we *do know* to have uses and ends, and to the production of which such wonderful contrivance and the combinations of so many things are required, be produced, and method and regularity be preserved *so far as it is*, if nothing but blind chance presided over all? Are not the innumerable instances of things which are undeniably made with reference to certain ends, and of those which are propagated and repeated by the same constant methods, enough to convince us that there are ends proposed, and rules observed, even where we do not see them? And, lastly, if we should descend to particulars, what are those seemingly useless or monstrous productions in respect of the rest, that plainly declare the ends for which they were intended, and that come into the world by the usual ways, with the usual perfection of their several kinds? If the comparison could be made, I verily believe these would be found to be almost infinituple of the other, which ought therefore to be reputed as nothing.

They, who content themselves with words, may ascribe the formation of the world to "fate" or "nature," as well as to chance, or better. And yet fate, in the first place, is nothing but a series of events, considered as necessarily following in some certain order, or of which it has always been true that they *would be* in their determinate times and places. It is called indeed a series of causes,[216] but then they are such causes as are also effects—all of them, if there is no First cause—and may be taken for such. So that in this description is nothing like such a cause as is capable of giving this form to the world. A series of events is the same with events happening *seriatim*: which words declare nothing concerning the *cause* of that concatenation of events, or why it is. Time, place, manner, necessity are but *circumstances* of things that come to pass, not causes of their existence, or of their being as they are. On the contrary, some external and superior cause must be supposed to put the series in motion, to project the order, to connect the causes and effects, and to *impose* the necessity.[217]

Then for "nature,"

1. If it be used for the intrinsic manner of existing—that constitution, make, or disposition, with which anything is produced or born, and from which result those properties, powers, inclinations, passions, qualities, and manners, which are called natural (and sometimes "nature"), in opposition to such as are acquired, adventitious, or forced (which use is common)—then to say that nature formed anything, or gave it

its manner of existence, is to say that it formed itself, or that the effect is the efficient.[218] Besides, how can *manner* (manner of existing) be the cause of existing, or properly do anything. An agent is an acting being, some substance, not a *manner* of being.

2. If it be used in that other sense, by which it stands for the *ideas* of things, what they are in themselves, and what in their circumstances, causes, consequences, respects; or, in short, that which determines them to be of this or that kind (as when we say, the *nature* of justice[219] requires this or that, i.e. the idea of justice requires or supposes it; a crime is of such a *nature*, that is, bears such a respect to the law, and is attended with such circumstances; or the like): then none of these senses can do an atheist any service.

3. If it be used for the *world*[220] (as, the laws of *nature* may be understood to be the laws of the world, by which it is governed, and the phenomena in it produced; after the same manner of speaking as when we say, the laws of England, France, etc.) then it stands for that very thing, the former and architect of which is the object of our inquiry, and therefore cannot be that architect itself. Under this sense may be comprehended that, when it denotes *reality of existence*, as when it is said that such a thing is not in *nature* (not to be found in the world).

4. If it signifies the forementioned laws themselves, or that course in which things by virtue of these laws proceed (as when the effects of these laws are styled the works of *nature*), then, laws suppose some legislator, and are posterior to that of which they are the laws. There can be no laws of any nation, till the people are of which that nation consists.

5. If it be used after the same manner as the word "habit" frequently is, to which many things are ascribed (just as they are to nature), though it be nothing existing distinct from the habits which particular men or beings contract, then nature is a kind of abstract notion, which can *do* nothing. Perhaps "nature" may be put for *natures*, all natures, after the manner of a collective noun; or it may be mentioned as an *agent* only as we personify virtues and attributes, either for variety, or the shorter and more convenient expressing of things.

6. Lastly, if it denotes the Author of nature, or God[221] (the effect seeming, though by a hard metonymy in this case, to be put for the efficient), then, to Him it is that I ascribe the formation of the world, etc.

To all which I must subjoin that there is an unaccountable liberty taken in the use of this word, and that frequently it is used merely as a word, and nothing more, they who use it not knowing themselves what they mean by it.[222] However, in no sense can it supersede the being of a Deity.

XV. *Life, sense, agitation, and the faculties of our own minds show the existence of some superior Being from whom they are derived,* Or, *God is that Being, without whom neither could these be, any more than the things before mentioned.* That they cannot flow from the nature of any matter about us, as matter, or from any modification, size, or motion of it, if it be not already apparent, may perhaps be proved more fully afterwards. And that our souls themselves are not self-existent, nor hold their faculties independently of all other beings, follows from propositions IV and VII. Therefore, we must necessarily be indebted for what we have, of this kind, to some great Benefactor who is the fountain of them. For, since we are conscious that we have them, and yet have them not of ourselves, we must have them from some other.

A man has little reason, God knows, to fancy the suppositum of his life, sense, and cogitative faculties to be an independent being, when he considers how transitory and uncertain at best his life and all his enjoyments are: what he is, whence he came, and whither he is going.[223] The mind acts not, or in the most imperceptible manner, *in animalculo*, or the seminal state of a man; only as a principle of vegetation in the state of an embryon; and as a sensitive soul in the state of infancy, at least for some time, in which we are rather below than above many other animals. By degrees indeed, with age and exercise and proper opportunities, it seems to open itself, find its own talents, and ripen into a rational being. But then it reasons not without labor, and is forced to take many tedious steps in the pursuit of truth; finds all its powers subject to great eclipses and diminutions, in the time of sleep, indisposition, sickness, etc., and at best reaching but a few objects in respect of all that are in the immensity of the universe; and, lastly, is obnoxious to many painful sensations and reflections. Had the soul of man the principle of its own existence and faculties within itself, clear of all dependence, it could not be liable to all these limitations and defects, to all these alterations and removes from one state to another: it must certainly be constant to itself, and persist in a uniform manner of being.

There may be, perhaps, who will say, that the soul, together with life, sense, etc., are propagated by traduction from parents to children, from them to their children again, and so from eternity,[224] and that therefore nothing can be collected from the nature of them as to the existence of a Deity. Answer: if there could be such a traduction, yet to suppose one traduced to come from another traduced, and so *ab æterno*, without any further account of the original of mankind, or taking in any author of this traductive power, is the same as to suppose an infinite series of moveds without a mover, or of effects without a cause, the absurdity of which is shown already, proposition I. But concerning this matter, I cannot but think further, after the following manner: What is meant by *tradux animæ* ought to be clearly explained, for it is not easy to conceive how thought, or thinking substances, can be propagated after the manner of branches, or in any manner that can be analogous to it, or even warrant a metaphorical use of that phrase.[225] It should also be told whether this traduction be made from one or from both the parents. If from one, from which of them is it? And if from both, then the same *tradux*, or branch, must always proceed from two stocks, which is a thing, I presume, that can nowhere else be found, nor has any parallel in nature. And yet such a thing may much better be supposed of vines, or plants, than of thinking beings, who are simple and uncompounded substances.[226]

This opinion of the traduction of souls seems to me to stand upon an unsound foundation. For I take it to be grounded chiefly on these two things: the similitude there is between the features, humors, and abilities of children and those of their parents;[227] and the difficulty men find in forming the notion of a spirit.[228] For, from hence, they are apt to conclude that there can be no other substance but matter, and that the soul, resulting from some disposition of the body, or some part of it, or being some merely material appendix to it, must *attend* it, and come along with it from the parent or parents; and as there is a derivation of the one, so there must be also of the other at the same time.

Now the former of these is not always true, as it ought to be to make the argument valid. Nothing more common than to see children differ from their parents, in their understandings, inclinations, shapes, complexions, and (I am sure) one from another. And this dissimilitude has as much force to prove there is *not* a traduction, as similitude, whenever that happens, can have to prove there is. Besides, it seems to me not hard to account for *some* likeness without the help of traduction. It is visible the meat and drink men take, the air they breathe, the objects they see, the sounds they hear, the company they keep, etc., will create changes in them, sometimes with respect to their intellectuals, sometimes to their passions and humors, and sometimes to their health and other circumstances of their bodies: and yet the original stamina and fundamental parts of the man remain still the same. If then the *semina*, out of which animals are produced, are (as I doubt not) *animalcula* already formed,[229] which, being distributed about, especially in some opportune places, are taken in with aliment, or perhaps the very air, being separated in the bodies of the males by strainers proper to every kind, and then lodged in their seminal vessels, do there receive some kind of addition and influence, and being thence transferred into the wombs of the females, are there nourished more plentifully, and grow, till they become too big to be longer confined;[230] I say, if this be the case, why may not the nutriment received from the parents, being prepared by their vessels, and of the same kind with that with which they themselves are nourished, be the same in great measure to the *animalcula* and *embrya* that it is to them, and consequently very much assimilate their young, without the derivation of anything else from them? Many impressions may be made upon the *fœtus*, and many tinctures given to the fluids communicated to it from the parents, and yet it, the *animal itself*, may not be originally begun in them, or traduced from them. This hypothesis (which has long been mine) suggests a reason why the child is sometimes more like the father, sometimes the mother: viz. because the vessels of the animalculum are disposed to receive a greater proportion of aliment sometimes from the one, sometimes from the other; or the fluids and spirits in one may ferment and operate more strongly than in the other, and so have a greater and more signal effect. (Here, it ought to be observed that though what the animalculum receives from the father is in quantity little, in respect of all that nutriment which it receives by the mother, yet the former, being the first accretion to the original stamina, adhering immediately, and being early interwoven with them, may affect it more.)

Since there cannot be a proper traduction of the child (one mind and one body) from both the *two* parents, all the similitude it bears to one of them must proceed from some such cause as I have assigned, or at least not from traduction. For the child being sometimes like the father, and sometimes the mother, and the traduction either always from the father, or always from the mother, there must sometimes be similitude where there is no traduction; and then, if the child may resemble one of them without it, why not the other too? The account I have given appears, many times at least, to be true in plants, which, raised from the same seed, but in different beds and soil, will differ. The different nutriment introduces some diversity into the seed or original plant, and assimilates it in some measure to the rest raised in the same place.

The other thing which I take to be one of the principal supports to this doctrine of traduction (a supposition that the soul is merely material, or but the result of some disposition in matter) has been undertaken to be refuted hereafter. But I may premise this here: though we can have no *image* of a spirit (because no being can be portrayed, or represented by an image, but what is material), yet we may have reason to assert the existence of such a substance.[231] Matter is a thing which we converse with, of which we know pretty well the nature and properties, and since we cannot find among them any that are cogitative, or such a thing as life, but several things *inconsistent* with them, we are under a necessity of confessing that there is some other species of substance beside that which is corporeal, and that our souls are of that kind (or rather of one of those kinds which are not merely corporeal, for there must be more than one), though we can draw no image of it in our own minds. Nor is it at all surprising that we should not be able to do this, for how can the mind be the object of itself?[232] It may contemplate the body which it inhabits, may be conscious of its own acts, and reflect upon the ideas it finds—but of its own substance it can have no adequate notion, unless it could be as it were object and spectator both. Only that perfect Being, whose knowledge is infinite, can thus intimately know himself.

They, who found the traduction of the soul upon this presumption, that it is material, and attends the body as some part or affection of it, seem further to be most woefully mistaken upon this account: because the body *itself* is not propagated by traduction. It passes indeed *through* the bodies of the parents, who afford a transitory habitation and subsistence to it; but it cannot be *formed by* the parents, or *grow out* of any part of them. For all the vital and essential parts of it must be one coeval system, and formed *at once* in the first article of the nascent animalculum; since no one of these could be nourished, or ever come to anything, without the rest: on the contrary, if any one of them could prevent and be before the rest, it would soon wither and decay again for lack of nourishment received by proper vessels, as we see the limbs and organs of animals do when the supply due from the animal economy is any way intercepted or obstructed. And since an organized body, which requires to be thus simultaneously made (fashioned, as it were, at one stroke) cannot be the effect of any natural and gradual process, I cannot but conclude that there were animalcula of every tribe originally formed by the almighty Parent, to be the seed of all future generations of animals. Any other manner of production would be like that which is usually called equivocal or spontaneous generation, and with great reason now generally exploded. And it is certain that the analogy of nature in other instances, and microscopical observations, do abet what I have said strongly.

Lastly, if there is no race of men that has been from eternity, there is no man who is not descended from two first parents: and then the souls of those two first parents could be traduced from no other. And that there is no such race (none that has been upon this earth from eternity), is apparent from the face of earthly things, and the history of mankind,[233] arts, and sciences. What is objected against this argument from fancied inundations, conflagrations, etc.[234] has no weight with me. Let us suppose some such great calamity to happen now. It must be either universal, or not. If universal, so that nobody at all could be saved, then either there must never be any more men, or they must begin again in some first parents. If it was only topical, affecting some one tract of the globe, or if the tops of mountains more eminent, or rocks more firm, remained unaffected, or if there were any natural means left by which men might escape, considerable numbers must certainly survive; and then it cannot be imagined that they should all be absolutely so ignorant of everything, that no one should be able to give an account of such things as were common; no one able to write, or read, or even to recollect that there were such things as letters; none that understood any trade; none that could tell what kind of habitations they had, how they used to be clothed, how their meat dressed, or even what their food was; nor can it be thought that all books, arms, manufactures of every kind, ships, buildings, and all the product of human skill and industry now extant in the world should be so universally and utterly abolished, that no part, no vestigium of them, should remain; not so much as to give a hint toward the speedy restoration of necessary arts at least. The people escaping must sure have clothes on, and many necessaries about them, without which they could not escape, nor outlive such a dreadful scene. In short, no conflagration, no flood, no destruction, can serve the objector's purpose to reduce mankind to that state which, by ancient memoirs and many undeniable symptoms, we find them to have been in not many thousands of years since; I say, no destruction can serve his purpose, but such an one as makes thorough work, only sparing two or three couples, stripped of everything, and the most stupid and veriest blocks[235] to be picked out of the whole number: natural fools, or mere *homines sylvestres*, would retain habits, and fall to their old way of living, as soon as they had the opportunity to do it. And suppose they never should have such an opportunity; yet neither would this serve him effectually, since without some supernatural Power interposing, such a revolution could not be brought about, nor the naked creatures preserved, nor the earth reformed out of its ashes and ruins after such a calcination, or dissolution, such a total demolition of everything. To this give me leave to add, that though many inundations, great earthquakes, volcanos, and fiery eruptions have been in particular countries, yet there is no memory or testimony of any such thing that has ever been universal,[236] except perhaps of one deluge: and as to that, if the genius of the language in which the relation is delivered, and the manner of writing history in it were well understood, some labored and moliminous attempts to account for it might have been prevented. And beside that, the same record which tells the thing was, tells also how immediately God was concerned in it, that some persons actually were saved, and that the people who then perished, as well as they who survived, all descended from two first parents: and if that authority be a sufficient proof of one part of the relation, it must be so of the rest.

We may conclude, then, that the human soul, with its faculties of cogitation, etc., depends upon a Superior being. And who can this be but the Supreme being, or God? Of whom I now proceed to affirm, in the next place, that,

XVI. *Though His essence and manner of being is to us altogether incomprehensible, yet we may say with assurance, that He is free from all defects: or One, from whom all defects must be removed.*

This proposition has in effect been proved already.[237] However I will take the liberty to enlarge a little further upon it here. As our minds are finite, they cannot, without a contradiction, comprehend what is infinite. And if they were enlarged, to ever so great a capacity, yet so long as they retain their general nature, and continue to be of the same kind, they would, by that, be only rendered able to apprehend more and more *finite* ideas; out of which, howsoever increased or exalted, no positive idea of the perfection of God can ever be formed. For a Perfect being must be infinite, and perfectly One; and in such a nature there can be nothing finite, nor any composition of finites.

How should we comprehend the nature of the Supreme incorporeal being, or how He exists, when we comprehend not the nature of the most inferior spirits, nor have any conception even of matter itself, divested of its accidents? How should we attain to an adequate knowledge of the Supreme author of the world, when we are utterly incapable of knowing the extent of the world itself, and the numberless undescried regions, with their several states and circumstances, contained in it, never to be frequented or visited by our philosophy; nor can turn ourselves any way, but we are still accosted with something above our understanding? If we cannot penetrate so far into effects, as to discover them and their nature thoroughly, it is not to be expected that we should—that we can ever be admitted to—see through the mysteries of His nature, who is the Cause, so far above them all. The Divine perfection, then, and manner of being, must be of a kind different from and above all that we can conceive.

However, notwithstanding our own defects, we may positively affirm there can be *none* in God: since He is perfect, as we have seen, He cannot be defective or imperfect. This needs no further proof. But what follows from it, I would have to be well understood and remembered: viz. that from Him must be removed want of life and activity, ignorance, impotence, acting inconsistently with reason and truth, and the like. Because these are defects: defect of knowledge, power, etc. These are defects and blemishes, even in us. And though his perfection is above all our ideas, and of a different kind from the perfections of men or any finite beings, yet what would be a defect in them, would be much more such in Him, and can by no means be ascribed to Him.[238]

Though we understand not His manner of knowing things, yet, ignorance being uniform and the same in every subject, we understand what is meant by that word, and can literally and truly deny that to belong to Him. The like may be said with respect to His power, or manner of operating, etc. And when we speak of the internal essential attributes of God positively, as that He is omniscient, omnipotent, eternal, etc. the intent is only to say, that there is no object of knowledge, or power, which He does not know, or cannot do; He exists without beginning and end; etc., and thus we keep still within the limits allowed by the proposition.[239] That is, we may speak thus without pretending to comprehend His nature. And so,

XVII. *We may consider God as operating in the production and government of the world, and may draw conclusions from His works, as they are called, notwithstanding anything which has been said.*[240] Because, this we can do without comprehending the manner of His existence. Nay, the contemplation of His works leads us into a necessity of owning that there must be an incomprehensible Being at the head of them.

Though I do not comprehend the mode in which the world depends upon Him and He influences and disposes things, because this enters into His nature, and the one cannot be understood without the other; yet if I see things which I know cannot be self-existent, and observe plainly an economy and design in the disposition of them, I may conclude that there is some Being, upon whom their existence does depend, and by whom they are modeled; may call this Being "God," or the Author and Governor of the world, etc., without contradicting myself or truth—as I hope it will appear from what has been said, and is going to be said in the next proposition.

XVIII. *God, who gives existence to the world, does also govern it by His providence.* Concerning this grand question, "Whether there is a Divine providence, or not," I use to think, for myself, after the following manner.

First: The world may be said to be *governed* (at least cannot be said to be ἀκυβέρνητος,[241] or left to fluctuate fortuitously), if there are laws by which natural causes act, the several phenomena in it succeed regularly, and, in general, the constitution of things is preserved—if there are rules observed in the production of herbs, trees, and the like—if the several kinds of animals are, in proportion to their several degrees and stations in the animal kingdom, furnished with faculties proper to direct and determine their actions (and when they act according to them, they may be said to follow the *law* of their nature)—if they are placed and provided for suitably to their respective natures and wants,[242] or (which amounts to the same thing) if their natures are adapted to their circumstances[243]—if, lastly, particular cases relating to rational beings are taken care of in such a manner as will at last agree best with reason.

Secondly: If there are such laws and provisions, they can come originally from no other being, but from Him who is the Author of nature. For those laws which result from the natures of things, their properties, and the use of their faculties, and may be said to be written upon the things themselves, can be the laws of no other; nor can those things whose very being depends upon God, exist under any condition repugnant to His will, and therefore can be subject to no laws or dispositions which He would not have them be subject to: that is, which are not *His*. Besides, there is no other being capable of imposing laws or any scheme of government upon the world, because there is no other who is not himself *part* of the world, and whose own existence does not depend upon Him.

Thirdly: By the "providence of God" I mean His governing the world by such laws, and making such provisions, as are mentioned above. So that if there are such, there is a Divine providence.

Lastly: It is not impossible that there should be such; on the contrary, we have just reasons to believe there are. It would be an absurd assertion to say that anything is impossible to a being whose nature is infinitely above our comprehension, if the terms do not imply a contradiction, but we may with confidence assert that it is impossible for anything, whose existence flows from such a being, ever to grow so far out of His reach, or be so emancipated from under Him, that the manner of its existence should not be regulated and determined by Him.

As to inanimate substances, we see the case to be really just as it was supposed before to be. The heavenly and greater bodies keep their stations, or persevere to go the same circuits over and over, by a *certain law*. Little bodies or particles, of the same kind, observe continually the same *rules* of attracting, repelling, etc. When there are any seeming variations in nature, they proceed only from the different circumstances and combinations of things, acting all the while under their ancient *laws*. We are so far acquainted with the laws of gravitation and motion, that we are able to calculate their effects, and serve ourselves of them, supplying upon many occasions the defect of power in ourselves by mechanical powers, which never fail to answer according to the establishment. Briefly, we see it so far from being *impossible* that the inanimate world should be governed by laws, that all the parts of it are obnoxious to laws by them *inviolable*.

As to vegetables, we see also how they are determined by certain methods prescribed them. Each sort is produced from its proper seed, has the same texture of fibers, is nourished by the same kind of juices out of the earth, digested and prepared by the same kind of vessels, etc. Trees receive annually their peculiar liveries, and bear their proper fruits; flowers are dressed, each family, in the same colors, or diversify their fashions after a certain manner proper to the kind, and breathe the same essences; and both these and all other kinds observe their seasons, and seem to have their several professions and trades appointed them, by which they produce such food and manufactures (pardon the catachresis), as may satisfy the wants of animals. Being so very necessary, they, or at least the most useful, grow easily: being fixed in the earth, insensible, and not made for society, they are generally ἀῤῥενοθήλεα;[244] being liable to a great consumption both of them and their seeds, they yield great quantities of these, in order to repair and multiply their race, etc. So that here is evidently a *regulation*, by which the several orders are preserved, and the ends of them answered according to their first establishment too.

Then as to animals, there are laws which *mutatus mutandis* are common to them with inanimate beings and vegetables, or at least such as resemble[245] their laws. The individuals of the several kinds of those, as of these, have the same (general) shape and members, to be managed after the same manner—have the same vessels replenished with the same kinds of fluids, and furnished with the same glands for the separation and distribution of such parts of them as answer the same intentions in them all—are stimulated by the same appetites and uneasinesses to take in their food, continue their breed, etc. And whatever it is, that proceeds thus in a manner so like to that of vegetables, according to fixed methods, and keeps in the same general track as they do, may be said to observe and be under some like rule or law, which either operates upon and limits it *ab extra*, or was given it with its nature. But there are, moreover, certain obligations resulting from the several degrees of reason and sense, or sense only, of which we cannot but be conscious in ourselves, and observe some faint indications in the kinds below us, and which can be looked upon as nothing less than *laws* by which animals are to move and manage themselves: that is, otherwise expressed, by which the Author of their natures *governs* them. 'Tis true these laws may not impose an absolute necessity, nor be of the same rigor with those of inanimate and merely passive beings, because the beings which are subject to these (men at least) may be supposed in some measure free, and to act upon some kind of principles or motives: yet still, they may have the nature of laws, though they may be broken; and may make a part of that providence by which God administers the affairs of the world. Whatever advantages I obtain by my own free endeavors, and right use of those faculties and powers I have, I look upon them to be as much the effects of God's providence and government as if they were given me immediately by Him, without my acting, since all my faculties and abilities (whatever they are) depend upon Him, and are as it were instruments of His providence to me in respect of such things as may be procured by them.[246]

To finish this head: it is so far from being *impossible* that the several tribes of animals should be so made and placed as to find proper ways of supporting and defending themselves (I mean, so far as it is consistent with the general economy of the world, for some cannot well subsist without the destruction of some others), that, on the contrary, we see men, beasts, birds, fishes, insects all have organs and faculties adapted to their respective circumstances and opportunities of finding their proper food or prey, etc., even to the astonishment of them who attend to the history of nature. If *men*, who seem to have more wants than any other kind, meet with difficulties in maintaining life, it is because they themselves, not contented with what is decent and convenient only, have by their luxuries and scandalous neglect of their reason *made* life expensive.

The world, then, being not left in a state of confusion or as a chaos, but reduced into order and methodized for ages to come—the several species of beings having their offices and provinces assigned them, plants and animals subsistence set out for them, and, as they go off, successors appointed to relieve them, and carry on the scheme, etc.—that the *possibility* only of a *general* providence should be allowed, is certainly too modest a demand. We see, or may see, that in fact there is such a providence.[247]

The great difficulty is, how to account for that providence which is called "particular," or that which respects (principally) particular men. For rational beings and free agents are capable of doing and deserving well or ill. Some will make a right use of their faculties and opportunities, some will not; the vicious may or may not repent, or repent and relapse; some fall into evil habits through inadvertence, bad examples, and the like, rather than any design, and these want to be reclaimed; some may be supposed to worship God and to crave His protection and blessing, etc., and then a proper answer to their prayers may be humbly expected. Hence many and great differences will arise, which will require from a governor suitable encouragements, rewards, correptions, punishments, and that some should be protected and fortunate, others not, or less. Now the good or ill state of a man here, his safety or danger, happiness or unhappiness, depend upon many things, which seem to be scarce all capable of being determined by providence. They depend upon what he does himself, and what naturally follows from his own behavior—upon what is done by others, and may either touch him at the same time, or reach him afterward—upon the course of nature, which must affect him—and, in fine, upon many incidents, of which no account is to be given.[248] As to what he does himself, it is impossible for him, as things are in this maze of life, to know always what tends to happiness, and what not; or, if he could know, that, which ought to be done, may not be within the compass of his powers. Then, if the actions of other men are free, how can they be determined to be only such as may be either good or bad (as the case requires) for some other particular man, since such a determination seems inconsistent with liberty? Besides, numbers of men—acting every one upon the foot of their own private freedom, and the several degrees of sense and ability which they respectively have—their acts (as they either conspire, or cross and obliquely impede, or perhaps directly meet and oppose each other, and have different effects upon men of different makes, or in different circumstances) must cause a strange embarras, and entangle the plot.[249] And, as to the course of nature, if a *good* man be passing by an infirm building, just in the article of falling, can it be expected that God should suspend the force of gravitation till he is gone by, in order to his deliverance; or can we think it would be increased, and the fall hastened, if a *bad* man was there, only that he might be caught, crushed, and made an example?[250] If a man's safety or prosperity should depend upon winds or rains, must new motions be impressed upon the atmosphere, and new directions given to the floating parts of it, by some extraordinary and new influence from God? Must clouds be so precipitated, or kept in suspense,[251] as the case of a particular man or two requires? To which, add that the differing, and many times contrary interests of men are scarce to be reconciled. The wind which carries one into the port, drives another back to sea; and the rains that are but just sufficient upon the hills, may drown the inhabitants of the valleys.[252] In short, may we expect miracles,[253] or can there be a particular providence, a providence that suits the several cases and prayers of individuals, without a continual repetition of them, and force frequently committed upon the laws of nature and the freedom of intelligent agents? For my part, I verily believe there may. For,

1. It seems to me not impossible that God should know what is to come; on the contrary, it is highly reasonable to think that He does and must know things future. Whatever happens in the world which does not come immediately from Him, must either be the effect of mechanical causes, or of the motions of living beings and free agents. For chance, we have seen already, is no cause. Now as to the former, it cannot be impossible for Him, upon whom the being and nature of everything depends, and who therefore must intimately know all their powers and what effects they will have, to see through the whole train of causes and effects, and whatever will come to pass in that way[254]— nay, it is is impossible that He should *not* do it. We ourselves, if we are satisfied of the goodness of the materials of which a machine is made, and understand the force and determination of those powers by which it is moved, can tell what it will do, or what will be the effect of it. And as to those things which depend upon the voluntary motions of free agents, it is well known that men (by whom learn how to judge of the rest) can only be free with respect to such things as are within their sphere—not great, God knows—and their freedom with respect to these can only consist in a liberty either to act, without any incumbent necessity, as their own reason and judgment shall determine them, or to neglect their rational faculties, and not use them at all, but suffer themselves to be carried away by the tendencies and inclinations of the body, which left thus to itself acts in a manner mechanically. Now He, who knows what *is* in men's power, what not; knows the make of their bodies, and all the mechanism and propensions of them; knows the nature and extent of their understandings, and what will determine them this or that way; knows all the process of natural (or second) causes, and consequently how these may work upon them:[255] He, I say, who knows all this, may know what men will do, if He can but know this one thing more, viz. whether they will use their rational faculties or not. And since even we ourselves, mean and defective as we are, can in some measure conceive how so much as this may be done, and seem to want but one step to finish the account, can we with any show of reason deny to a Perfect being this one article more, or think that He cannot do that too, especially if we call to mind that this very power of using our own faculties is held of Him?[256]

Observe what a sagacity there is in some men—not only in respect of physical causes and effects, but also of the future actings of mankind—and how very easy it is, many times (if the persons concerned, their characters, and circumstances are given) to foresee what they will do; as also to foretell many general events, though the intermediate transactions upon which they depend are not known.[257] Consider how much more remarkable this penetration is in some men than in others; consider further, that if there be any minds more perfect than the human (and who can be so conceited of himself as to question this?), they must have it in a still more eminent degree, proportionable to the excellence of their natures; in the last place, do but allow (as you must) this power of discerning to be, in God, proportionable to His nature, as in lower beings it is proportionable to theirs, and then it becomes infinite; and then again, the future actions of free agents are at once all unlocked and exposed to His view. For, that knowledge is not infinite which is limited to things past or present or which come to pass necessarily.

After all, what has been said is only a feeble attempt to show how far even we can go, toward a conception of the manner in which future things may be known; but as we have no adequate idea of an infinite and perfect Being, His powers, and among them His power of knowing, must infinitely pass all our understanding. It must be something different from, and infinitely transcending, all the modes of apprehending things which we know anything of.[258]

We know matters of fact by the help of our senses, the strength of memory, impressions made upon fancy, or the report of others (though that indeed is comprehended under *senses*. For that which we know only by report, in proper speaking we only know the report of, or we have heard it); and all these ways do suppose those matters either to be present, or once to have been. But is it therefore impossible that there should be any *other* ways of knowing? This is so far from being true, that, since God has no organs of sensation, nor such mean faculties as the best of ours are, and consequently cannot know things in the way which we know them in, if He does not know them by some other way, He cannot know them at all, even though they were present; and therefore there must be other ways, or at least another way, of knowing even matters of fact. And since the difficulty we find, in determining whether future matters of fact may be known, arises chiefly from this: that we in reality consider, without minding it, whether they may be known in *our way* of knowing; it vanishes, when we recollect that they are and must be known to God by some other way, and not only so, but this must be some way that is perfect and worthy of Him. Future, or what to us is future, may be as truly the object of Divine knowledge, as present is of ours; nor can we[259] tell what respect "past," "present," "to come," have to the Divine mind, or wherein they differ. To deaf men there is no such thing as sound; to blind no such thing as light or color: nor, when these things are defined and explained to them in the best manner which their circumstances admit, are they capable of knowing how they are apprehended. So here, we cannot tell how future things are known, perhaps, any more than deaf or blind people what sounds or colors are and how they are perceived; but yet there may be a way of knowing those, as well as there is of perceiving these. As they want a fifth sense to perceive sounds or colors, of which they have no notion, so perhaps we may want a sixth sense, or some faculty of which future events may be the proper objects. Nor have we any more reason to deny that there is in nature such a sense or faculty, than the deaf or blind have to deny that there is such a sense as that of hearing or seeing.

We can never conclude that it is impossible for an infinitely perfect Being to know what a free agent will choose to do, till we can comprehend all the powers of such a Being, and that is till we ourselves are infinite and perfect.[260] So far are we from being able to pronounce, with any show of reason, that it is impossible there should be such knowledge in God.

In the last place, this knowledge is not only not impossible, but that which has been already proved concerning the Deity and His perfection does necessarily infer that nothing can be hid from Him. For if ignorance be an imperfection, the ignorance of future acts and events must be so: and then if all imperfections are to be denied of Him, this must.

There is indeed a common prejudice against the prescience (as it is usually called) of God, which suggests that if God foreknows things, He foreknows them infallibly or certainly, and if so, then they are *certain*, and if certain, then they are no longer matter of freedom. And thus prescience and freedom are inconsistent. But sure the nature of a thing is not changed by being known, or known beforehand. For if it is known truly, it is known to be what it is, and therefore is not altered by this. The truth is, God foresees, or rather sees the actions of free agents, because they will be—not that they will be because He foresees them.[261] If I see an object in a certain place, the veracity of my faculties supposed, it is certain that object is there; but yet, it cannot be said it is there *because* I see it there, or that my seeing it there is the cause of its being there; but because it is there, therefore I see it there. It is the object that determines my sensation; and so in the other case, it is a future choice of the free agent that determines the prescience, which yet may be infallibly true.[262]

Let us put these two contradictory propositions—"B (same particular man) will go to church next Sunday," and "B will not go to church next Sunday"—and let us suppose withall, that B is free, and that his going or not going depends merely upon his own will. In this case he may indeed do either, but yet he can do but one of these two things: either go, or not go; and one he must do. One of these propositions therefore is now true, but yet it is not the truth of that proposition which forces him to do what is contained in it; on the contrary, the truth of the proposition arises from what he shall choose to do. And if that truth does not force him, the *foreknowledge* of that truth will not. We may sure suppose B himself to know certainly beforehand which of the two he will choose to do, whether to go to church or not (I mean so far as it depends upon his choice only), and if so, then here is B's own foreknowledge consistent with his freedom; and if we can but, further, suppose God to know as much in this respect as B does, there will be God's foreknowledge consistent with B's freedom.

In a word, it involves no contradiction to assert that God certainly knows what any man will choose; and therefore, that he should do this cannot be said to be impossible.

2. It is not impossible that such laws of nature, and such a series of causes and effects, may be originally designed, that not only general provisions may be made for the several species of beings, but, even particular cases, at least many of them, may also be provided for without innovations or alterations in the course of nature.[263] It is true, this amounts to a prodigious scheme, in which all things to come are, as it were,

comprehended under one view, estimated, and laid together; but, when I consider what a mass of wonders the universe is in other regards; what a Being God is, incomprehensibly great and perfect; that He cannot be ignorant of anything, no not of the future wants and deportments of particular men; and that all things which derive from Him as the First cause, must do this so as to be consistent one with another, and in such a manner as to make one compact system, befitting so great an Author: I say, when I consider this, I cannot deny such an adjustment of things to be within His power.[264] The order of events, proceeding from the settlement of nature, may be as compatible with the due and reasonable success of my endeavors and prayers (as inconsiderable a part of the world as I am),[265] as with any other thing or phenomenon how great soever.

Perhaps my meaning may be made more intelligible thus: Suppose M (some man) certainly to foreknow, some way or other, that, when he should come to be upon his deathbed, L would petition for some particular legacy in a manner so earnest and humble, and with such a good disposition, as would render it proper to grant his request; and upon this M makes his last will, by which he devises to L that which was to be asked, and then locks up the will—and all this many years before the death of M, and while L had yet no expectation or thought of any such thing. When the time comes, the petition is made and granted—not by making any new will, but by the old one already made, and without alteration; which legacy had, notwithstanding that, never been left had the petition never been preferred. The grant may be called an effect of a future act, and depends as much upon it as if it had been made after the act. So if it had been foreseen that L would not so much as ask, and had therefore been left out of the will, this preterition would have been caused by his carriage, though much later than the date of the will. In all this is nothing hard to be admitted, if M be allowed to foreknow the case.[266] And thus the prayers which good men offer to the All-knowing God, and the neglects of others, may find fitting effects already forecasted in the course of nature. Which possibility may be extended to the labors of men, and their behavior in general.

It is obvious to everyone's observation, that in fact particular men are very commonly (at least in some measure) rewarded or punished by the general laws and methods of nature. The natural (though not constant) attendants and consequences of virtue are peace, health, and felicity; of vice, loss of philosophical pleasures, a diseased body, debts, and difficulties. Now then, if B be virtuous and happy, C vicious and at last miserable, laboring under a late and fruitless remorse—though this comes to pass through the natural tendence of things, yet these two cases, being supposed such as require, the one that B should be favored, the other that C should suffer for his wickedness, are as effectually *provided for*, as if God exerted his power in some peculiar way on this occasion.

3. It is not impossible that men, whose natures and actions are foreknown, may be

introduced into the world in such times, places, and other circumstances, as that their acts and behavior may not only coincide with the general plan of things, but also answer many private cases too.[267] The planets and bigger parts of the world, we cannot but see, are disposed into such places and order that they together make a noble *system*, without having their natural powers of attraction (or the force of that which is equivalent to attraction) or any of the laws of motion restrained or altered. On the contrary, being rightly placed, they, by the observation of these, become subservient to the main design. Now why may there not be in the Divine mind something like a projection of the future history of mankind, as well as of the order and motions and various aspects of the greater bodies of the world? And then why should it not be thought possible for *men*, as well as for *them*, by some secret law, though of another kind, or rather by the presidence and guidance of an unseen governing power, to be brought into their places in such a manner as that by the free use of their faculties; the conjunctions and oppositions of their interests and inclinations; the natural influence and weight of their several magnitudes and degrees of parts, power, wealth, etc.; they may conspire to make out the scheme? And then again, since generals consist of particulars, and in this scheme are comprehended the actions and cases of particular men, they cannot be so situated respectively among the rest of their species as to be serviceable to the principal intention, and fall properly into the general diagram of affairs, unless they and their several actings and cases do in the main correspond one to another, and fit among themselves, or at least are not inconsistent.

Here is no implication of any contradiction or absurdity in all this: and therefore it may at least be fairly *supposed*. And if so, it will follow, that a particular providence may be compatible with the natural freedom of men's actions. Such a supposition is certainly not beyond the power of an almighty, perfect Being; it is moreover worthy of Him, and what they who can dwell a while upon those words, and take their import, must believe.

The ancients, I am persuaded, had some such thoughts as these. For they were generally fatalists, and yet do not seem to have thought that they were not masters of their own actions.[268]

4. It is not *impossible* (for this is all that I contend for here), that many things, suitable to several cases, may be brought to pass by means of secret and sometimes sudden influences on our minds,[269] or the minds of other men whose acts may affect us. For instance: if the case should require that N should be delivered from some threatening ruin, or from some misfortune which would certainly befall him if he should go such a way at such a time as he intended, upon this occasion some new reasons may be presented to his mind why he should not go at all, or not then, or not by that road—or he may forget to go. Or, if he is to be delivered from some dangerous enemy, either some new turn given to his thoughts may divert him from going where the enemy will be, or the enemy may be after the same manner diverted from coming where he shall

be, or his (the enemy's) resentment may be qualified, or some proper method of defense may be suggested, or degree of resolution and vigor excited. After the same manner, not only deliverances from dangers and troubles, but advantages and successes may be conferred; or, on the other side, men may, by way of punishment for crimes committed, incur mischiefs and calamities. I say, these things and suchlike *may be*. For since the motions and actions of men, which depend upon their wills, do also depend upon their judgments, as these again do upon the present appearances or nonappearances of things in their minds, if a new prospect of things can be any way produced, the lights by which they are seen altered, new forces and directions impressed upon the spirits, passions exalted or abated, the power of judging enlivened or debilitated, or the attention taken off, without any suspension or alteration of the standing laws of nature, than without that *new* volitions, designs, measures, or a cessation of thinking may also be produced, and thus many things prevented that otherwise would be, and many brought about that would not. But, that this is far from being impossible seems clear to me. For the operations of the mind following in great measure the present disposition of the body, some thoughts and designs, or absences of mind, may proceed from corporeal causes, acting according to the common laws of matter and motion themselves; and so the case may fall in with no. 2, or they may be occasioned by something said or done by other men; and then the case may be brought under no. 3, or they may be caused by the suggestion, and impulse, or other silent communications of some spiritual being— perhaps the Deity himself. For that such imperceptible influences and still whispers may be, none of us all can positively deny: that is, we cannot know certainly that there are no such things. On the contrary, I believe there are but few of them who have made observations upon themselves and their affairs, but must, when they reflect on life past and the various adventures and events in it, find many instances in which their usual judgment and sense of things cannot but seem to themselves to have been overruled, they knew not by what, nor how,[270] nor why, (i.e. they have done things, which afterwards they wonder how they came to do), and that these actions have had consequences very remarkable in their history.[271] I speak not here of men demented with wine, or enchanted with some temptation: the thing holds true of men even in their sober and more considering seasons.

That there may be possibly such inspirations of new thoughts and counsels may perhaps further appear from this: that we so frequently find thoughts arising in our heads, into which we are led by no discourse, nothing we read, no clue of reasoning, but they surprise and come upon us from we know not what quarter.[272] If they proceeded from the mobility of spirits, straggling out of order, and fortuitous affections of the brain, or were of the nature of dreams, why are they not as wild, incoherent, and extravagant as they are? Not to add, that the world has generally acknowledged, and therefore seems to have experienced, some assistance and directions given to good men by the Deity; that men have been many times infatuated, and lost to themselves, etc. If anyone should object that if men are thus overruled in their actings, then they are deprived of their liberty, etc., the answer is that though man is a free agent, he may not be free as to *everything*. His freedom may be restrained, and he only accountable for those acts in respect of which he is free.

If this then be the case, as it seems to be, that men's minds are susceptive of such insinuations and impressions as frequently, by ways unknown, do affect them and give them an inclination toward this or that, how many things may be brought to pass by these means without fixing and refixing the laws of nature—any more than they are unfixed when one man alters the opinion of another by throwing a book, proper for that purpose, in his way? I say, how many things may be brought about thus, not only in regard of ourselves, but other people who may be concerned in our actions, either immediately,[273] or in time through perhaps many intermediate events? For the prosperity or improsperity of a man, or his fate here, does not entirely depend upon his own prudence or imprudence, but in great measure upon his situation among the rest of mankind, and what they do. The natural effect of his management, meeting with such things as are the natural effects of the actions of other men, and being blended with them, the result may be something not intended or foreseen.

5. There possibly may be, and most probably are, beings invisible and superior in nature to us, who may by other means be in many respects ministers of God's providence, and authors under Him of many events to particular men, without altering the laws of nature. For it implies no contradiction or absurdity to say there are such beings—on the contrary, we have the greatest reason to think what has been intimated already: that such imperfect beings as we are, are far below the top of the scale. The pictures of spiritual beings cannot be drawn in our imagination, as of corporeal, yet to the upper and reasoning part of the mind the idea of spiritual substance may perhaps be as clear as that of corporeity.[274] For what penetrability is must be known just as well as what impenetrability is, and so on.

And since it has been proved (see this part of proposition XIII), that all corporeal motions proceed originally from something incorporeal, it must be as certain that there are incorporeal substances as that there is motion. Besides, how can we tell but that there may be above us beings of greater powers, and more perfect intellects, and capable of mighty things, which yet may have corporeal vehicles as we have, but finer and invisible? Nay, who knows but that there may be even of these many orders, rising in dignity of nature and amplitude of power, one above another? It is no way below the philosophy of these times, which seems to delight in enlarging the capacities of matter, to assert the possibility of this. But, however, my own defects sufficiently convince me that I have no pretension to be one of the first rank, or that which is next under the All-perfect.

Now then, as we ourselves, by the use of our powers, do many times interpose and alter the course of things within our sphere from what it would be if they were left entirely to the laws of motion and gravitation, without being said to alter those *laws*; so may these superior beings likewise, in respect of things within their spheres (much larger be sure, the least of them all, than ours is), only with this difference: that as their knowledge is more extensive, their intellects purer, their reason better, they may be much properer instruments of Divine providence with respect to us, than we can be with respect one to another, or to the animals below us. I cannot think indeed that the power of these beings is so large as to alter or suspend the general laws of the world, or that the world is like a bungling piece of clockwork which requires to be oft set backward or forward by them, or that they can at pleasure change their condition to ape us or inferior beings, and consequently am not apt hastily to credit stories of portents, etc., such as cannot be true unless the natures of things and their manner of being be quite reversed; yet (I will repeat it again) as men may be so placed as to become, even by the free exercise of their own powers, instruments of God's particular providence to other men (or animals), so may we well suppose that these higher beings may be so distributed through the universe, and subject to such an economy (though I pretend not to tell what that is), as may render them also instruments of the same providence, and that they may, in proportion to their greater abilities, be capable, consistently with the laws of nature, some way or other, though not in our way, of influencing human affairs in proper places.

6. Lastly, what I have ventured to lay before you I would not have to be so understood, as if I peremptorily asserted things to be just in this manner, or pretended to impose my thoughts upon anybody else; my design is only to show how I endeavor to help my own narrow conceptions. There must be other ways, above my understanding,[275] by which such a Being as God is may take care of private cases without interrupting the order of the universe or putting any of the parts of it out of their channels. We may be sure He regards everything as being what it is, and that therefore His laws must be accommodated to the true genius and capacities of those things which are affected by them. The purely material part of the world is governed by such as are suited to the state of a being which is insensible, passive only, and everywhere and always the same; and these seem to be simple and few, and to carry natural agents into one constant road. But intelligent, active, free beings must be under a government of another form. They must, truth requiring it, be considered as beings who may behave themselves as they ought, or not; as beings susceptive of pleasure and pain; as beings who not only owe to God all that they are or have, but are (or may be) sensible of this, and to whom therefore it must be natural upon many occasions to supplicate Him for mercy, defense, direction, assistance; lastly, as beings whose cases admit great variety: and therefore that *influence*, by which He is present to them, must be different from that by which gravitation and common phenomena are produced in matter. This seems to be, as it were, a public influence, the other private, answering private cases, and prayers; this to operate directly upon the body, the other more especially upon the mind, and upon the

body by it, etc. But I forbear, lest I should go too far out of my depth, only adding in general that God cannot put things so far out of His own power, as that He should not forever govern transactions and events in His own world; nor can perfect knowledge and power ever want proper means to achieve what is fit to be done. So that, though what I advanced should stand for nothing, there may still be a particular providence notwithstanding the forementioned difficulty. And then, if there *may be* one, it will unavoidably follow that there *is* one: because in the description of providence, see proposition XVIII, nothing is supposed with respect to particular cases but that they should be provided for in such a manner as will at last agree best with reason; and to allow that this may be done, and yet say that it is not done, implies a blasphemy that creates horror: it is to charge the Perfect being with one of the greatest imperfections, and to make Him not so much as a *reasonable* being.

I conclude, then, that it is as certain that there is a particular providence, as that God is a Being of perfect reason. For if men are treated according to reason, they must be treated according to what they are: the virtuous, the just, the compassionate, etc., as such, and the vicious, unjust, cruel, etc., according to what they are; and their several cases must be taken and considered as they are, which cannot be done without such a providence.

Against all this, it has been (as one might well expect) objected of old, that things do not seem to be dealt according to reason: virtuous and good men very often laboring under adversity, pains, persecutions, while vicious, wicked, cruel men prevail and flourish.[276] But to this an answer (in which I shall a little further explain myself) is ready. It might be taken out of that which has been given to the Manichean objection under proposition VII. But I shall here give one more direct, and let that and this be mutually assisting and supplements each to the other:

1. We are not always certain who are good, who wicked.[277] If we trust to fame and reports, these may proceed, on the one hand, from partial friendship, or flattery; on the other, from ill-natured surmises and constructions of things, envy, or malice; and on either, from small matters aggrandized, from mistake, or from the unskillful relation even of truth itself. Opposite parties make a merit of blackening their adversaries[278] and brightening their friends, undeservedly and unmeasurably, and to idle companions and gossips it is diversion, and what makes the principal part of their conversation,[279] to rehearse the characters of men, dressed up out of their own dreams and inventions. And besides all this, the good or bad repute of men depends in great measure upon mean people, who carry their stories from family to family, and propagate them very fast, like little insects, which lay apace, and the less the faster. There are few, very few, who have the opportunity and the will and the ability to represent things truly.[280] Beside the matters of fact themselves, there are many circumstances which, before sentence is passed, ought to be known and weighed, and yet scarce ever can be known,

but to the person himself who is concerned. He may have other views, and another sense of things, than his judges have; and what he understands, what he feels, what he intends, may be a secret confined to his own breast. A man may, through bodily indispositions and faults in his constitution which it is not in his power to correct, be subject to starts and inadvertancies, or obnoxious to snares, which he cannot be aware of; or, through want of information or proper helps, he may labor under invincible errors, and act as in the dark: in which cases, he may do things which are in themselves wrong, and yet be innocent, or at least rather to be pitied than censured with severity. Or perhaps the censurer, notwithstanding this kind of men talk as if they were infallible, may be mistaken himself in his opinion, and judge that to be wrong which in truth is right.[281] Nothing more common than this. Ignorant and superstitious wretches measure the actions of lettered and philosophical men by the tattle of their nurses or illiterate parents and companions, or by the fashion of the country, and people of differing religions judge and condemn each other by their own tenets, when both of them cannot be in the right, and it is well if *either* of them are. To which may be added that the true characters of men must chiefly depend upon the unseen part of their lives, since the truest and best religion is most private and the greatest wickedness endeavors to be so.[282] Some are modest, and hide their virtues; others hypocritical, and conceal their vices under shows of sanctity, good nature, or something that is specious. So that it is, many times, hard to discern to which of the two sorts, the good or the bad, a man ought to be aggregated.

2. It rarely happens that we are competent judges of the good or bad fortune of other people.[283] That which is disagreeable to one, is many times agreeable to another, or disagreeable in a less degree. The misery accruing from any infliction or bad circumstance of life is to be computed as in section II, or according to the resistence and capacity of bearing it which it meets with. If one man can carry a weight of four or five hundred pounds as well as another can the weight of one hundred, by these different weights they will be equally loaded. And so the same poverty or disgrace, the same wounds, etc. do not give the same pain to all men. The apprehension of but a vein to be opened is worse to some, than the apparatus to an execution is to others; and a word may be more terrible and sensible to tender natures, than a sword is to the senseless or intrepid breed. The same may be said with respect to enjoyments: men have different tastes, and the use of the same things does not beget equal pleasure in all. Besides, we scarce ever know the whole case. We do not see the inward stings and secret pains which many of those men carry about them, whose external splendor and flourishing estate is so much admired by beholders,[284] nor perhaps sufficiently consider the silent pleasures of a lower fortune, arising from temperance, moderate desires, easy reflections, a consciousness of knowledge and truth, with other pleasures of the mind, much greater many times than those of the body.[285] Before one can pronounce another happy or

otherwise, he should know all the other's enjoyments and all his sufferings.[286] Many misfortunes are compensated[287] by some larger endowments, or extraordinary felicities in other respects. But suppose the pleasures of some, and the sufferings of some others, to be just as they appear: still we know not the consequences of them.[288] The pleasures of those men may lead to miseries greater than those of the latter, and be in reality the greater misfortune; and, again, the sufferings of these may be preludes to succeeding advantages.[289] So that, indeed, we know not how to name these outward appearances of particular men, nor which to call happiness, which the contrary, unless we knew the inward sense of the persons themselves, all their true circumstances, and what will be hereafter consequent upon their present success or adversity.

3. Men ought to be considered as members of families, nations, mankind, the universe, from which they cannot be separated; and then from the very condition of their being it will appear that there must be great inequalities:[290] that the innocent cannot but be sometimes involved in general calamities or punishments, nor the guilty but share in public prosperities,[291] and that the good of the whole society or kind is to be regarded preferably to the present pleasure of any individual, if they happen to clash.[292]

4. Lastly, if the virtuous man has undergone more, in this life, than it would be reasonable he should suffer, if there was no other, yet those sufferings may not be unreasonable if there *is* another. For they may be made up to him by such enjoyments as it would be reasonable for him to prefer, even with those previous mortifications, before the pleasures of this life with the loss of them. And moreover, sometimes the only way to the felicities of a better state may lie through dark and difficult passes, discipline to some men being necessary to bring them to reflect, and to force them into such methods as may produce in them proper improvements, such as otherwise and of themselves they would never have fallen into. On the other side, if vicious and wicked men do prosper and make a figure, yet it is possible their sufferings hereafter may be such as that the excess of them above their past enjoyments may be equal to the just mulct of their villanies and wickedness. And further, their worldly pleasures (which must be supposed to be such as are not philosophical, or moderated and governed by reason and habits of virtue) being apt to fill the mind, and engross the whole man, and by that means to exclude almost all right reflections, with the proper applications of them, may be the very causes of their ruin, while they leave them under such defects at the end of their days, as we shall see afterward tend to unhappiness.

If what is objected be in many instances true, this only infers the *necessity* of a future state: that is, if good and bad men are not respectively treated according to reason in *this life*, they may yet be so treated if this and another to follow be taken together into the account.[293] And perhaps it is (as I have been always apt to think) in order to convince us of the certainty of a future state, that instances of that kind have been so numerous. For he must not only be guilty of blasphemy, but reduced to the greatest absurdity, who, rather than he will own there is such a state, is forced to make God an unreasonable Being:[294] which I think amounts to a strong demonstration that there is one. But of that, more hereafter.

XIX. *If we would behave ourselves as being what we cannot but be sensible we are, towards God as being what He is according to the foregoing propositions; or, if we would endeavor to behave ourselves towards him according to truth, we must observe these following and the like particulars:*

1. We must not pretend to represent Him by any picture or image whatsoever.[295] Because this is flatly to deny his incorporeity, incomprehensible nature, etc.[296]
2. We ought to be so far from doing this, that even the language we use when we speak of Him, and especially of his positive nature and essential properties, ought not only to be chosen with the utmost care, but also to be understood in the sublimest sense; and the same is true with respect to our thoughts, *mutatis mutandis*.[297] Or, thus: we must endeavor to think and speak of Him in the most reverent terms and most proper manner we are able;[298] keeping withal this general conclusion and, as it were, habitual reflection in our minds: that, though we do the best we can, He is still something above all our conceptions; and desiring that our faint expressions may be taken as aiming at a higher and more proportionable meaning. To do otherwise implies not only that His mode of existence and essential attributes are comprehensible by us, but also (which is more) that our words and phrases, taken from among ourselves[299] and the objects of our faculties, are adequate expressions of them: contrary to truth.

   To explain myself by a few instances: When we ascribe *mercy* to God, or implore His *mercy*, it must not be understood to be mercy like that which is called "compassion" in us. For though this be a very distinguishing affection in human nature,[300] to which we are made subject for good reasons—the constitution of the world and circumstances of our present state making it necessary for us to compassionate each the sufferings of another—yet it is accompanied with uneasiness, and must therefore not be ascribed strictly to God in that sense in which it is used when ascribed to ourselves. It perhaps may not be amiss to call it "Divine mercy," or the like, to distinguish it, and to show that we mean something, which, though in our low way of speaking and by way of analogy we call it by the same name, is yet in the perfect nature of God very different. Or we may consider it in general as the manner in which God respects poor supplicants and proper objects for their good. For certainly the respect or relation which lies between God, considered as an unchangeable Being, and one that is humble and supplicates and endeavors to qualify himself for mercy, cannot be the same with that which lies between the same unchangeable God and one that is obstinate, and will not supplicate or endeavor to qualify himself:[301] that is, the same thing, or Being, cannot respect opposite and contradictory characters in the same manner: him who does behave himself as before, and him who does not. Therefore, when we apply to the mercy of God, and beg of him to pity our infirmities and wants, the design is not to move His affections—as good speakers move their auditors by the pathetic arts of rhetoric, or hearty beggars theirs by importunities and tears—but to express our own sense of ourselves and circumstances in such a manner as may render us more capable of the emanations of Divine goodness, and fit to receive such instances of His beneficence as to us may seem to be the effects of compassion, though they proceed not from any alteration in the Deity. For it may be, and no doubt is, agreeable to perfect reason always and without alteration, that he who labors under a sense of his own defects, honestly uses his best endeavors to mend what is amiss, and (among other things) flies for relief to Him upon whom his being and all that he has do depend, should have many things granted him which are not given to the careless, obdurate, unasking[302] part of mankind; though his expressions and manner of address, with all his care, are still inadequate, and below the Divine nature. In short, by our applications, we cannot pretend to produce any alteration in the Deity, but by an alteration in ourselves, we may alter the relation or respect lying between him and us.

As God is a pure, uncompounded Being, His attributes of mercy, justice, etc. cannot be as we conceive them, because in him they are one. Perhaps they may more properly be called together "Divine reason," which, as it exerts itself upon this or that occasion, is by us variously denominated.

Here it must not be forgot that "mercy" or "mercies" are many times taken for advantages or benefits enjoyed by us, and then they are properly ascribed to God, from whom they proceed as the effects of His beneficence and providence.

When we speak of the knowledge of God, we must not mean that He knows things in the way that we do, that any intention or operation of His mind is requisite to produce it: that He apprehends things by any impressions made upon Him, that He reasons by the help of ideas, or even that the knowledge which in us is most intuitive and immediate does in any degree come up to the mode in which He knows things. We must rather intend, in general, that there is nothing of which He is, or can be, ignorant, which has been said already and is, I am afraid, as much as we can safely say.

When *glory, honor, praise*[303] are given to God, or He is said to do anything for His own glory, or we to propose the glory of His name in what we do, those words should not be taken as standing for that kind of glory and applause which is so industriously sought, and capriciously[304] distributed, among us mortals, and which I will take this opportunity to handle a little more largely, in order to give here a specimen of the world and save that trouble in another place. Among us, some are celebrated for small matters, either through the ignorance of the multitude, the partiality of a faction, the advantage of great friendships, the usual deference paid to men in eminent stations, or mere good luck;[305] and others for achieving such things as, if they were duly weighed, and people were not imposed upon by false notions—first introduced in barbarous times, and since polished and brought into fashion by historians, poets, and flatterers—would appear rather to be a disgrace to savages than any recommendation of rational and civilized natures. Strength, and courage, and beauty, and parts, and birth are followed with encomiums and honors, which, though they may be the felicities and privileges of the possessors, cannot be their merit, who received them gratis, and contributed nothing[306] themselves toward the acquisition of them; while real virtue and industry (which, even when unsuccessful, or oppressed by ill health or unkind fortune, give the truest title to praise) lie disregarded. Thirst after glory, when that is desired merely for its own sake, is founded in ambition and vanity;[307] the thing itself is but a dream and imagination; since, according to the differing humors and sentiments of nations and ages, the same thing may be either glorious or inglorious, the effect of it, considered still by itself, is neither more health, nor estate, nor knowledge, nor virtue to him who has it, or, if that be anything, it is but what must cease when the man[308] dies, and, after all, as it lives but in the breath of the people, a little sly envy or a new turn of things extinguishes it,[309] or perhaps it goes quite out of itself.[310] Men please themselves with notions of immortality, and fancy a perpetuity of fame secured to themselves by books and testimonies of historians; but, alas! it is a stupid delusion when they imagine themselves present, and enjoying that fame at the reading of their story after their death. And besides, in reality the man is not known ever the more to posterity, because his name is transmitted to them: *he* does not live because his *name* does. When it is said Julius Cæsar subdued Gaul, beat Pompey, changed the Roman commonwealth into a monarchy, etc., it is the same thing as to say, the conqueror of Pompey, etc., was Cæsar: that is, Cæsar and the conqueror of Pompey are the same thing; and Cæsar is as much known by the one designation as by the other. The amount then is only this: that the conqueror of Pompey conquered Pompey; or somebody conquered Pompey; or rather, since Pompey is as little known now as Cæsar, somebody conquered somebody.[311] Such a poor business is this boasted immortality,[312] and such as has been here described is the thing called "glory" among us! The notion of it may serve to excite them who, having abilities to serve their country in time of real danger or want, or to do some other good, have yet not philosophy enough to do this upon principles of virtue, or to see through the glories of the world (just as we excite children by praising them, and as we see many good inventions and improvements proceed from emulation and vanity); but to discerning men this fame is mere air, and the next remove from nothing:[313] what they despise, if not shun. I think there are two considerations which may justify a desire of some glory or honor, and scarce more. When men have performed any virtuous actions, or such as sit easy upon their memories, it is a reasonable pleasure to have the testimony of the world added to that of their own consciences, that they have done well:[314] and more than that, if the reputation acquired by any qualification or action may produce a man any real comfort or advantage (if it be only protection from the insolencies and injustice of mankind, or if it enables him to do by his authority more good to others), to have this privilege must be a great satisfaction, and what a wise and good man may be allowed, as he has opportunity, to propose to himself. But then he proposes it no farther than it may be useful; and it can be no farther useful than he wants it. So that upon the whole, glory, praise, and the like, are either mere vanity, or only valuable in proportion to our defects and wants. If then those words are understood according to the import and value they have among men, how dares anyone think that the Supreme being can propose such a mean end to himself as our praises? He can neither want nor value them. Alexander, according to his taste of things, it may well be supposed would have been proud to have heard that he should be the subject of some second Homer,[315] in whose sheets his name might be embalmed for ages to come, or to have been celebrated at Athens, the mother of so many wits and captains—but sure even he, with all his vanity, could not propose to himself as the end of all his fatigues and dangers only to be praised by children, or rather by worms and insects, if they were capable of showing some faint sense of his greatness.[316] And yet how far short is this comparison! In conclusion therefore, though men have been accustomed to speak of the Deity in terms taken from princes, and such things as they have, in their weakness, admired; though these are now incorporated into the language of Divines; and though, considering what defects there are in our ways of thinking and speaking, we cannot well part with them all; yet we must remember to *exalt* the sense of them, or annex some mental qualification to the use of them. As, if God be said to do things for His own glory, the meaning I humbly conceive must be that the transcendent excellence of His nature may be collected from the form of the world and administration of things in it, where there occur such marks of inexpressible wisdom and power that He needed not to have given us greater, had He only intended His own glory: or something to this purpose. Or, if the glory of what *we* do be ascribed to Him, by this must be signified that no glory is due to us, who have no powers but what originally depend upon Him, and that we desire therefore to acknowledge Him to be the true author of all that which is laudable in us.[317]

When we *thank* God for any deliverance or enjoyment, this must not be so understood as if He could value Himself upon our ceremonious acknowledgments, or wanted complements or any return from us. It is rather a profession of the sense we have of our wants and defects, of the beneficience of His nature, and the greatness or reasonableness of the mercies received: an effort of a poor dependent being who desires to own things, as far as he is able, to be what they are,[318] and especially to beget in himself such a disposition of mind as he ought to have towards his Almighty benefactor.

When we are said to be *servants* of God, or to *serve* Him, or do Him *service*, these phrases are not to be taken as when one man is said to be servant of another, or to do him service. For here it implies the doing of something which is useful and beneficial to the man who is served, and what he wants, or fancies he wants: but nothing of *want* can be supposed in God, nor can we any way be profitable or serviceable to Him. To serve Him, therefore, must rather be to worship or adore Him (of which something by and by). And thus that word in another language, of which our serve is but the translation, is frequently used: as "to serve a graven image"[319] is to worship the image, but cannot signify the doing of anything which may be serviceable or useful to the dead stone. Or "to serve God" may be understood in a sense something like that: "Serve the king of Babylon."[320] For they were said to serve the king of Babylon, who owned his authority and lived according to his laws, though they did nothing, nor had anything perhaps, which could be particularly serviceable to him; and so they may be said to serve God, or to be His servants, who live in a continual sense of His sovereign nature and power over them, and endeavor to conform themselves to the laws which He has imposed upon them.[321] In these senses we pray, that we may live to serve Him: that is, we pray, that we may live to worship Him, and practice those laws of reason and virtue to which rational natures are by Him subjected.[322]

Many more reflections might be made upon epithets and ways of speaking introduced by custom, from rude antiquity, or by necessity following from the narrowness either of men's minds or their language. It is plain that "love," "anger," "hands," "eyes," etc. when ascribed to God, cannot import such bodily parts or passions as are found in us. Even the pronouns, "my," "thy," "his" (as His people, His house, etc.) require much temper in the use of them.[323]

3. We shall find ourselves bound to worship Him, in the best manner we can. For by worshipping Him I mean nothing but owning Him to be what He is, and ourselves to be what we are, by some more solemn and proper act: that is, by addressing ourselves as His dependents to Him as the Supreme cause and Governor of the world, with acknowledgments of what we enjoy, petitions for what we really want, or He knows to be convenient for us,[324] and the like. As if, e.g. I should in some humble and composed manner[325] pray to that "Almighty being, upon whom depends the existence of the world, and by whose providence I have been preserved to this moment and enjoyed many undeserved advantages, that He would graciously accept my grateful sense and acknowledgments of all His beneficience toward me; that he would deliver me from the evil consequences of all my transgressions and follies; that He would endow me with such dispositions and powers as may carry me innocently and safely through all future trials, and may enable me upon all occasions to behave myself conformably to the laws of reason, piously, and wisely; that He would suffer no being to injure me, no misfortune to befall me, nor me to hurt myself by any error or misconduct of my own; that He would vouchsafe me clear and distinct perceptions of things, with so much health and prosperity as may be good for me; that I may at least pass my time in peace, with contentment, and tranquility of mind; and that, having faithfully discharged my duty to my family and friends, and endeavored to improve myself in virtuous habits and useful

knowledge, I may at last make a decent and happy exit, and then find myself in some better state." Not to do this, or something like it, will certainly fall among those criminal omissions mentioned in section I, proposition V. For never to acknowledge the enjoyments and privileges we have received and hold of God, is in effect to deny that we receive them from Him; not to apply to Him for what we want is to deny either our wants, or His power of helping us; and so on: all contrary to truth.[326]

It must ever be owned, that no worship can be proportionable to the Divine nature and perfections; but yet, that we are obliged to do what we can: therefore I added those words, "in the best manner we can." And it must be acknowledged further, that those words do not oblige us to be *always* at our devotions neither.[327] For as in the worship of God we own Him to be what He is, so must we do this as not denying ourselves to be what we are: beings not capable of bearing continual intention of mind; beings that are encompassed with many wants, which by the constitution of our nature require to be supplied, not without care and activity joined to our prayers; beings that are made for many harmless enjoyments; beings that have many offices to perform one for another; and beings in whom, all things considered, it would be less respect to be constantly in the formal act of devotion, than it is to address ourselves to Him with prepared minds, at certain times, or upon certain occasions. To be always thus engaged, if it could be, would be to make God what He is not: since it seems to suppose that He wants it and we merit Him by it; or that He is bound to give what we ask, without our endeavoring; or, at least, that He is a Being obnoxious to importunity and teasing. For these reasons I have also in the explication of my meaning inserted that limitation, "by some solemn and proper act."

Though every man knows best his own opportunities and circumstances, and therefore may be most able to judge for himself how he may best perform this duty, yet in general it may be said that, to the doing of it solemnly and in the best manner we can, these things are required: an intent mind,[328] proper times and places, a proper form of words, and a proper posture. For if the mind be absent, or attends not to what is said, it is not the man that prays: this is only as it were the noise of a machine, which is put into motion indeed, but without any consciousness of its own act. To repeat one's prayers with moving lips, but alienated thoughts, is not to pray in the best manner we can, because it is not in a manner agreeable to what we are, or to truth. For this is to do it only as *speaking*, and not as *thinking* beings.

Upon this account, it will be certain that all times and places cannot be equally proper.[329] Some times are engrossed by the business of life, and some places lie exposed to interruptions. Those of retreat and silence ought to be sought, and, as far as fairly it may be, contrived. And for this further reason: because the farther we are removed from the notice of others, the clearer we stand of all ostentation; that is, the more we do it upon the score of truth and duty; and this is, again, the more truly and dutifully we do it.

Our next care is a proper form of words. All prayer must either be vocal or mental. Now even that which is called mental can scarce be made without words,[330] or something equivalent.[331] (I believe that even the deaf and dumb form to themselves some kind of language: I mean something which supplies the room of language.) For thoughts in their naked state, divested of all words and taken merely by themselves, are such subtle and fleeting things as are scarce capable of making any appearance in the mind; at least of being detained, compared together, and arranged into sentences. If a sentence may be so made up of sensible ideas as to subsist in the mind by the help of those images which remain in the fantasy, after the manner of a sentence expressed in pictures or by hieroglyphics, yet such a sentence must be very imperfect—through the want of grammatical inflections, particles, and other additions necessary to modify and connect the ideas, of which (particles, etc.) there can be no images[332]—and indeed little more than a set of disjointed conceptions, scarce exhibiting any sense without the assistance of language to fill up the blanks; and besides that, a prayer cannot be made out of such sentences as those. It is by the help of words, at least in great measure, that we even reason and discourse within ourselves, as well as communicate our thoughts and discourse with others; and if anyone observes himself well, he will find that he thinks, as well as speaks, in some language, and that in thinking he supposes and runs over silently and habitually those sounds which in speaking he actually makes. This is the cause why men can scarce write well in any language but their own: for while they think in their own, their style and speech, which is but the portraiture of their thoughts, must have the turn and genius of their own language, to what language soever the particular words belong. In short, words seem to be, as it were, bodies or vehicles to the sense or meaning, which is the spiritual part,[333] and which without the other can hardly be fixed in the mind. Let any man try ingenuously, whether he can think over but that short prayer in Plato, Τὰ μὲν ἐθλὰ, κτλ.,[334] abstracted quite from those and all other words. One may apply his mind to the words of a prayer pronounced by another, and by taking them in make them his own; or he may be, as it were, his own reader, and pronounce them himself; or he may lay before him a prayer in writing, and so carry his eyes and his mind together through it; or he may go over a form of words imprinted on his memory; or he may put words together in his mind *ex tempore*: but still, in all these ways, words and language are used. And since to think over a set of words cannot be a more adequate manner of addressing to God (who neither speaks, nor thinks like us) than to speak it over and think too; and moreover, since the very sound of the words affects us, and, when the form is ready prepared, and the mind freed from the labor of composing, does really help attention:[335] I say, since this is the case, it must be better, when we have opportunity, to pronounce a prayer,[336] than only to think it over. But then it should be spoken no louder (I mean when we pray privately) than just to make it audible to ourselves.[337] It is not upon God's account that we speak, since he would know even our thoughts: but it is upon our own account, and to make our adoration, though imperfect at the best, as complete as we are able. (Which, by the way, is an answer to them who object, against prayer, the impertinence of talking to God.) This being premised, and it being found that we must make use of words, it cannot be denied that we ought to use the best and properest we can. This cannot be done in extemporaneous effusions, and therefore there must be forms premeditated: the best that we are capable of making or procuring, if we would worship God to the best of our capacity. As a prayer ought to have all the marks of seriousness and being in earnest, it ought to be the plainest, and at the same time is perhaps the hardest of all compositions. It ought to take in a general view of what we have enjoyed, what we want, what we have done, etc., and everything ought to be expressed with method, in phrases that are grave and pointing, and with such a true eloquence as engages all our attention and represents our deepest sense, without affectation or needless repetitions. These considerations have caused me many times to wonder at those men who dispute against preconceived forms of prayer. They, who talk so much of the spirit of prayer, seem to know but little of it.

As to the posture, that is best which best expresses our humility, reverence,[338] and earnestness, and affects us most. Though perhaps some regard is to be paid to the customs of the place where we are, or of our own country to which we have been most used. Several nations may denote the same thing by different gestures, and we may take these as we do their words: i.e. as having that signification which they put upon them.

Though I have not hitherto mentioned it, there ought to be also a *public worship* of the Deity. For a man may be considered as a member of a society, and *as such* he ought to worship God (if he has the opportunity of doing it: if there are proper prayers used publicly which he may resort to, and his health, etc. permit). Or the society may be considered as one body that has common interests and concerns, and as such is obliged to worship the Deity, and offer one common prayer. Besides, there are many who know not of themselves how to pray; perhaps cannot so much as read. These, too, must be taken as they are, and consequently some time and place appointed where they may have suitable prayers read to them, and be guided in their devotions. And further, toward the keeping mankind in order, it is necessary there should be some religion professed, and even established; which cannot be without some public worship. And were it not for that sense of virtue, which is principally preserved (so far as it is preserved) by national forms and habits of religion, men would soon lose it all, run wild, prey upon one another, and do what else the worst of savages do.

But how does this public worship, it may be demanded, comport with that retreat and privacy recommended above? Answer: I spoke there of prayer *in general*, to which those circumstances give a great advantage; but then they are recommended no farther than they can be had and the nature of the prayer admits of them. Excuse a short reflection here, which if it be not directly for the purpose, is not altogether foreign to it: Though he who reads the form of public prayer reads it to all at the same time, that all may unite in one common act which otherwise they could not do, yet still, every particular person who minds the prayers at all has a separate perception of the words in his mind, and there he offers them, or the sense contained under them, with more or less application and ardor. And since no man can be said to pray any further than he does this, and it cannot be known to anybody in the congregation besides himself how far he does do it, his prayer is in reality as private as if he was enclosed within a thousand walls. So that, though there are reasons for a public worship, yet I will venture to affirm that all true prayer is private; and the true seat of it being in the mind, toward the interesting of whose powers all the circumstances of worship are mainiy designed to contribute, it may be said upon that account to be always made in the most retired and undiscerned of all retreats;[339] nor can more be said in respect of a worship which, by the terms, is in other respects public. A man may be present in a congregation, and either pray the same prayer in which others seem to join, or some other, or none at all,[340] for ought anybody there can tell besides himself.

I am not insensible how much I may expose myself by these things to the laughter of some who are utter strangers to all this language. What a stir is here, say they, about *praying*? Who ever observed that they who pray are more successful or happy than they are who do not? Answer: All observations of this kind must be very lubricous and uncertain. We neither know what other men are inwardly and really,[341] nor how they pray,[342] nor what to call success.[343] That which is good for one, may be bad for another; and that which seems good at present, may at length be evil, or introduce something which is so.[344] And as to the prosperity of them who endeavor to worship God in a proper and reasonable manner, whatever it is, perhaps it might be less if they did not, or their misfortunes might be greater; who can be certain of the contrary? If these gentlemen have any way of discovering it, I wish they would impart their secret. In the meantime, sure they cannot expect that, even in the most imperfect sketch of natural religion, the worship of the Deity should be omitted: that very thing which has been principally intended by the word "religion."[345]

4. And lastly, to deliver what remains, summarily: Rational beings, or they to whom reason is the great law of their nature, if they would behave themselves as above, should consider in earnest what a mighty being He is, who by the constitution of their nature has laid them under an obligation of being governed by it, and whose laws the dictates of right reason may be said to be. They ought to keep it well impressed upon their minds that He is the being upon whom their very existence depends; that it is He who superintends and administers the affairs of the world by His providence; that the effects of His power and influence are visible before their faces, and round about them, in all the phenomena of nature, not one of which could be without Him; that they are always

in His presence; that He is a being of perfect reason; that, if it be reasonable that the transgressors of reason should be punished, they will most certainly, one time or other, be punished, etc. And then, if they do this, it is easy to see what effect it must have upon their thoughts, words,[346] and actions.

By what is said here, no superstition is intended to be introduced; it is only the practice of reason and truth which is required, and anything that is not inconsistent with them may be freely done, though under the inspection of our great Lawgiver himself.

VI
Truths Respecting Mankind in General, Antecedent to All Human Laws

In this and the following sections I shall proceed as in the foregoing.

I. *Every man has in himself a principle of individuation, which distinguishes and separates him from all other men, in such a manner as may render him and them capable of distinct properties in things* (or *distinct subjects of property*). That is: B and C are so distinguished, or exist so distinctly, that if there be anything which B can call his, it will be for that reason not C's; and, vice versa, what is C's will for that reason not be B's. The proof of this I put upon every man's own conscience. Let us see, then, whether there is anything which one man may truly call his.

II. *There are some things, to which (at least before the case is altered by voluntary subjection, compact, or the like) every individual man has, or may have, such a natural and immediate relation, that he only of all mankind can call them his.*

The life, limbs, etc. of B are as much his, as B is himself.[347] It is impossible for C, or any other, to see with the eyes of B: therefore they are eyes only to B; and when they cease to be *his* eyes, they cease to be eyes at all. He then has the sole property in them, it being impossible in nature that the eyes of B should ever be the eyes of C.

Further, the labor of B cannot be the labor of C: because it is the application of the organs and powers of B, not of C, to the effecting of something; and therefore the labor is as much B's, as the limbs and faculties made use of are his.

Again, the effect or produce of the labor of B is not the effect of the labor of C, and therefore this effect or produce is B's, not C's; as much B's, as the *labor* was B's and not C's.[348] Because, what the labor of B causes or produces, B produces by his labor; or it is the product of B by his labor: that is, it is B's product, not C's, nor any other's. And, if C should pretend to any property in that which B only can truly call his, he would act contrary to truth.[349]

Lastly, there may be many things which B may truly call *his* in some such sense, or upon some such account, as no other can, and to which C has no more right than D, nor D than F, etc. the *property* of which will therefore be in B. Because C has no more title than D, nor D than F, etc., and that to which everyone besides B has an equal title, no one besides B can have any title to at all,[350] their pretences mutually balancing and destroying each other, while his only remains. And in this case, a small matter, being opposed to nothing, will be strong enough to maintain the claim of B.

III. *Whatever is inconsistent with the general peace and welfare (or good) of mankind, is inconsistent with the laws of human nature, wrong, intolerable.* Those maxims may be esteemed the natural and true laws of any particular society, which are most proper to procure the *happiness* of it. Because happiness is the end of society and laws: otherwise we might suppose unhappiness to be proposed as the right end of them; that is, unhappiness to be desirable, contrary to nature and truth. And what is said of a particular society is not less true, when applied to the universal society of mankind. Now, those things are most apt to produce happiness, which make the most men happy. And therefore those maxims or principles which promote the general tranquility and well-being of mankind, if those words express the happiness of mankind, must be the true laws of humanity, or the basis of them; and all such practices as interfere with these, must also interfere with those. It is contradictory to say that anything can be a general law of human nature, which tends only to favor the pleasures of some particulars, to the prejudice of the rest who partake of the same common nature—and especially if these pleasures are of the lower and brutal kind. As a million of men are more than one, so in fixing the public laws of human nature, and what ought to be or not to be, they must in reason be more regarded by a million of times: for here we consider men only as men.

It will be easy now to show that the transgression, of these laws conducing to the general good of the world, is wrong and morally evil. For if mankind may be said in general to be a rational animal, the general welfare of it must be the welfare of a rational nature: and therefore that, and the laws which advance it, must be founded in reason; nor can be opposed by anything but what is opposite to reason, and consequently to truth.

Let us suppose some rule by which, if all mankind would agree to govern themselves, it would be in general good for the world: that is, such a practice would be agreeable to the nature and circumstances of mankind. If all men should transgress this rule, what would be the consequence of such a universal revolt? A general evil, or something disagreeable to our nature and the truth of our circumstances: for of contrary practices there must be contrary effects; and contraries cannot both be agreeable to the same thing. This then would be wrong by the terms. And as wrong it would be in any *one* man: because all the individuals have equal right to do it—one as much as another, and therefore all as much as any one. At least it is certain that whoever should violate that rule, would contribute his share towards the introduction of universal disorder and misery, and would for his part deny human circumstances to be what they are, public happiness to be what it is, and the rule to be what it really is, as much as if all others conspired with him in this iniquity and madness.

With what face can any *particular* man put his own humor or unreasonable pleasure into the scale against such a weight of happiness as that of *all the world?* Does not he—who thus centers in himself, disregards the good of everybody else, and entirely separates his enjoyments and interests from those of the public—does not he, I say, strike himself out of the roll of mankind?[351] Ought he to be owned as one of them? Ought he not rather to be repelled, and treated as an alien and enemy to the common happiness and tranquility of our species?

IV. *Whatever is either reasonable or unreasonable in B with respect to C, would be just the same in C with respect to B, if the case was inverted.*[352] Because reason is universal, and respects cases,[353] not persons. (See section III, proposition II.)

Corollary: Hence it follows, that a good way to know what is right or wrong, in relation to other men, is to consider what we should take things to be were we in their circumstances.[354]

V. *In a state of nature, men are equal in respect of dominion.*[355] I except for the present the case of parents and their children, and perhaps of some few other near relations. Here, let me be understood to mean only those between whom there is no family relation (or between whom all family relation is vanished).

In a state where no laws of society make any subordination or distinction, men can only be considered *as men*, or only as individuals of the same species, and equally sharing in one common definition.[356] And since, by virtue of this same definition, B is the same to C that C is to B, B has no more dominion over C than C reciprocally has over B: that is, they are in this regard *equal.*

Personal excellencies or defects can make no difference here: because,

1. Who must judge on which side the advantage lies? To say B (or D, or anybody else) has a right to judge to the disadvantage of C, is to *suppose* what is in question—a dominion over him—not to *prove* it.
2. Great natural or acquired endowments may be privileges to them who have them, but this does not deprive those who have less of *their title* to what they have; or, which is the same, give anyone who has greater abilities a right to take it, or the use of it, from them. If B has better eyes than C, it is well for him; but it does not follow from this that C should not therefore see for himself, and use *his* eyes, as freely as B may his. C's eyes are accommodated by nature to his use, and so are B's to his, and each has the sole property in his own; so their respective properties are equal. The case would be parallel to this if B should happen to have better *intellectual* faculties than C. And further, if B should be *stronger* than C, he would not yet for that reason have any right to be his lord. For C's less degree of strength is as much his, as B's greater is his: therefore C has as much right to his, and (which is the natural consequence) to use his, as B has to use his: that is, C has as much right to resist, as B has to impose or command, by virtue of his strength: and where the right (though nor the power) of resisting is equal to the right of commanding, the right of commanding or dominion is nothing.
3. Since strength and power are most apt to pretend a title to dominion,[357] it may be added further that *power* and *right*, or a power of doing anything and right to do it, are quite different ideas, and therefore they may be separated; nor does one infer the other. Lastly, if power, quà power, gives a right to dominion, it gives a right to everything that is obnoxious to it; and then nothing can be done that is wrong. (For nobody can do anything which he has not the *power* to do.) But this is not only contrary to what has been proved in section I, but to assert it would be to advance a plain absurdity, or contradiction rather. For then to oppose the man who has this power, as far as one can,

or (which is the same) as far as one has the power to do it, would not be wrong: and yet so it must be, if he has a right to dominion, or to be not opposed. Moreover, that a man should have a right to anything, merely because he has the power to take it, is a doctrine indeed which may serve a few tyrants, or some banditti and rogues, but directly opposite to the peace and general good of mankind; and therefore to be exploded, by proposition III. It is also what the powerful themselves could not allow, if they would but imagine themselves to be in the state of the weak and more defenceless; and therefore unreasonable, by proposition IV.[358]

VI. *No man can have a right to begin to interrupt the happiness of another.* Because, in the first place, this supposes a dominion over him, and the most absolute too that can be. In the next, for B to begin to disturb the peace and happiness of C is what B would think unreasonable, if he was in C's case. In the last, since it is supposed that C has never invaded the happiness of B, nor taken anything from him, nor at all meddled with him, but the whole transaction begins originally from B (for all this is couched in the word "begin"), C can have nothing that is B's, and therefore nothing to which C has not at least as good a title as B has, or, in other words, nothing which C has not as much right to keep as B to claim. These two rights being then at least equal, and counterpoising each other, no alteration in the present state of things can follow from any superiority of right in B; and therefore, it must of right remain as it is, and what C has must, for any right that B has to oppose this settlement, remain with C in his undisturbed possession. But the argument is still stronger on the side of C, because he seems to have such a property in his own happiness, as is mentioned in proposition II—such a one as no other can have.[359]

VII. *Though no man can have a right to begin to interrupt another man's happiness, or to hurt him; yet every man has a right to defend himself and his against violence, to recover what is taken by force from him, and even to make reprisals, by all the means that truth and prudence permit.*[360] We have seen already that there are some things which a man may truly call his; and let us for the present only suppose that there may be more. This premised, I proceed to make good the proposition.

To deny a man the privilege mentioned in it, is to assert, contrary to truth, either that he has not the faculties and powers which he has, or that the Author of nature has given them to him in vain. For to what end has he them, if he may not use them? And how may he use them, if not for his own preservation when he is attacked, and like to be abused or perhaps destroyed?

All animals have a principle of self-preservation, which exerts itself many times with an uncontrollable impetuosity. Nature is uniform in this, and everywhere constant to itself. Even inanimate bodies, when they are acted upon, react. And one may be sure that no position can have any foundation in nature, or be consistent with it and truth (those inseparable companions), which turns upon nature itself, and tends to its destruction.

Great part of the general happiness of mankind depends upon those means by which the innocent may be saved from their cruel invaders—among which, the opportunities they have of defending themselves may be reckoned the chief. Therefore, to debar men of the use of these opportunities, and the right of defending themselves against injurious treatment and violence, must be inconsistent with the laws of nature by proposition III.

If a man has no right to defend himself and what is his, he can have no right to *anything* (the contrary to which has been already in part, and will by and by be more amply, proved), since that cannot be his right which he may not *maintain* to be his right.

If a man has no right to defend himself against insults, etc., it must be because the aggressor has a right to assail the other and usurp what is his. But this pretension has been prevented in the foregoing proposition. And, more than that, it includes a great absurdity: to commence an injury, or to begin the violence, being in nature more than only to repel it. He who begins is the true cause of all that follows; and whatever falls upon him, from the opposition made by the defending party, is but the effect of his own act: or, it is that violence of which he is the author, reflected back upon himself. It is as when a man spits at heaven, and the spittle falls back upon his own face.

Since he who begins to violate the happiness of another, does what is wrong, he who endeavors to obviate or put a stop to that violence, does in that respect what is right, by the terms.

Lastly, since every man is obliged to consult his own happiness, there can be no doubt but that he not only may, but even *ought* to defend it (section II, proposition IX); in such a manner, I mean, as does not interfere with truth,[361] or his own design of being happy. He ought indeed not to act rashly, or do more than the end proposed requires—that is, he ought, by a prudent carriage and wise forecast, to shut up, if he can, the avenues by which he may be invaded; and when that cannot be done, to use arguments and persuasives, or perhaps withdraw out of the way of harm: but when these measures are ineffectual or impracticable, he must take such other as he can, and confront force with force. Otherwise he will fail in his duty to himself, and deny happiness to be happiness.

By the same means that a man may *defend* what is his, he may certainly endeavor to *recover* what has been by any kind of violence or villainy taken from him. For it has been shown already that the *power* to take anything from another gives no *right* to it. The *right*, then, to that which has been taken from its owner against his will, remains still where it was: he may still truly call it his; and if it be his, he may use it as his: which, if he who took it away, or any other, shall hinder him from doing, that man is even here the aggressor, and the owner does but defend himself and what is his. Besides, he who uses anything as his, when it is his, acts on the side of truth; but that man who opposes him in this, and consequently asserts a right to that which is not his, acts contrary to truth. The former, therefore, does what cannot be amiss; but what the latter does, is wrong by that fundamental proposition, section I, proposition IV.

Then further, if a man has still a right to what is forcibly or without his consent taken from him, he must have a right to the *value* of it. For the thing is to him what it is *in value* to him:

and the right he has to it, may be considered as a right to a thing of *such a value*. So that if the very thing which was taken be destroyed, or cannot be retrieved, the proprietor nevertheless retains his right to a thing of such a value to him, and something must be had *in lieu* of it: that is, he has a right to make *reprisals*. Since everything is to every man what it is in value to him, things of the same value to anyone may be reckoned as to him *the same*, and to recover the *equivalent* the same as to recover the thing itself: for otherwise it is not an equivalent. If the thing taken by way of reprisal should be, to the man from whom it is taken, of greater value than what he wrongfully took from the recoverer, he must charge himself with that loss. If injustice be done him, it is done by himself; the other has no more than what he has a right to. To which add, that as a man has a right to recover what is his, or the equivalent, from an invader; so he seems for the same reasons to have a right to an equivalent for the expense he is at in recovering his own, for the loss of time and quiet, and for the trouble, hazards, and dangers undergone: because all these are the effects of the invasion, and therefore to be added to the invader's account.

VIII. *The first possession of a thing gives the possessor a greater right to it than any other man has, or can have, till he, and all that claim under him, are extinct.*

1. For till then, no other man can be the first possessor again: which is more than nothing; since he comes into it by God's providence, and as it were donation.
2. That which no man has yet any title to,[362] the finder may take without the violation of any truth. He does not deny that to be another man's, which is another man's; he does not begin to interrupt the happiness of anybody; etc. Therefore to possess himself of it is not wrong. So far from it, that, since every man is obliged to consult his own happiness (that is, his own interest and advantages, whenever he can do it without the violation of truth), not to act consonantly to this obligation is an omission that would be wrong. What he does, therefore, is right. And then if he does right in taking possession of it, he must from thence be the rightful possessor; or, it becomes his.
3. There are many things which cannot be possessed without cultivation and the contrivance and labor of the first possessor. This has generally been the case of lands, and these are indeed more eminently meant by the word possessions. Now, to deprive a man of the fruit of his own cares and sweat, and to enter upon it as if it was the effect of the intruder's pains and travel, is a most manifest violation of truth. It is asserting in fact that to be his, which cannot be his. See proposition II.
4. The contrary doctrine, viz. that prime occupancy gives no right, interferes with proposition III, for it must certainly be inconsistent with the peace and happiness of mankind in general to be left in endless wars and struggles for that which no man can ever have any right to. And yet, thus it must be if that doctrine was true: because it has been demonstrated that power confers no right, and therefore the first right to many things can only accrue from the first possession of them.
5. If B should endeavor by force (or fraud) to eject C out of the possession of anything which C enjoys (and obtained without expelling or disturbing anybody), he would

certainly do that which he himself would judge unreasonable, were he in C's place. Therefore, he acts as if that was not reason with respect to C, which would be reason in respect of B; contrary to the nature of reason, and to proposition IV.
6. To endeavor to turn a man violently out of his possessions is the same as to command him to leave them, upon pain of suffering for non-obedience. But this is usurping a dominion which he has no right to, and is contrary to section V, proposition VII. No man can expel another out of his possession without beginning to interrupt his happiness; nor can anyone do this without contravening the truth contained in proposition VI. This therefore secures the possessor in his possession forever: that is, it confirms his right to the thing possessed.
7. Lastly, the first possessor, of whom I have been speaking, has undoubtedly a right to defend his person, and such other things as can only be his, against the attempts of any aggressor (see proposition II); therefore, these no one can have a right to violate. And therefore again, if he cannot be forcibly dispossessed without violence offered to these, no one has any right to dispossess him. But this must be the case, where the possessor does not quit his possession willingly. The right, consequently, must remain solely in him, unless he consents to quit it.

Note: The successors of an invader, got into possession wrongfully, may acquire a right *in time*,[363] by the failure of such as might claim under him who had the right. For he who happens to be in possession, when all these are extinct, is in the place of a prime occupant.

IX. *A title to many things may be transferred by compact or donation.*[364] If B has the sole right in lands, or goods, nobody has any right to the disposal of them besides B—and he has a right. For disposing of them is but using them as his. Therefore the act of B in exchanging them for something else, or bestowing them upon C, interferes not with truth: and so B does nothing that is wrong. Nor does C do anything against truth, or that is wrong, in taking them, because he treats them as being what they are: as things which come to him by the act of that person in whom is lodged the sole power of disposing of them. Thus C gets the title innocently.

But in the case of *compact*, the reason on which this transaction stands is more evident still. For the contractors are supposed to receive, each from other, the equivalent of that which they part with, or at least what is equivalent to them retrospectively, or perhaps by each party preferable. Thus neither of them is hurt; perhaps both advantaged. And so each of them treats the thing, which he receives upon the innocent exchange, as being what it is: better for him, and promoting his convenience and happiness. Indeed he who receives the *value* of anything, and what he likes as well, in effect has it still. His *property* is not diminished: the situation and matter of it is only altered.

Mankind could not well subsist without bartering one thing for another; therefore, whatever tends to take away the benefit of this intercourse is inconsistent with the general good of mankind, etc. If a man could find the *necessaries* of life without it, and by himself, he must at least want many of the *comforts* of it.

X. *There is, then, such a thing as property, founded in nature and truth:*[365] *or, there are things which one man only can, consistently with nature and truth, call his:* by propositions II, VIII, IX.[366]

XI. *Those things which only one man can truly and properly call his, must remain his till he agrees to part with them (if they are such as he may part with) by compact or donation;* or (which must be understood) till they fail, or death extinguishes him and his title together, and he delivers the lamp to his next man. Because no one can deprive him of them without his approbation, but the depriver must use them as his when they are not his, in contradiction to truth. For,

XII. *To have the property of anything and to have the sole right of using and disposing of it are the same thing: they are equipollent expressions.* For, when it is said that P has the property, or that such a thing is proper to P, it is not said, that P and Q, or P and others, have the property (*proprium* limits the thing to P only); and when anything is said to be *his*, it is not said that *part of it only* is his. P has therefore the all or all-hood[367] of it, and consequently all the use of it. And then, since the all of it to him, or all that P can have of it, is but the use and disposal of it,[368] he who has this has the thing itself, and it is his.[369]

Laws, indeed, have introduced a way of speaking, by which the *property* and the *usufruct* are distinguished; but in truth, the usufructuary has a *temporary* or *limited* property, and the proprietary has a *perpetual* usufruct, either at present, or in reversion. Propriety without the use (if the use is never come to the proprietary) is an empty sound.

I have before, upon some occasions, taken it as granted, that he who uses anything as his, when it is not his, acts against truth, etc., but now I say further, that,

XIII. *He who uses or disposes of anything, does by that declare it to be his.* Because this is all that he, whose it *really* is, can do. Borrowing and hiring afford no objection to this. When the borrower or hirer uses the thing borrowed or hired, he uses what is his own for the time allowed, and his doing so is only one of those ways in which the true proprietary disposes of it.

XIV. *To usurp or invade the property of another man is injustice:* or, more fully, *to take, detain, use, destroy, hurt, or meddle*[370] *with anything that is his without his allowance, either by force or fraud or any other way, or even to attempt any of these, or assist them who do, are acts of injustice. The contrary—to render and permit quietly to everyone what is his—is justice.* Definition.

XV. *He that would not violate truth, must avoid all injustice:* or, *all injustice is wrong and evil.* It interferes with the truths[371] here before laid down, and perhaps more. It denies men to be subjects capable of distinct properties; in some cases it denies them to have a property even in their own bodies, life, fame, and the like; the practice of it is incompatible with the peace and happiness of mankind; it is what every man thinks unreasonable in his own case, when the injury is done to himself; to take anything from another only because I think I want it, or because I have power to take it and will have it, without any title to it, is the highest pretence to dominion, and denial of our natural equality; it is setting up a right to begin to distub the happiness of others; and lastly, it is to deny there is any such thing as property, contrary to truth.

Briefly, if there be anything which P can truly and properly call his, then, if T takes or uses it without the consent of P, he declares it to be his (for if it was his he could do no more) when it is not his, and so acts a lie,[372] in which consists the idea and formal ratio of moral evil.

The very attempting any instance of injustice, or assisting others in such an attempt, since it is attempting and promoting what is wrong, is being in the wrong as much as one is able to be, or doing what one can to achieve that which is evil, and to do this, by the terms, must be wrong and evil.

Even the *desire* of obtaining anything unjustly is evil: because to desire to do evil, by the terms again, is an evil or criminal desire. If the act follows such a desire, it is the child and product of it; and the desire, if anything renders the fulfilling of it impracticable, is the act obstructed in the beginning and stifled in the womb.

Let it be observed here, by way of scholion concerning the thing called "covetousness," that there seem to be three sorts of it. One is this here mentioned: a desire of getting from others, though it be unjustly. This is wrong and wicked. Another is an immense desire of heaping up what one can, by just methods, but without any reasonable end proposed,[373] and only in order to keep,[374] and, as it were, bury it;[375] and the more he accumulates, the more he craves.[376] This also entrenches upon truth, and seems to be a vice. But to covet to obtain what is another man's, by just means and with his consent, when it may contribute to the happiness of ourselves or families, and perhaps of the other person too, has nothing surely that looks unfriendly upon truth, or is blameable, in it. This, if it may be called covetousness, is a virtuous covetousness.

XVI. *When a man cares not what sufferings he causes to others, and especially if he delights in other men's sufferings and makes them his sport, this is what I call cruelty. And not to be affected with the sufferings of other people, though they proceed not from us, but from others or from causes in which we are not concerned, is unmercifulness. Mercy and humanity are the reverse of these.*

XVII. *He, who religiously regards truth and nature, will not only be not unjust, but (more) not unmerciful, and much less cruel.* Not to be affected with the afflictions of others, so far as we know them, and in proportion to the several degrees and circumstances of them, though we are not the causes of them, is the same as to consider the afflicted as persons not in affliction: that is, as being not what they are, or (which is the same) as being what they are not—and this contradicts matter of fact.

One can scarce know the sufferings of another without having at least some image of them in his mind: nor can one have these images without being conscious of them and, as it were, feeling them. Next to suffering itself is to carry the representation of it about with one. So that he who is not affected with the calamities of others, so far as they fall within his knowledge, may be said to know and not to know, or at least to cancel his knowledge, and contradict his own conscience.

There is something in human nature,[377] resulting from our very make and constitution—while it retains its genuine form, and is not altered by vicious habits, not perverted by transports of revenge or fury, by ambition, company, or false philosophy,[378] nor oppressed by stupidity and neglecting to observe what happens to others—I say, there is something which renders us obnoxious to the pains of others, causes us to sympathize with them, and almost comprehends us in their case. It is grievous to see or hear (and almost to hear of) any man, or even any animal whatever, in torment. This compassion appears eminently in them who, upon other accounts, are justly reckoned among the best of men:[379] in some degree it appears in almost all—nay, even sometimes, when they more coolly attend to things, in those hardened and execrable monsters of cruelty themselves, who seem just to retain only the least tincture of humanity that can be. The Pheræan tyrant, who had never wept over any of those murders he had caused among his own citizens, wept when he saw a tragedy but acted in the theatre:[380] the reason was, his attention was caught here, and he more observed the sufferings of Hecuba and Andromache than ever he had those of the Pheræans, and more impartially, being no otherwise concerned in them but as a common spectator. Upon this occasion, the principle of compassion, implanted in human nature, appeared, overcame his habits of cruelty, broke through his petrifaction, and would show that it could not be totally eradicated. It is therefore according to nature to be affected with the sufferings of other people, and the contrary is inhuman and unnatural.

Such are the circumstances of mankind, that we cannot (or but very few of us, God knows) make our way through this world without encountering dangers and suffering many evils; and therefore, since it is for the good of such as are so exposed, or actually smarting under pain or trouble, to receive comfort and assistance from others, without which they must commonly continue to be miserable or perish, it is for the common good and welfare of the majority, at least, of mankind that they should compassionate and help each other.[381] To do the contrary must therefore be contrary to nature and wrong by proposition III. And besides, it is by one's behavior and actions to affirm that the circumstances of men in this world are not what they are, or that peace, and health, and happiness, and the like, are not what they are.

Let a man substitute himself into the room of some poor creature dejected with invincible poverty, distracted with difficulties, or groaning under the pangs of some disease or the anguish of some hurt or wound, and without help abandoned to want and pain. In this distress, what reflections can he imagine he should have, if he found that everybody neglected him, nobody so much as pitying him or vouchsafing to take notice of his calamitous and sad condition? It is certain that what it would be reasonable or unreasonable for others to do in respect of him, he must allow to be reasonable or unreasonable for him to do in respect of them, or deny a manifest truth in proposition IV.

If unmercifulness, as before defined, be wrong, no time need to be spent in proving that *cruelty* is so. For all that is culpable in unmercifulness is contained in cruelty, with additions and aggravations. Cruelty not only denies due regard to the sufferings of others, but *causes* them, or perhaps *delights* in them, and (which is the most insolent and cruel of all cruelties) makes them a jest and subject of raillery. If the one be a *defect* of humanity, the other is diametrically opposite to it.[382] If the one does no good, the other does much evil. And no man, how cruel soever in reality he was, has ever liked to be reckoned a cruel man: such a confession of guilt does nature extort, so universally does it reject, condemn, abhor this character.

XVIII. *The practice of justice and mercy is just as right, as injustice, unmercifulness, and cruelty are wrong.* This follows from the nature of contraries. Besides, not to be just to a man is to be not just, or unjust, to him; and so not to be merciful is to be unmerciful, or perhaps cruel.

Here I might end this section, but perhaps it may not be improper to be a little more particular. Therefore,

XIX. *From the foregoing propositions may be deduced the heinousness of all such crimes as murder, or even hurting the person of another anyhow, when our own necessary defense does not require it,* (it being not possible that anything should be more his than his own person, life and limbs); *robbing, stealing, cheating, betraying, defamation, detraction, defiling the bed of another man, etc. with all the approaches and tendencies to them.* For these are not only comprised within the definition of injustice, and are therefore violations of those truths which are violated by that, but commonly (and some of them always) come within the description of cruelty too. All which is evident at first light with respect to murder, robbery, cheating, slandering, etc., especially if a man brings himself into the case, and views himself in his own imagination as rendered scandalous by calumniators and liars, stripped by thieves, ruined in his fortunes and undone by knaves, struggling to no purpose, convulsed and agonizing under the knife of some truculent ruffian, or the like.

The same is altogether as plain in the case of adultery,[383] when anyone[384] ensnares and corrupts the wife of another—notwithstanding the protection it gains from false notions, great examples,[385] and the commonness of the crime.[386] For (the nature of matrimony being, for the present, supposed to be such as it will appear by and by to be) the adulterer denies the property a husband has in his wife by compact, the most express and sacred that can possibly be made; he does that which tends to subvert the peace of families, confounds relation, and is altogether inconsistent with the order and tranquility of the world and therefore with the laws of human nature; he does what no man in his wits could think reasonable, or even tolerable, were he the person wronged;[387] briefly, he impudently treats a woman as his own woman (or wife[388]), who is not his but another's, contrary to justice, truth, and fact.[389] Nor is this simple injustice only, but injustice for which no reparation can be made, if the injured man thinks so, as he generally does (see [section II, proposition I, observation 4](#))—injustice accompanied with the greatest cruelty, so complicated as scarce any other can be. The husband is forever robbed of all that pleasure and satisfaction which arises from the wife's fidelity and affection to him,[390] presuming upon which he took her to be not only the partner of his bed, but the companion of his life and sharer in all his fortunes;[391] and into the room of them succeed painful and destructive passions. The poor woman[392] herself, though she may be deluded,[393] and not see at present her guilt or the consequences of it, usually pays dear for her security and want of guard, the husband becoming cold[394] and averse to her, and she full of apprehensions and fears,[395] with a particular dread of his further resentment. And their affairs, in this disjointed and distracted condition, are neglected: innocent children slighted, and left unprovided for, without so much as the comfort of any certain relations to pity them,[396] etc.

The adulterer may not be permitted to extenuate his crime by such impertinent similes and rakish talk as are commonly used for that purpose.[397] When anyone wrongs another of his property, he wrongs him of *what it is to him*, the proprietor: and the value must be set according to what *he* esteems it to be, not what the injurer—who perhaps has no taste of virtuous pleasures—may think it to be. (See section II, proposition 1, observations [3] and [4].) Nor may these thefts be excused from their secrecy:

1. For the injustice of the fact is the same in itself, whether known or not. In either case truth is denied, and a lie is as much a lie when it is whispered as when it is proclaimed at the market-cross.
2. It has been shown (section II) that the rectitude of our actions and way to happiness are coincident, and that such acts as are disagreeable to truth, wrong in themselves, tend to make men ultimately unhappy.[398] Things are so ordered and disposed by the Author of nature, or such a constitution of things flows from him, that it must be so. And since no retreat can be impervious to his eye, no corner so much out of the way as not to be within his plan, no doubt there is to every wrong and vicious act a suitable degree of unhappiness and punishment annexed, which the criminal will be sure to meet with same time or other.[399] For his own sake, therefore, he ought not to depend upon the darkness of the deed.
3. But lastly, it can hardly be but that it must be discovered.[400] People generally rise in vice, grow impudent and vain and careless, and discover themselves;[401] the opportunities contrived for it must be liable to observation; some confidents must be trusted, who may betray the secret, and upon any little distaste probably will do it; and besides, love is quick of apprehension.[402]

It will be easily perceived, from what has been said, that if to murder, rob, etc. are unjust and crimes of a heinous nature, all those things which have any tendency toward them, or affinity with them, or any way countenance them, must be in their degree criminal[403] because they are of the same complexion with that which they tend to, though not of the same growth, nor matured into the gross act, or perhaps do not operate so presently, apparently, or certainly. Envy, malice, and the like, are *conatus* toward the destruction or ruin of the person who is the object of these unhappy passions. To throw dust[404] upon a man's reputation by innuendos, ironies, etc. may not indeed sully it all at once, as when dirt is thrown, or gross calumnies, yet it infects the air, and may destroy it by a lingering poison. To expose another by the strength of a jesting talent, or harder temper of face, is to wound him, though it be in an invisible place.[405] Many freedoms and reputed civilities of barbarian extract, and especially gallantries,[406] that proceed not to consummate wickedness, nor perhaps are intended to be carried so far, may yet divert people's affections from their proper object, and debauch the mind.[407] By stories or insinuations to sow the seeds of discord and quarrels between men is to murder or hurt them by another hand. Even for men to intermeddle in other people's affairs, as busybodies and ἀλλοτριοεπίσκοποι[408] do, is to assume a province which is not theirs; to concern themselves with things in which they are not concerned; to make that public which in itself is private; and perhaps to rob the person, into whose business they intrude themselves, of his quiet, if of nothing else. For indeed this intermeddling looks like setting up a pretence to something further: like an unjust attack begun at a distance. All which declares what an enemy, and how irreconcilable to truth, this pragmatical humor is. And so on.

If these things are so, how guilty must they be who are designedly the *promoters* or *instruments* of injustice and wickedness, such as mercenary-swearers and false witnesses, traders in scandal, solicitors in vice, they who intend by their conversation to relax men's principles too much, and (as it seems) prepare them for knavery, lewdness, or any flagitious enterprise.[409]

There are other crimes, such as infidelity to friends or them who entrust us with anything, ingratitude, all kinds of wilful perjury, and the like, which might have been mentioned in the proposition, being great instances of injustice; but because they are visibly such, and their nature cannot be mistaken, I comprise them in the *et cetera* there. Anyone may see that he who acts unfaithfully, acts against his promises and engagements, and therefore denies and sins against truth, does what it can never be for the good of the world should become a universal practice, does what he would not have done to himself, and wrongs the man who depends upon him of what he justly might expect. So the ungrateful man treats his benefactor as not being what be is, etc. And the false-swearer respects neither things, nor himself, nor the persons affected, nor mankind in general, nor God himself, as being what they are. All this is obvious.[410]

VII
Truths Respecting Particular Societies of Men, or Governments

I. *Man is a social creature: that is, a single man or family cannot subsist, or not well, alone out of all society.* More things are necessary to sustain life, or at least to make it in any degree pleasant and desirable, than it is possible for any one man to make and provide for himself merely by his own labor and ingenuity. Meat, and drink, and clothing, and house, and that frugal furniture which is absolutely requisite, with a little necessary physic, suppose many arts and trades, many heads, and many hands. If he could make a shift, in time of health, to live as a wild man under the protection of trees and rocks, feeding upon such fruits, herbs, roots, and other things as the earth should afford and happen to present to him, yet what could he do in *sickness*, or *old age*, when he would not be able to stir out, or receive her beneficence.

If he should take from the other sex such a help as the common appetite might prompt him to seek, or he might happen to meet with in his walks, yet still if the hands are doubled the wants are doubled too—nay, more: additional wants, and great ones, attending the bearing and education of children.

If we could suppose all these difficulties surmounted, and a family grown up and doing what a single family is capable of doing by itself: supporting themselves by gardening, a little agriculture, or a few cattle, which they have somehow got and tamed (though even this would be hard for them to do, having no markets where they might exchange the produce of their husbandry, or of their little flock or herd, for other things; no shops to repair to for tools; no servant or laborer to assist; nor any public invention, of which they might serve themselves in the preparation of their grain, dressing their meat, manufacturing their wool, and the like); yet still, it is only the cortex of the man which is provided for: what must become of the interior part, the *minds* of these people? How would those be fed and improved?[411] Arts and sciences, so much of them as is necessary to teach men the use of their faculties and unfold their reason, are not the growth of single families so employed. And yet for men to lay out all their pains and time in procuring only what is proper to keep the blood and humors in circulation, without any further views or any regard to the nobler part of themselves, is utterly incongruous to the idea of a being formed for rational exercises.

If all the exceptions against this separate way of living could be removed, yet, as mankind increases, the little plots which the several families possess and cultivate must be enlarged or multiplied. By degrees they would find themselves straitened, and there would soon be a collision of interests, from whence disputes and quarrels would ensue. Other things, too, might minister matter for these. And besides all this, some men are naturally troublesome, vicious, thievish, pugnacious, rabid—and these would always be disturbing and flying upon the next to them—as others are ambitious, or covetous, and, if they happen to have any advantage or superiority in power, would not fail to make themselves yet greater or stronger by eating up their neighbors, till by repeated encroachments they might grow to be formidable.[412]

Under so many wants, and such apprehensions or present dangers, necessity would bring some families into terms of friendship with others for mutual comfort and defense; and this, as the reason of it increased, would become stronger, introduce stricter engagements, and at last bring the people to mix and unite. And then, the weak being glad to shelter themselves under the protection and conduct of the more able, and so naturally giving way for these to ascend, the several sorts would at length settle into their places, according to their several weights and capacities with respect to the common concern. And thus some form of a society must arise: men cannot subsist otherwise.

But if it was possible for a man to preserve life by himself, or with his petit company about him, yet nobody can deny that it would be infinitely *better* for him, and them, to live in a society, where men are serviceable to themselves and their neighbors at the same time, by exchanging their money, or goods, for such other things as they want more—where they are capable of doing good offices each for other in time of need—where they have the protection of laws, and a public security against cheats, robbers, assassins, and all enemies to property—where a common force or army is ready to interpose between them and foreign invaders—and where they may enjoy those discoveries which have been made in arts and learning, may improve their faculties by conversation and innocent conflicts of reason, and (to speak out) may be made men.

If, when we have the privilege of society and laws, we can scarce preserve our own or be safe, what a woeful condition should we be in *without them*: exposed to the insults, rapines, and violence of unjust and merciless men, not having any sanctuary, anything to take refuge in? So again, if notwithstanding the help of friends and those about us, and such conveniencies as may be had in cities and peopled places, we are forced to bear many pains and melancholy hours, how irksome would life be, if in sickness or other trouble there was nobody to administer either remedy or consolation?

Lastly, society is what men generally *desire*. And though much company may be attended with much vanity, and occasion many evils,[413] yet it is certain that absolute and perpetual solitude has something in it very irksome and hideous.[414] Thus the social life is natural to man, or what his nature and circumstances require.

II. *The end of society is the common welfare and good of the people associated.* This is but the consequence of what has been just said. For because men cannot subsist well, or not *so well*, separately, therefore they unite into greater bodies: that is, the end of their uniting is their better subsistence; and by how much their manner of living becomes better, by so much the more effectually is this end answered.

III. *A society, into which men enter for this end, supposes some rules or laws, according to which they agree all to be governed, with a power of altering or adding to them as occasion shall require.* A number of men, met together without any rules by which they submit to be governed, can be nothing but an irregular multitude. Everyone being still *sui juris*, and left entirely to his own private choice, by whatever kind of judgment or passion or caprice that happens to be determined, they must needs interfere one with another; nor can such a concourse of people be anything different from an indigested chaos of dissenting parts, which by their confused motions would damnify and destroy each other. This must be true if men differ in the size of their understandings, in their manner of thinking, and the several turns their minds take from their education, way of living, and other circumstances; if the greatest part of them are under the direction of bodily affections, and if these differ as much as their shapes, their complexions, their constitutions do.[415] Here then we find nothing but confusion and unhappiness.

Such a combination of men, therefore, as may produce their common good and happiness, must be such a one as, in the first place, may render them compatible one with another, which cannot be without *rules* that may direct and adjust their several motions and carriages towards each other, bring them to some degree of uniformity, or at least restrain such excursions and enormities as would render their living together inconsistent.

Then, there must be some express declarations and *scita* to ascertain properties and titles to things by common consent: that, so when any altercations or disputes shall happen concerning them (as be sure many must in a world so unreasonable and prone to iniquity), the appeal may be made to their own settlements, and by the application of a general undisputed rule to the particular case before them, it may appear on which side the obliquity lies, the controversy may be fairly decided, and all mouths eternally stopped. And then again, that they may be protected and persevere in this agreeable life, and the enjoyment of their respective properties be secured to them, several things must be forecasted by way of precaution against foreign invasions; punishments must be appointed for offences committed among themselves, which, being known, may deter men from committing them, etc. These rules, methods, and appointments of punishments, being intelligibly and honestly drawn up, agreed to, and published, are the mutual compacts[416] under which the society is confederated, and the laws of it.

If, then, to have the members of a society capable of subsisting together, if to have their respective properties ascertained, if to be safe and quiet in the possession of them be for the general good of the society, and these things cannot be had without laws; then a society whose foundation and cement is the public good must have such laws, or be supposed at least to design such.

As to the making of any further laws, when the public interest and welfare require them, that is but repeating the same power, in other instances, which they made use of before in making their first laws; and as to altering or repealing, it is certain the power of making and unmaking here are equal. Besides, when men are incorporated and live together for their mutual good, this end is to be considered at one time as much as at another: not only in their first constitution and settlement.

IV. *These laws and determinations must be such as are not inconsistent with natural justice.* For

1. To ordain anything that interferes with truth is the same as to ordain that what is true shall be false, or vice versa,[417] which is absurd.
2. To pretend by a law to make that to be just, which before and in itself was unjust, is the same as to ordain that which interferes with truth, because justice is founded in truth (as before) and everywhere the same.[418]
3. Therefore, by a law to enact anything which is naturally unjust is to enact that which is absurd: that which by section I is morally evil, and that which is opposite to those laws by which it is manifestly the will of our Creator we should be governed.[419] And to enact what is thus evil must be evil indeed.
4. Lastly, to establish injustice must be utterly inconsistent with the general good and happiness of any society—unless to be unjustly treated, pilled, and abused can be happiness.[420] And if so, it is utterly inconsistent with the end of society; or, it is to deny that to be the end of it, which is the end of it.

V. *A society limited by laws supposes magistrates, and a subordination of powers: that is, it supposes a government of some form or other.* Because where men are to act by rules or laws for the public weal, some must of necessity be appointed to judge when those laws are transgressed, and how far; to decide doubtful cases, and the like; there must be some armed with authority to execute those judgments, and to punish offenders; there must be persons chosen not only to punish and prevent public evils, but also to do many other things which will be required in advancement of the public good; and then the power of making new laws, and abrogating or mending old ones, as experience may direct or the case at any time require; as also of providing presently and legally for the safety of the public in time of sudden danger, must be lodged somewhere.

If there are no executors of the laws, the laws cannot be executed; and if so, they are but a dead letter, and equal to none; and if the society has none, it is indeed no society, or not such a one as is the subject of this proposition. Guardians and executors of laws are therefore the vitals of a society, without which there can be no circulation of justice in it, no care of it taken, nor can it continue. And since men can be but in in one place at once, there must be numbers of these proportionable to the bigness and extent of it.

And further, since the concerns of a whole society, and such things as may fall within the compass of a statute book, are various, requiring several sorts and sizes of abilities, and lying one above another in nature; since not only private men want to be inspected, but even magistrates and officers themselves, who (though they oft forget it) are still but men; and since the whole society is to be *one*, one compact body: I say, since the case is thus, there must be men to act in several elevations and qualities as well as places, of which the inferior sort in their several quarters must act immediately under their respective superiors, and so this class of superiors in their several provinces under others above them, till at last the ascent is terminated in some head, where the legislative power is deposited and from whence spirits and motion are communicated though the whole body. An army may as well be supposed to be well disciplined, well provided, and well conducted without either general or officers, as a society without governors and their subalterns, or (which is the same) without some form of government, to answer the end of its being.

VI. *A man may part with some of his natural rights, and put himself under the government of laws, and those who in their several stations are entrusted with the execution of them, in order to gain the protection of them and the privileges of a regular society.* Because by this he does but exchange one thing for another, which he reckons equivalent, or indeed preferable by much, and this he may do without acting against any truth. For the liberties and natural rights which he exchanges are his own, and therefore no other man's property is denied by this; nor is the nature of happiness denied to be what it is, since it is happiness which he aims at in doing this. On the contrary, he would rather offend against truth, and deny happiness to be what it is, if he did not do it; especially seeing that here his own happiness coincides with the *general* happiness and more convenient being of the kingdom or commonwealth where his lot falls, or his choice determines him to live.

If the question should be asked, *what* natural rights a man may part with, or *how far* he may part with them, the general answer, I think, may be this: Some things are essential to our being, and some it is not in our power to part with. As to the rest, he may depart from them so far as it is consistent with the end for which he does this: not further, because beyond that lies a contradiction. A man cannot give away the natural right and property he has in anything, in order to preserve or retain that property: but he may consent to contribute part of his estate, in order to preserve the rest, when otherwise it might all be lost; to take his share of danger in defense of his country, rather than certainty perish, be enslaved, or ruined by the conquest or oppression of it; and the like.

VII. *Men may become members of a society (i.e. do what is mentioned in the foregoing proposition) by giving their consent, either explicitly or implicitly.* That a man may subject himself to laws, we have seen. If he does this, he must do it either in his own person; or he must do it by some proxy, whom he substitutes in his room to agree to public laws; or his consent must be collected only from the conformity of his carriage, his adhering to the society, accepting the benefits of its constitution, and acquiescing in the established methods and what is done by virtue of them. By the two first ways he declares himself explicitly and directly; nor can he after that behave himself as if he was no member of the society, without acting as if he had not done what he has done. And this is the case not only of them who have been concerned in the first formation of any government, but also of them who have in the said manners[421] given their consent to any subsequent acts, by which they owned, confirmed, and came into what their ancestors had done, or who have by oaths put themselves under obligations to the public. By the last of the three ways mentioned, a man's consent is given indeed implicitly, and less directly—but yet it is given, and he becomes a party. For suppose him to be born in some certain kingdom or commonwealth, but never to have been party to any law, never to have taken any oath to the government, nor ever formally to have engaged himself by any other act. In this case he cannot methinks but have some love and sympathy for that place which afforded him the first air he drew, some gratitude towards that constitution which protected his parents while they educated and provided for him, some regard to those obligations under which perhaps they have laid him, and with which limitations, as it were, they (or rather the Governor of the world by them) conveyed to him his very life.

If he inherits or takes anything, by the laws of the place, to which he has no indefeasible right in nature—or which, if he had a natural right to it, he could not tell how to get, or keep, without the aid of laws and advantage of society—then, when he takes this inheritance, or whatever it is, with it he takes and owns the laws which give it him.

Indeed, since the security he has from the laws of the country in respect of his person, and rights, whatever they either are or may happen to be hereafter, is the general equivalent for his submission to them, he cannot accept that without being obliged in equity to pay this.

Nay, lastly, his very continuing and settling in any place shows that either he likes the constitution, or likes it better than any other, or at least thinks it better in his circumstances to conform to it than to seek any other: that is, he consents to be comprehended in it.[422]

VIII. *When a man is become a member of a society, if he would behave himself according to truth, he ought to do these things:*viz. to consider property as founded not only in nature, but also in law, and men's titles to what they have as strengthened by that, and even by his own concession and covenants, and therefore by so much the more inviolable and sacred; instead of taking such measures to do himself right when he is molested or injured, as his own prudence might suggest in a state of nature, to confine himself to such ways as are with his own consent marked out for him; and, in a word, to behave himself according to his subordination or place in the community, and to observe the laws of it. For it is contained in the *idea* of a law, that it is intended to be observed: and therefore he who is a party to any laws, or professes himself member of a society formed upon laws, cannot willingly transgress those laws without denying laws to be what they are, or himself to be what he is supposed or professes himself to be: and indeed without contradicting all or more of those truths contained in the foregoing propositions.

IX. *In respect of those things which the laws of the place take no cognizance of, or when if they do take cognizance of them, the benefit of those laws cannot be had* (for so it may sometimes happen. I say, in respect of such things), *he who is a member of a society in other respects retains his natural liberty, is still as it were in a state of nature, and must endeavor to act according to truth and his best prudence.* For in the *former* case there is nothing to limit him, by the suppositiom, but truth and nature. And in the *other* it is the same as if there was nothing, since in effect there is no law where no effect or benefit from it is to be had. As, for example, if a man should be attacked by thieves or murderers, and has no opportunity or power to call the proper magistrate or officer to his assistance.

There is a third case which perhaps may demand admission here, and that is when laws are plainly contrary to truth and natural justice. For though they may pass the usual forms, and be styled laws, yet, since no such law can abrogate that law of nature and reason to which the

Author of our being has subjected us, or make falsehood to be truth, and two inconsistent laws cannot both oblige, or subsist together, one of them must give way, and it is easy to discern which ought to do it.[423]

There remains one truth more to be annexed here, which may be contradicted by the practices and pretences of Enthusiasts.[424]

X. *The societies intended in this section, such as kingdoms and commonwealths, may defend themselves against other nations: or, war may lawfully be waged in defense and for the security of a society, its members and territories, or for reparation of injuries.* For if one man may in a state of nature have a right to defend himself (see section VI, proposition VII), two may, or three, and so on. Nay, perhaps two may have a double right, three a threefold right, etc. At least, if the right be not greater, the concern is greater, and there will be more reason, that two, or three, or more should be saved, than one only; and therefore that two, or three, or more should defend themselves, than that one should. And if this may be done by men in a state of nature, it may be done by them when confederated among themselves, because with respect to other nations they are still in that state—I mean, so far as they have not limited themselves by leagues and alliances.

Besides, if a man may defend himself, he may defend himself by what methods he thinks most proper—provided he trespasses against no truth—and therefore, by getting the aid and assistance of others. Now when war is levied in defense of the public and the people in general, the thing may be considered as if every particular man was defending himself with the assistance of all the rest, and so be turned into the same case with that of a single man.

In truth, the condition of a nation seems to be much the same with that of a single person when there is no law, or no benefit of law, to be had. And what one man may do to another in that position, may be done by one nation or politic body with respect to another. And perhaps by this rule, regard being had to what has been delivered in section VI, the justice of foreign wars may be not untruly estimated.

Mutual defense is one of the great ends of society, if not the greatest, and in a particular and eminent manner involves in it defense against foreign enemies. And whoever signalizes himself, when there is occasion for his service, merits the grateful acknowledgements and celebrations of his countrymen, so far at least as he acts generously and with a public spirit, and not in pursuance only of private views.

As to those wars which are undertaken by men out of ambition[425]—merely to enlarge empire, or to show the world how terrible they are, how many men they are able to slay, how many slaves to make,[426] how many families to drive from their peaceful habitations, and, in short, how much mischief and misery they are able to bring upon mankind—these are founded upon false nations of glory: embellished indeed by servile wits and misplaced eloquence, but condemned by all true philosophy and religion.

VIII
Truths Concerning Families and Relations

This section I shall begin, as relation itself does, with marriage.

I. *The end of marriage is the propagation of mankind and joint happiness of the couple intermarrying, taken together, or the latter by itself.*[427] The difference of the sexes, with the strong inclination they have each to the enjoyment of the other,[428] is plainly ordained by the Author of nature for the continuance of the species, which without that must be soon extinguished. And though people, when they marry, may have many times not so much the increase of their family in their design or wishes, as the gratification of an importunate appetite; yet since nature excites the appetite, and that tends to this end, nature (or rather its great Author) may be said to make this an end of the marriage, though the bridegroom and bride themselves do not.

And then as to that other thing, which either accompanies the aforesaid end of marriage, or is (as in many cases it can only be) the end itself[429]—the joint happiness of the *conjuges*—nobody can be supposed to marry in order and on set purpose to make him or herself *unhappy*, no nor without a presumption of being *more happy*. For without an apprehension of some degree of happiness to accrue, or what presents itself to the imagination as such and is taken for such, what can induce people to alter their condition? Something there must be, by which (however things prove upon trial) they think to better it. And indeed if their circumstances are such as may enable them to maintain a family and provide for children, without difficulties and an overburden of cares, and if they in good earnest resolve to behave themselves as they ought, and reciprocally to be helpful and loving each to other, much comfort and happiness[430] may justly be expected from this intimate union,[431] the interchange of affections, and a conspiration of all their counsels and measures,[432] the qualities and abilities of the one sex being fitted and, as it were, tallying to the wants of the other. For to pass over in silence those joys which are truest when most concealed,[433] many things there are which may be useful, perhaps necessary, to the man, and yet require the delicater hand or nicer management and genius of the woman:[434] and so, *vicissim*, the woman cannot but want many things which require the more robust and active powers or greater capacity of the man.[435] Thus, in lower life, while the wheel, the needle, etc. employ her, the plough or some trade perhaps demands the muscles and hardiness of him; and, more generally, if she inspects domestic affairs, and takes care that everything be provided regularly, spent frugally, and enjoyed with neatness and advantage, he is busied in that profession, or the oversight and improvement of that estate, which must sustain the charge of all this; he presides and directs in matters of greater moment; preserves order in the family by a gentle and prudent govemment; etc.[436]

As then I founded the greater societies of men upon the mutual convenience which attends their living regularly together, so may I found this less, but stricter, alliance between the man and the woman in their joint-happiness.[437] Nature has a further aim: the preservation of the kind.

II. *That marriages are made by some solemn contract, vow, or oath (and these perhaps attended with some pledge, or nuptial rites),*[438] *by which the parties mutually engage to live together in love, and to be faithful, assisting, and the like, each to other, in all circumstances of health and fortune, till death parts them,*[439] I take for granted. For all nations have some form or other upon these occasions, and even private contracts cannot be made without some words in which they are contained, nor perhaps without some kind of significant, though private, ceremony between the lovers, which lose nothing of force with respect to them by their being both parties and witnesses themselves. Something must pass between them, that is declarative of their intentions, expresses their vows, and binds them each to the other. There is no coming together after the manner of man and wife upon any other foot.

III. *That intimate union, by which the* conjuges *become possessed each of the other's person,*[440] *the mixture of their fortunes,*[441] *and the joint relation they have to their children,*[442] all strengthen the bonds and obligations of matrimony. By every act done in pursuance of a covenant, such as the matrimonial is, that covenant is owned, ratified, and, as it were, made *de integro* and repeated.

Possession is certainly more than nothing. When this therefore is added to a former title, the title must needs be corroborated.

When two persons throw their all into one stock as joint-traders for life, neither of them can consistently with truth and honesty take his share out and be gone (i.e. dissolve the partnership) without the concurrence of the other; and sometimes it may not be easy, perhaps possible, to do it at all. Each therefore is even by this bound, and becomes obnoxious to the other.

And as to the present case, if the marriage be not altogether unfruitful, since both the parents are immediately related to the same child, that child is the medium of a fixed, unalterable relation between them. For, being both of the same blood with the child,[443] they themselves come to be of the same blood; and so that relation, which at first was only moral and legal, becomes natural: a relation in nature which can never cease or be disannulled. It follows now that,

IV. *Marrying, when there is little or no prospect of true happiness from the match,*[444] *and especially if there are plain presages of unhappiness; after marriage, adultery; all kinds of infidelity; transferring that affection, which even under the decays of nature ought to preserve its vigor, and never to degnerate (at worst) but into a friendship of a superior kind;*[445] *and the like, are all wrong.*[446] Because the first of these is belying one's own sense of things, and has an air of distraction—or however it is to act as if that was the least and most trifling of all transactions in life, which is certainly one of the greatest and most delicate. And to offend in any of the other ways is to behave as if the end of marriage was not what it is; as if no such league had been made between the persons married, as has been made, actually, and solemnly, and is still subsisting between them; as if they were not possessed each of the other; their fortunes not interwoven; nor their children so equally related to them, as they are; and therefore the misbehavior, being repugnant to truth, is a sin against it, and the mighty Patron of it.

If the most express and solemn contracts, upon which persons, when they marry, do so far depend as, in confidence of their being religiously observed, to alter quite their condition, begin a new thread of life, and risk all their fortune and happiness: I say, if such sacred compacts as these are allowed to be broken, there is an end of all faith; the obligation of oaths (not more binding than marriage vows) ceases; no justice can be administered; and then what a direful influence must this have upon the affairs of mankind, upon that and other accounts?[447]

Allowance, by section IV ought to be made for inabilities, and involuntary failings. A person's age, health, estate, or other circumstances may be such, and without any fault, that he or she cannot do what they would; or perhaps instead of that, one of them may come to want the pity and assistance of the other. In this case (which requires the philosophy and submission proper in afflictions) it is the duty of the one not only to bear with, but also to comfort, and do what may be done for the other. This is part of the happiness proposed, which consists not only in positive pleasures, but also in lessening pains and wants, while the pair have each in the other a refuge at hand.

Note: I have designedly forborn to mention that authority of a husband over his wife which is usually given to him—not only by private writers, but even by laws—because I think it has been carried much too high. I would have them live so far upon the level, as (according to my constant lesson) to be governed both by reason.[448] If the man's reason be stronger, or his knowledge and experience greater (as it is commonly supposed to be), the woman will be obliged upon that score to pay a deference, and submit to him.[449]

Having now considered the man and woman between themselves, I proceed in the order of nature to consider them as parents, and to see (in a few propositions following) how things will be carried between them and their children, as also between other relations, coming at first from the same bed, if truth and matters of fact (to be named, where the argument shall call for them) are not denied.

V. *Parents ought to educate their children, take the best care of them they can, endeavor to provide for them, and be always ready to assist them.* Because otherwise they do not carry themselves towards their children as being what they are: children and theirs; they do not do what they would desire to have done to themselves, were they again to pass through that feeble and tender state, or perhaps what has been done to them;[450] and besides, they transgress the law established by nature for the preservation of the race, which, as things are, could not without a parental care and affection be continued—a law which is in force among all the other tribes of animals, so far as there is occasion for it.

Not to do what is here required, is not *barely* to act against truth and nature, not *only* such an omission as is mentioned in section I, proposition V, but a heinous instance of *cruelty*. If anyone can deny this, let him better consider the case of an infant, neglected, helpless, and having nothing so much as to solicit for him but his cries and (that which will do but little in this world) his innocence; let him think what it would be to turn a child, though a little grown up, out of doors, destitute of everything, not knowing whither to fly,[451] or what to do; and whether it is not the same thing if he be left to be turned out by anybody else hereafter, or (in general) to conflict with want and misery—let him reflect a while upon the circumstances of poor orphans[452] left unprovided for, to be abused by everybody,[453] etc.—and then let him say whether it is possible for a parent to be so void of bowels as not to be moved with these considerations, or what epithet he deserves if he is not. If any of them who have been thus abandoned and turned adrift have done well, those instances ought to be placed among particular providences: as when a vessel at sea, without pilot or sailor, happens to be blown into the port.

Not only the care, but the early care of parents is required, lest death should prevent them: death, which skips none, and surprises many. Not to remember this, and act accordingly, is in practice to contradict one of the most certain and obvious of all truths.

VI. *In order to the good of children, their education, etc., there must be some authority over them lodged by nature in the parents:* I mean, *the nature of the case is such, as necessarily requires there should be in the parents an authority over their children in order to their good.* At first if somebody did not nurse, feed, clothe, and take care of children, the interval between their first and last breath would be very short. They on whom it is incumbent to do this are undoubtedly their parents; to do this is their duty, by the foregoing proposition. But then they must do it as they can, and according to their judgment; and this is plainly an act of authority, to order and dispose of another according to one's judgment, though it be done according to the best of one's judgment.

As the child grows up, the case is still the same in some degree or other, till he arrives at the age reckoned mature (and very often longer). He is become able perhaps to walk by himself, but what path to choose he knows not—cannot distinguish his safety and his danger, his advantages and disadvantages, nor, in general, good and evil—he must be warned, and directed, and watched still by his parents, or somebody entrusted by them, or else it might have been possibly much better for him to have expired under the midwife's hands, and prevented the effects of his own ignorance.

When he not only runs about, but begins to fancy himself capable of governing himself: by how much the more he thinks himself capable, by so much the less capable may he be, and the more may he want to be governed. The avenues of sense are opened, but the judgment and intellectual faculties are not ripened but with time and much practice. The world is not easily known by persons of *adult* abilities, and, when they become tolerably acquainted with it, yet they find things in it so intricate, dubious, difficult, that it is many times hard for *them* to resolve what measures are fittest to be taken: but they who are not (or but lately) past their nuts, cannot be supposed to have any extent of knowledge, or to be, if they are left to themselves, anything else but a prey to the villain who first seizes upon them. Instead of judgment and experience, we find commonly in youth such things as are remotest from them—childish appetites, irregular passions, peevish and obstinate humors—which require to be subdued, and taught to give way to wholesome counsels. Young people are not only obnoxious to their own humors and follies, but also to those of their companions. They are apt to hearken to them, and to imitate one and anothers misconduct; and thus folly mingles with folly, and increases prodigiously. The judgment, therefore, of the parents must still interpose, and preside, and guide through all these stages of infancy, childhood, and youth; according to their power, improving the minds of their children, breaking the strength of their inordinate passions, cultivating rude nature, forming their manners, and showing them the way which they ought to be found in.

These things are so in fact, and a parent cannot acquit himself of the duty imposed upon him in the preceding proposition, if he acts so as to deny them; but then he cannot act so as not to deny them (that is, so as to subdue the passions of the child, break his stomach, and cause him to mind his instructions) without some sort of discipline, and a proper severity (at least very rarely).[454]

To all this, and much more that might be urged, must be superadded that the fortunes of children, and their manner of setting out in the world, depending (commonly) upon their parents, their parents must upon this account be their directors, and govern their affairs.

Note 1: It appears now from the premisses, that even parents have not properly a *dominion* over their children such as is intended in [section VI, proposition V](), from which this parental authority is a very different thing. This only respects the good of the children, and reaches not beyond the means which the parents, acting according to the best of their skill, abilities, and opportunities, find most conducive to that end; but dominion only respects the will of the lord, and is of the same extent with his pleasure. Parents may not, by virtue of this authority, command their children to do anything which is in itself evil—and if they do, the children ought not to obey.[455] Nor may they do anything what they please to them. They may not kill, or maim, or expose them,[456] and when they come to be men or women, and are possessed of estates, which either their parents (or anybody else) have given them, or they have acquired by their own labor, management, or frugality, they have the same properties in these with respect to their parents, which they have with respect to other people: the parents have no more right to take them by force from them than the rest of the world have.[457] So that what occurs in the place abovementioned remains firm, notwithstanding anything that may be objected from the case of parents and children. And moreover,

Note 2: They who found monarchy in paternal authority, gain little advantage with respect to despotic or absolute power. A power to be exercised for the good of subjects (like that of parents for the good of their children), and that principally where they are incapable of helping themselves, can only be derived from hence. The father of his country cannot by this way of reasoning be demonstrated to be the absolute lord[458] of the lives, and limbs, and fortunes of the people, to dispose of them as he pleases.[459] The authority of parents goes not this length. Besides, if a parent has an authority over his children, it does not follow that the eldest son should have the same authority, be it what it will, over his brothers and sisters; and much less, that the heir of the first parent should in succeeding generations have it over all the collaterals. The very relation between them soon vanishes, and comes at last in effect to nothing, and this notion with it.

VII. *As parents are obliged to educate their children, etc., so children ought to consider parents as the immediate authors (authors under the first and great Cause*[460]*) of their being; or, to speak more properly, of their being born.* I know children are apt (not very respectfully, or prudently) to say that their parents did not beget them for *their sakes*, whom they could not know before they were born, but for their *own pleasure*. But they who make this a pretext for their disobedience or disregard, have not sufficiently thought what pain, what trouble, how many frights and cares,[461] what charges, and what self-denials parents undergo upon the score of their children—and that all these, if parents only rushed into pleasure and consulted nothing else, might easily be avoided by neglecting them and their welfare.[462] For as to those parents who do this, let them speak for themselves; I shall not be their advocate.

VIII. *A great submission and many grateful acknowledgements, much respect and piety, are due from children to their parents.* For if there is an authority in parents (as before) this must be answered by a proportionable submission on the other side, since an authority to which no obedience is due, is equal to no authority.

If the thought of annihilation be generally disagreeable, as it seems to be, then merely to be conscious of existence must have in it something desirable.[463] And if so, our parents must be considered as the authors, or at least the instruments, of that good to us, whatever it is—which cannot be done unless they are treated with distinction and great regard, being to us what no other is, or ever can be.

God, as the first cause of all beings, is often styled metaphorically, or in a large sense of the word, the *Father* of the world, or of us all, and, if we behave ourselves towards Him as being such, we cannot (according to section V, proposition XIX, no. 3) but adore Him. Something analogous, though in a low degree, to the case between God and his offspring there seems to be in the case between parents and their children. If that requires divine worship, this will demand a great respect and reverence.[464] Nor can I believe that a child who does not honor his parent can have any disposition to worship his Creator.[465] The precept of honoring parents, to be found in almost all nations and religions, seems to proceed from some such sentiment: for in books we meet with it commonly following, or rather adhering to, that of worshipping the Deity.[466] In laying children under this obligation, they have all conspired, though scarce in anything else.[467]

The admonitions of a parent must be of the greatest weight with his children, if they do but remember that he has lived longer, and had repeated occasions to consider things and observe events; has cooler passions as he advances in years, and sees things more truly as they are; is able in a manner to predict what they themselves will desire to have done when they shall arrive at his age; may upon these accounts, ordinarily, be presumed to be a more competent judge than themselves;[468] and lastly, from his relation to them must be more sincerely inclined to tell them truth than any other person in the world can be supposed to be.[469] I say, if young people reflect well upon these things, they cannot in prudence, or even kindness to themselves, but pay the utmost deference to the advertisements and directions of a parent.

And to conclude: if parents want the assistance of their children, especially in the declension of their age and when they verge towards a helpless condition again, they cannot deny or withhold it, but they must at the same time deny to requite the care and tenderness shown by their parents towards them in *their* helpless and dangerous years; that is, without being ungrateful, and that is, without being unjust, if there be injustice in ingratitude.[470] Nor (which is more still) can they do this without denying what they may in their turn require of their children.[471] In effect, they do thus, by their actions, deny that to have been, which has been, and those things to be possible, which may be hereafter.

Not only bodily infirmities of parents, but such decays of their minds as may happen, ought to be pitied—their little hastinesses and mistakes dissembled, and their defects supplied, decently.[472]

IX. *That* στοργὴ *or affection on both sides, which naturally and regularly is in parents towards their children, and* vicissim,[473] *ought to be observed and followed, when there is no reason to the contrary.*

We have seen before, and it is evident from the terms, that sense ought to govern when reason does not interpose, i.e. when there is no reason why it should not. If then this στοργὴ or mutual affection be an inward sense of the case between parents and children, which, without much thinking upon it, is felt by them and sits upon their natures,[474] it may be comprised in propositions XIV and XV of section III. But whether it is or not, the same may be said (which must be repeated in another place) of every affection, passion, inclination in general. For when there is no reason why we should not comply with them, their own very solicitation, and the agreeableness we apprehend to be in complying, are preponderating arguments. This must be true, if something is more than nothing, or that ought to be granted which there is no reason to deny. So that if this στοργὴ be only taken as a kind of attraction, or tendence, in the mere matter of parents and children, yet still this physical motion or sympathy ought not to be overruled, if there be not a good reason for it. On the contrary, it ought to be taken as a suggestion of nature, which should always be regarded when it is not superseded by something superior, that is, by reason. But further, here reason does not only not gainsay, by its silence and consent, and so barely leave its right of commanding to this bodily inclination; but it comes in strongly to *abet* and *enforce* it, as designed for a reasonable end: and therefore, not to act according to it is not to act according to reason, and to deny that to be which is,

X. *The same is true of that affection which other relations naturally have, in some proportion or other, each for other.* To this they ought to accommodate themselves where reason does not prohibit. The proof of this assertion is much the same with that of the foregoing *mutatis mutandis*.

The foundation of all natural relation is laid in marriage.[475] For the husband and wife having solemnly attached themselves each to other, having the same children, interests, etc., become so intimately related as to be reckoned united: one flesh, and in the laws of nations many times, one person.[476] Certainly they are such with respect to the posterity, who proceed from them jointly.[477] The children of this couple are related between themselves by the mediation of the parents. For every one of them being of the same blood with their common parents, they are all of the same blood (truly *consanguinei*), the relations which they respectively bear to their parents meeting there as in their center. This is the nearest relation that can be,[478] next to those of man and wife, parents and their children, who are immediately related by contact or rather continuity of blood, if one may speak so. The relation between the children of these children grows more remote and dilute, and in time wears out. For at every remove the natural tincture or sympathy may be supposed to be weakened, if for no other reason, yet for this: Every remove takes off half the common blood derived from the grandparents. For let C be the son of A and B, D the son of C, E of D, F of E; and let the relation of C to A and B be as 1: then the relation of D to A and B will be but ½, because C is but one of the parents of D, and so the relation of D to A and B is but the half of that, which C bears to them. By proceeding after the same manner it will be found, that the relation of E to A and B is ¼ (or half of the half), of F ⅛, and so on. So that the relation which descendents in a direct line have by blood to their grandparents, decreasing thus in geometrical proportion,[479] the relation between them of collateral lines, which passes and is made out through the grandparents, must soon be reduced to an inconsiderable matter.[480]

If, then, we suppose this affection or sympathy—when it is permitted to act regularly and according to nature, no reason intervening to exalt or abate it—to operate with a strength nearly proportionable to the quantity or degree of relation, computed as above, we may perhaps nearly discern the degrees of that obligation which persons related lie under, to assist each other, from this motive.

But there are many circumstances and incidents in life capable of affecting this obligation, and altering the degrees of it. A man must weigh the wants of himself and his own family against those of his relations; he must consider their sex, their age, their abilities and opportunities, how capable they are of good offices, how they will take them, what use they will make of them, and the like. He, who designs to act agreeably to truth, may find many such things demanding his regard: some justly moving him to compassion, others holding back his hand. But, however, this may in general be taken as evident: that next after our parents and own offspring,[481] nature directs us to be helpful in the first place to brothers and sisters, and then to other relations according to their respective distances in the genealogy of the family, preferably to all foreigners.[482] And, though our power or opportunities of helping them in their wants should be but little, yet we ought to preserve our affection towards them, and a disposition to serve them, as far as we honestly and prudently can, and whenever the proper opportunity shall present itself. This nature and truth require.

IX
Truths Belonging to a Private Man, and Respecting (Directly) Only Himself

I. *Every man knows (or may[483] know) best what his own faculties and personal circumstances are, and consequently what powers he has of acting and governing himself.* Because he only, of all mankind, has the internal knowledge of himself and what he is, and has the only opportunity, by reflection and experiments of himself, to find what his own abilities, passions, etc. truly are.[484]

II. *He that well examines himself, I suppose, will find these things to be true:*[485]

1. That there are some things common to him not only with sensitive animals and vegetables, but also with inanimate matter: as, that his body is subject to the general law of gravitation, that its parts are capable of being separated or dislocated, and that therefore he is in danger from falls and all impressions of violence.
2. That there are other things common to him with vegetables and sensitive animals: as, that he comes from a seed (such the original animalculum may be taken to be); grows, and is preserved by proper matter, taken in and distributed through a set of vessels; ripens, flourishes, withers, decays, dies, is subject to diseases, may be hurt, or killed; and therefore wants, as they do, nourishment, a proper habitation, protection from injuries, and the like.
3. That he has other properties, common only to him and the sensitive tribe: as, that he receives by his senses the notice of many external objects and things; perceives many affections of his body; finds pleasure from some and pain from others; and has certain powers of moving himself and acting: that is, he is not only obnoxious to hurts, diseases, and the causes of death, but also *feels* them;[486] is not only capable of nourishment, and many other provisions made for him, but also *enjoys* them; and, besides, may contribute much, himself, to either his enjoyments or his sufferings.
4. That beside these, he has other faculties—which he does not apprehend to be either in the inert mass of matter, or in vegetables, or even in the sensitive kind, at least in any considerable degree—by the help of which he investigates truth or probability, and judges whether things are agreeable to them or not, after the manner set down in section III, or, in a word, that he is *animal rationale*.[487]
5. That he is conscious of a liberty in himself to act or not to act, and that therefore he is such a being as is described in section I, proposition I: a being whose acts may be morally good or evil. Further,
6. That there are in him many inclinations and aversions, from whence flow such affections as desire, hope, joy, hatred, fear, sorrow, pity, anger, etc., all which prompt him to act

this or that way,
7. That he is sensible of great defects and limitations in the use of his rational faculties and powers of action, upon many occasions; as also, that his passions are many times apt to take wrong turns, to grow warm, irregular, excessive.[488] In other words, that he is, in many respects, fallible and infirm.[489]
8. Lastly, that he desires to be happy: as everything must, which understands what is meant by that word.

III. *If he does find those things to be so, then if he will act as he ought to do (that is, agreeably to truth and fact) he must do such things as these:*

1. He must subject his sensual inclinations, his bodily passions, and the motions of all his members[490] to reason, and try everything by it. For in the climax set down, he cannot but observe that as the principle of vegetation is something above the inertia of mere matter, and sense something above that again, so reason must be something above all these;[491] or, that his uppermost faculty is reason.[492] And from hence it follows, that he is one of those beings mentioned in section III, proposition XI and that the great law imposed upon him is to be governed by reason.

   Any man may prove this to himself by experiment, if he pleases. Because he cannot (at least without great violence to his nature) do anything if he has a greater reason against the doing of it than for it. When men do err against reason, it is either because they do not (perhaps *will not*) advert, and use their reason, or not enough; or because their faculties are defective.

   And further, by section III, proposition X, to endeavor to act according to right reason, and to endeavor to act according to truth, are in effect the same thing. We cannot do the one, but we must do the other. We cannot act according to truth, or so as not to deny any truth—and that is, we cannot act *right*—unless we endeavor to act according to *right reason*, and are led by it.

   Therefore, not to subject one's sensitive inclinations and passions to reason is to deny either that he is rational, or that reason is the supreme and ruling faculty in his nature: and that is to desert mankind,[493] and to deny himself to be what he knows himself, by experience and in his own conscience upon examination, to be, and what he would be very angry if anybody should say he was not.

   If a beast could be supposed to give up his sense and activity, neglect the calls of hunger and those appetites by which he (according to his nature) is to be guided, and, refusing to use the powers with which he is endowed in order to get his food and preserve his life, lie still in some place, and expect to grow and be fed like a plant, this would be much the same case, only not so bad, as when a man cancels his reason, and, as it were, strives to metamorphize himself into a brute. And yet, this he does, who pursues only sensual objects, and leaves himself to the impulses of appetite and passion.

For as in that case, the brute neglects the law of his nature and affects that of the order below him, so does the man disobey the law of his nature and put himself under that of the lower animals, to whom he thus makes a defection.[494]

If this be so, how wretchedly do they violate the order of nature and transgress against truth, who not only reject the conduct of reason to follow sense and passion, but even make it subservient to them;[495] who use it only in finding out means to effect their wicked ends,[496] but never apply it to the consideration of those ends, or the nature of those means: whether they are just or unjust, right or wrong? This is not only to deviate from the path of nature, but to *invert* it, and to become something more than brutish—*brutes with reason*—which must be the most enormous and worst of all brutes. When the brute is governed by sense and bodily appetites, he observes his proper rule; when a man is governed after that manner, in defiance of reason, he *violates* his; but when he makes his rational powers to *serve* the brutish part—to assist and promote it— he heightens and increases the brutality, enlarges its field, makes it to act with greater force and effect,[497] and becomes a monster.

His duty then, who is conscious to himself of the truth of those things recounted under the foregoing proposition, is to examine everything carefully, and to see that he complies with no corporeal inclination at the expense of his reason, but that all his affections, concupiscible and irascible, be directed towards such objects, and in such measure, time, and place, as that allows. Every word[498] and action, every motion and step in life, should be conducted by reason.[499] This is the foundation, and indeed the sum, of all virtue.

2. He must take care not to bring upon himself[500] want, diseases, trouble; but, on the contrary, endeavor to prevent them, and to provide for his own comfortable subsistence, as far as be can without contradicting any truth[501] (that is, without denying matters of fact, and such propositions as have been already, or will in the sequel, here be shown to be true concerning God, property, the superiority of reason, etc.). To explain this limitation: if a man should consider himself as obnoxious to hunger, weather, injuries, diseases, and the rest; then, to supply his wants, take what is his neighbor's property; and at last, in vindication of himself, say, "I act according to what I am, a being obnoxious to hunger, etc., and to act otherwise would be incompliance with truth;" this would not be sufficient to justify him. The grand rule requires that what he does should interfere with no truth, but what he does interferes with several. For by taking that which (by the supposition) is his neighbor's, he acts as if it was not his neighbor's but his own, and therefore plainly contradicts fact, and those truths in sections VI and VII respecting property: when by not taking what is his neighbor's, he would contradict no truth, he would not deny himself to be obnoxious to hunger, etc. There are other ways of furnishing himself with conveniencies, or at least necessaries, which are consistent

with property and all truth, and he can only be said to deny himself to be what he is by omitting to provide against his wants when he omits to provide against them by some of *those ways*, and then indeed he does do it. (See the answer to objection 3 above.)

So again, when a man does anything to avoid present suffering or dangers *contrary* to the express dictates of reason and the tenor of forementioned truths, he acts as a sensitive being only, not as being what he really is: *sensitivio-rationalis*. But when there is no good argument against his doing of anything that may gain him protection from evil, or a better condition of life, he may then look upon himself only as a being who needs that which is to be obtained by doing it; and in that case, if he should not do it, he would be false to himself, and deny the circumstances of his own nature.

Certainly, when a man may, without transgressing the limits prescribed, consult his own safety, support, and reasonable satisfaction, and does not—and especially when he takes a counter-course, and exposes himself[502]—he forgets many of the foregoing truths, and treats himself as not being what he is. This is true with respect to futurity, as well as the present time; and indeed, by how much future time is more than the present, by so much the more perhaps ought that to be regarded. At least enjoyments ought to be taken and adjusted in such a manner that no one should preclude or spoil *more or greater* to come.

It may easily be understood here, that those evils which it is not in a man's power to prevent, he must endeavor to bear patiently and decently, i.e. as such; and moreover, such as are made by this means lighter[503]—for when they cannot be totally prevented, as much of the *effect* must be prevented, or taken off, as can be. And in order to this, it is good to be prepared for all attacks, especially the last great one.[504]

3. He must consider even bodily and sensual affections, passions, and inclinations as intimations which *many times* he not only may, but ought to hearken to. What is said before of the subjection of passions and appetites to reason must always be remembered. They are not to proceed from unjustifiable causes, or terminate in wrong objects; not be unseasonable or immoderate. Being thus regulated, set to a true bias, and freed from all eruptions and violence, they become such as are here intended: gentle ferments working in our breasts without which we should settle in inactivity,[505] and what I think may be taken for just motives and good arguments to act upon.

For if a man finds that he has not only a superior faculty of reason, but also an inferior appetitive faculty, under which are contained many propensions and aversions, these cannot be denied *to be* any more than that; though they must be taken indeed for what they *really are*, and not more. When they are checked by reason and truth, or there lies a reason against them (as there always will, when they are not within the foresaid restrictions), they must be taken as clogged with this circumstance, as things overruled and disabled; but when they are under no prohibition from the superior powers and truth, then they are to be considered as unfettered and free, and become governing principles. For (as it has been observed upon a particular occasion before), when there is no reason against the complying with our senses, there is always one for it by proposition XIV, section III; the inclination itself, being precluded by nothing above it, is in this case uppermost, and in course takes the commanding post, and then a man must act as being what he is in number 3 under proposition II of this section.

The springs of all human actions are in fact either a sense of duty, or a prospect of some pleasure or profit to be obtained, some evil or danger to be avoided; that is: either the reasonableness of what is done, or the manner in which something does or is like to affect the agent; and that is, again: human actions are founded either in reason, or passion and inclination. (I need not add they may be in both.) This being so, what should hinder, when reason does not work, but that the inferior springs should retain their nature, and act?

Bodily inclinations and passions, when they observe their due subordination to reason, and only take place where that leaves it open for them, or allows them to be, as it were, assessors to it upon the throne, are of admirable use in life, and tend many times to noble ends. This is applicable to the irascible as well as the concupiscible affections, and the whole animal system. Love of that which is amiable, compassion[506] toward the miserable and helpless, a natural abhorrence and resentment[507] of that which is villainous or vicious or base,[508] fear[509] of evils, are things which, duly tempered, have laudable effects, and without them mankind could not well subsist. By which it appears, that the Author of nature has placed these *conatus*, these tendencies and reluctancies, in us to dispose us for action when there are no arguments of a higher nature to move us. So far are they, *rightly managed*, from being mere infirmities. And certainly the philosopher who pretends to absolute *apathy* maims nature, and sets up for a half-man, or I don't know what.[510]

I must confess, however, that our passions are so very apt to grow upon us and become exorbitant, if they are not kept under an exact discipline, that by way of prevention or caution it is advisable rather to affect a *degree* of apathy, or to recede more from the worse extreme.[511] This very proposition itself, which, when reason is absent, places sense and inclination in the chair, obliges not to permit the reins to our passions or give them their full career, because, if we do, they may (and will) carry us into such excesses, such dangers and mischiefs, as may sadly affect the sensitive part of us: that part itself which now governs. They ought to be watched, and well examined: if reason is on their side, or stands neuter, they are to be heard (this is all that I say); in other cases we must be deaf to their applications, strongly guard against their emotions, and in due time prevent their rebelling against the sovereign faculty.

I cannot forbear to add, though I fear I shall tire you with repetitions, that from what is said here, and just before, not only the liberty men take in preferring what they like best among present enjoyments, meats, drinks, etc., so far as they are innocent, but all those prudential and lawful methods by which they endeavor to secure to themselves a comfortable and pleasant being, may be justified, and that observation under proposition XIII in section II strengthened.

If the gratification of an appetite be incompatible with reason and truth, to treat that appetite according to what it is, is to *deny* it; but if it is not, to use it as it is, is to consider it as an appetite clear of all objections, and this must be to *comply* with it. The humoring of such appetites, as lie not under the interdict of truth and reason, seems to be the very means by which the Author of nature intended to sweeten the journey of life, and a man may, upon the road, as well muffle himself up against sunshine and blue sky, and expose himself bare to rains and storms and cold, as debar himself of the innocent delight of his nature for affected melancholy, want, and pain. Yet,

4. He must use what means he can to cure his own defects, or at least to prevent the effects of them; learn to deny temptations, or keep them at a proper distance;[512] even mortify, where mortification is necessary;[513] and always carry about him the sense of his being but a man. He who does not do this, does not conform himself to the seventh particular under the preceding proposition (does not own that to be true, which he is supposed to have found true in himself), denies a defect to be what it is (to be something which requires to be supplied, or amended), and is guilty of an omission that will fall under section I, proposition V.

I might here mention some precautions with some kinds and degrees of mortification, or self-denial, which men will commonly find to be necessary. But I shall not prescribe: leaving them, who best know their own weak places and diseases, to select for themselves the proper remedies.

I shall only take notice that, since the self-denial here recommended can only respect things in themselves lawful and not unreasonable, and in favor of such our bare inclinations have been allowed to be taken for arguments and directions, it looks as if this advice to deny one's self or inclinations inferred a contradiction. But this knot will be quickly untied. For when we deny our inclinations in order to better our natures, or prevent crimes, though to follow those inclinations might otherwise be right, yet in these circumstances and under this view there arises a good reason against it, and they, according to the established rule, must therefore give way: which is all that is intended.[514]

The last clause of the proposition takes in a great compass. It will oblige men, if they do but think well what they are, and consequently what others of the same kind with themselves also are, not to be proud, conceited, vain; but modest, and humble, and rather diffident of themselves: not to censure the failings of others too hardly, not to be over-severe in punishing or exacting justice,[515] and particularly not to be revengeful; but candid, placable, mansuete; and so forth.

5. He ought to examine[516] his own actions and conduct, and where he finds he has transgressed,[517] to repent. That is, if the transgression be against his neighbor, and the

nature of it admits, to make reparation, or at least as far as he can; in other cases, when that which is done cannot be recalled, or repaired, or terminates in himself only, to live however under a sense of his fault, and to prove, by such acts as are proper, that he desires forgiveness, and heartily wishes it undone—which is, as it were, an essay towards the undoing of it,[518] and all that now can be;[519] and lastly, to use all possible care not to relapse. All this is involved in the *idea* of a fault, or action that is wrong, as it presents itself to a rational mind. For such a mind cannot approve what is unreasonable and repugnant to truth—that is, what is wrong, or a fault—nay more, it cannot but disapprove it, detest it. No rational animal therefore can act according to truth—the true nature of himself, and the idea of a crime—if he does not endeavor not to commit it; and, when it is committed, to repair it, if he can, or at least show himself to be penitent.[520]

If, when a man is criminal, he does not behave himself *as such*, or, which is the same, behaves himself as being *not such*, he opposes truth confidently.

And further, to act agreeably to what he is supposed to find himself to be, is to act as one who is in danger of relapsing: which is to be upon his guard for the future.

6. He must labor to improve his rational faculties by such means as are (fairly) practicable by him and consistent with his circumstances. If it be a disadvantage to be obnoxious to error, and act in the dark, it is an advantage to know such truths as may prevent this; if so, it is a greater advantage to know, or be capable of knowing, more such truths;[521] and then again: not to endeavor to improve those faculties by which these truths are apprehended, is to shut them out, as being not what they are.[522]

And moreover, by the enlargement of our rational faculties we become more rational: that is, we advance our natures,[523] and become more attentive to rational enjoyments.

The ordinary means indeed of improving our minds, are the instruction of able men, reading, observation, meditation. But every man has not proper opportunities or capacity for these, or but in some low degree, and no man is obliged beyond his abilities and opportunities (by section IV, proposition II). Therefore, that mollification is added, "by such means," etc.

Besides health, a comfortable and suitable provision of externals is so necessary to the well-being of the whole man, that without it, the rational part cannot dwell easy, all pursuits of knowledge will be liable to interruption, and improvements (commonly) imperfect.[524] And so reason itself (which cannot betray its own interest) must, for its own sake, concur in seeking and promoting that which tends to the preservation and happiness of the whole. But the doing of this engrosses time and industry, and before that which is sought can be obtained (if it is ever obtained), probably the *use* of it is lost, except where men live by the profession of some part of learning.

And as to them who are more free from worldly cares, or whose business and employment brings them into a stricter acquaintance with letters, after all their endeavors (such is the great variety of human circumstances in other respects), they must be contented with several *degrees* and *portions* of knowledge. Some are blessed with clean and strong constitutions, early instructions and other helps, succeeding encouragements, useful acquaintance, and freedom from disturbance; while others, under an ill state of body, or other disadvantages, are forced to be their own guides, and make their way as well as they can.

But notwithstanding all this, every man may, in some degree or other, endeavor to cultivate his nature, and possess himself of useful truths. And not to do this is (again) to cast off reason (which never can be reasonable), apostatize from humanity, and recoil into the bestial life.[525]

7. He must attend to instruction,[526] and even ask advice, especially in matters of consequence. Not to do this is to deny that his faculties are limited and defective, or that he is fallible (which is contrary to that which he is presumed to be conscious of), and perhaps that it is possible for another to know what he does not.

Advice every man is capable of hearing; and the meaner a man's own improvements are, the more does truth press him to submit to the counsel and opinions of others. Nor is everyone only *capable*, but everyone *wants* upon some occasions to be informed. In how many country affairs must the scholar take the rustic for his master? In how many, other men of business, traders, and mechanics? And on the other side, in respect of how many things does the generality of the world want to be taught by them who are learned and honest?

There is, or should be, a commerce or interchange of counsel and knowledge, as well as of other things: and where men have not these of their own growth, they should thankfully receive what may be imported from other quarters.

I do not mean that a man ought implicitly and blindly to follow the opinion of another[527] (this other being fallible too, as well as himself), unless he has in himself a good reason so to do, which many times happens; but by the assistance of another, and hearing what he has to say, to find out more certainly on which side reason, truth, and happiness (which always keep close together) do lie. And thus it is indeed a man's *own reason* at last which governs.

He who is governed by what another says (or does) without understanding it and making the reason of it his own, is not governed by his own reason, and that is, by no reason that he has. To say one is led by the nose (as we commonly speak[528]) gives immediately the idea of a brute.[529]

8. Lastly: He must labor to clear his mind of those preoccupations and incumbrances which hang about it and hinder him from reasoning freely and judging impartially. We set out in life from such poor beginnings of knowledge, and grow up under such remains of superstition and ignorance, such influences of company and fashion, such insinuations of pleasure, etc. that it is no wonder if men get habits of thinking only in one way, that

these habits in time grow confirmed and obstinate, and so their minds come to be overcast with thick prejudices, scarce penetrable by any ray of truth or light of reason. He, therefore, who would use his rational faculties, must in the first place disentangle them, and render them *fit* to be used; and he who does not do this, does hereby declare that he does not *intend* to use them: that is, he proclaims himself irrational, contrary to truth, if supposition the fourth be true.

The sum of all is this: it is the duty of every *man* (if that word expresses such a being as is before described) to behave himself in all respects (which I cannot pretend to enumerate) as far as he is able according to reason. And from hence it will follow, further, that,

IV. *Every man is obliged to live virtuously and piously.* Because to practice reason[530] and truth[531] is to live after that manner. For, from the contents of the foregoing sections, it is apparent that one cannot practice reason (or act according to truth) without behaving himself reverently and dutifully toward that Almighty being on whom he depends, nor without justice and a tender regard to the properties of other men: that is, unless his enjoyments be free from impiety, virtuous, and harmless. And as to those virtues which respect a man's self, the same thing[532] will be as apparent when I have told what I mean by some of the principal ones.

Prudence, the queen of virtues, is nothing but choosing (after things[533] have been duly weighed), and using the most reasonable means to obtain, some end that is reasonable. This is therefore *directly* the exercise of reason.

Temperance permits us to take meat and drink not only as physic for hunger and thirst, but also as an innocent cordial and fortifier against the evils of life, or even, sometimes, reason not refusing that liberty, merely as matter of pleasure. It only confines us to such kinds, quantities, and seasons, as may best consist with our health,[534] the use of our faculties,[535] our fortune, etc., and show that we do not think ourselves made only to eat and drink here;[536] that is, such as speak us to be what we are.

Chastity does not pretend to *extinguish* our tender passions, or cancel one part of our nature: it only bids us not to indulge them against reason and truth;[537] not give up the *man* to humor the *brute*,[538] nor hurt others to please ourselves; to divert our inclinations by business, or some honest amusement, till we can gratify them lawfully, conveniently, regularly;[539] and even then to participate of the mysteries of love with modesty, as within a veil or sacred enclosure, not with a canine impudence.[540]

Frugality indeed looks forward, and round about; not only considers the man himself, but compassionates his family; knows, that when the exactest computation is made that can be beforehand, there will still be found many unforeseen desiderata in the calendar of his expenses; is apprehensive of the world, and accidents, and new occasions, that may arise, though they are not yet in being;[541] and therefore endeavors wisely to lay in as much as may give him some kind of security against future wants and casualties, without which provision no man, whose sense is not quite lost or circumscribed within the present minute, can be very easy.[542] To this end, it not only cuts off all profusion and extravagance, but even deducts something from that which, according to the present appearance, might be afforded[543]—and chooses rather that he should live upon half allowance now, than be exposed (or expose anybody else) to the danger of starving hereafter,[544] when full meals and former plenty shall make poverty and fasting more insupportable. But still it forbids no instance of generosity, or even magnificence, which is agreeable to the man's station and circumstances, or (which is tantamount) to the truth of his case.[545]

After the same manner, I might proceed upon other particular virtues. But my notion of them must by this time be sufficiently understood, and therefore I shall only give this general advice: That you may take the truer prospect of any act, place yourself in your imagination beyond it (beyond it in time), and suppose it already done, and then see how it looks—always remembering that a long repentance is a disproportionate price for a short enjoyment. Or: fancy it done by some other man, and then view it in that speculum; we are commonly sharper-sighted in discerning the faults of others than of ourselves.[546] And further, as to those virtues which are said to consist in the mean, it may be sometimes safer to incline a little more to one of the extremes than to the other, as: rather to stinginess, than prodigality; rather to inflexibility and even a degree of ill nature, than to dangerous complaisance or easiness in respect of vice and such things as may be hurtful; and so on.[547]

Since, then, to live virtuously is to practice reason and act conformably to truth, he who lives so must be ultimately happy, by section II, proposition XIV, and therefore not only the commands of reason, but even the desire of happiness (a motive that cannot but work strongly upon all who think) will oblige a man to live so.

It may be collected, even from experience, that the virtuous life compared with the contrary (if one looks no further than the present state) is the happier life;[548] or, that the virtuous pleasures, when the whole account is made up, are the truer.[549] Who sees not that the vicious life is full of dangers and solicitudes, and usually ends ill: perhaps in rottenness and rags, or at least in a peevish and despicable discontent?[550]

I am not of opinion that virtue can make a man happy upon a rack,[551] under a violent fit of the the stone, or the like;[552] or that virtue and prudence can always exempt him from wants and sufferings, mend a strait fortune, or rectify an ill constitution. Amidst so many enemies to virtue, so many infirmities as attend life, he cannot but be sometimes affected. But I have said, and say again, that the natural and usual effect of virtue is happiness, and if a virtuous man should in some respects be unhappy, yet still his virtue will make him *less unhappy*: for at least he enjoys inward tranquility, and a breast conscious of no evil. And which kind of life, I pray, ought one to prefer: that which naturally tends to happiness, though it may be disturbed, or that which naturally tends to unhappiness? In brief: virtue will make a man here, in any given circumstances, as happy as a man can be in those circumstances, or however it will make him happy hereafter in some other state: for ultimately, all taken together, happy he must be.

Some may possibly wonder why, among virtues, I have not so much as once named one of the *cardinal*, and the only one perhaps which they pretend to: I mean *fortitude*. That that by which so many heroes have triumphed over enemies (even the greatest: death itself)—that which distinguishes nations, raises empires, has been the grand theme of almost all wits, attracts all eyes, opens all mouths, and assumes the name of virtue by way of excellence—that *this* should be forgot!

To atone for this omission, I will make this appendix to the foregoing brief account: If *fortitude* be taken for natural courage (i.e. strength, activity, plenty of spirits, and a contempt of dangers resulting from these), this is constitution and the gift of God,[553] not any virtue in us: because if it be *our* virtue, it must consist in something which we produce or do ourselves.[554] The case is the same with that of fine features and complexion, a large inheritance, or strong walls, which may indeed be great *advantages*, but were never called *virtues*.[555] To *have these* is not virtue; but to *use them rightly*, or according to reason, if we have them.

That this is justly said, may perhaps appear from what is to be said on the other side. It may be a man's misfortune that he has not more courage, a greater stock of spirits, firmer health, and stronger limbs, if he has a just occasion to use them; but it never can be reckoned a vice or fault not to use what he has not: for otherwise it might be a crime not to be able to carry a ten thousand pound weight or outrun a cannonball.

Fortitude considered as a virtue consists in standing and endeavoring to overcome dangers and oppositions, when they cannot be avoided without the violation of reason and truth. Here it is that he who is endowed with natural bravery, a healthful constitution, good bones and muscles, ought to use them, and be thankful to the Doner; and he, who is not so favored, must yet do what he can: if he cannot conquer, he must endeavor to be patient and prudent. And thus, he who is naturally timorous, or weak, or otherwise infirm, may have as much or more of the virtue of fortitude than the hero himself, who apprehends little and feels little, compared with the other, or possibly may find pleasure in a scene of dangerous action.

If a man can prevent or escape any peril or trouble, *salvâ veritate*, he ought to do it, otherwise he neither considers himself, nor them, as being what they are—them not as unnecessary, himself not as capable of being hurt by them—and so dashes against truth on the worse side.[556] But where that cannot be done, he must exert himself according to his abilities, whether great or little, and refer the success to the Divine providence. This is the true virtue of fortitude, which is nothing but *endeavoring* firmly and honestly to act as truth requires, and therefore is directly deducible from that notion on which we have founded the morality of human acts.

It has for its object not only adversaries, noxious animals, and bold undertakings, but in general all the evils of life[557] which a man must labor by prudence to ward off; and where this cannot be done, to bear with resignation, decency, and a humble expectation of an adjustment of all events in a future state: the belief of which I am now going to prove, in my manner, to be no vain nor groundless conceit.

V. *Everyone that finds himself, as before in proposition I, finds in himself at the same time a consciousness of his own existence and acts (which is life), with a power of apprehending, thinking, reasoning, willing, beginning and stopping many kinds and degrees of motion in his own members, etc.*[558] He who has not these powers, has no power to dispute this with me, therefore I can perceive no room for any dispute here, unless it be concerning the power of beginning motion. For they, who say there is always the same quantity of motion in the world, must not allow the production of any new, and therefore must suppose the animal spirits not to be put into motion by the mind, but only, being already in motion, to receive from it their directions into these or those canals, according as it intends to move this or that limb. But to this may be answered that if the mind can give these new directions and turns to the spirits, this serves my purpose as well, and what I intend will follow as well from it. And besides, it could not do this, if it could not excite those spirits being at rest.

It is plain I can move my hand upward or downward or horizontally, faster or slower or not at all, or stop it when it is in motion, just as I will. Now if my hand, and those parts and spirits by which it is put into motion, were left to be governed by the law of gravitation, or by any motions already impressed upon them, the effects would be determined by rules of mechanism, and be necessary; the motion or rest of my hand would not attend upon my will and be alterable upon a thought at my pleasure. If, then, I have (as I am sensible I have) a *power of moving* my hand, in a manner which it would not move in by those laws that mere bodies already in motion or under the force of gravitation would observe, this motion depends solely upon *my will*, and *begins* there.[559]

VI. *That, which in man, is the subject or suppositum of self-consciousness, thinks, and has the foresaid faculties, must be something different from his body or carcass.*

For, first, he does not, I suppose, find himself to think, see, hear, etc. *all over*, in any part of his body, but the seat of cogitation and reflection he finds in his *head*;[560] and the nerves, by which the knowledge of external objects is conveyed to him, all tend to the same place. It is plainly something which resides there,[561] in the region of the brain, that by the mediation of these nerves governs the body and moves the parts of it (as by so many reins or wires),[562] feels what is done to it, sees through the eyes, hears through the ears, etc.[563]

Upon amputation of a limb[564] this thing (whatever it is) is not found to be diminished,[565] nor any of its faculties lost. Its sphere of acting, while it is confined to the body, is only contracted, and part of its instrument lost. It cannot make use of that which is not, or which it has not.

If the eyes be shut, or the ears stopped, it cannot then see, or hear—but remove the obstruction, and it instantly appears that the faculty by which it apprehends the impressions made upon the organs of sensation, remained all that while entire: and that so it might have done if the eyes, or ears, had never been opened again, or if the eyes had been out, or the ears quite disabled. This shows, in general, that when any sense or faculty seems to be impaired or lost—by any bodily hurt, after a fever, or through age—this does not come to pass because it is *the body* that perceives and has these faculties in itself, but because the body loses its *instrumentality*, and gives that which is the true subject of these faculties no opportunity of exerting them, or of exerting them well, though it retains them as much as in the case before, when the eyes or ears were only shut.[566] Thus distinct are it and its faculties from the body and its affections. I will now call it the "soul."

Again, as a man peruses and considers his own body, does it not undeniably appear to be something different from the considerer? And when he uses this expression "my body," or "the body of me," may it not properly be demanded: who is meant by "me," or what "my" relates to? It cannot be the body itself; that cannot say of itself, "it is my body," or "the body of me." And yet this way of speaking we naturally fall into, from an inward and habitual sense of ourselves and what we are, even though we do not advert upon it.

What I mean is this: A man being supposed a person consisting of two parts—soul and body—the whole person may say of this or that part of him, "the soul of me" or "the body of me," but if he was either all soul, or all body, and nothing else, he could not then speak in this manner, because it would be the same as to say "the soul of the soul," or "the body of the body," or "the I of me." The pronoun therefore (in that saying "my body," or "the body of me") must stand for something else, to which the body belongs,[567] or at least for something of which it is only a part, viz. the person of the whole man.[568] And then even this implies that there is another part of him, which is not body.

It is plain there are two different interests in men[569]—on the one side reason, on the other passion—which, being many times directly opposite, must belong to different subjects. There are, upon many occasions, contests and, as it were, wars between the mind and the body: so far are they from being the same thing.

Lastly, there is, we may perceive, something within us which supports the body (keeps it up), directs its motion for the better preservation of it when any hurts or evils befall it, finds out the means of its cure, and the like; without which, it would fall to the ground and undergo the fate of common matter. The body, therefore, must be considered as being under the direction and tuition of some other thing, which is (or should be) the governor of it, and consequently upon this account must be concluded to be different from it.

VII. *The soul cannot be mere matter.* For if it is, then either *all matter* must think, or the difference must arise from the different modification, magnitude, figure, or motion[570] of some parcels of matter in respect of others, or a faculty of thinking must be superadded to some systems of it which is not superadded to others. But,

In the first place, that position which makes all matter to be cogitative is contrary to all the apprehensions and knowledge we have of the nature of it; nor can it be true, unless our senses and faculties be contrived only to deceive us. We perceive not the least symptom of cogitation or sense in our tables, chairs, etc.

Why does the scene of thinking lie in our heads, and all the ministers of sensation make their reports to something there, if *all* matter be apprehensive and cogitative? For in that case, there would be as much thought and understanding in our heels, and everywhere else, as in our heads.

If all matter be cogitative, then it must be so *quatenùs* matter, and thinking must be of the essence and definition of it; whereas, by "matter" no more is meant but a substance extended and impenetrable to other matter. And since, for this reason, it cannot be necessary for matter to think (because it may be matter without this property), it cannot think as matter only.

If it did, we should not only continue to think always, till the matter of which we consist is annihilated (and so the assertor of this doctrine would stumble upon immortality unawares), but we must also have thought always in time past, ever since that matter was in being; nor could there be any the least intermission of actual thinking, which does not appear to be our case.

If thinking, self-consciousness, etc. were essential to matter, *every part* of it must have them: and then no *system* could have them. For a system of material parts would be a system of things, conscious every one by itself of its own existence and individuality, and consequently thinking by itself: but there could be no *one act* of self-consciousness or thought common to the whole. Juxtaposition in this case could signify nothing; the distinction and individuation of the several particles would be as much retained in their vicinity as if they were separated by miles.

In the next place, the faculties of thinking, etc. cannot arise from the size, figure, texture, or motion of it, because bodies by the alteration of these only become greater or less; round or square, etc.; rare, or dense; translated from one place to another, with this or that new direction or velocity; or the like: all which ideas are quite different from that of thinking; there can be no relation between them.[571] These modifications and affections of matter are so far from being principles or causes of thinking and acting, that they are themselves but effects, proceeding from the action of some other matter or thing upon it, and are proofs of its passivity, deadness, and utter incapacity of becoming cogitative. This is evident to sense.

They who place the essence of the soul in a certain motion given to some matter (if any such men there really be) should consider, among many other things, that to move the body spontaneously is one of the faculties of the soul,[572] and that this, which is the same with the power of beginning motion, cannot come from motion already begun, and impressed *ab extra*.

Let the materialist examine well whether he does not feel something within himself that acts from an internal principle; whether he does not experience some liberty, some power of governing himself and choosing; whether he does not enjoy a kind of invisible empire, in which he commands his own thoughts, sends them to this or that place, employs them about this or that business,[573] forms such and such designs and schemes; and whether there is anything like this in bare matter,[574] however fashioned or proportioned, which, if nothing should protrude or communicate motion to it, would forever remain fixed to the place where it happens to be, an eternal monument of its own being dead. Can such an active being as the soul is,⁵⁷⁵ the subject of so many powers, be itself nothing but an accident?

When I begin to move myself, I do it for some reason, and with respect to some end, the means to effect which, I have, if there be occasion for it, concerted within myself: and this does not at all look like motion *merely material* (or, in which matter is only concerned), which is all mechanical. Who can imagine matter to be moved by arguments, or ever placed syllogisms and demonstrations among levers and pulleys?

We not only move ourselves upon reasons which we find in ourselves, but upon reasons imparted by words or writing from others, or perhaps merely at their desire or bare suggestion. In which case, again, nobody sure can imagine that the words spoken or written (the sound in the air, or the strokes on the paper) can by any natural or mechanical efficience cause the reader or hearer to move in any determinate manner (or at all). The reason, request, or friendly admonition, which is the true motive, can make no impression upon matter. It must be some other kind of being that apprehends the force and sense of them.

Do not we see in conversation how a pleasant thing said makes people break out into laughter, a rude thing into passion, and so on? These affections cannot be the physical effects of the words spoken, because then they would have the same effect whether they were understood or not. And this is further demonstrable from hence: that though the words do really contain nothing which is either pleasant, or rude (or perhaps words are thought to be spoken, which are not spoken), yet if they are *apprehended* to do that, or the sound to be otherwise than it was, the effect will be the same. It is therefore the *sense* of the words, which is an immaterial thing, that, by passing through the understanding and causing that which is the subject of the intellectual faculties to influence the body, produces these motions in the spirits, blood, muscles.

They who can fancy that matter may come to live, think, and act spontaneously—by being reduced to a certain magnitude, or having its parts placed after a certain manner, or being invested with such a figure, or excited by such a particular motion—they, I say, would do well to discover to us that degree of fineness, that alteration in the situation of its parts, etc. at which matter may begin to find itself alive and cogitative, and which is the critical minute that introduces these important properties. If they cannot do this, nor have their eye upon any particular crisis, it is a sign they have no good reason for what they say. For if they have no reason to charge this change upon any particular degree or difference, one more than another, they have no reason to charge it upon any degree or difference at all, and then they have no reason by which they can prove that such a change is made at all. Besides all which, since magnitude, figure, motion are but *accidents* of matter, not matter, and only the substance is truly matter; and since the substance of any one part of matter does not differ from that of another, if any matter can be by nature cogitative, all must be so. But this we have seen cannot be.

So then in conclusion, if there is any such thing as matter that thinks, etc., this must be a particular privilege granted to it, that is: a faculty of thinking must be *superadded* to certain parts or parcels of it. Which, by the way, must infer the existence of some Being able to confer this faculty, who, when the ineptness of matter has been well considered, cannot appear to be less than omnipotent, or God. But the truth is, matter seems not to be capable of such improvement: of being made to think. For since it is not the essence of matter, it cannot be made to be so without making matter another kind of substance from what it is. Nor can it be made to arise from any of the modifications or accidents of matter—and in respect of what else can any matter be made to differ from other matter?

The accidents of matter are so far from being made by any power to produce cogitation, that some *even of them* show it incapable of having a faculty of thinking superadded. The very *divisibility* of it does this. For that which is made to think must either be one part, or more parts joined together. But we know no such thing as a part of matter purely one (or indivisible). It may indeed have pleased the Author of nature that there should be atoms whose parts are actually indiscerptible, and which may be the principles of other bodies—but still they consist of parts, though firmly adhering together. And if the feat of cogitation be in more parts than one (whether they lie close together, or are loose, or in a state of fluidity, it is the same thing), how can it be avoided, but that either there must be so many several minds, or thinking substances, as there are parts (and then the consequence, which has been mentioned, would return upon us again); or else, that there must be something else superadded for them to center in, to unite their acts, and make their thoughts to be one? And then what can this be, but some other substance which is purely one?

Matter by itself can never entertain *abstracted* and *general* ideas, such as many in our minds are.[576] For could it reflect upon what passes within itself, it could possibly find there nothing but material and particular impressions; abstractions and metaphysical ideas could not be printed upon it.[577] How could one abstract *from matter* who is himself nothing *but matter*? And then, as to material images themselves, which are usually supposed to be impressed upon the brain (or some part of it), and stock the fantasy and memory, that which peruses the impressions and traces there (or anywhere) must be something distinct from the brain, or that upon which these impressions are made: otherwise it must contemplate itself, and be both reader and book. And this other distinct contemplating being cannot be merely corporeal, any more than the body can perceive and think without a soul. For such a corporeal being must require sense, and suitable organs to perceive and read these characters and vestigia of things, and so another organized body would be introduced, and the same questions and difficulties redoubled concerning the soul of that body and its faculties.[578]

If my soul was mere matter, external visible objects could only be perceived within me according to the impressions they make upon matter, and not otherwise. E.g. the image of a cube in my mind (or my idea of a cube) must be always under some particular prospect, and conform to the rules of perspective, nor could I otherwise represent it to myself; whereas now I can form an idea of it as it is *in itself*, and almost view all its *hedræ* at once—as it were, encompassing it with my mind.

I can, within myself, correct the external appearances and impressions of objects, and advance, upon the reports and hints received by my senses, to form ideas of things that are *not extant* in matter. By seeing a material circle I may learn to form the idea of a circle, or figure generated by the revolution of a ray about its center; but then, recollecting what I know of matter upon other occasions, I can conclude there is no exact material circle. So that I have an idea, which perhaps was raised from the hints I received from without, but is not truly to be found there. If I see a tower at a great distance, which according to the impressions made upon my material organs seems little and round, I do not therefore conclude it to be either: there is something within that reasons upon the circumstances of the appearance, and, as it were, commands my sense, and corrects the impression; and this must be something superior to matter, since a *material soul* is no otherwise impressible itself, but as *material organs* are. Instances of this kind are endless. (See section III, proposition XIII.)

If we know anything of matter, we know that by itself it is a lifeless thing—inert, and passive only—and acts *necessarily* (or rather is acted) according to the laws of motion and gravitation. This passiveness seems to be essential to it. And if we know anything of ourselves, we know that we are conscious of our own existence and acts (i.e. that we live), that we have a degree of freedom, that we can move ourselves spontaneously, and, in short, that we can, in many instances, take off the effect of gravitation and impress new motions upon our spirits (or give them new directions) only by a thought. Therefore, to make mere matter do all this is to change the nature of it: to change death into life, incapacity of thinking into cogitativity, necessity into liberty. And to say that God may superadd a faculty of thinking, moving itself, etc. to matter—if by this be meant that he may make matter to be the suppositum of these faculties (that substance, in which they inhere)—is the same in effect as to say that God may superadd a faculty of thinking to incogitativity, of acting freely to necessity, and so on. What sense is there in this? And yet so it must be, while matter continues to be matter.

That faculty of thinking, so much talked of by some as superadded to certain *systems* of matter, fitly disposed, by virtue of God's omnipotence, though it be so called, must in reality amount to the same thing as another *substance* with the faculty of thinking. For a faculty of thinking alone will not make up the idea of a human soul, which is endowed with many faculties—apprehending, reflecting, comparing, judging, making deductions and reasoning, willing, putting the body in motion, continuing the animal functions by its presence, and giving life—and therefore, whatever it is that is superadded, it must be something which is endowed with all those other faculties. And whether that can be a faculty of thinking, and so these other faculties be only faculties of a faculty,[579] or whether they must not all be rather the faculties of some substance,[580] which, being (by their own concession) superadded to matter, must be different from it, I do leave the unprejudiced to determine.

If men would but seriously look into themselves, I am persuaded the soul would not appear to them as a *faculty* of the body, or kind of *appurtenance* to it, but rather as some *substance*, properly placed in it, not only to use it as an instrument, and act by it, but also to govern it (or the parts of it; as the tongue, hands, feet, etc.) according to its own reason. For I think it is plain enough that the mind, though it acts under great limitations, does however in many instances govern the body arbitrarily—and it is monstrous to suppose this governor to be nothing but some fit disposition or accident (superadded) of that matter which is governed. A ship, it is true, would not be fit for navigation if it was not built and provided in a proper manner, but then, when it has its proper form, and is become a system of materials fitly disposed, it is not this *disposition* that governs it. It is the man—that other substance—who sits at the helm, and they who manage the sails and tackle, that do this. So *our vessels*, without a proper organization and conformity of parts, would not be capable of being acted as they are; but still it is not the shape, or modification, or any other accident, that can govern them. The *capacity* of being governed or used can never be the *governor* applying and using[581] that capacity. No, there must be at the helm something distinct that commands the body, and without which it would run adrift, or rather sink.

For the foregoing reasons, it seems to me that matter cannot think; cannot *be made* to think. But if a faculty of thinking can be superadded to a system of matter, without uniting an immaterial substance to it[582]—I say, if this can be, yet a human body is not such a system: being plainly void of thought, and organized in such a manner as to transmit the impressions of sensible objects up to the brain, where the percipient, and that which reflects upon them, certainly resides; and therefore that, which there apprehends, thinks, and wills, must be that system of matter to which a faculty of thinking is superadded. All the premises then well considered, judge I beseech you whether instead of saying that this inhabitant of our heads (the soul) is a system of matter to which a faculty of thinking is superadded, it might not be more reasonable to say, it is "a thinking substance intimately united to some fine material vehicle, which has its residence in the brain." Though I understand not perfectly the manner how a cogitative and spiritual substance can be thus closely united to such a material vehicle, yet I can understand this union as well, as how it can be united to the body in general (perhaps, as how the particles of the body itself cohere together), and much better than how a thinking faculty can be superadded to matter. And besides, several phenomena may more easily be solved by this hypothesis, which (though I shall not pertinaciously maintain it) in short is this: viz. that the human soul is a cogitative substance, clothed in a material vehicle, or rather united to it, and as it were inseparably mixed (I had almost said "incorporated") with it;[583] that these act in conjunction, that which affects the one affecting the other; that the soul is detained in the body (the head or brain) by some sympathy or attraction between this material vehicle and it, till the habitation is spoiled, and this mutual tendency interrupted (and perhaps turned into an aversion, that makes it fly off) by some hurt or disease, or by the decays and ruins of old age, or the like, happening to the body; and that in the interim, by means of this vehicle motions and impressions are communicated to and fro. But of this perhaps something more by and by.

VIII. *The soul of man subsists after the dissolution of his body* or, *is immortal*. For,

1. If it is immaterial, it is indiscerptible, and therefore incapable of being dissolved or

demolished, as bodies are.[584] Such a being can only perish by annihilation: that is, it will continue to subsist and live if some other being, able to do this, does not by a particular act annihilate it. And, if there is any reason to believe that at the death of every man there is always such a particular annihilation, let him that knows it produce it. Certainly to reduce any substance into nothing requires just the same power as to convert nothing into something: and, I fancy, they who deny the immortality of the soul will be cautious how they admit any such power.

2. If the soul could be material—that is, if there could be any matter that might be the subject of those faculties of thinking, willing, etc.—yet still, since we cannot but be sensible that all these are faculties of the selfsame thing, and that all the several acts of the mind are acts of the same thing, each of them individual and truly one; I say, since it is so, this matter must be so perfectly united in itself, so absolutely one, as no matter knowable by us can be. And then the least that can be allowed is that it should be truly solid, and not actually divisible: that is, such as no natural cause could destroy.

To introduce matter with a faculty of thinking, or a "thinking matter," is to introduce matter with a new and opposite property, and that is to introduce a new species of matter[585] which will differ as essentially from the other, common, unthinking kind, as any species whatsoever does from its opposite in *scala prædicamentali*; even as body does from spirit. For thinking and unthinking differ as corporeal and incorporeal. And if so, this "thinking matter" must always continue to think, till either it is annihilated, or there is a transmutation of one species into another: and to take refuge in either of these expectations is at least to expect omnipotence should interpose to help out a bad cause.

If anyone should say that God might, by virtue of his omnipotence, superadd to certain parcels of matter a fourth dimension, I should not perhaps dispute the Divine power, but I might say that such matter, existing under four dimensions, would essentially differ from that which cannot exist under four, or which can exist but only under three, and that this four-dimensioned matter must always remain such, because no substance can be changed into or become another, essentially different, nor do we know of any that by the course of nature ceases totally to be, or is reduced to nothing.

3. The next argument shall proceed by way of objection and answer, because a removal of the principal objection against anything is a good argument for it. Objection: It seems as if *thinking* was not essential to the soul, but rather a *capacity of thinking* under certain circumstances. For it does not think when it lies concealed in the primitive rudiment of the man, in the womb, perhaps in the beginnings of infancy, in sleep, in a swoon; and the reason of this seems to lie in the circumstances of the body, which either is not sufficiently attended and prepared, or for a while employs the spirits wholly in the digestion of its aliment and other offices in the animal economy, or by some external attack, or the working of some enemy got into it has its parts disordered and the passages so possessed that the blood and other fluids can scarce break through, or after

some such manner is preternaturally affected. And therefore, the question to be resolved is not whether the soul is material or immaterial, and much less whether it will be annihilated at death, but whether that soul (be it what it will), which ceases to think when the body is not fitly disposed, can think at all when the body is quite dissolved and leaves the soul no opportunity of actuating it any more or operating by it.[586] Answer: If this objection cannot be fully answered, till we know more of the nature of beings, and of that *vinculum* by which the soul and body are connected, than we do at present, it must not therefore be looked upon as certainly unanswerable in itself; and much less, if only it cannot be answered *by me*. It may perhaps be possible to turn it even into an argument for the immortality of the soul.

The soul, it cannot be denied, is a limited being, or a being which acts under limitations. These limitations at different times are different; its activity and faculties being more obstructed or clogged at one time than another, and most of all in sleep, or a deliquium. As these obstructions are removed, it acts more clearly and freely, and therefore if the state of the soul in the body (its confinement there) may be considered as one general and great limitation, why, when this limitation shall be taken off (this great obstruction removed), may it[587] not be allowed to act with still greater freedom and clearness: the greatest it is capable of? While it remains in the brain, it can, as it were, look out at a few apertures: that is, receive the notices of many things by those nerves and organs which are the instruments of sensation; but if any of those avenues to it be stopped, that branch of its knowledge is for a time cut off. If those tracks in the brain, or those marks, whatever they are and wherever they are imprinted, upon which our memory and images of things seem to depend, are filled up or overcast by any vapor, or otherwise darkened, it can read them no more till the cloud is dispersed. (For it cannot read what is not legible, and indeed for the present not there.) And since even in abstracted reflections the mind is obliged to make use of words,[588] or some kind of signs, to fix its ideas and to render them tractable and stable enough to be perused, compared, etc., and this kind of language depends upon memory, while this is intermitted, the use of the other is taken away, with all that depends upon it. This is the present state of the soul, and from hence the reason appears in some measure: why we do not think in sound sleep, etc.; but it does not follow from hence, that the soul cannot subsist and act under more enlarged circumstances. That, which being confined to the body, and able to act only according to the opportunities this affords, can now perceive visible objects only with two eyes (at two windows[589]), because there are no more, might doubtless see with four if there were so many properly placed and disposed; or, if its habitation were *all eye* (window all round), might see all round. And so, in general, that which now can know many things by the impressions made at the ends of the nerves, or by the intervention of our present organs, and in this situation and inclosure can know them no other way, may for all that, when it comes to be loosed out of that prison,[590] know them *immediately*, or by some other medium. That which is now forced to make shift with words and signs of things in its reasonings, may, when it shall be set at liberty and can come at them, reason upon the intuition of things themselves, or use a language more spiritual or ideal. I say, it is not *impossible* that this should be the case; and therefore no one can say, with reason, that it is not: especially, since we find by experience that the soul is limited, that the limitations are variable, that we know not enough of the nature of spirit to determine how these limitations are effected, and therefore cannot tell how far they may be carried on or taken off. This suffices to remove the force of the objection. But further,

A man when he wakes, or "comes to himself" (which phrase implies what I am going to say), immediately knows this, and knows himself to be the same soul that he was before his sleep or fainting away. I will suppose that he is also conscious to himself that in those intervals he thought not at all (which is the same the objector must suppose)— that is, if his body had been cut to pieces or mouldered to dust, he could not have thought less—for there is no thinking less than thinking not at all. From hence, then, I gather that the soul preserves a capacity of thinking, etc. under those circumstances and indispositions of the body in which it thinks no more than if the body was destroyed, and that therefore it may, and will, preserve it when the body is destroyed. And if so, what can this capacity be preserved for? Certainly not that it may never be exerted. The Author of nature does not use to act after that manner. So that here is this dilemma to be opposed to the objection: In sleep and swoonings the soul does either think, or not. If it does, the objection has no foundation; and if it does not, then all that will follow which I have just now said.

If we should suppose the soul to be a being by nature made to inform some body, and that it cannot exist and act in a state of total separation from all body, it would not follow from hence that what we call death must therefore reduce it to a state of absolute insensitivity and inactivity, which to it would be equal to nonexistence. For that body, which is so necessary to it, may be some fine vehicle that dwells with it in the brain (according to that hypothesis [some paragraphs back](#)) and goes off with it at death. Neither the answers to the objection, nor the case after death, will be much altered by such a supposition. And since I confess I see no absurdity in it, I will try to explain it a little further: We are sensible of many material impressions (impressions made upon us by material causes, or bodies); that there are such, we are sure. Therefore there must be some matter within us, which, being moved or pressed upon, the soul apprehends it immediately. And therefore, again, there must be some matter to which it is immdiately and intimately united, and related in such a manner as it is not related to any other. Let us now suppose this said matter to be some refined and spirituous vehicle,[591] which the soul does immediately inform, with which it sympathizes, by which it acts and is acted upon, and to which it is vitally and inseparably united; and that this animated vehicle has its abode in the brain, among the heads and beginnings of the nerves.

Suppose we also, that when any impressions are made upon the organs or parts of the body, the effects of them are carried by the nerves up to their fountain, and the place where the soul in its vehicle is, and there they communicate their several motions or tremors to this material vehicle (or by their motions, or tendency to motion, press upon it), so that the soul, which inhabits it in a peculiar manner and is thoroughly possessed of it, shall be apprehensive of these motions or pressures; and moreover, that this vehicle, so guarded and encompassed by the body as it is, can be come at or moved by external objects no other way but by the mediation of the nerves; nor the soul, by consequence, have any direct intelligence concerning them, or correspondence with them, any other way. And as we suppose the soul to receive notices of things from without in this manner, so let us suppose, on the other side, that by moving its own vehicle it may produce motion in the contiguous spirits and nerves, and so move the body: I mean, when nothing renders them unfit to be moved. Let us suppose further that the soul, by means of this vehicle, feels or finds those prints and portraits, or those effects and remains left by objects on the mind in some manner or other, which cause the remembrance of words and things: I mean again, when they are not filled up or obscured by anything; or, when there are any such to be felt. And lastly, let us suppose that if the soul in its more abstracted and purer reasonings, or more spiritual acts, has any occasion for matter to serve it, the matter of this vehicle is that which is always with it, and serves it. All which it is easy to understand, and perhaps not very difficult to suppose. On the contrary, by many symptoms it appears most probable that that matter to which the mind is immediately present, and in which is its true *shekinah*, is not the whole gross body, but some *subtle body*, placed (as I have said) in the region of the brain. For there all the conveyances of sensible species conspire to meet, and there in reflection we find ourselves: when a limb is lost, the soul, 'tis true, loses an opportunity of receiving intelligence from or by it, and of using it, but perceives no loss *in itself*: and though the body, many parts of it at least, are in a perpetual flux and continually altering, yet I know that the substance which thinks within me now (or rather, which is I) is, notwithstanding all the changes my body has undergone, the very same which thought above fifty years ago, and ever since: when I played in such a field, went to such a school, was of such a university, performed such and such exercises, etc.[592] If you would permit me to use a school term, I would say the "egoity"[593] remains. Now to answer the objection, and apply all this to our purpose: Why do we not perceive external objects in our sleep or a swoon? Because the passages are become impracticable, the windows shut, and the nerves, being obstructed or somehow rendered for the time useless, can transmit no information to it. Why, however, does it not reason and think about something or other? Because, all the marks by which things are remembered, being for the present choked up or disordered, the remembrance of those objects about which it is wont to employ itself, and even of the words (or other signs) in which it uses to reason and to preserve the deductions and conclusions it makes, is all suspended and lost for the time; and so, its tables being covered, its books closed, and its tools locked up, the requisites for reasoning are wanting, and no subject offers itself to exercise its thoughts, it having yet had little or no opportunity to take in higher objects and more refined matter for contemplation. And to conclude, if it be demanded, why anyone should imagine that the soul may think, perceive, act after death, when it does not do this in sleep, etc. the answer is: because those enclosures and impediments which occasioned the forementioned intermissions, and those great limitations under which it labors at all times, will be removed with its enlargement out of the body. When it shall in its proper vehicle be let go, and take its flight into the open fields of heaven, it will then be bare to the immediate impressions of objects: and why should not those impressions which affected the nerves that moved and affected the vehicle and soul in it, affect the vehicle immediately when they are immediately made upon it, without the interposition of the nerves? The hand, which feels an object at the end of a staff, may certainly be allowed to feel the same much better by immediate contact, without the staff. Nay, why should we not think that it may admit of *more* objects and the knowledge of more things than it can now, since, being exposed all round to the influences of them, it may be moved not only by visible objects just at the extremities of the optic nerves, by sounds at the ends of they auditory, etc., but become, as it were, all eye to visible objects, all ear to audible, and so on? And why should we not think this the rather, because then the soul may be also perceptive of finer impressions and ethereal contacts, and consequently of more kinds of objects, such as we are now incapable of knowing? And then, this being so, why should we not presage that other endowments, as faculties of reasoning, communicating thoughts, and the like, will be proportionable to such noble opportunities of knowledge? There seems to be nothing in this account *impossible*, and therefore nothing but what *may be*.

If we do but attend, we must see everywhere that many things are by ways which we do not, nor can, understand; and therefore we must be convinced, even from hence, that more may be, and therefore that the objection before us (though we could salve the difficulties in it, and what is supposed here should be all rejected as chimerical) yet ought to be no prejudice against the belief of the immortality of the soul, if there is any (but *one*) good reason for it.

But if we can, in any tolerable manner (which in our present circumstances is as much as can be expected), account for the difficulties objected, and those the greatest belonging to this matter, and show how it is possible that they may consist with immortality, this will greatly corroborate the arguments for it, if not be one itself. This I hope is done; or, if I have not spoke directly to every part of the objection, from what has been done that defect may easily be supplied.

4. We may conclude the souls of men to be immortal from the nature of God. For if he is (which sure nobody doubts) a Perfect being, He, as such, can do nothing inconsistent with perfect or right reason. And then no being, nor circumstance of any being, can come, from Him as its cause, which it is not agreeable to such reason should be; or

(which is the same): He cannot but deal *reasonably* with all His dependents. And then again, if we are in the number of these, and the mortality of the human soul does not consist with reason, we may be sure it is immortal: as sure as we can be of anything by the use of our faculties, and that is as sure as we can be of anything. Whether therefore that does consist with reason or not, is to be inquired.

To produce a being into a state of clear happiness, in any degree, can be no injury to it—or into a state of mixed happiness, provided the happiness certainly overbalances the contrary, and the unhappy or suffering part be not greater than what that being would choose in order to obtain the happiness, or rather than lose it. Nor, again, can any wrong be done by producing a being subject to more misery than happiness, if that being has it in his own power to avoid the misery, or so much of it as may leave the remainder of misery not greater than what he would rather sustain than miss the proportion of happiness. The only case then, by which wrong can be done in the production of any being, is when it is necessarily and irremediably to be miserable, without any recompense or balance of that misery:[594] and this indeed is a case so grievous, so utterly irreconcilable to all reason, that the heart of a reasoning and considering man can scarce bear the thought of it. So much everyone must understand of the nature of reason and justice, as to allow these things for truths incontestable.

Now then, he who says the soul of man is mortal must say one of these two things: either that God is an unreasonable, unjust, cruel Being; or that no man in respect of this life (which according to him is *all*), has a greater share of misery, unavoidable, than of happiness. To say the former is to contradict that which I presume has been proved beyond contradiction. To which I may add here that this is to avow such an unworthy, impious notion of the Supreme being, as one would not entertain without caution even of the worst of men; such a one, as even the person himself, who says this, must know to be false. For he cannot but see, and must own, many instances of the reasonableness and beneficence of the Deity, not one of which could be, if cruelty and unreasonableness were His inclination: since He has power to execute His own inclinations thoroughly, and is a Being uniform in his nature. Then to say the latter, is to contradict the whole story of mankind, and even one's own senses. Consider well the dreadful effects of many wars, and all those barbarous desolations, which we read of: what cruel tyrants there are, and have been, in the world, who (at least in their fits) divert themselves with the pangs and convulsions of their fellow-creatures;[595] what slavery is,[596] and how men have been brought into that lamentable state; how many have been ruined by accidents unforeseen; how many have suffered or been undone by unjust laws, judges, witnesses, etc.;[597] how many have brought incurable diseases, or the causes of them and of great torments, into the world with them; how many more, such bodily infirmities and disadvantages, as have rendered their whole lives uneasy; how many are born to no other inheritance but invincible poverty and trouble? Instances are endless: but, for a little taste of the condition of mankind here, reflect upon that story related by Strabo (from Polybius) and Plutarch, where, even by order of the Roman senate, Paullus Æmylius, one of the best of them too, at one prefixed hour sacked and destroyed seventy cities, unawares, and drove fifteen myriads of innocent persons into captivity, to be sold only to raise pay for the merciless soldiers and their own executioners. Peruse that account of the gold-works in the confines of Egypt given by Diodorus, and think over the circumstances of the unfortunate laborers there, who were not only criminals or men taken in war, but even such as calumny or unjust power had doomed (perhaps for being too good) to that place of torment, many times with all their relations and poor children.[598] Or, once for all, take a view of servitude as it is described by Pignorius. To pass over the Sicilian tyrants, him of Pheræ, Apollodorus,[599] and the like, of which history supplies plenty; consider those terrible proscriptions among the Romans,[600] with the reigns of most of their emperors, more bloody than Lybic lion or Hyrcanian tiger—even some of the Christian emperors not excepted. Read the direful and unjust executions reported by Ammianus Marcellinus; among hundreds of others that of Eusebius.[601] Every whisper in those times, or light suspicion, brought upon men the question and tortures inconceivable. Men's very dreams were once interpreted to be treason, and they durst scarce own that they had ever slept.[602] What inhuman punishments were used among the Persians,[603] in an arbitrary manner too, and many times extended to whole families and all the kindred, though not concerned?[604] But instead of enumerating here burnings, crucifixions, breakings upon the wheel, impalings, σκαφισμοὺς,[605] etc. I choose to refer you to those authors who have designedly treated of the torments and questions of the ancients. Look into the history of the Christian Church, and her martyrologies; examine the prisons of the inquisition, the groans of which those walls are conscious, and upon what slight occasions men are racked and tortured by the tormentors there; and, to finish this detail (hideous indeed, but too true) as fast as I can, consider the many massacres, persecutions, and miseries consequent upon them, which false religion has caused, authorized, sanctified. Indeed the history of mankind is little else but the history of uncomfortable, dreadful passages: and a great part of it, however things are palliated and gilded over, is scarcely to be read by a good-natured man without amazement, horror, tears. One can scarce look into a newspaper, or out at his window, but hardships and sufferings present themselves in one shape or other. Now, among all those millions who have suffered eminently, can it be imagined that there have not been multitudes whose griefs and pangs have far outweighed all their enjoyments, and yet who have not been able, either by their innocence, their prudence, or any power in them, to escape that bitter draught which they have drunk? And then, how can we acquit the justice and reasonableness of that Being upon whom these poor creatures depend, and who leaves them such great losers by their existence, if there be no future state where the proper amends may be made?

So that the argument is brought to this undeniable issue: if the soul of man is not immortal, either there is no God upon whom we depend, or He is an unreasonable Being, or there never has been any man whose sufferings in this world have exceeded his enjoyments without his being the cause of it himself. But surely no one of these three things can be said. Ergo...

That which aggravates the hard case of the poor sufferers mentioned above—if there be no future state in which their past sufferings may be brought into the account and recompensated—is that many times their persecutors and tormentors pass their lives in plenty and grandeur: that is, the innocent have not only the portion that properly belongs to the criminal and unreasonable part of mankind, but the guilty have that which belongs rather to the innocent.[606] Such a transposition of rewards and punishments, ending in itself, without any respect to something which is to follow hereafter, can never consist with the nature of a Governor who is not very much below rational: a thought which God forbid anyone should dare to admit of Him. To suppose the virtuous and wise left ultimately but in the same state with the unjust and profligate is to suppose such a constitution of nature as never can flow from a principle of reason, a God of truth and equity; and therefore, such a constitution as leaves the former in a worse condition than the other, can much less be supposed.

Objection: It has been said that virtue tends to make men's lives happy even here, etc., and how then can the virtuous be supposed ever to be so very miserable? Answer: In ordinary cases virtue does produce happiness; at least it has indeed a natural tendency to it, is the mean by which it is most likely to be attained, and is therefore the way which a wise man would choose for his own sake. But then it does not follow from hence that there are no perturbations in human affairs: no cases in which the usual effect of virtue may be overpowered by diseases, violence, disasters. It does not render men invulnerable, cannot command the seasons, nor prevent many great calamities under which virtue and vice must fall undistinguished. (There may be a direct road to a place, and such a one, as he who sets out for that place ought to be found in, and yet it is possible he may meet with robbers or accidents in it, that may incommode, or hurt him in his journey.) On the other side, vice and wickedness may be so circumstantiated as to be attended with much greater pleasure than pain, contrary to the tendency of its nature; that is, a wicked man may be of a healthful make, born to riches or power, or fortunately placed for attaining them, and from the advantage of a strong body, an ample fortune, many friends, or lucky hits, he may derive pleasures which shall exceed the present inconveniences and sufferings naturally following from his vices.[607]

Men's circumstances have a natural influence with respect to the present pleasures or sufferings, as well as their virtue or vice. Nobody, sure, ever said that all depends only upon these; nor, when the natural tendence of them is asserted, is the natural tendence or effect of the other denied. Therefore indeed, when it is said that virtue naturally tends to make men happy even here, the meaning only is that it tends to make men happy in proportion to their circumstances; and vice does the contrary. It is naturally productive of that part of happiness which is in our own power and depends upon ourselves; makes men more truly happy, whatever their circumstances are, than they could be without it; and commonly tends to mend their worldly circumstances too—but it is not asserted that virtue can always entirely correct them, or make men so completely happy in this life, as that their enjoyments shall exceed their mortifications: no more than the vices of some particular men, though they bereave them of many solid pleasures, and bring troubles upon them too, do hinder their worldly enjoyments from being greater than their present sufferings. Not only our being, but our place, with the time and manner of our being in this world, depend upon the Author of the scheme; the manner of behaving ourselves in our station (according to our endowments, and the talents we have) only depends upon us. And perhaps (which has been hinted already) He has so ordered things on purpose, that from the various compositions of men's circumstances with the natural effects of their virtues and vices, and the many inequalities arising thence, they might see the necessity and certainty of another state: and that for this reason there should always be some remarkable instances of oppressed innocence and flourishing wickedness.

The upshot is that upon comparing those pleasures which are the natural effects of virtue, with those sufferings which are the natural effects of ill constitution or other calamity, these are many, very many times found to exceed; and, è contrario, upon balancing those evils which are the genuine effects of vice, against the advantages resulting from a fortunate estate, these may often be found to outdo the other. Both contrary to reason, if all ends with this life, and after death be nothing. For my part, if there were only some few, nay but *one* instance of each kind in the world (unfortunate virtue, and prosperous wickedness), it would be to me a sufficient argument for a future state, because God cannot be unjust or unreasonable in any one instance. It must not be forgot here, that many times men of great vices have also great virtues, and the natural effect of these may qualify that of the other, and being added to their favorable circumstances may help to turn the scale.

If there is no other besides the present being, the general and usual state of mankind is scarce consistent with the idea of a reasonable cause. Let us consider it a little.[608] Not to mention what we must suffer from the very settlement and condition of this world by hunger, thirst, heat, cold, and indispositions; like leaves one generation drops, and another springs up, to fall again, and be forgotten.[609] As we come into the world with the labor of our mothers, we soon go out of it with our own. Childhood and youth are much of them lost in insensibility or trifling, vanity and rudeness; obnoxious to many pains and accidents; and, when they are spent in the best manner, are attended with labor and discipline. When we reach that stage of life which usually takes us from our nearest relations and brings us out into the world, with what difficulty are proper employments and stations found for us? When we are got out and left to scramble for ourselves, how many hardships and tricks are put upon us before we get the sagacity and dexterity to save ourselves? How many chances do we stand? How troublesome is business made by unreasonableness, ill nature, or trifling and want of punctuality in the persons with whom we deal? How do we find ourselves instantly surrounded with snares from designing men, knaves, enemies (of which the best men have some), opposite interests, factions, and many times from a mischievous breed whose childish or diabolical humor seeks pleasure in the uneasiness of other people? Even in many of those enjoyments which men principally propose to themselves, they are greatly disappointed, and experience shows how unlike they are to the antecedent images of them. They are commonly mixed:[610] the apparatus to most of them is too operose; the completion of them seldom depends upon ourselves alone, but upon a concurrence of things, which rarely hit all right;[611] they are generally not only less in practice than in theory, but die almost as soon as they are; and perhaps they entail upon us a tax to be paid after they are gone. To go on with the history of human life: though affairs go prosperously, yet still perhaps a family is increasing, and with it new occasions of solicitude are introduced, accompanied with many fears and tender apprehensions. At length, if a man, through many cares and toils and various adventures, arrives at old age, then he feels most commonly his pressures rather increased than diminished, and himself less able to support them.[612] The business he has to do grows urgent upon him and calls for dispatch; most of his faculties and active powers begin now to fail him apace; relations and friends, who might be helpful to him (and among them perhaps the dear Consort of all his joys, and all his cares[613]) leave him, never to return more; wants and pains all the while are multiplying upon him; and under this additional load he comes melancholy behind, tottering, and bending toward the earth, till he either stumbles upon something which throws him into the grave,[614] or, fainting, falls of himself. And must he end here? Is this the period of his being? Is this all? Did he come into the world only to make his way through the press, amidst many justlings and hard struggles, with at best only a few deceitful, little, fugacious pleasures interspersed, and so go out of it again? Can this be an end worthy a first Cause perfectly reasonable? Would even any *man*, of common sense and good nature, send another upon a difficult journey in which—though he might perhaps now and then meet with a little smooth way, get an interval for rest and contemplation, or be flattered with some verdures and the smiles of a few daisies on the banks of the road—yet upon the whole he must travel through much dirt, take many wearisome steps, be continually inquiring after some clue or directions to carry him through the turnings and intricacies of it, be puzzled how to get a competent *viaticum* and pay his reckonings, ever and anon be in danger of being lost in deep waters, and besides, forced all the while to fence against weather, accidents, and cruel robbers, who are everywhere lying in wait for him: I say, would anyone send a man upon such a journey as this, only that the man might faint and expire at the end of it, and all his thoughts perish: that is, either for no end at all, or for the punishment of one whom I suppose never to have hurt him, nor ever to have been capable of hurting him? And now, can we impute to God that which is below the common size of men?[615]

I am apt to think that even among those whose state is beheld with envy, there are many who, if at the end of their course they were put to their option whether, without any respect to a future state, they would repeat all the pleasures they have had in life, upon condition to go over again also all the same disappointments, the same vexations and unkind treatments from the world, the same secret pangs and tedious hours, the same labors of body and mind, the same pains and sicknesses, would be far from accepting them at that price.[616]

But here the case, as I have put it, only respects them who may be reckoned among the *more fortunate* passengers, and for one that makes his voyage so well, thousands are tossed in tempests and lost.[617] How many never attain any comfortable settlement in the world? How many fail, after they have attained it, by various misfortunes? What melancholy, what distractions are caused in families by inhumane or vicious husbands, false or peevish wives, refractory or unhappy children; and, if they are otherwise, if they are good, what sorrow by the loss of them? How many are forced by necessity upon drudging and very shocking employments for a poor livelihood? How many subsist upon begging, borrowing, and other shifts, nor can do otherwise? How many meet with sad accidents, or fall into deplorable diseases? Are not all companies, and the very streets, filled with complaints, and grievances, and doleful stories? I verily believe that a great part of mankind may ascribe their deaths to want and dejection. Seriously, the present state of mankind is unaccountable if it has not some connection with another, and be not, as it were, the porch or entry to it.[618]

There is one thing more, of which notice ought to be taken. To one who carefully peruses the story and face of the world, what appears to prevail in it? Is it not corruption, vice, iniquity, folly, at least? Are not debauching,[619] getting *per fas aut nefas*,[620] defaming one another, erecting tyrannies of one kind or other, propagating empty and senseless opinions with bawling and fury, the great business of this world? And are not all these contrary to reason? Can anyone then, with reason, imagine that reason should be given, though it were but to a few, only to be run down and trampled upon and then extinguished? May we not rather conclude that there must be some world where reason will have its turn, and prevail and triumph? Some kingdom of reason to come?[621]

5. In the last place, that great expectation which men have of continuing to live in another state beyond the grave, has, I suppose, been commonly admitted as one proof that they *shall* live, and does seem indeed to me to add some weight to what has been said. That they generally have had such an expectation, can scarce be denied. The histories of mankind, their deifications, rites, stories of apparitions, the frequent mention of a hades,

with rewards and punishments hereafter, etc. all testify that even the Heathen world believed that the souls of men survived their bodies. Their ignorance, indeed, of the seats and circumstances of the departed has begot many errors and superstitions, and these have been multiplied by licentious poets and idle visionaries, but this, being no more than what is usual in the like cases, ought to be no prejudice against the fundamental opinion itself.

Cicero,[622] though he owns there were different opinions among the Greek philosophers about this matter, that *quod literis extet, Pherecydes Syrus primum dixit, animos hominum esse sempiternos*, that Pythagoras and his school confirmed this opinion; that Plato was the man who brought a reason for it, etc., yet tells us plainly, *naturam ipsam de immortalitate animorum tacitam judicare*, that *nescio quomodo inhæret in mentibus quasi sæculorum quoddam augurium*, that *permanere animos arbitramur consensu nationum omnium*,[623] and more to this purpose. Now if this consent was only the effect of some tradition handed from parents to their children, yet since we meet with it in all the quarters of the world (where there is any civility or sense), and in all ages, it seems to be coeval to mankind itself, and born with it. And this is sufficient to give a great authority to this opinion of the soul's immortality. But this is not all. For it is supported by all the foregoing arguments, and many other reasonings and symptoms which we may find within ourselves. All which, put together, may at least justify an expectation of a future state—that is, render it a just or reasonable expectation—and then this reasonable expectation grows, by being such, into a further argument, that there *will be* such a state.

Fancy a man walking in some retired field, far from noise, and free from prejudice, to debate this matter with himself; and then judge whether such meditations as these would not be just: "I think I may be sure that neither lifeless matter, nor the vegetative tribe—that stone, that flower, that tree—have any reflex thoughts; nor do the sensitive animals—that sheep, that ox—seem to have any such thing, or but in the lowest degree, and in respect of present objects only. They do not reason, nor discourse. I may, therefore, certainly pretend to be something much above all these things.[624] I not only apprehend and consider these external objects acting at present upon my nerves, but have *ideas* raised within myself of a higher order, and many: I can not only represent to myself things that are, or have been, but deduce many other from them, make excursions into futurity, and foresee much of what will be, or at least may be—by strict thinking I had almost said, 'get into another world beforehand'—and, whether I shall live in some other state after death or not, I am certainly a being capable of such an expectation, and cannot but be solicitious about it; none of which things can be said of these clods, or those brutes.[625] Can I then be designed for nothing further than just to eat, drink, sleep, walk about, and act upon this earth:[626] that is, to have no further being than what these brutes have, so far beneath me? Can I be made capable of such great expectations, which those animals know nothing of (happier by far in this regard than I am, if we must die alike), only to be disappointed at last? Thus placed, just upon the confines of another better world, and fed with hopes of penetrating into it and enjoying it, only to make a short appearance here[627] and then to be shut out and totally sunk? Must I then, when I bid my last farewell to these walks, when I close these lids, and yonder blue regions and all this scene darken upon me and go out—must I then only serve to furnish dust to be mingled with the ashes of these herds and plants, or with this dirt under my feet? Have I been set so far above them in life, only to be leveled with them at death?"

This argument grows stronger in the apprehension of one who is conscious of abilities and intellectual improvements which he has had no opportunity, here, of showing and using: through want of health, want of confidence,[628] want of proper place, want of liberty. Such improvements, and the knowledge consequent upon them, cannot ultimately respect this state; they can be only an enlargement, and preparation for another. That is all they can be, and if they are not that, they are nothing. And therefore, he may be supposed thus, further, to argue within himself: "Can the Author of my reasoning faculties be himself so *unreasonable* as to give me them, either not to employ them, or only to weary myself with useless pursuits, and then drop me? Can He, who is privy to all my circumstances, and to these very thoughts of mine, be so insensible of my case as to have no regard to it, and not provide for it?"

It grows stronger still upon the mind of one who, reflecting upon the hard treatment he has met with from this world, the little cause he has given for it, the pains and secret uneasiness he has felt upon that score, together with many other sufferings which it was not in his power to prevent, cannot but make a silent, humble appeal to that Being who is his last and true refuge, and who he must believe will not defeat him thus.

Lastly, it is strongest of all to one who, besides all this, endeavors in the conduct of his life to observe the laws of reason (that is, of his nature; and that is, of the Author of nature upon whom he depends); laments and labors against his own infirmities; implores the Divine mercy; prays for some better state hereafter; acts and lives in the hopes of one; and denies himself many things upon that view: one who, by the exaltation of his reason and upper faculties—and that which is certainly the effect of real and useful philosophy: the practice of virtue—is still approaching toward a higher manner of being, and does already taste something spiritual and above this world. To such a one there must be a strong expectation, indeed, and the argument built upon it must be proportionable. For can he be endowed with such capacities, and have, as it were, *overtures* of immortality made him, if after all there is no such thing? Must his private acts and concealed exercises of religion be all lost?[629] Can a perfect Being have so little regard to one who, however inferior and nothing to Him, yet regards Him according to his best abilities in the government of himself?

Are such meditations and reflections as these well founded, or not? If they are, it must be reasonable to think that God will satisfy a reasonable expectation.

There are other arguments for the immortality of the soul, two of which I will leave with you, to be at your leisure pondered well. The one is that, if the souls of men are mortal (extinguished at death), the case of brutes is by much preferable to that of men. The pleasures of brutes, though but sensual, are more sincere, being palled or diminished by no diverting consideration. They go wholly into them, and when they have them not, they seem less to want them, not thinking of them. Their sufferings are attended with no reflection,[630] but are such as they are said to be section II, proposition I, observation 8. They are void of cares; are under no apprehension for families and posterity; never fatigue themselves with vain inquiries, hunting after knowledge which must perish with them; are not anxious about their future state,[631] nor can be disappointed of any hopes or expectations; and at last some sudden blow (or a few minutes of unforeseen pain) finishes them, having never so much as known that they were mortal.

The other is that the soul is a principle of life: that which brings vitality to the body. For how should that which has been proved to be a substance, and at the same time is also a principle of life, and as such (as being what it is) is alive—I say, how can that die,[632] unless it is annihilated?

Here I begin to be very sensible how much I want a guide. But as the religion of nature is my theme, I must at present content myself with that light which nature affords; my business being, as it seems, only to show what a Heathen philosopher, without any other help, and almost αὐτοδίδακτος,[633] may be supposed to think. I hope that neither the doing of this, nor anything else contained in this Delineation, can be the least prejudice to any other true religion. Whatever is immediately revealed from God must, as well as anything else, be treated as being *what it is*, which cannot be if it is not treated with the highest regard, believed, and obeyed. That, therefore, which has been so much insisted on by me, and is, as it were, the burden of my song, is so far from undermining true *revealed* religion, that it rather paves the way for its reception. This I take this opportunity to remark to you once for all. And so, returning to my philosopher, I cannot imagine but that even he would have at least some such general thoughts as these which make up almost the remainder of this last section.

IX. *The soul, when it parts from this gross body, will pass by some law into some new seat, or state, agreeable to the nature of it.*[634] Every species of beings must belong to some region, or state. Because nothing can be, but it must be *somewhere* and *somehow*, and there being different kinds of abodes and manners of subsisting in the universe, and the natures of the things that are to exist in them being also different, there will be a greater congruity between these several natures respectively and some particular places or states, than there is between them and others; and indeed, such a one that out of those, perhaps, they cannot subsist, or not naturally. To those, therefore, must be their respective tendencies; to those they are adjudged by the course of nature and constitution of things, or rather by the Author of them.[635]

While the soul is in the body, it has some powers and opportunities of moving it spontaneously, or otherwise than it would be moved by the mere laws of gravitation and mechanism. This is evident. But yet, notwithstanding this, the weight of that body to which at present it is limited (among other causes) constrains it to act for a while upon this stage. That general law to which bodies are subjected, makes it sink in this fluid of air, so much lighter than itself; keeps it down; and so determines the seat of it, and of the soul in it, to be upon the surface of this earth where, or in whose neighborhood, it was first produced. But then, when the soul shall be disengaged from the gross matter which now encloses and encumbers it, and either become naked spirit or be only veiled in its own fine and obsequious vehicle, it must at the same time be either freed from the laws of bodies and fall under some other, which will carry it to some proper mansion or state,[636] or at least by the old ones be capable of mounting upwards[637] in proportion to the volatility of its vehicle, and of emerging out of these regions into some medium more suitable and (if the philosopher may say so) equilibrious. Thus much as to the general state of souls after death. But then,

X. *In this new state, or place of abode, there may be different stations befitting the differences of particular souls among themselves, as they are more or less perfect in their kind.* We see even inanimate bodies, which have different gravities, figures, impulses, etc., settle into some order among themselves, agreeable to these differences. And so by the same universal rule in nature (viz. that differences in things are attended with answerable relations and effects) souls must also take their situation in some kind of order according to their differences

XI. *The great difference of human souls, with respect to perfection and imperfection, lies in their different degrees and habits*[638] *of reasonableness or unreasonableness.*[639] That is to say: not only in men's different improvements, or neglects and abuse, of their rational faculties; but also in the greater or less influence of these upon their actions, and by consequence in their different degrees of virtue or vice. For a man is accounted a *reasonable* man when he reasons rightly and follows his reason: in which expression virtue must be included, being (as proposition IV, et al.) nothing but the practice of reason and truth.

That men are reasonable, or the contrary, in *different degrees* is plain. Some reason well upon some subjects but, in respect of others to which they have not been accustomed, are dim and confused; or they are partial to their vices and passions, their old impressions and parties, and so their reason is not general, nor has its due extent or influence. Others, whose reason is uncultivated and weak, though they have virtuous inclinations, many times fall into superstition and absurdities: misled by authorities and overawed by old, or formal, modes of speaking, and grave nonsense. Many, if not the most, seem to have scarce any notion of reason or virtue at all, but act fortuitously, or as they see other folks act: moved either by bodily propensions or by example. Some few there are who endeavor to improve their understandings, to discover what is agreeable to reason, and to fix their opinions—and conduct their lives accordingly. And in all these several kinds there are various degrees of elevation in knowledge and virtue and of immersion in vice and ignorance, and new differences arising endlessly. All this is visible.

Now the soul, reflecting, finds in itself two general faculties: one by which it understands, and judges, and reasons (all which I comprehend under the term "rational faculties," or "reason"); and another, by which it wills, or determines to act, according to the judgments and conclusions made in the upper part of it. And the more perfectly it performs these operations (i.e. the more truly it reasons, and the more readily it wills and executes the decisions of reason), the more perfect, certainly, it must be in its kind; and the more imperfectly, the more imperfect. The accomplishments, therefore, and perfections of human souls, and the contrary, must be in proportion to the forementioned differences.

XII. *According to these differences, then, it is reasonable to think the souls of men will find their stations in the future world.*[640] This is but a corollary from what goes before.

Objection: Why should we think that God causes things to be in such a manner as that in the future state, men shall be placed and treated according to their merit and the progress they have made in reason and virtue, when we see the case to be widely different in *this*? Answer: It must be remembered that this is one of those very *reasons* on which the belief of the soul's immortality is founded. Now, if it be reasonable to believe there is a future state, because things are dealt unequally now, upon that very score it will be reasonable to think that they are dealt equally[641] in that other state.

Here, bodily wants and affections, and such things as proceed from them, do intermix with human affairs, and do confound merit with demerit, knowledge with ignorance: and hence it comes to pass, many times, that bad men enjoy much and good men suffer, and both are, if there is no other state, in their wrong places. But, when the corporeal causes of misplacing shall be removed, spirits (or spirits and their σώματα πνευματικά[642]) may be supposed more regularly to take their due posts and privileges: the impudent and vicious will have no such opportunities of getting into circumstances of which they are unworthy, nor improved and virtuous minds find such obstructions to keep them down in circumstances unworthy of them. Be sure: the more advanced and pure any state is, the more properly will the inhabitants be ranked, and the juster and more natural will the subordination of its members be.

Even *here* we commonly find men in that kind of business for which they are educated and prepared, men of the same professions generally keeping together, the virtuous and reasonable desiring to be (though they not always can be) with their like,[643] and the vicious (as they scarcely cannot be) with theirs. And why should we not think that an association and communion of souls with those of their own size, disposition, and habits may be more *universal* and *complete*, when those things which in great measure hinder it, here, shall be no more? If we may think this, certainly those fields or states in which the virtuous and wise[644] shall meet must be different from those in which the foolish and wicked shall herd together.[645] The very difference of the company will itself create a vast difference in the manner of their living.

XIII. *The mansions and conditions of the virtuous and reasoning part must be proportionably better than those of the foolish and vicious.* The proposition cannot be inverted, or the case be otherwise, if the constitution of things depends upon a reasonable cause—as I have endeavored to show it does.

Corollary: Hence it follows that the practice of reason (in its just extent) is the great preparative for death, and the means of advancing our happiness through all our subsequent duration. But moreover,

XIV. *In the future state, respect will be had not only to men's reasoning and virtues, or the contrary, but also to their enjoyments and sufferings here.*[646] Because the forementioned inequalities of this world can by no means be redressed, unless men's enjoyments and sufferings, taken together with their virtues and vices, are compared and balanced. I say "taken together" because no reason can be assigned why a vicious man should be recompensed for the pains and mischiefs and troubles which he brings upon himself by his vices, as the natural consequences of them; nor, on the other side, why any deductions should be made from the future happiness of a good man upon the score of those innocent enjoyments which are the genuine fruit of his moderation, regularity, other virtues, and sound reasoning.

Corollary: Wicked men will not only be less happy than the wise and virtuous, but be really unhappy in that state to come. For when all the happiness, that answers to those degrees of virtue which they had, and those sufferings which they underwent, above what was the natural effect of their wickedness—I say, when that is subtracted, what remains upon the account will be something below no-happiness: which must be some quantity of positive unhappiness, or misery.

Thus there will be rewards and punishments hereafter, and men will be happy or unhappy according to their behavior, enjoyments, and sufferings in this present life. But,

XV. *If the immortality of the soul cannot be demonstrated, yet it is certain the contrary cannot.*[647] To say, when a house is ruinous and fallen, that it once had an inhabitant, and that he is escaped out of it and lives in some other place, can involve no contradiction or absurdity.[648] And,

XVI. *If the immortality of the soul should be considered only as a probability, or even as a chance possible, yet still a virtuous life is to be preferred before its contrary.* For if the soul be mortal, and all perception perishes forever at our death, what in this case does a good man lose by his virtue? Very rarely more than some acts of devotion and instances of mortification, which too by custom grow habitual and easy,[649] and it may be pleasant by being (or seeming at least to be) reasonable. On the other hand, what does a vicious man gain? Only such enjoyments as a virtuous man leaves, and those are such as most commonly owe their being to a vitiated taste, grow insipid in time, require more trouble and contrivance to obtain them than they are worth, go off disagreeably, are followed many times by sharp reflections and bitter penances in the rear, and at best: after a short time end in nothing, as if they had never been. This is all.[650] But then if the soul prove to be immortal (as we have all the reason in the world to think it will), what does the virtuous man gain? His present pleasures (if not so many) are more sincere[651] and natural,[652] and the effect of his self-denials and submission to reason, in order to prepare himself for a future state, is the happiness of that state, which, without pretending to describe it, may be presumed to be immortal, because the soul is so, and to be purer and of a more exalted nature (i.e. truer and greater) than any of these low enjoyments here, because that state is every way in nature above this. And again: what does the wicked man lose? That happiness which the virtuous gain as such; and he sinks, besides, into some degree of the unhappiness of that future state, of which one may say in general that it may be as much greater than the unhappiness or sufferings of this world, as the happiness and joys of that are above those of this.

In a state that is spiritual and clear, everything will be purer and operate more directly and strongly and (if the expression may be tolerated) with more spirit; there will be fewer obstructions to either happiness or unhappiness, the soul will lie more open, and have more immediate and acute perceptions of either, so that each of them in their kind will be more intense: the one nearer to pure or mere happiness, the other to the contrary.[653] But to enter further into the nature and economy of the yet unknown world is too arduous an undertaking for my philosopher.

I shall only add that the reasoning and virtuous man has at least this advantage over the foolish and profligate: that, though his wisdom and virtue cannot always rectify that which is amiss in himself or his circumstances, they will find means to alleviate his pressures and disadvantages, and support him under all the anomalies of life, with comforts of which the other knows nothing—particularly this: the enjoyment of a humble but well-grounded expectation of felicity hereafter, sincere and durable.[654]

XVII. *He, therefore, who would act according to truth, must, in the last place, not only consider what he is, and how circumstantiated in this present state, and provide accordingly, but further, must consider himself also as one whose existence proceeds on into another, and provide for that too.* How I think this is to be done, by this time I hope you fully apprehend.

For a conclusion of the whole matter: let our conversation in this world, so far as we are concerned and able, be such as acknowledges everything to be *what it is* (what it is in itself, and what with regard to us, to other beings, to causes, circumstances, consequences); that is: let us by no act deny anything to be true which is true; that is: let us act according to reason; and that is: let us act according to the law of our nature. By honestly endeavoring to do this, we shall express our duty[655] to Him who is the Author of it, and of that law, and at the same time prosecute our own proper happiness (the happiness of rational beings); we shall do what tends to make us easy here, and be qualifying ourselves and preparing for our removal hence to our long home: that great revolution, which, at the farthest, cannot be very far off.

And now, Sir, the trouble is almost over for the present, not properly which I give you, but which you have brought upon yourself, these being the Thoughts which you desired—unless I have anywhere misrepresented myself through inadvertence, which I own may be. At the foot of the page I have in some places subjoined a few little strictures, principally of antiquity, after the manner of annotations, such as, when I came to revise these sheets, I could recollect upon the sudden,[656] having no commonplace book to help me, nor thought of any such thing before that time. They may serve perhaps sometimes a little to explain the text, and sometimes to add weight, but chiefly to divert you, who know very well how to improve any the least hint out of the Ancients, and I fear will want to be diverted. I have also printed a few copies of this Sketch, not with any design to make it public, but merely to save the trouble of transcribing[657]—being minded, since I have made it, to leave it not only with you, but perhaps also with two or three other friends, or, however, with my Family, as a private monument of one that meant well. Though, as to the disposal and fate of it, much will depend upon your judgment and manner of acceptance.

—William Wollaston.

מכ"אות"ל

"Who is like unto God?" And "Praised be God."[658]

Endnotes

1. So, in Plato, Socrates requires of Euthyphro not to teach him ἕν τι ἢ δύο με διδάξαι τῶν πολλῶν ὁσίων, ἀλλ' ἐκεῖνο αὐτὸ τὸ εἶδος ᾧ πάντα τὰ ὅσια ὅσιά ἐστιν: "one or two particulars of the multitude of things that are just and right; but to show him the original pattern itself, by which everything that is just and good becomes so." And again, ταύτην τοίνυν με αὐτὴν δίδαξον τὴν ἰδέαν τίς ποτέ ἐστιν, ἵνα εἰς ἐκείνην ἀποβλέπων καὶ χρώμενος αὐτῇ παραδείγματι, ὃ μὲν ἂν τοιοῦτον ᾖ ὧν ἂν ἢ σὺ ἢ ἄλλος τις πράττῃ φῶ ὅσιον εἶναι, ὃ δ' ἂν μὴ τοιοῦτον, μὴ φῶ: "Show me the original image or picture, that I may see what sort of a thing it is, and when I look upon it, and make use of it as the original pattern, I may be able to affirm that an action performed by you or any other person, if it be of such a sort, is just and good; and, if it be not of such a sort, then I cannot affirm it to be so." (*Euthyphro.*) *Posce exemplar honesti*: "Enquire after the original pattern of virtue." (Lucan, *Pharsalia.*) ↩

2. Οἶδε τό γ' αἰσχρὸν, χανόνι τοῦ χαλοῦ μαθών: "He knows what vice is, having been taught by the rule of virtue." (Euripides, *Fabulae.*) *Adsit Regula, peccatis quæ pœnas irroget æquas*, says Horace (*Satirae* 3.) Now by the same *rule* by which punishments are justly proportioned, crimes must be distinguished amongst themselves; and therefore much more, crimes from no-crimes, and crimes from good actions. So that it is at bottom a *rule* which can do this, that is required. ↩

3. *Formula quædam constituenda est: quam si sequemur in comparatione rerum, ab officio nunquam recedemus*: "There ought to be some rule established: which if we follow in comparing things with each other, we shall never fall short of our duty." (Cicero, *De Officiis.*) ↩

4. Πῶς οἷόν τε ἀτέκμαρτα εἶναι καὶ ἀνεύρετα τὰ ἀναγκαιότατα ἐν ἀνθρώποις; Ἔστιν οὖν [κανών τις]: "How is it possible that those things which are necessary for men [to know or to do] should be such, as they can have no certainty of knowing or finding out? There must then be [some rule]." (Arrian, *Discourses of Epictetus.*) ↩

5. *Ubi virtus, si nihil situm est in ipsis nobis?* "Where is virtue then, if there be nothing within our own power?" (Cicero, *Academica.*) הוא עמוד התורה והמצוה... רשות לכל אדם נתונה אם רצה להטות עצמו לדרך טובה: "There is a power given to every man, if he be but willing to incline himself to the way that is good... This is the support of the law and the commandments." (Maimonides, *Mishneh Torah*, Hilkot Teshubah, V, 1, 3.) הרשות היא הבחירה: "This power is what we call free will." (Isaac Abravanel, *Nahalot Abot.*) ↩

6. *Lacrymæ pondera* vocis *habent*: "Tears have the force of words." (Ovid, *Epistulæ Ex Ponto*, III.) ↩

7. *Oculi, supercilia, frons, vultus denique totus, qui sermo qui dam tacitus mentis est, etc.*: "The eyes, the eyebrows, and indeed the whole countenance are a kind of tacit speech of the mind, etc." (Cicero, *Against Piso*.) *Nutu signisque loquuntur*: "They [Piramus and Thisbe] speak to each other by nods and signs." (Ovid, *Metamorphoses*.) *Est actio quasi sermo corporis*: "Every action is a sort of a speech of the body." (Cicero, *De Oratore*, and often repeated by him.) ↩

8. איש און מולל ברגליו: "A wicked man speaks by his feet." (Proverbs 6:12–13.) ↩

9. Τὸν κατὰ τῆς κινήσεως λόγον σιωπῶν περιεπάτησεν: "Without saying anything against the argument about motion, he got up and walked about." (Sextus Empiricus, *Outlines of Pyrrhonism*.) So Menedemus reproved luxury by eating only olives (Diogenes Laërtius, *Life of Menedemus*.) And others are mentioned by Plutarch, who ἄνευ φωνῆς ἃ δεῖ φράζειν, did declare "what they had to say without making use of words." (*De garrulitate*.) ↩

10. Roscius, in Macrobius's *Saturnalia*. ↩

11. Where we find φίλοι τε φίλοις καὶ πολῖται πολίταις... ἐς χεῖρας ἀλλήλοις ἐλθόντες: "that friends and fellow-citizens fell into each other's hands." (Thucydides, *The Peloponnesian War*.) ↩

12. Τοὶς οἰκείους ὡς πολεμίους ἠμύνοντο: "They revenged themselves upon their own people, as if they had been their enemies." (Diodorus Siculus *Bibliotheca historica*.) ↩

13. Valerius Maximus, *Facta et dicta memorabilia*. ↩

14. Cicero. (Editor's note.) ↩

15. Ἀνθρώποισιν οὐκ ἐχρῆν ποτὲ τῶν πραγμάτων τὴν γλῶσσαν ἰσχύειν πλέον: "There never could be any necessity that men's tongues should be of more force [to declare their intentions] than their actions." (Euripides, *Hecuba*.) *Quasi intersit, audiam, an videam*: "As if there were any difference whether I hear you, or see you." (Cicero, *Ad Atticum*.) ↩

16. Ἡμεῖς τὸν ὠνούμενον βιβλία Πλάτωνος ὠνεῖσθαί φαμεν Πλάτωνα κτλ.: "He who buys Plato's books, we say, buys Plato." (Plutarch, *Isis and Osiris*.) ↩

17. Virgil (in *The Eclogues*) and Theocritus (in *The Idyls*). ↩

18. ותתם שמשמ: "On the bed together." (Rashi, *Commentary on the Torah*, on Genesis 26:8.) ↵

19. Only ענון נשוק וחיבוק, "kissing and embracing her," according to Moses Alshek. (*Torat Mosheh*, on Genesis 26:8.) ↵

20. Ὦτα γὰρ τυγχάνει ἀνθρώποισι ἐόντα ἀπιστότερα ὀφθαλμῶν: "Men do not usually give so much credit to their ears, as to their eyes." (Herodotus, *The Persian Wars*.) ↵

21. That instance of Menelaus and his guest Alexander, in Arrian, might be subjoined to this. Εἴ τις αὐτοὺς εἶδεν φιλοφρονουμένους ἀλλήλους, ἠπίστησεν ἂν τῷ λέγοντι οὐκ εἶναι φίλους αὐτούς: "If anyone saw them treating each other in a very friendly manner, he would not believe a person who should say that they were not friends." (Arrian, *Discourses of Epictetus*.) ↵

22. *De duplici martyrio ad Fortunatum*, Desiderius Erasmus. ↵

23. Something like this is that in one of Gregory Nazinzen's orations (*Contra Julianum imperatorem*.) When some Christians, who had been ensnared by Julian, asked, πῶς Χριστὸν ἠρνήμεθα: "How have we denied Christ?" They were answered, ὅτι κατὰ τοῦ πυρὸς ἐθυμιάσατε: "you have offered incense on the altar." ↵

24. Τὰ ψευδῆ πράγματα διώκων: "Pursuing things that are false." (Johannes Chrysostom, *Expositiones in Psalmos*.) Καὶ στολισμὸς ἀνδρός, καὶ γέλως, καὶ βῆμα ποδὸς ἀναγγέλλει περὶ αὐτοῦ: "Nay the habit of a man, or his laugh, or the step of his foot, will discover who he is," as Basil speaks: and therefore greater things must do it more. (Chrysostom, *The Prayer*.) ↵

25. As that word Βλιτρι (*Blitri*) in Diogenes Laërtius's *Life of Zeno*, which word has no meaning at all. ↵

26. Αἰγύπτιοι... τὰ πολλὰ πάντα ἔμπαλιν τοῖσι ἄλλοισι ἀνθρώποισι ἐστήσαντο ἤθεά τε καὶ νόμους, κτλ.: "The Egyptians... have established a great many laws and customs, quite contrary to those of other people." (Herodotus, *The Persian Wars*.) ↵

27. המתפלל לא יעמוד בתפלה ... בראש מגולה: "He that prays, must not have his head uncovered while he is praying." (Maimonodes in *Mishneh Torah*, Hilkot Tefillah, V, 5, and others everywhere.) ↵

28. Θεὸν ὁμολογοῦσιν εἰδέναι, τοῖς δὲ ἔργοις ἀρνοῦνται: "They profess to know God, but in works they deny him." (Epistle to Titus 1:16.) And τὸ ἔργοις ἀρνεῖσθαι Θεὸν ὑπερ τὸ εἰπεῖν ἐν στόματι: "To deny God by our works is worse than to deny him by our words." (Johannes Chrysostom, *Commentary on the Psalms*.) ↵

29. Λόγος ἔργου σκιή: "Words are the images of our deeds." (Plutarch, *Moralia*.) *Res loquitur ipsa: quæ semper valet plurimum*: "The thing speaks itself, which is always of very great force." (Cicero, *Pro Tito Annio Milone*.) *Quid verba audiam, cum facta videam?* "What signifies my hearing of words, when I see the facts?" (Cicero, *Tusculan Disputations*.) Αὐτὰ βοᾷ τὰ πράγματα, κἂν τῇ φωνῇ σιωπᾷς: "The facts themselves speak out aloud, though you are silent with your voice." (Basil of Caesarea.) ↵

30. This we know. For they are different to different nations; we coin them as we please, etc. φύσει τῶν ὀνομάτων οὐδέν ἐστιν, ἀλλ᾽ ὅταν γένηται σύμβολον: "The names of things are not founded in nature, but are only artificial signs." (Aristotle, *Organon*.) And though Plato seems to be of another mind, yet when Cratylus says, Ὀνόματος ὀρθότητα εἶναι ἑκάστῳ τῶν ὄντων φύσει πεφυκυῖαν, "that the propriety of the name is founded in the nature of every thing," it is as much to be questioned whether anything more be meant than this, that some names of things are more natural or proper than others. For he says that this rectitude of names is the same καὶ Ἕλλησι καὶ βαρβάροις, "with the Greeks and with the Barbarians;" that it is [only] such as is sufficient δηλοῦν οἷον ἕκαστόν ἐστι τῶν ὄντων, "to signify what every thing is;" such as may render them κατὰ τὸ δυνατὸν ὅμοια*hellip;* τοῖς πράγμασιν, etc. "as like the things as is possible, etc." (Plato, *Cratylus*.) That *lepidum et festivum argumentum*, "that witty and jocular argument," which Publius Nigidius in Aulus Gellius makes use of to show, *cur videri possint verba esse naturalia magis quam arbitraria*, "why words seem rather to be natural than arbitrary," deserves only to be laughed at. (*Attic Nights*.) ↵

31. ריש, the Hebrew word *Resh*. ↵

32. ريش, the Arabic word *Resh*. So Aben Ezra observes that אבה, *Abab*, in Hebrew is to "will," in Arabic to "nill" (though in Arabic the word is written אבי, *Abi*): and in another place, that the *same* word even in the *same* language sometimes signifies דבר והפכו, a thing and its contrary. And everyone knows, that the greater part of our words have different senses and uses. The word עגו (*Gnigon*) in Arabic, according to Giggeius and Golius, has 70 or 80, and some (two at least) contrary the one to the other. ↵

33. This is ποιεῖν ψεῦδος: "to act a lie." (Revelation 21:27.) Plato uses the same way of speaking. Ψεῦδος, says he, μηδεὶς μηδὲν… μήτε λόγῳ μήτε ἔργῳ πράξειεν: "No man should tell a lie either by word or deed." (*Laws*.) The contrary to this is in Aristotle: ἀληθεύειν… ὁμοίως ἐν λόγοις καὶ πράξεσιν: "to perform the truth both in words and in deeds;" and ἐν βίῳ ἀληθεύειν: "to live in the truth." (*Nicomachean Ethics*.) And in *Sefer Bereshit* לכת באמת: "to walk in the truth," and דרך אמת: "in the way of truth." ↵

34. *Actum generale verbum est, sive verbis sive re quid agatur*: "An act is a general expression, and signifies anything that is acted either by words or deeds." (Justinian,

Digest.) ↩

35. As it must be, because Ὀρθὸν ἡ ἀληθεί ἀεί: "Truth is always right." (Sophocles, *Antigone.*) ↩

36. Τῷ λογικῷ ζώῳ ἡ αὐτὴ πρᾶξις κατὰ φύσιν ἐστὶ καὶ κατὰ λόγον: "An action which is done according to nature, or according to reason, is the same in a creature endowed with reason"; that is, according to truth, which it is the office of reason to discover. (Marcus Aurelius, *Meditations.*) *Nunquam aliud* natura, *aliud* sapientia *dicit*: "*Nature never dictates one thing, and reason a different thing.*" (Juvenal, *Satires.*) ↩

37. Ἔδωκεν [ὁ Θεὸς] ἀντὶ δέλτου τὸν κόσμον: "[God] has given us the world, as it were for a book to read in." (Johannes Chrysostom, *Homilies on First Corinthians.*) ↩

38. What Hierocles says of his ἐγκόσμιοι Θεοί, "Gods that govern this world," is true in respect of everything. Τῷ Θείῳ νόμῳ κατακολουθούντων ἐστί… τοῦτο αὐτοὺς εἶναι τίθεσθαι, ὃ γεγόνασι: "The supposing them to be what they are… is paying obedience to the law of God." (*Commentary on the Carmen Aureum.*) There is a passage somewhere in *Sefer ha-Ikkarim* (II, 28) much like this: where it is said (as I remember) that he, who worships an Angel מצד מה הוא שליח ה ("as being what he is, the messenger of God") is not guilty of idolatry. (Joseph Albo.) ↩

39. הקב״ה נקרא אמת וכו׳: "The holy Being is called truth." In *Reshit Hokmah* and others (Elijah ben Moses de Vidas). And St. Chrysostom defines truth in the same words, which philosophers apply to the Deity. Ἀλήθεια τὸ ὄντως ὄν: "Truth is that which has a real existence." (Paraphrasing the Eleatic in Plato's *Sophist.*) ↩

40. Ἀλήθεια γὰρ ὀπαδὸς θεοῦ: "For truth is the companion of God." (Philo Judaeus, *On the Life of Moses.*) ↩

41. Ποίμνας… ὡς ἄνδρας… ἔχων: "Treating his flocks… like men," is in Sophocles the character of Ajax, when his head was turned, in a fit of raving. And among the monstrous and mad extravagances of Caesar Caligula, one is that he treated his horse Incitatus as a man. (Suetonius, *The Lives of the Caesars.*) ↩

42. Horace argues after the same manner: *Si quis lectica nitidam gestare amet* agnam; *Huic vestem, ut* gnatæ, *paret, etc.… Interdicto huic omne adimat ius Prætor, etc.… Quid? si quis* gnatam *pro mutâ devovet* agnâ *Integer est animi? Ne dixeris*: "If anyone should take pleasure in carrying a very pretty lamb about with him in his chariot, and clad it like his daughter, etc., ought not the magistrate to take the power out of such a one's hands? etc. But what if any man should attempt to offer his daughter as a sacrifice instead of a dumb lamb, would you say that he was in his right senses? I am sure you would not." (*Satires.*) If it be against truth and nature to use a lamb as a daughter, it

will be as much against truth to use a daughter as a lamb. ↵

43. Καθ' αὐτο... μὲν ψεῦδος φαῦλον καὶ ψεκτόν τὸ δ' ἀληθει καλὸν καὶ ἐπαινετόν: "A lie is base and blameworthy of itself, and truth is beautiful and praiseworthy." (Aristotle, *Nicomachean Ethics*.) *Est quiddam, quod suâ vi nos alliciat ad sese, non emolumento captans aliquo, sed trahens sua dignitate; quod genus, virtus, scientia,* veritas *est*: "There is something that wins our affections by its own native force, something that does not catch us by any profit that it brings, but attracts us by its superior excellency; something of this kind is virtue, knowledge, *truth*." (Cicero, *De Inventione*.) "Truth is a sweet thing" (a festival saying in Plutarch). ↵

44. *O magna vis veritatis, etc.*: "O the great force of truth, etc." (Cicero, *For Marcus Cœlius*.) A good man עושה האמת מפני שהוא אמת: "does the truth, because it is the truth." (Maimonides.) ↵

45. *Plura vera discrepantia esse non possunt*: "Be there never so many truths, they cannot be inconsistent with each other." (Cicero, *Academica Priora*.) ↵

46. *Oblivione voluntaria*: "By a voluntary forgetfulness." (Cicero, *Letters to Friends*.) ↵

47. In the Civil Law he is said to act, who does omit. *Qui* non facit *quod facere debet,* videtur facere *adversus ea qua non facit*. (*Digestorum, seu Pandectarum*.) ↵

48. *Est quodam prodire tenus*: "It is something to go, though it be but a little way, or to make a small progress." (Horace, *Epistles*.) ↵

49. *Disces quamdiu voles: tamdiu autem velle debebis quoad te, quantum proficias, non pœnitebit*: "You may learn as long as you please, and you ought to please, so long as you are not uneasy at any improvement of yourself," says Cicero to his son. (*De Officiis*.) ↵

50. *Nulla virtus virtuti contraria est*: "No one virtue can be contradictory to any other virtue." (Seneca, *De Clementi*.) ↵

51. עגי באותה שעה: "Poor at that particular time:" according to that determination in a case something like this, which occurs in *Mishnah* Peah V, 4. ↵

52. *Utrique simul consulendum est. Dabo egenti; sed ut* ipse *non egeam, etc.*: "Regard is to be had to both at the same time; I will give to one in want, yet so that I may not want myself, etc." (Seneca, *De Beneficiis*.) *Ita te aliorum miserescat, ne tui alios misereat*: "Take pity of others, but do it in such a manner as not to stand in need of the pity of others yourself." (Plautus, *Trinummi*.) ↵

53. Sextus Empiricus seems to be fond of that filthy saying of Zeno, in relation to what is

storied of Jocasta and Oedipus: μὴ ἄτοπον εἶναι τὸ μόριον τῆς μητρὸς... τρῖψαι, κτλ. any more, than to rub with the hand any other part of her, when in pain. Here only τρῖψις is considered; as if all was nothing more, but *barely* τρῖψις; but this is an incomplete idea of the act [Clarke chastely refuses to translate this, but the gist of it is that Sextus Empricus, in *Outlines of Pyrrhonism*, claims that Zeno says that rubbing your mother's naughty bits with your own shouldn't be considered any stranger than rubbing some more mundane part of her with your hand —Editor]. For τρῖψις τοῦ μόριον is more than τρῖψις by itself: and τρῖψις τοῦ μόριον τῆς μητρὸς is still more: and certainly τρίβειν τὴν χεῖρα τῇ χειρὶ is a different thing from τρίβειν τὸ μόριον τῷ μορίῳ, etc. He might as well have said, that to rub a red hot piece of iron with one's bare hand is the same as to rub one that is cold, or any other innocent piece of matter: for all is but τρῖψις. Thus men, affecting to appear freethinkers, show themselves to be but half-thinkers, or less: they do not take in the whole of that which is to be considered. ↩

54. *Sunt res quædam ex tempore, et ex consilio, non ex sua natura considerandæ... Quid tempora petant, aut quid personis dignum sit, considerandum est, etc.*: "Some things are to be considered, not as they are in their own nature, but the particular time and the intention are to be taken into the account... We are to consider what the times require, and what is proper, for such and such persons, etc." (Cicero, *De Inventione*.) ↩

55. Οὐ λέγεις φιλόπονον τὸν διὰ παιδισκάριον ἀγρυπνοῦντα: "You will not say that a person is industrious, because he once watched all night with his daughter." (Arrian, *Discourses of Epictetus*.) *Amico ægro aliquis assidet: probamus. At hoc si hereditatis causâ facit, vultur est, cadaver expectat*: "A man watches with a sick friend: it is allowed to be a good action; but if he did it in order to make himself his heir, he is a vulture, and watched for the carcass." (Seneca, *Epistles*.) ↩

56. Οὐ γὰρ εἷς ἀρνήσεώς ἐστι τρόπος: "There are more ways than one of denying a thing." (Johannes Chrysostom, *De Anna*.) ↩

57. Τὸ κράτιστον τῶν ἀγαθῶν, ἡ ἀλήθεια, καὶ ὁ ἔσχατος ὅρος τῆς πονηρίας, τὸ ψεῦδος: "Of all the good things in the world, truth is the best, and falsehood is the utmost boundary of all evil." (Basil.) ↩

58. Notwithstanding that paradox of the Stoics, Ὅτι ἴσα τὰ ἁμαρτήματα, καὶ τὰ κατορθώματα, "That all sins are equal, and all duties equal," in Cicero, Plutarch, Diogenes Laërtius, and others, which might easily be confuted from their own words in Cicero. For if sinning be like passing a line, or limit; that is, going over or beyond that line: then, to sin being equal to going beyond that line, to go more (or farther) beyond that line must be to sin more. Who sees not the falsity of that, *nec bono viro meliorem ... nec forti fortiorem, nec sapiente sapientiorem posse fieri*, "that it is impossible for a good man to be better... or a strong man to be stronger, or a wise man wiser?" (Cicero,

Paradoxa Stoicorum) and so on. *Nullum inter scelus et erratum discrimen facere*, "to make no difference betwixt notorious wickedness and mere mistakes" (as St. Jerome expresses their opinion: if that epistle to Celantia be his) is to alter or destroy the natures of things. ↩

59. Sure that Wiseman was but a bad accountant, who reckoned, τὴν μεγίστην οὐσίαν ἀποβαλὼν, δραχμὴν μίαν ἐκβεβληκέναι: "that he who throws away the greatest estate, throws away but a drachm." (Plutarch, *De Stoicorum Repugnantiis*.) ↩

60. This is confessed in Cicero. *Illud interest, quod in servo necando, si adsit injuria, semel peccatur: in patris vita violanda multa peccantur, etc. Multitudine peccatorum præstat, etc.*: "There is this difference: that he who kills a slave, if it be done wrongfully, is guilty of sin in that one respect only; but he that wickedly takes away the life of his father, sins in many respects, etc. He excels in the multitude of his sins, etc." (*Paradoxa Stoicorum*.) ↩

61. This may serve for an answer to Chrysippus, and them who say, εἰ ἀληθὲς ἀληθοῦς μᾶλλον οὐκ ἔστιν, οὐδὲ ψεῦδος ψεύδους · οὕτως οὐδὲ ἀπάτη ἀπάτης, οὐδὲ ἀμάρτημα ἁμαρτήματος, κτλ.: "That if no one truth be greater than another truth, nor no one falsehood greater than another falsehood; then neither is one fraud nor one sin greater than another." (In Diogenes Laërtius, *Life of Zeno of Citium*.) ↩

62. *Queis paria esse ferè placuit peccata, laborant, Cùm ventum ad verum est: sensus moresque repugnant, Atque ipsa utilitas*: "They, who would have all sins to be equal, labor under great difficulty when they come to the truth; for they find it contrary to reason, to morality, and to the interest of mankind." (Horace, *Satires*.) ↩

63. Therefore they, who denied there was either good or evil (Φύσει ἀγαθὸν καὶ κακόν: "good or evil in the nature of things"), were much in the right to make thorough work, and to say there was nothing in nature either true or false. See Sextus Empiricus (*Pros Ethikous*) and Diogenes Laërtius (*Life of Pyrrho*). ↩

64. *Quod [extremum, et ultimum bonorum] omnium philosophorum sententiâ tale debet esse, ut ad id omnia referri oporteat: ipsum autem nusquàm*: "That which is the [ultimate end or final good] according to the opinion of all philosophers, must be something to which all other things ought to be referred, but itself referred to nothing." (Cicero, *De finibus bonorum et malorum*.) ↩

65. There was among the old philosophers such an uncertainty and variety of opinions concerning the *fines bonorum et malorum*, "the limits of good and evil," that if Varro computes rightly, the number might be raised to 288. (St. Augustine, *City of God*.) ↩

66. *Quod honestum est, id bonum solum habendum est*: "That which is truly honorable, and

valuable upon its own account, is the only thing that ought to be esteemed really good." (Cato, in Cicero's *De finibus bonorum et malorum*.) ↩

67. *Qui [omnes] permulta ob eam unam causam faciunt... quia honestum est*: "Who [everybody] do abundance of things for this reason only... because they are honorable in themselves." (Cicero, *De finibus bonorum et malorum*.) ↩

68. It is commonly placed among ends, and is considered as such in those ways of speaking; *honestum esse propter se expetendum*: "that which is honorable ought to be sought after for its own sake." (Cicero, *De finibus bonorum et malorum*.) Finem *bonorum esse honestè vivere*: "*The perfection* of all goodness and virtue is to live by the rules of true honor." (Ibid., and the like.) ↩

69. To say *Quod laudabile est, omne honestum est*: "what is truly praiseworthy, is truly honorable," or anything like that, is, to say nothing. For how shall one know what is truly *laudabile*, "praiseworthy?" ↩

70. Τέλος εἶπε *[Ζήνων]* τὸ ὁμολογουμένως al. ἀκολούθως τῇ φύσει ζῆν, ὅπερ ἐστὶ κατ' ἀρετὴν ζῆν· Ἄγει γὰρ πρὸς ταύτην ἡμᾶς ἡ φύσις: "The perfection of man says [Zeno] is to live agreeably to, or to follow, nature; and that is to live virtuously, for nature leads us to that." (Diogenes Laërtius, *Life of Zeno*.) ↩

71. *Vivere ex hominis naturâ*: "To live agreeably to the nature of man." (Cicero, *De finibus bonorum et malorum*.) It is true, he adds *undique perfectâ et nihil requirente*: "every way perfect and wanting nothing," but those words have either no meaning, or such as will not much mend the matter. For what is *natura undique perfecta et nihil requirens*: "a nature every way perfect and wanting nothing?" Besides, moral religion does not consist in following nature already perfect, but by the practice of religion we aim at the perfecting of our natures. ↩

72. Celebrated everywhere. ↩

73. Τὸ μὲν οὖν οὕτω διορίσασθαι τὰς οἰγαθὰς πράξεις, τὰς κατα τὸν ὀρθὸν γινομένας λόγον, τὰς πονηρὰς τοὐναντίον, ἀληθὲς μέν, οὐκ ἔστι δὲ ἱκανὸν τὰς πράξεις σημᾶναι: "To define good actions thus, viz. that they are done according to right reason, and bad actions the contrary; is indeed true, but is not sufficient to declare the nature of them by showing what actions are truly such." (Andronicus of Rhodes [from a commentary on Aristotle's *Nicomachean Ethics* sometimes attributed to Andronicus —Editor].) ↩

74. *Nec solum jus et injuria a natura dijudicatur, sed omnino omnia honesta et turpia. Nam communis intelligentia nobis notas res efficit easque in animis nostris inchoavit, ut honesta in virtute ponantur, in vitiis turpia*: "Not only right and wrong are different in the nature of things, but all sorts of honorable and base actions are so likewise: for

common sense makes us understand things, and lays the first rudiments of them in our minds, in such a manner that we make honorable things to consist in their being virtuous, and base things to consist in their being vicious." (Cicero, *De Legibus*.) Κριτήριά φησιν *[ὁ Χρύσιππος]* εἶναι αἴσθησιν καὶ πρόληψιν: "Chrysippus says that sensation and reflection are the rules by which we form our judgment of things." (Diogenes Laërtius, *Life of Zeno*.) ↵

75. They are usually called *principia naturæ*, *lex* (or *leges*) *naturæ*, προλήψεις κοιναὶ, or φυσικαὶ ἔννοιαι, νόμος φυσικὸς, etc. "the principles of nature, the law (or laws) of nature, first apprehensions of things, universal or natural notions, the law of nature, etc." ↵

76. The set of these practical principles (or a habit flowing from them) is what, I think, goes by the name of *Synteresis*. ↵

77. *Unaquæque gens hoc legem naturæ putat, quod didicit*: "Every nation think that to be the law of nature, which they have been taught." (St. Jerome, *Against Jovianus*.) ↵

78. Under which word these delicate men comprehend *labor*. When Epicurus, in Lucian's *The Double Indictment*, is asked, Κακὸν ἡγῇ τὸν πόνον: "Whether he thought labor an evil?" he answers, Ναί: "Yea." And Mindyrides (Σμενδυρίδης, according to Herodotus in his *Histories*, ὃς ἐπὶ πλεῖστον δὴ χλιδῆς εἷς ἀνὴρ ἀπίκετο: "Smyndirides... a man who carried luxury to the highest degree") proceeded so far in his aversion to labor, that *ejus latus* alieno labore *condoluit... qui cum vidisset fodientem, et altiùs rastrum allevantem, lassum se fieri* (ῥῆγμα λαβεῖν in Athenæus) *questus vetuit illum opus in conspectu suo facere*: "it gave him a pain in his side *to see another man labor...* : when he saw anyone digging or lifting a heavy rake, he complained that it made him weary ('demolished him,' it is in Athenæus) and forbade the person doing any more work in his sight." (Seneca, *De Ira*.) ↵

79. *Ad hæc [voluptatem, et dolorem] et quæ sequamur, et quæ fugiamus, refert omnia [Aristippus]*: "[Aristippus] referred everything [to pleasure and pain] which we pursue or avoid." (Cicero, *De finibus bonorum et malorum*.) ↵

80. *Velim definias, quid sit voluptas: de quo omnis hæc quæstio est*: "I would have you define what pleasure is, for this whole question is about that." (Cicero, *De finibus bonorum et malorum*.) The disputes about pleasure between the Cyrenaics, Epicurus, Hieronymus, etc. are well known: whether the end was pleasure of body or mind; whether it was *voluptas in motu*, or *in statu (stabilitate); quae suavitate aliqua naturam ipsam movet*, or *quae percipitur, omni dolore detracto*; ἡ ἐν κινήσει, or ἡ καταστηματικὴ etc. (Cicero, Diogenes Laërtius, et al.) ↵

81. *Negat Epicurus jucundè vivi posse, nisi cum virtute vivatur*: "Epicurus denies that

anyone can live pleasantly that does not live virtuously." (Cicero, *Tusculan Disputations*.) But for all that, their pleasures have not continued to be always like those in the little gardens of Gargettus. Nor indeed do they seem to be very virtuous even there. For Epicurus not only had his Leontium (or, as he amorously called her, Λεοντάριον, "his pretty poppet"), a famous harlot; but she πᾶσί τε τοῖς Ἐπικουρείοις συνῆν ἐν τοῖς κήποις: "laid with all the Epicureans in the gardens." (Athenæus, *Deipnosophistae*.) And in his book περὶ τέλους ("Of Perfection") he is said to have written thus, Οὐ γὰρ ἔγωγε ἔχω τί νοήσω τἀγαθόν, ἀφαιρῶν μὲν τὰς διὰ χυλῶν (χειλῶν Athenæus) ἡδονάς, ἀφαιρῶν δὲ καὶ τὰς δι᾽ ἀφροδισίων, κτλ.: "There is nothing that I esteem good, if you take away the pleasure which arises from eating and drinking and women." (See this and more in Diogenes Laërtius, *Life of Epicurus*.) ↩

82. St. Jerome uses the plural number, as if this was the prevailing notion in his time. *Philosophorum sententia est*, μεσότητας ἀρετάς, ὑπερβολὰς κακίας εἶναι: "It is the opinion of the philosophers that virtues consist in the middle, and vices in the extremes." (*Letter to Demetrias*.) ↩

83. Ἡ μὲν ὑπερβολὴ ἁμαρτάνεται, ἁμαρτάνεταικαὶ ἡ ἔλλειψις ψέγεται, τὸ δὲ μέσον ἐπαινεῖται... Ἔστιν ἄρα ἡ ἀρετὴ ἕξις προαιρετικὴ ἐν μεσότητι οὖσα, κτλ. ... Μεσότης δὲ δύο κακιῶν, τῆς μὲν καθ᾽ ὑπερβολὴν τῆς δὲ κατ᾽ ἔλλειψιν: "Every excess is a crime, and every defect is blameworthy, but the medium is commendable. ... Virtue then is a habit of our own procuring, and consists in the middle. ... Which middle is between the two extremes; the one of excess, and the other of defect." (Aristotle, *Nicomachean Ethics*.) Perhaps Pythagoras (and after him Plato, and others), when he said (in Diogenes Laërtius, *Life of Pythagoras*) τὴν ἀρετὴν ἁρμονίαν εἶναι, "that virtue was a kind of harmony," might have some such thought as this. ↩

84. When he says it must be taken οὕτως ὡς ἂν ὁ ὀρθὸς λόγος προστάξῃ, "according to the direction of right reason" (Aristotle, *Nicomachean Ethics*), it is not by that acertained. See note 82. ↩

85. Οὐ γὰρ ῥᾴδιον διορίσαι τὸ πῶς καὶ τίσι, κτλ.: "It is not easy to determine the particular manner and the particular persons." (Aristotle, *Nicomachean Ethics*.) Therefore Rabbi Albo might have spared that censure, where he blames himself for expressing himself too generally, when he says, כמו שראוי יבעת הראוי ובמקוס הראוי, "after a due manner, in a convenient time, and in proper place," without telling him what that manner, time, place is. (*Sefer ha-Ikkarim* I, 8.) ↩

86. That man, says he, cannot be neglected, who endeavors δίκαιος γίγνεσθαι, καὶ ἐπιτηδεύων ἀρετήν, εἰς ὅσον δυνατὸν ἀνθρώπῳ ὁμοιοῦσθαι θεῷ: "to make himself a righteous man, by laboring after virtue, that he may be as like God as it is possible for a man to be." (*Republic*.) And in another place, our φυγὴ ἐνθένδε is ὁμοίωσις θεῷ κατὰ

τὸ δυνατόν: "fleeing from thence is being like unto God so far as we can be." (*Theaetetus.*) St. Augustine seems to agree with him, in that sentence of his, *Religionis summa est imitari quem colis*: "The highest pitch of religion is to imitate the being you worship." (*The City of God.*) ↩

87. Πυθαγόρας ἐρωτηθεὶς τί ποιοῦσιν ἄνθρωποι θεῷ ὅμοιον, ἔφη, Ἐὰν ἀληθεύωσι: "Pythagoras, being asked what it was that any man could do like what God does, answered: Speak the truth." (Joannes Stobaeus, *On Truth.*) ↩

88. There is certainly not that difficulty or perplexity in morality, which Cicero seems to suppose, when he says, *Consuetudo exercitatioque capienda, ut boni ratiocinatores officiorum esse possimus*: "That use and exercise are necessary to make us good reasoners about what is our duty." (*De Officiis.*) ↩

89. What it is in nature. כפי מה שיהואבא: "According to what the thing is," to use Maimonides's words. And thus that in Arrian is true, Νόμος βιωτικός ἐστιν οὗτος, τὸ ἀκόλουθον τῇ φύσει πράττειν: "The rule of life is, to do whatever is agreeable to nature." (*Discourses of Epictetus.*) *Omni in re quid sit veri, videre et tueri decet*: "We ought to find out and to maintain what is true, about everything." (Cicero, *De Officiis.*) This is indeed the way of truth. ↩

90. Because there is scarce anything which one or other will not say. *Quid enim dici potest de illo, qui nigram dixit esse nivem, etc.*: "What can we say of a man that affirms black to be white, etc." (Lactantius, *Divine Institutes.*) ↩

91. *Conveniet cùm in dando munificum esse, tum in exigendo non acerbum:... à litibus verò quantùm liceat, et nescio an paulo plus etiam quàm liceat, abhorrentem.... Habenda autem est ratio rei familiaris, quam quidem dilabi finere flagitiosum est*: "It is but reasonable that we should be liberal in giving, and not severe in our demands:... we should be averse to any contention, as far as is lawful, nay I don't know if we should not go a little farther.... But we must have regard to our own private circumstances, for it is a wicked thing in us to hurt them." (Cicero, *De Officiis.*) ↩

92. Τὸν φιλέοντ' ἐπὶ δαῖτα καλεῖν, τον δ' ἐχθρὸν ἐᾶσαι: "Invite your friend to supper, but let your enemy alone." (Hesiod, *Works and Days.*) ↩

93. Τὸ πένεσθαι οὐκ ὁμολογεῖν τινὶ αἰσχρόν, ἀλλὰ μὴ διαφεύγειν ἔργῳ αἴσχιον: "For a poor man not to own himself to be poor is a base thing; but for him not to endeavor to be otherwise is a baser thing still." (Thucydides, *History of the Peloponnesian War.*) ↩

94. For ἔργον δ' οὐδὲν ὄνειδος: "no endeavor is any reproach." (Hesiod, *Works and Days.*) ↩

95. *Suum cuique incommodum ferendum est potius, quam de alterius commodis detrahendum*: "Every man ought to bear the evils he is under, rather than deprive others of their advantages." (Cicero, *De Officiis*.) According to Plato, a man should choose to die, πρὸ τοῦ ἀδικεῖν, "rather than do an unjust thing." ↵

96. Οὕτω καὶ ἰατρὸς νοσοῦντα ἐξαπατᾷ, ... καὶ δεινὸν οὐδέν: "Thus a physician deceives a sick person, ... and there is nothing shocking in it." (Maximus Tyrius, *Dissertations*.) ↵

97. To that question, *Si quis ad te confugiat, qui mendacio tuo possit à morte liberari, non es mentiturus?* "If a man should come to you who should be saved from death by your telling a lie, would you tell one?" St. Augustine answers in the negative, and concludes, *Restat ut nunquam boni mentiantur. ... Quanto fortiùs, quanto excellentiùs dices, nec prodam, nec mentiar*: "It remains then that good men should never tell a lie. ... How much more courageous, how much better is it to say: I will neither betray him nor tell a lie." (*De Mendacio*.) ↵

98. In such pressing cases, under imminent danger, the world is wont to make great allowances. Οὐκ αἰσχρὸν ἡγῇ δῆτα τὰ ψευδῆ λέγειν; ... Οὐκ, εἰ τὸ σωθῆναί γε τὸ ψεῦδος φέρει: "Is it not then a base thing to say what is false? ... No, not if the falsity will save anyone." (Sophocles, *Philoctetes*.) Even they, who say, השח שיחה בטלה עובר במעשה: "that he who speaks falsehood transgresses indeed," and, עשה לדבר אמת אפילו במילי דעלמא: "that it is a positive precept to speak the truth in common discourse;" and, חמשקר כאלו עובד ע"ז: "that a liar is like an idolater;" say also, אבל לשים שלום מותר: "that it is better to preserve peace." (Eliezer Azkari, *Sefer Haredim* and various places.) And Aben Ezra says of Abraham, דחה אבימלך בדברים כפי צורך השעה: "that he urged Abimelech with such words as the necessity of that time required." (*Commentary on the Torah* on Genesis 20:12.) In short, some have permitted, in desperate cases, *mendacio tanquam veneno uti*, "to make use of a lie as you do of poison." (Sextus the Pythogorean, *Sentences of Sextus*.) ↵

99. אסור ... לשבר כליו בחמתו וכו': "It is forbidden ... to break your own vessels in your anger." (Judah ben Samuel, *Sefer Hasidim*.) ↵

100. Who does not detest that thought of Caligula, *de Homeri carminibus abolendis*, etc.? about destroying Homer's verses, etc. (Suetonius, *Lives of the Caesars*.) ↵

101. The Stoics must certainly therefore be much too scrupulous, when they affirm (if they were in earnest), that οὐδὲ τὸν δάκτυλον ὡς ἔτυχε σαλεύειν τῷ σοφῷ ὁ λόγος ἐπιτρέπει: "reason commands a wise man, not so much as to move his fingers, as it were by chance." (Clemens Alexandrinus, *Paedagogus*.) Especially since this is, at least ordinarily, a thing perfectly indifferent by proposition IX. ↵

102. *Tu si hic sis, aliter sentias*: "You would be of another opinion, if you were in my

circumstances." (Terence, *The Andrian*.) ↩

103. *Felicitas cui præcipua fuerit homini, non est humani judicii: cùm prosperitatem ipsam alius alio modo, et suopte ingenio quisque terminet*: "No man can judge what the happiness of another man consists in; because some make their happiness to consist in one thing, and some in another, according to their several dispositions." (Pliny the Elder, *Natural History*.) ↩

104. It is not possible, in Joseph Albo's words, לתת לאיש כדרכיו שוה בשוה ולשער העונשים במדה במשקל וכו׳: "to give to every man according to equity, with regard to his ways, and to estimate punishments by measure and weight." (*Sefer ha-Ikkarim* I, 8.) ↩

105. *Inter hominem et belluam hoc maximè interest, quod hæc... ad id solum quod adest, quodque præsens est, se accommodat, paululum admodum sentiens præteritum aut futurum, etc.*: "Herein lies the chief difference between a man and a beast, that this latter conforms itself to that only which is present and before it, having but a very small sense of what is past or to come, etc." (Cicero, *De Officiis*.) *Nos et venturo torquemur et præterito. Timoris enim tormentum memoria reducit, providentia anticipat. Nemo tantum præsentibus miser est*: "But we torment ourselves with what is to come, and with what is past: for by our foresight we anticipate the torment of fear, and by our memory we bring back that torment which is past. No man is miserable by the present things alone." (Seneca, *Epistles*.) ↩

106. *Præsens tempus brevissimum est, adeo quidem, ut quibusdam nullum videatur, etc.*: "The present time is as short as is possible, insomuch that some have imagined it to be a mere nothing, etc." (Seneca, *De Brevitate Vitae*.) ὅταν γὰρ μηδὲν αὐτοὶ μεταβάλλωμεν τὴν διάνοιαν, ἢ λάθωμεν μεταβάλλοντες, οὐ δοκεῖ ἡμῖν γεγονέναι χρόνος: "When we have no succession of thoughts, or if we have, but forget them, then time seems to us to be nothing." (Aristotle, *Physics*.) ↩

107. אין השם חפץ שתמות בהמה הגם וכו׳: "God takes no delight that a beast should die, if there be no reason for its dying." (Aben Ezra.) עושה צער לבהמה תנם ... בא לדין וכו׳: "He that put a beast to any pain, without a just reason for so doing, shall be accountable for it." (Judah ben Samuel, *Sefer Hasidim*.) ↩

108. The rants of those men, who assert, μὴ διαφέρειν ἡδονῆν ἡδονῆς, μηδὲ ἡδεῖόν τι εἶναι, "that there is no difference in pleasures, that nothing can be more than pleasant," nay, Φύσει οὐδὲν ἡδὺ, ἢ ἀηδές, "that there is nothing that is naturally pleasant or unpleasant," in Diogenes Laërtius (*Life of Aristippus*), can surely affect nobody who has sense, or is alive. Nor that of the Stoics, in Plutarch, ὅτι ἀγαθὸ ὁ χρόνος οὐκ αὔξει προσγιγνόμενος, κτλ., "That the continuance of any good makes no addition to it."

(*Moralia.*) As if an age was not more than a moment, and (therefore) an age's happiness more than a moment's. ↩

109. *Nocet [fit noxa] empta dolore voluptas*: "Pleasure, that is procured by pain, is so much real hurt." (Horace, *Epistles.*) And, *multo corrupta dolore voluptas*: "Pleasure vitiated by much pain." (Horace, *Sermons.*) ↩

110. As when that Pompey, mentioned by Valerius Maximus, by burning his finger, escaped the torture. (*Facta et dicta memorabilia.*). ↩

111. *Bona malis paria non sunt, etiam pari numero: nec lætitia ulla minimo mærore pensanda*: "Good things are not equal to evil things, though they were the same in number; nor is any joy an equivalent for the least sorrow." (Pliny the Elder, *Natural History.*) ↩

112. Οἰόμεθά τε δεῖν ἡδονὴν παραμεμῖχθαι τῇ εὐδαιμονίᾳ: "We think that happiness must have some pleasure mixed with it." (Aristotle, *Nicomachean Ethics*). ↩

113. Or οἱονεὶ καθεύδοντός κατάστασις: "like a man in a deep sleep." (Aristippus, in Diogenes Laërtius's *Life of Aristippus.*) ↩

114. This is truly *Bonum summum, quò tendimus omnes*: "the chief good, which we all aim at." (Lucretius, *De Rerum Natura*). Ἅπαντα γὰρ ὡς εἰπεῖν, ἑτέρου χάριν αἱρούμεθα, πλὴν τῆς εὐδαιμονίας τέλος γὰρ αὕτη: "We choose all other things, except happiness, for the sake of something else; but that is itself the end." (Aristotle, *Nicomachean Ethics.*) ↩

115. *Non dat Deus beneficia. Unde ergo quæ possides? quae…*: "God does not give us any good things, whence then comes all that we have? which.…" (Seneca, *De Beneficiis.*) ↩

116. Παντὶ τὸ παρὰ φύσιν αὐτοῦ κακία καὶ κακοδαιμονία ἐστίν: "Everything that is contrary to the nature of any being, is evil and misery to it." (Arrian, *Enchiridion of Epictetus.*) ↩

117. Τίνων ἡδονῶν καὶ κατὰ λόγον ὀρθὸν μεταλαμβάνομεν: "There are some pleasures which we claim by the dictates of right reason." (Simplicius). *Rectè facit, animo quando obsequitur suo: quod omnes homines facere oportet, dum id modo fiat bono*: "He does right who follows the dictates of his own mind, as all men ought to do, if they do it in a proper manner." (Plautus, *Amphitryon.*) ↩

118. *Habebit philosophus amplas opes; sed nulli detractas etc.*: "A philosopher would have large possessions, but then he would not have them taken from others, etc." (Seneca, *De Vita Beata.*) Here he seems to confess the folly of the Stoics, who denied themselves many pleasures that were honest and almost necessary; living in tubs, feeding upon raw

herbs and water, going about in a sordid garment, with a rough beard, staff, and satchel, etc. ↩

119. *Quid rectum sit, apparet: quid expediat, obscurum est: ita tamen, ut… dubitare non possimus, quin ea maximè conducant, quæ sunt rectissima*: "It is very evident what right is; but it is very difficult to say what is expedient; but yet there can be no doubt, but that those things which are most right are most conducive to our happiness." (Cicero, *Letters to Friends*.) ↩

120. *Quis hoc statuit, quod æquum sit in Quinctium, id iniquum esse in Nævium?* "Who has decreed that what is equitable with regard to Quinctius, should be unjust with respect to Nævius?" (Cicero, *For Publius Quinctius*.) ↩

121. That question in Plato, Τί ἄν τις ἔχοι τεκμήριον ἀποδεῖξαι, εἴ τις ἔροιτο νῦν οὕτως ἐν τῷ παρόντι, πότερον καθεύδομεν καὶ πάντα ἃ διανοούμεθα ὀνειρώττομεν, κτλ., "If anyone should affirm that all our thoughts are only mere dreams, and that we are now asleep, what demonstrative proof could be brought to the contrary?" may have place among the velitations of philosophers: but a man can scarce propose it seriously to himself. If he does, the answer will attend it. (*Theaetetus*.) ↩

122. = a. ↩

123. = e. ↩

124. = ae. ↩

125. See André Tacquet's *Elementa Geometriæ* 1.5, page 3, Number XII. But the thing appears from the bare inspection of these quantities: b, ab, aeb, aeib, aeiob, etc. ↩

126. "Things that are equal to the same thing, are equal to one another," and "things that are each equal to a third thing, are also equal to each other" (versions of Euclid's first postulate). If men, in their inferences, or in comparing their ideas, do many times not actually make use of such maxims; yet the thing is really the same. For what these maxims express, the mind sees without taking notice of the words. ↩

127. Under the word "reason" I comprehend the intuition of the truth of axioms. For certainly to discern the respect which one term bears to another, and from thence to conclude the proposition necessarily true, is an act of reason, though performed quick, or perhaps all at once. ↩

128. If many believed, according to Socrates (in Lucian's *Halcyon*) that ὅσην ἔχει τὸ μέγεθος τοῦ κόσμου τὴν ὑπεροχὴν πρὸς τὸ Σωκράτους ἢ Χαιρεφῶντος εἶδος, τηλικοῦτον καὶ τὴν δύναμιν αὐτοῦ, καὶ τὴν φρόνησιν, καὶ διάνοιαν ἀνάλογον διαφέρειν τῆς περὶ ἡμᾶς διαθέσεως, "so much as the magnitude of the world exceeds the bulk of Socrates and

Chærophon; so far are their powers, reason, and understanding beyond the capacity of one of us," what may we think of the God of the world? Therefore Cicero seems to express himself too boldly where he writes, *Est... homini cum Deo rationis societas. Inter quos autem ratio, inter eosdem etiam recta ratio communis est*: "That God and man are allied to each other by reason. And where reason is in common to any persons, right reason is so likewise." (*De Legibus.*) ↩

129. Upon this account it is, that I add the word "given" at the end of my description of reason. ↩

130. *Simplex et nuda veritas est luculentior; quia satis ornata per se est: adeoque ornamentis extrinsecus additis fucata corrumpitur: mendacium verò specie placet alienâ, etc.*: "Pure and naked truth is so much the clearer, because it has ornaments enough of its own; and therefore, when it is daubed over with external additional ornaments, it is corrupted by them, so that a lie is therefore pleasing, because it appears in the shape that is not its own, etc." (Lactantius, *Divine Institutes.*) ↩

131. That way, which some Sceptics take to prove the inexistence of truth, has nothing in it, unless it be a contradiction. If anything, say they, is demonstrated to be true, how shall it be known that that demonstration is true? Εἰ ἐξ ἀποδείξεως, ζητηθήσεται πάλιν, πῶς ὅτι καὶ τοῦτο ἀληθές ἐστι, καὶ οὕτως εἰς ἄπειρον: "If by another demonstration, how shall we know that this is true? and so on forever." (Sextus Empiricus, *Against the Logicians.*) Nor do I well comprehend St. Chrysostom's meaning, when he says, Τὸ λογισμοῖς ἀποδεχθέν, κἄν ἀληθὲς ᾖ, οὐδέπω πληροφορίαν τῇ ψυχῇ παρέχει καὶ πίστιν ἱκανήν: "That what is demonstrated by reasoning, though it may indeed be true, yet it does not afford sufficient proof or conviction to the mind." (*Against the Anomoeans.*) For as no man truly believes anything, unless he has a reason for believing it: so no reason can be stronger than demonstration. ↩

132. *Haud alio fidei proniore lapsu, quàm ubi falsæ rei gravis autor existit*: "Men being never more easily drawn into a wrong belief, than when the author of a falsity is a grave person." (Pliny the Elder, *Natural History.*) ↩

133. That manner of demonstration, in which it has been pretended truth is deduced directly from that which is false, is only a way of showing that an assertion is true, because its contradictory is false; founded in that known rule, *Contradictoriæ nec simul veræ, nec simul falsæ esse possunt, etc.*, "That contradictory propositions can neither be true at the same time, nor false at the same time, etc." ↩

134. *Cujus [summi rectoris et domini] ad naturam apta ratio vera illa et summa lex à philosophis dicitur*: "The reason [of the supreme lord and governor] which is accommodated to the nature of things, is, by philosophers, called the true and chief

law." (Cicero, *De finibus bonorum et malorum*.) Νόμος ἀψευδὴς ὁ ὀρθὸς λόγος, οὐχ ὑπὸ τοῦ δεῖνος ἢ τοῦ δεῖνος, θνητοῦ φθαρτός, ἐν χαρτιδίοις ἢ στήλαις, ἄψυχος ἀψύχοις, ἀλλ' ὑπ' ἀθανάτου φύσεως ἄφθαρτος ἐν ἀθανάτῳ διανοίᾳ τυπωθείς: "Right reason is an unerring law, not to be defaced by any mortal man, as if it were a lifeless thing written upon paper or pillars which must decay: but it proceeds from an immortal being, and is itself immortal, and engraven on an immortal soul." (Philo Judaeus, *Every Good Man is Free*.) More to this purpose might easily be collected. ↩

135. Λόγος ἐστὶν εἰκὼν Θεοῦ: "reason is the image of God." (Philo Judaeus, *De Monarchia*.) ↩

136. Τὸ ἡγεμονικὸν καὶ κυριεῦον τῆς ψυχῆς σου μέρος: "The governing part of the soul." (Marcus Aurelius, *Meditations*.) Or as it is in [Pseudo-]Plutarch, τῆς ψυχῆς ἀνώτατον μέρος: "the supreme part of the soul." (*Placita Philosophorum*.) *Principatus*, "the principal part," in Cicero. *Summus in anima gradus*. (Tertullian, *De Anima*.) ↩

137. Criterion. (Editor's note.) ↩

138. *Religio cogi non potest, verbis potiùs quàm verberibus res agenda est, ut sit voluntas*: "Religion cannot be forced upon anyone, it must be done by words and not by blows, that it may be a thing of choice." (Lactantius, *Divine Institutes*.) ↩

139. *Tantulus ille... sol*: "The sun... that small thing." (Lucretius, *De Rerum Natura*.) Poor creature! ↩

140. *Nec nimio solis major rota... Esse potest, nostris quàm sensibus esse videtur*: "The orb of the sun cannot be much bigger than it appears to our senses." (Lucretius, *De Rerum Natura*.) *Epicurus autem posse putat etiam minorem esse quàm videatur, etc.*: "Epicurus thought it might be less than it appears, etc." (Cicero, *Academica*.) ↩

141. *Natura etiam nullo docente profecta ab iis, quorum, ex prima et inchoata intelligentia, genera cognovit, confirmat ipsa per se rationem, et perficit*: "For nature, without any teaching, proceeds upon those general truths which we are convinced of, as soon as we begin to have any understanding, and confirms and perfects them by reason." (Cicero, *De Legibus*.) ↩

142. *Semina nobis scientiæ dedit [natura] scientiam non dedit*: "The seeds or principles of knowledge are given us [by nature], but not knowledge itself." (Seneca, *Epistles*.) ↩

143. *Si sani sunt [sensus], et valentes, et omnia removentur, quæ obstant et impediunt*: "If [the senses] be sound and strong, and if everything be removed out of the way that might obstruct or hinder them." (Cicero, *Academica Priora*.) ↩

144. Socrates's saying, in Cicero, *nihil se scire, nisi id ipsum*: "that he knew nothing but

this," viz. that he knew nothing, savors of an affected humility, and must not be understood strictly. But they, who followed, went further (... *omnes pæne veteres: qui nihil cognosci, nihil percipi, nihil sciri posse dixerunt*: "... almost all the ancients, who affirmed, that nothing could be known, nothing perceived, nothing understood"): and particularly *Arcefilas negabat esse quidquam quod sciri posset, ne illud quidem ipsum, quod Socrates sibi reliquisset*: "Arcefilas denied that anything could be certainly known, *not so much as that* which Socrates reserved to himself." And thus the absurdity grew to a size that was monstrous. For no man can act, or even be alive, if he knows nothing at all. Besides, to know that one knows nothing is a contradiction, and not to know that he knows even that, is not to know whether he knows anything or not; and that is to know for ought he knows. (Quotes from Cicero's *Academica*.) ↩

145. *Nec scire fas est omnia*: "Nor is it possible to know all things." (Horace, *Odes*.) ↩

146. This was the opinion of a wise man. חגוך לנער על פי דרכו גם כי יזקין לא יסור ממנה: "Train up a child in the way that he should go; and when he is old, he will not depart from it." (Proverbs 22:6.) For הלימד בימי הנערות הוא כפתוח, על האבן... והלימד בימי הזקנה כפתוח על החול: "learning in the days of youth, is like graving upon a stone... and learning, in the days of old age, is like marking upon the sand." (Elisha ben Abraham ben Judah, *Kab we-Naki*.) Οὐ μικρὸν διαφέρει τὸ οὕτως ἢ οὕτως εὐθὺς ἐκ νέων ἐθίζεσθαι ἀλλὰ πάμπολυ, μᾶλλον δὲ τὸ πᾶν: "It is not a small but a very great advantage, or indeed all that can be, to be accustomed to such and such things from our very youth." (Aristotle, *Nicomachean Ethics*.) ↩

147. Τετράκις ἔλεγον ἐξ ἠθέων τὸν ἥλιον ἀνατεῖλαι · ἔνθα τε νῦν καταδύεται, ἐνθεῦτεν δὶς επαντεΤλαι, και ενθεν νῦν ανατελλει, ενθαῦτα δὶς καταδῦναι: "That the sun had risen four times contrary to what it usually does, viz. risen twice where it now sets, and set twice, where it now rises." (*Histories*: Euterpe.) ↩

148. עולם כמנהגו הולך: "The world goes on in its usual course." (*Avodah Zarah*.) ↩

149. פתי יאמין לכל דבר: "A fool believes everything that he hears." (Proverbs 14:15) (which sure one may convert thus, המאמין לכל דבר פתי הוא: "He that believes everything that he hears, is a fool"). ↩

150. *Statuere enim, qui sit sapiens, vel maximè videtur esse sapientis*: "It seems requisite that a man must be himself wise, in order to determine who is a wise man." (Cicero, *Academica Priora*.) ↩

151. *Non numero hæc judicantur, sed pondere*: "these are to be judged of, not by number, but by weight," as Cicero speaks upon another occasion (*De Officiis*). Therefore I cannot, without a degree of indignation, find a sort of writers pleasing themselves with having discovered some uncivilized nations, which have little or no knowledge of the

Deity, etc., and then applying their observations to the service of atheism. As if ignorance could prove anything, or alter its nature by being general! ↵

152. Aristotle's known rule is Ἔνδοξα, τὰ δοκοῦντα πᾶσιν, ἢ τοῖς πλείστοις, ἢ τοῖς σοφοῖς, καὶ τούτοις, ἢ τοῖς πᾶσιν, ἢ τοῖς πλείστοις, ἢ τοῖς μάλιστα γνωρίμοις καὶ ἐνδόξοις: "Those things are probable, which seem so to all men, or to most men, or to wise men: or which seem so to such as these, viz. to all, or to a great many, or to the most knowing and those of the best reputation." (*Topics*.) But it is not applicable to all cases. ↵

153. Δοκεῖ μοι χρῆναι παρ αὐτῶν [πρεσβυτῶν] πυνθάνεσθαι, ὥσπερ τινὰ ὁδὸν προεληλυθότων, ἣν καὶ ἡμᾶς ἴσως δεήσει πορεύεσθαι, ποία τίς ἐστι: "It seems best to enquire of old men, who have gone over the way that you are to go, what sort of a way it is." (Plato, *Republic*.) ↵

154. When Sophocles, now grown old, was asked, Πῶς ἔχεις πρὸς τ' ἀφροδίσια, "What relish he had of women," he answered, Εὐφήμει, ὦ ἄνθρωπε ἀσμενέστατα μέν τοι αὐτὸ ἀπέφυγον, ὥσπερ λυττῶντά τινα καὶ ἄγριον δεσπότην ἀποφυγών.... παντάπασι γὰρ τῶν γε τοιούτων ἐν τῷ γήρᾳ πολλὴ εἰρήνη γίγνεται καὶ ἐλευθερία: "Be quiet, Sir. I flee from them as gladly as I would run away from a mad or a cruel master.... there is great ease and freedom from all such things when a man is grown old." (Plato, *Republic*, et al.) ↵

155. Prerequisites. (Editor's note.) ↵

156. Ἐν βραχεῖ σφυρήλατον νοῦν περιεχούτα: "That contains solid sense in a small compass." (Plutarch, *De Garrulitate*.) ↵

157. *Sicut* ἀμαθία μὲν θράσος, λογισμὸς δὲ ὄκνον φέρει (è Thucydides) *ita recta ingenia debilitat verecundia, perversa confirmat audacia*: "As ignorance carries impudence along with it (out of Thucydides's *History of the Peloponnesian War*) and reputation makes men lazy; so modesty weakens great geniuses, and impatience confirms the obstinate." (Pliny, the younger, *Epistles*.) ↵

158. Ὅταν τι βουλόμεθα ἀκριβὲς νοῆσαι, εἰς ἐρημίαν ἀποδιδράσκομεν, τὰς ὄψεις, τὰ ὦτα ἐπιφράττομεν, ἀποταττόμεθα ταῖς αἰσθήσεσι: "When we would consider a thing very exactly, we retire into some private place, we wink our eyes, and stop our ears, and renounce all our bodily senses." (Philo Judaeus, *Legum Allegoriæ*.) ↵

159. *Aliis nullus est deorum respectus, aliis pudendus*: "Some do not worship the Gods at all, and others do it in a shameful manner." (Pliny the Elder, *Natural History*.) The former part of this observation is in truth the effect of the latter. ↵

160. *Pudet dicere frequentiam salutandi, etc.*: "I am ashamed to relate what sort of visits they make to each other, etc." (Jerome, *Epistles*.) ↩

161. Τὰ χρηστ' ἐπιστάμεθα, καὶ γιγνώσκομεν, Οὐκ ἐκπονοῦμεν δ' οἱ μὲν ἀργίας ὕπο, κτλ.: "We know and understand what is good, but we do not labor after it; some out of laziness, etc." (Euripides, *Hippolytus*.) ↩

162. פאת, "fate" in Arabic is "to die": and from hence the word *fatum*, "fate," seems to come (as many Latin words do, from that and other Eastern languages), death, if anything, being fatal and necessary. Yet, it does not follow that therefore the time or manner of dying is unmoveably fixed. Οὐ πάντα καθαρῶς οὐδὲ διαρρήδην ἡ εἱμαρμένη περιέχει, ἀλλ᾽ ὅσα καθόλου: "Fate does not contain in it all things clearly and distinctly, but only general things." (Plutarch, *Moralia*.) Chrysippus, in Aulus Gellus, seems to explain himself much after the same manner. The ancients moreover seem many times to make fate conditional. *Similis si cura fuisset, Nec pater omnipotens Trojam, nec fata vetabant Stare, etc.*: "If the same care had been taken, neither Jupiter nor fate would have hindered Troy from standing at this time, etc. (Virgil, *Aeneid*.) ↩

163. What the Pharisees say, according to Josephus, seems to be right. Οἱ μὲν οὖν Φαρισαῖοι τινὰ καὶ οὐ πάντα τῆς εἱμαρμένης εἶναι λέγουσιν ἔργον, τινὰ δ᾽ ἐφ᾽ ἑαυτοῖς ὑπάρχειν, συμβαίνειν τε καὶ οὐ γίνεσθαι: "The Pharisees say some things, but not all, are the work of fate, for some are in our own power, and some may by accident not come to pass." (*Antiquities of the Jews*.) Rabbi Albo, in relation to human actions (and the consequent events), explains this opinion thus: מקצתן בחיריות ומקצתן מכרחות ומקצתן מעודבות מן ההכרח והבחירה וכו': "Some of them are perfectly free, some of them are forced, and some of them have a mixture of choice and force." (*Sefer ha-Ikkarim* IV, 5.) But for men to charge their own faults upon fate or fortune has been an old practice: ἐθελοκακήσαντας... ἐπὶ τὴν κοινὴν ἐκείνην ἀπολογίαν, κτλ.: "voluntary evildoers... have recourse to that common apology." (Lucian, *Apologia*.) ↩

164. *Dimidium dacti, qui cœpit, habet. Sapere aude*: "He that has made a good beginning, has half finished his work: take courage then enough to be wise." (Horace, *Epistles*.) Aristotle goes further than that old adagial saying (ἀρχὴ ἥμισυ παντός: "The beginning is half the work"). His words are, Δοκεῖ πλεῖον ἢ τὸ ἥμισυ τοῦ παντὸς εἶναι ἡ ἀρχή: "The beginning is more than half the whole business." (*Nicomachean Ethics*.) ↩

165. Οὐδὲν γὰρ οὕτω κακῶς συντέτακται τῶν ψυχὴν ἐχόντων, ὥστ᾽ ἀβουλοῦντος αὐτοῦ προϊέναι πόδας ἢ φθέγγεσθαι γλῶτταν κτλ.: "No living creatures are so badly constituted, as that their feet will move, and their tongues speak, whether they will or no." (Plutarch, *De Communibus Notitiis Adversus Stoicos*.) That in Tibullus, *Cùm bene juravi, pes tamen ipso redit*: "Though I had directly sworn to the contrary, yet my feet would come back again," is a little poetic sally. (*Elegies*.) ↩

166. Ὅλως δὲ πᾶσα ἀργία καὶ τῆς τυχούσης πράξεώς ἐστιν εὐμαρεστέρα · οἷον, Οὐ φονεύσεις, οὐ μοιχεύσεις, κτλ.: "In general, the forbearing to do a thing is very easy: as thou shalt not kill, thou shalt not commit adultery." (Basil of Caesarea, *Homily on Psalm 1*.) ↩

167. Z + Y + X, that is, Z, Y, and X added together. ↩

168. One might with the Στασιῶται, "stationary philosophers," (so called by Aristotle, in Sextus Empiricus, in opposition to those philosophers who maintained that nothing continued fixed, but everything was in motion) as well deny that there is any such thing as motion, as say there is motion without a mover; or, which is the same, a First mover. ↩

169. Ἡρῶτον μεταβάλλον: "Something that first emits any alteration to be made in a thing." (Plato.) Ἀρχὴ κινήσεως ἁπάσης: "The principle of all motion." (Plato.) Πρῶτον κινοῦν: "The First mover." (Aristotle.) ↩

170. The greatest men among the ancients denied the possibility of such an ascent. Οὔτε γὰρ τόδ' ἐκ τοῦδε δυνατὸν ἰέναι εἰς ἄπειρον: "it is impossible for one thing to proceed from another and so on forever." If there could be such a process, then all the parts of it but the last would be μέσα, "intermediate ones"; and then εἴπερ μηδέν ἐστι τὸ πρῶτον, ὅλως αἴτιον οὐδέν ἐστι, κτλ.: "if there be no first, there can be no cause at all." (Aristotle, *Metaphysics*.) To suppose one thing moved by another, this by another, and so on ἐπ' ἄπειον, "infinitely," is to suppose ὅπερ ἐστὶν ἀδύνατον· οὐδὲν γὰρ οὕτως οὔτε κινοῦν ἔσται οὔτε κινούμενον, μὴ οὔσης ἀρχῆς τῆς κινούσης: "a thing that is impossible; for nothing can either move or be moved in this manner, without any beginning of motion." (Simplicius, *On Aristotle's On The Heavens*.) Not only those Arabian philosophers called מדברים (Hebrew) אלמחכלמון (Arabic), "the rational" (a sect who maintained that the world was eternal), but many of the elder Jews have agreed with the Greeks in this matter, and added arguments of their own. Of the former see *The Guide for the Perplexed* I (Maimonides) et. al. and particularly *Sefer Ha-Kuzari* V (Jehudah Ha-Levi): where their first argument seems to be strong (and much the same with the fourth in *Emunoth ve-Deoth* I, Saadya Gaon) אם היה חולף אין לו ראשית הנה האישים הנמצאים בזמן החולף עד העת הזאת אין תכלית להם ומה שאין לו תכלית לא יצא אל הפועל: "If there be any succession which has no beginning, then the number of those men, who existed during that whole succession down to the present time, must be infinite, and that which is infinite cannot be the effect of any other thing." For though, as Joseph Moscato observes, these reasonings of the Medabberim לא לרצון היו לפניו /המורה/, "rational philosophers, were not agreeable to him" (*Kol Jehudah*); yet most certainly, let the series of causes and effects be what it will, it is just as long downward as upward; and if they are infinite and inexhaustible one way, they must be so the other too: and then what Saadya Gaon says, takes place אם לא תגיע ההויה

אלינו נהיה וכו: "If we had no beginning, we could not now exist." There is another argument of this kind in [Pseudo-]Justin Martyr, which deserves notice, what stress soever may be laid upon it. Εἰ τὸ μέλλον μέρος τοῦ χρόνου, οὔπω ἐστίν· ἦν δὲ καὶ τὸ γελονὸς μέρος τοῦ χρόνου πρὸ τοῦ γενέσθαι μέλλον· ἦν ἄρα ὅτε οὐκ ἦν τὸ γεγονὸς μέρος τοῦ χρόνου: "If the future part of time, says he, has no existence, and the part of time that is past was future before it was present, then there was a time when that part of time which is past had no existence." (*Confutatio Dogmatum Quorundam Asistotelicorum.*) ↩

171. Aristotle himself, who asserts the eternity of motion, asserts also the necessity of a first and eternal mover. ↩

172. Σειρὴν χρυσείην ἐξ οὐρανόθεν: "A golden chain hanging down from heaven…" (Homer, *Iliad.*) *Aurea de cœlo… funis*: "a golden rope reaching down from heaven" is mentioned too by Lucretius. (*De Rerum Natura.*) ↩

173. אי אפשר שישתלשל ענין מעלה ועלול אל בלתי תכלית: "It is impossible that causes and effects can be connected with each other without end." (Joseph Albo, *Sefer ha-Ikkarim* II, 11.) Where more may be seen of this השתלשלות, "concatenation," out of Ibn Sinai, Maimonides, etc. ↩

174. The chain must be fastened περὶ ῥίον Οὐλύμποιο: "to the top of Olympus." *Invenietur pressius intuenti à summo Deo usque ad ultimam rerum fæcem… connexio: et hæc est Homeri catena aurea, quam pendere de cœlo in terras Deum jussisse commemorat*: "Whoever considers the thing closely (says Macrobius in his *Commentary on Somnium Scipionis*) will see that there is a connection of things from the supreme God to the lowest dregs that are… : and this is Homer's golden chain, which he tells you God commanded to hang down from heaven to the earth." This matter might be illustrated by other similitudes (even שלשלת הקבלה, "the chain of the Kabbalah," might serve for one): but I shall set down but one more: and in that indeed the motion is inverted, but the thing is the same taken either way. It occurs in *Hobot Ha-Lebabot* I, and afterward in *Reshit Hokmah*. Suppose a row of blind men, of which the last laid his hand upon the shoulder of the man next before him, he on the shoulder of the next before him, and so on till the foremost grew to be quite out of sight; and somebody asking what guide this string of blind men had at the head of them, it should be answered that they had no guide, nor any head, but one held by another, and so went on, *ad infinitum*, would any rational creature accept this for a just answer? Is it not to say that infinite blindness (or blindness, if it be infinite) supplies the place of sight, or of a guide? ↩

175. So Aristotle says of the First Mover, Οὐκ ἐνδέχεται ἄλλως ἔχειν ἐξ ἀνάγκης ἐστι, κτλ.: "It is impossible for it to be otherwise; it is necessary." (*Metaphysics.*) And after him

the Arabic philosophers, Maimonides, Albo, among others teach all that God exists necessarily: מן השקר העדרו: "To suppose him not to be implies a falsity;" or "He cannot be supposed not to be." This seems to be the import of that name by which God calls himself, in Moses's history: אהיה אשר אהיה, "I am that I am;" or in one word, אהיה, "I will be;" which, in the mouth of one who speaks of Him in the third person, is יחיה or יהוה, "He will be." So Philo explains it: Εἶναι πέφυκα: "Existence belongs to his very nature." So Abravanel: אני אהיה בעבור שאהיה כי אין מציאותי תלוי בזולתי אלא בעצמי: "I am, because I am; for my existence does not depend upon anything without me, but is from myself," adding moreover that it showed God to be, not like other beings, איפשרי המציאות: "a being that might or might not have existed," but מחויב המציאות מצד עצמו: "whose existence flows necessarily from himself," a *Necessary being*. And so Levi ben Gershom, יורה זה השם שהוא הנמצא אשר ימצא מעצמותו: "The very name (of God) shows this, for it signifies a being that exists of itself, or from its own nature." I omit others who write after the same manner. There have been even Heathens who seemed to think that some such name as this belonged to the Deity, and for the same reason. For as אהוה: *Eheveh*, "I shall be," and thence יהוה: *Jehovah*, "He shall be," are used above, so Plutarch says that in addressing to Him the second person Εἶ (תהיה or תהוה—*Tehejeh* or *Teheveh*) "Thou shalt be," is αὐτοτελὴς τοῦ Θεοῦ προσαγόρευσις καὶ προσφώνησις, "the most complete appellation or title of God," and that by this compellation we give him ἀληθῆ καὶ ἀψευδῆ καὶ μόνην μόνῳ προσήκουσαν τὴν τοῦ εἶναι προσαγόρευσιν. Ἡμῖν μὲν γὰρ ὄντως τοῦ εἶναι μέτεστιν οὐδέν: "the true, the certain, and the only title that is peculiar to the self-existent being; for self-existence does not belong to any of us." (Plutarch, *Moralia*.) It is τὸ ἀίδιον καὶ ἀγενητὸν καὶ ἄφθαρτον: "that which is eternal, which never had any beginning, and which is incorruptible," that is, ὄντως ὄν, "the being that truly exists." ↵

176. Something must be מחויב המציאות, "necessarily existent," otherwise לא יהיה דבר נמצא כלל, "there could be no beings at all;" everything cannot be אפשר מציאות: "precarious or such as might not have existed, etc." (*The Guide for the Perplexed* et. al.) ↵

177. This needs no demonstration. But there is a very old one in *Emunoth ve-Deoth* and after in *Sefer Hobot Ha-Lebabot*: עושה את עצמו אל ימלט מאחד משני דברים שעשה את עצמו קודם היותו או אחר היותו ושניהם אי אפשר וכ׳: "He, who makes himself, must be said to do one of these two things, viz. either to have made himself before he existed, or else to have made himself after he existed, either of which is impossible." ↵

178. What relation or analogy there is between time (a flux of moments) and eternal (unchangeable) existence, how any being should not be older now than he was 5,000 years ago, etc., are speculations attended with insuperable difficulties. Nor are they at all cleared by that of Timæus in Plato: Ὡς ποτ᾽ ἀΐδιον παράδειγμα τὸν ἰδανικὸν κόσμον ὅδε ὠρανὸς ἐγεννάθη, οὕτως ὡς πρὸς παράδειγμα τὸν αἰῶνα ὅδε χρόνος σὺν κόσμῳ

ἐδαμιουργήθη: "As the heavens were formerly made according to the eternal pattern of the world in the intellectual mind, so time was made with this world according to the pattern of an age;" or that in Philo: Αἰὼν ἀναγράφεται τοῦ νοητοῦ βίος κόσμου, ὡς αἰσθητοῦ χρόνος: "An age is described to be the length of the intellectual world, as time is the length of the visible world." Many philosophers therefore have thought themselves obliged to deny that God exists in time. Τὸ, τ' ἦν, τὸ, τ' ἔσται, χρόνου γεγονότος εἴδη, φέροντες λανθάνομεν ἐπὶ τὴν ἀίδιον οὐσίαν οὐκ ὀρθῶς, κτλ.: "Past and future are parts of that time which is made (with the world), and it is very wrong to apply these to an eternal being." (Plato.) Ἔστιν ὁ Θεός, χρὴ φάναι, καὶ ἔστι κατ' οὐδένα χρόνον ἀλλὰ κατὰ τὸν αἰῶνα τὸν ἀκίνητον, καὶ ἄχρονον καὶ ἀνέγκλιτον, καὶ οὗ πρότερον, οὐδέν ἐστιν, οὐδ' ὕστερον οὐδὲ νεώτερον · ἀλλ' εἷς ὢν ἑνὶ τῷ νῦν τὸ ἀεὶ πεπλήρωκε, κτλ.: "We must allow that God exists, though not in any time, but in a duration that has no succession, that is eternal and invariable, before which there was nothing, nor will there be any after or later than it; and that he is a single being who fills all eternity as if it were a single moment." (Plutarch.) השם יתעלה אין יחם בינו ובין הזמן וכו': "That name (Jehovah) shall be exalted; there is no proportion betwixt it and the present time." (Maimonides, *The Guide for the Perplexed* I, 52.) אינו מצוי בזמן: "He (God) does not exist in time." (Maimonides, *The Guide for the Perplexed.*) Joseph Albo has a whole chapter to show שה"י אינו נופל תחת הזמן: "that he, whose name is blessed, cannot be compared (as to his duration) with the time that now is." But then he owns that their Rabbis do not mean הזמן בשלוח, "time in general," or זמן סתם, "mere duration," or that בלתי נספר ומשוער והוא המשך שהיה קודם מציאות הגלגל וכו': "time which cannot be reckoned, and which is duration itself, and was before the world was;" but הזמן המשוער בתנועת הגלגל נקרא סדר זמנים לא זמן בשלוח וכו', "that time which is reckoned by the motion of the world, and is called the order or succession of time, and not absolute time." (*Sefer ha-Ikkarim*, II, 18.) In short, they reckon (to use Gedalyah ben Solomon Lipschütz's words in *Ez Shatul*) שזמן האמתי הוא נברא והמשך אינו קרוי זמן: "that time, properly so called, is created, and that duration is not called time." And so, what they say does not include all the present difficulty; "time," in their use of the word, being confined to the duration of this world, which according to them is new. Yet see *Sefer ha-Ikkarim* II, 19. הש"י א"א שיאמר עליו שיש לו יותר זמן היום ממה שהיה לו בימי דויד וממה שהיה לו כשברא העולם: "Blessed be that name (Jehovah), it is not possible to affirm, concerning him, that he is older today than he was in the days of David, or than he was when he first created this world." (Joseph Albo, *Sefer ha-Ikkarim* II, 19.) ↩

179. Οἶδα μὲν πολλὰ οὐκ ἐπίσταμενος δὲ αὐτῶν τὸν τρόπον.… ὅτι ἄναρχός ἐστιν [ὁ Θεός], καὶ ἀγέννητος, καὶ ἀΐδιος, οἶδα · τὸ δὲ πῶς οὐκ οἶδα: "There are a great many things that I understand, without knowing the particular manner how they are so.… I know that God is without beginning and unbegotten, but I know not the manner how he is so." So Chrysostom, *De Incomprehensibili Dei Natura.* ↩

180. Simonides had good reason still to double upon Hiero the number of days allowed for answering that question, *Quid, aut quale sit Deus?* "What or what sort of a being is God?" (in Cicero, *De Natura Deorum.*) ↵

181. *Nec viget quidquam simile aut secundum*: "Nor is there any being in the world like or anything near to him." (Horace, *Odes.*) ↵

182. In *The Guide for the Perplexed* (I, 57) Maimonides, having proved that there must be some Being who exists necessarily, or whose existence is necessary בבחינת עצמו "if we examine into his nature," proceeds from this necessity of existence to derive incorporeity, absolute simplicity, perfection, and particularly unity, המחויב המציאות אי אפשר בו השניות כלל לא דומה ולא הפך וכו: "It is impossible that the number two can be applied to that which exists necessarily; there is nothing that can be compared to it, nor no reverse of it." ↵

183. Therefore, by Plato He is called ὁ εἷς: "the One." ↵

184. *Deus, si perfectus est,… ut esse debet, non potest esse nisi unus, ut in eo sint omnia*: "God, if He is a perfect being,… as He must be, can be but One, that all things may be in Him." If there could be more Gods than one, *tantum singulis deerit, quantum in cæteris fuerit*: "everyone would want what the other had." (Lactantius, *Divine Institutes.*) ↵

185. As light and darkness are. Δύο γὰρ ἐξισάζοντα ἀλλήλοις κατ᾽ ἐναντίωσιν, φθαρτικὰ ἔσται πάντως τῆς ἀλλήλων συστάσεως: "For two things that are equal, and directly contrary, destroy each other entirely." (St. Basil, *Hexaemeron.*) There can be no such law between them, as is said to be among the Heathen deities. Θεοῖσι δ᾽ ὧδ᾽ ἔχει νόμος. Οὐδεὶς ἀπαντᾶν βούλεται προθυμίᾳ Τῇ τοῦ θέλοντος, κτλ.: "The law amongst the Gods is this, that when any one of them would have anything, no other God contradicts what he desires." (Euripides, *Hippolytus.*) ↵

186. Ἀπόλωλεν ἡ ἀλήθει᾽, ἐπεὶ σὺ δυστυχεῖς: "So that, because things go ill with you, there must be an end of truth." (Euripides, *The Phoenician Women.*) ↵

187. Ψυχὴν ἔχεις αὐτεξούσιον᾽… οὐ γὰρ κατὰ γένεσιν ἁμαρτάνεις, οὔτε κατὰ τύχην πορνεύεις, κτλ.: "You have a soul that is absolutely free:… you were not created a sinner, nor do you commit whoredom by chance." (Cyril of Jerusalem, *Catecheses Ad Illuminandos.*) ↵

188. Ὧν αὐτὸς εἶ κύριος, τούτων τὰς ἀρχὰς μὴ ζητήσῃς ἑτέρωθεν: "Do not seek without you for the causes of the things which are entirely in your own power." (St. Basil, *Hexaemeron.*) ↵

189. "Must God extinguish sun, moon, and stars, because some people worship them?" (*Mishnah*, Abodah zarah IV, 7.) Αὐτοῦ τοῦ ἑλομένου αἰτία, Θεὸς ἀναίτιος: "The fault lies in him who chooses to do the thing; God is not to blame." (Maximus Tyrius, *Dissertations*.) ↩

190. Ἡ δίψα μὲν σώματι παρασκευάζει ἡδονὴν ποτοῦ, κτλ.: "It is thirst that makes the pleasure of drinking agreeable to the body." (Maximus Tyrius, *Dissertations*.) This observation might be extended a great way. If there was, e.g., no such thing as poverty, there could be no riches, or no great benefit by them; there would be scarce any arts or sciences, etc. Ἂν γὰρ ἀνέλῃς τὴν πενίαν, τοῦ βίου τὴν σύστασιν ἀνεῖλες ἅπασαν, κτλ.: "Take away poverty, and you destroy the whole state of life." (St. Chrysostom, *De Anna*.) ↩

191. Τὰ μέρη πρὸς αὐτὸ τὸ ὅλον δεῖ σκοπεῖν, εἰ σύμφωνα καὶ ἁρμόττοντα ἐκείνῳ: "The parts must be compared with the whole, if we would see whether they are agreeable and fitted thereto," with more to this purpose. (Plotinus, *Enneads*.) ↩

192. See Maimonides, *The Guide for the Perplexed* III, 12. ↩

193. Πολυειδὴς ἡ τοῦ Θεοῦ ἰατρική: "God has provided several sorts of physic." (Simplicius.) ↩

194. Κακία βλάστημα τῆς ὕλης: "Evil is a bud that springs from matter." (Plutarch, *Moralia*.) ↩

195. To that question—Why are we not so made ὥστε μηδὲ βουλομένοις ἡμῖν ὑπάρχειν τὸ ἁμαρτάνειν, "as to be incapable of committing sin?"—St. Basil answers: Because ἀρετὴ ἐκ προαιρέσεως καὶ οὐκ ἐξ ἀνάγκης γίνεται: "virtue is from our own choice, and not from any necessity." And he who blames the Deity because we are not impeccable, οὐδὲν ἕτερον ἢ τὴν ἄλογον φύσιν τῆς λογικῆς προτιμᾷ, καὶ τὴν ἀκίνητον καὶ ἀνόρμητον τῆς προαιρετικῆς καὶ ἐμπράκτου, "does the very same thing as he does, who prefers a creature not endowed with reason to one that is, and a creature that has not the power of moving itself, and is void of all appetites, to a free agent and one that can choose what he will do." (*Homilia Quod Deus Non Est Auctor Malorum*.) ↩

196. Ἀθληταὶ ἀρετῆς: "Champions for virtue," as Philo Judaeus. ↩

197. In Chrysostom's style, ἀρετῆς ἐπιμελεῖσθαι, καὶ καθάπερ ἐν παλαίστρᾳ ἐπὶ τοῦ παρόντος βίου ἀγωνίζεσθαι, ἵνα μετὰ τὸ λυθῆναι τὸ θέατρον λαμπρὸν ἀναδήσασθαι δυνηθῶμεν τὸν στέφανον: "To be industrious after virtue, and to strive in this present life, as in a place where exercises are to be performed; that, when we go off the stage, we may be crowned with a crown of glory." (*Homilies on Genesis*.) ↩

198. Εἰ σῶμά ἐστι, φύσις δὲ σώματος μεριζομένη εἰς πλείω, ἕκαστον τῶν μὴ τὸ αὐτὸ εἶναι (f. ἔσται) τῷ ὅλῳ: "If it be made of matter, and if it be the property of matter to be divided into a multitude of parts, every single part will not be the same as the whole," says Plotinus, even of the soul. (*Enneads.*) ↩

199. Δέδεικται δὲ καὶ ὅτι μέγεθος οὐδὲν ἐνδέχεται ἔχειν ταύτην οὐσίαν ἀλλὰ ἀμερὴς καὶ ἀδιαίρετός ἐστιν: "It has been shown before that nobody can be of this nature; it must be something indivisible, and whose parts cannot be separated from each other." (Aristotle, *Metaphysics.*) ↩

200. They, who call God מקום, "space," do it לפי שהוא מקום הכל ואין הכל מקומו, "because He is the space in which the whole universe is contained, and not because the universe is the space in which He is contained." (Elijah Levita, *Tishbi.*) Or, as Phil. Aquin. from the ancients, הקב"ה מקום של עולם ואין עולמו מקימו: "The holy and blessed Being is the space in which the universe is contained, and not the universe the space in which He is contained." (Rashi, on Exodus 34:21.) Οὐ γὰρ περιέχεται ὁ Θεός], ἀλλὰ περιέχει τὸ πᾶν: "For He (God) is not comprehended in any thing, but He comprehends all things." (Philo Judaeus, *Legum Allegoriæ.*) By which ways of speaking (though there is a Kabbalistic reason assigned too) they intend chiefly to express his omnipresence and immensity. That, in Acts of the Apostles (17:28), seems to be of the same kind: Ἐν αὐτῷ γὰρ ζῶμεν, καὶ κινούμεθα, καὶ ἐσμεν: "In him we live, and move, and have our beings." ↩

201. Such things as these, how incongruous and wild soever they are, have been affirmed: that God is infinite duration, space, etc. What can be meant by that, Καλῶς ἂν λέγοιτο ὁ αἰὼν θεός: "God may be properly called eternity," in Plotinus (*Enneads*)? ↩

202. Were not they, who converse with books, accustomed to such trials, it would be shocking to find Balbus in Cicero asserting, *esse mundum deum*, "that the world was God;" and yet in another place, that it is *quasi communis deorum, atque hominum domus, aut urbs utrorumque*: "as it were the common house of the Gods and of men, or the city of both of them;" and *deorum, hominumque cause factus*: "was made for the sake of the Gods and of men;" in another, *providentia deorum mundum, et omnes mundi partes et initio constitutas esse, et omni tempore administrari*: "that the world, and all the parts of the world, were in the beginning made by the providence of the Gods, and were always governed by the same;" in another, *mundum ipsum naturâ administrari*: "that the world itself is governed by nature;" with other like inconsistences. (*De Natura Deorum.*) ↩

203. Ἄτοπον εἰ μία ἡ ἐμὴ /ψυχὴ/ καὶ ἡ ὁτιοῦν ἄλλου · ἐχρῆν γὰρ ἐμοῦ αἰσθανομένου καὶ ἄλλον αἰσθάνεσθαι... καὶ ὅλως ὁμοπαθεῖν ἡμᾶς τε πρὸς ἀλλήλους, καὶ πρὸς τὸ πᾶν: "It is absurd that my (soul) and the soul of any other person should be one and the same;

for then, it must needs be that when I perceived anything, he would perceive it also… and he, and I, and all the whole universe would be affected alike." (Plotinus, *Enneads.*) Here this author is clear, though at some other times very dark. ↩

204. *Cur quidquam ignoraret animus hominis, si esset Deus?* "If the soul of man were a God, how could it be ignorant of anything?" (Cicero, *De Natura Deorum.*) ↩

205. The system of Spinoza is so apparently false, and full of impieties and contradictions, that more needs not be said against it, though much might be. What Velleius says in Cicero (*De Natura Deorum*), is not only true, *Si mundus est deus… dei membra partim ardentia partim refrigerata dicenda sunt*, "that if the world be God… then the members of God may be said to be some of them hot, and some of them cold;" but if there is but one substance, one nature, one being, and this being is God, then all the follies, madnesses, wickednesses that are in the world, are in God; then all things done and suffered are both done and suffered by Him; He is both cause and effect; He both wills and nills, affirms and denies, loves and hates the same things at the same time, etc. That such gross Atheism as this should ever be fashionable! Atheism: for certainly when we inquire whether there is a God, we do not inquire whether we ourselves, and all other things which are visible about us, do exist: something different from them must be intended. Therefore to say there is no God different from them, is to say there is no God at all. ↩

206. What Censorinus charges upon many great men (but upon some of them surely unjustly) is to me unintelligible. He says they believed *semper homines fuisse, etc.*, "mankind always existed, etc.," and then, *Itaque et omnium, quæ in sempiterno isto mundo semper fuerunt, futuraque sunt, aiunt principium fuisse nullum; sed orbem esse quemdam generantium, nascentiumque, in quo uniuscujusque geniti initium simul et finis esse videatur*: "They say that there was no beginning of all those things, which have existed in that world which was from eternity, but that there is a certain round of things generated and springing up, which round seems to be both the beginning and the end of everything that is produced." (*De Die Natali.*) ↩

207. So what we call attraction and aversion (centripetal and centrifugal forces) seem to have been called by Empedocles: φιλία ᾗ συγκρίνεται [τὰ στοιχεῖα], καὶ νεῖκος ᾧ διακρίνεται: "a kind of friendship by which they (the elements) are united together, and a sort of discord whereby they are separated from each other." (Diogenes Laërtius *Life of Empedocles*, *Life of Arist.*, Cicero, et al.) ↩

208. So far is that from being true, *Nequaquam… divinitus esse creatam Naturam mundi, quæ tantâ est prædita culpâ*: "That the world could never be created by a divine Being, there are so many faults in it." (Lucretius, *De Rerum Natura.*) Men rashly (impiously) censure what they do not understand. Like that king of Castile who fancied himself able

to have contrived a better system of the world, because he knew not what the true system is, but took it to be as ascribed to him by Rabbi Isaac ibn Sid and other astronomers of those times. ↵

209. Since they have, or may have, great effects upon the several parts of the solar system, one may speak thus without falling into the superstition of the multitude, or meaning what is intended by that, *Nunquam cœlo spectatum impune cometen*: "A comet is never seen in the heavens but for some punishment"; (in Claudian, *De Bello Gothico*) or the like. ↵

210. *Finitus, et infinito similis*: "Finite, but very near to infinite." (Pliny the Elder, *Natural History*.) ↵

211. Ποικίλη θαυματουργία: "Variety of surprising things." (Plotinus, *Enneads*.) ↵

212. If anyone, sitting upon mount Ida, had seen the Greek army coming on in proper order (μετὰ πολλοῦ κόσμου καὶ τάξεως τοῖς πεδίοις προσιοῦσαν: "marching over the fields in rank and file"), he ought most certainly, nowithstanding what Sextus Empiricus says, to have concluded that there was some commander under whose conduct they moved. (*Against the Physicists*.) ↵

213. Τίς ὁ ἁρμόζων τὴν μάχαιραν πρὸς τὸ κολεὸν, καὶ τὸ κολεὸν πρὸς τὴν μάχαιραν, κτλ.: "Who was it that fitted the sword to the scabbard, and the scabbard to the sword?" (Arrian, *Discourses of Epictetus*.) Even such a thing as this does not come by accident. ↵

214. *Hoc qui existimat fieri potuisse, non intelligo cur non idem putet, si innumerabiles unius et viginti formæ literarum, ... aliquè conjiciantur, posse ex his in terram excussis annales Ennij, ut deinceps legi possint, effici: quod nescio anne in uno quidem versu possit tantum valere fortuna*: "He who thinks that this is possible to be, I don't see but he may as well think that an infinite number of alphabets, ... cast anywhere upon the ground at a venture, might come up the annals of Ennius, so as anyone might read them; whereas I question whether chance is capable of producing one verse of them." (Cicero, *De Natura Deorum*.) But alas, what are Ennius's annals to such a work as the world is! ↵

215. He was πολυγραφώτατος, πάντας ὑπερβαλλόμενος πλήθει βιβλίων: "a great writer, and exceeded all others in the quantity of books." (Diogenes Laërtius, *Life of Epicurus*.) But that part of his physics is here meant, in which he treated of the origin of the world, or rather of infinite worlds, which makes his thought the grosser still. For infinite worlds require infinite chances infinitely repeated. ↵

216. *Series implexa causarum*: "A series of causes connected with each other." (Seneca, *De*

Beneficiis.) ↵

217. Seneca says himself that, in this series, God is *prima omnium causa, ex quâ cæteræ pendent,* "the first of all the causes, and upon him the rest depend." (*De Beneficiis.*) Indeed, it is many times difficult to find out what the ancients meant by "fate." Sometimes it seems to follow the motions of the heavenly bodies and their aspects. Of this kind of fate is that passage in Suetonius to be understood, where he says that Tiberius was *addictus mathematicæ, persuasionisque plenus cuncta fato agi*: "given to mathematics, and fully persuaded that all things were governed by fate." (*Lives of the Caesars.*) Sometimes it is confounded with "fortune." So in Lucian we find τὴν τύχην πράξουσαν τὰ μεμοιραμένα, καὶ ἃ ἐξ ἀρχῆς ἑκάστῳ ἐπεκλώσθη: "fortune doing the things which are determined by fate and destined to everyone from the beginning." (*The Parliament of the Gods.*) And sometimes it is the same with God: as when the Stoics say, ἕν τε εἶναι θεὸν καὶ νοῦν καὶ εἱμαρμένην καὶ Δία: "God, and mind, and fate, and Jupiter, are all the same." (In Diogenes Laërtius's *Life of Zeno* and the like elsewhere.) ↵

218. As when Strato of Lampsacus, according to Cicero, *docet omnia esse effecta naturâ*: "teaches that all things are the effects of nature." (*Academica.*) ↵

219. *Vis et natura justitiæ*: "The force and nature of justice." (Cicero, *Academica.*) ↵

220. Almost as if it stood for *nata*, or *res natæ*; "all things that are produced." (So *fœtura* seems to be put sometimes for *fœtus*: "the child in the womb.") *Sunt, qui omnia naturæ nomine appellent;... corpora, et inane, quæque his accidant*: "Some persons use the word 'nature' for everything;... bodies and space, and all the properties of these." (Cicero, *De Natura Deorum.*) ↵

221. *Natura, inquit, hæc mihi præstat. Non intelligis te, cùm hoc dicis, mutare nomen Deo? Quid enim aliud est Natura, quàm Deus, et divina ratio, etc.*: "Nature, says he, gives me these things. Do you not see, when you say this, that you only put another name for God? For what else is nature, but God, and the divine reason, etc." (Seneca, *De Beneficiis.*) When it is said, *Necesse est mundum ipsum natura administrari*, "that the world must necessarily be governed by nature" (in Cicero, *De Natura Deorum*), what sense are those words capable of, if by "nature" be not really meant God? For it must be something different from the world, and something able to govern it. ↵

222. *Alii naturam censent esse vim quandam sine ratione, cientem motus in corporibus necessarios, etc.*: "Some think nature to be a certain power or force without reason, producing the necessary motions in bodies, etc." says Balbus in Cicero (*De Natura Deorum*). What can this *vis* ("power") be: *vis* by itself, without the mention of any subject in which it inheres, or of any cause from whence it proceeds? A soul of the

world, plastic nature, hylarchic principle, שכל פועל, "an understanding principle," and the like, are more intelligible than that. ↵

223. דע מאין באת ולאן אתה הולך וכו: "Search out from whence you came, and whither you are going." (*Mishnah*, Abot III, 1.) ↵

224. For I cannot think that anybody will now stand by that way of introducing men first into the world, which is mentioned by Diodorus Siculus but asserted by Lucretius (*De Rerum Natura*). *Ubi quæque loci regio opportuna dabatur, Crescebant uteri terræ radicibus apti, etc.*: "Where the country was proper for it, there grew wombs out of the earth, fixed to it by their roots, etc." ↵

225. What by Tertullian in one place is called *animæ ex Adam tradux*, "a soul derived from Adam," in another is *velut surculus quidam ex matrice Adam in propaginem deducta*, "as it were, a shoot derived from the womb of Adam, that the race might be continued," and equally unintelligible. Nor does he explain himself better, when he confesses there to be *duas species seminis, corporalem et anamalem (al. corporis semen et animæ)*, "two sorts of seed: corporeal and animal (or a seed of the soul, and another of the body)," or more fully, *semen animale ex animæ distillatione, sicut et virus illud, corporale semen, ex carnis defæcatione*, "an animal seed flowing from the soul, as the bodily seed does from the body." (*De Anima*.) ↵

226. According to the fore-cited author, the soul is derived from the father only, *et genitalibus fœminæ foveis commendata*, "delivered to the womb of the mother," and all souls from that of Adam. *Definimus animam, Dei flatu natam, ex una redundantem*: "We, says he, define the soul to spring from the breath of God, and all souls to proceed from one;" and in another place, *ex uno homine tota hæc animarum redundantia agitur*: "all the souls that are, come originally from one man." But this does not well consist with his principal argument for traduction, that children take after their parents. For besides what will here be said by and by, if there is a traduction of all men from one man, and traduction causes likeness, then every man must be like the first, and (consequently) every other. (Tertullian, *De Anima*.) ↵

227. *Unde, oro te, similitudine animæ quoque parentibus de ingeniis respondemus,… si non ex animæ femine educimur?* "Whence is it, I beseech you, says the same author, that we are so like our parents in the dispositions of our minds,… if we be not produced from the seed of the soul?" Then to confirm this, he argues like a father indeed, thus; *in illo ipso voluptatis ultimo æstu quo genitale virus expellitur, nonne aliquid de anima quoque sentimus exire?*: "Do we not in the act of generation perceive some part of our very souls to go out of us?" I am ashamed to transcribe more. (Tertullian, *De Anima*.) ↵

228. Therefore the said father makes the soul to be corporeal. ↵

229. This might seem to be favored by them who hold that all souls were created in the beginning (an opinion mentioned by Isaac Abravanel in *Nahalot Abot*, et al., often), did not the same authors derive the body מטפה סרוחה, "from a small seed," as may be seen in *Abot, et passim*. Particularly Rabbi David Kimhi says of man, נופו נברא מטיפת הזרע אשר תהפך לדם, ומשם יגדל מעט מעט עד שישתלמו איבריו: "That his body is produced out of a small seed, which is first converted into blood, and then increases by degrees, till all the members of it are complete." ↩

230. This account destroys that argument, upon which Censorinus says many of the old philosophers asserted the eternity of the world: *quod negent omnino posse reperiri, avesne ante, an ova generata sint; cùm et ovum sine ave, et avis sine ovo gigni non possit*: "Because they denied the possibility of finding out which is first generated, the birds or the eggs; because an egg cannot be produced without a bird, nor a bird without an egg." (*De Die Natali*.) This question was once much agitated in the world, as may be seen by Macrobius and Plutarch, who calls it, τὸ ἄπορον καὶ πολλὰ πράγματα τοῖς ζητητικοῖς παρέχον … πρόβλημα: "a problem that cannot be solved, and which put the curious to great difficulties." (*Moralia*.) ↩

231. This is as much as Epicurus had to say for his atoms, for they were only σώματα λόγῳ θεωρητά, κτλ.: "imaginary bodies." (Justin Martyr.) ↩

232. Οὐ γὰρ τῷ θεωρουμένῳ τὸ θεωρεῖν: "For the thing which is speculated upon, cannot speculate." (Plotinus, *Enneads*.) ↩

233. *Si nulla fuit genitalis origo terrai et cœli… Cur supra bellum Thebanum et funera Trojæ Non alias alii quoque res cecinere poctæ?*: "If the earth and the heavens never had any beginning,… how comes it to pass that the poets never celebrated any other matters before the wars of Thebes and the destruction of Troy?" (Lucretius, *De Rerum Natura*.) ↩

234. Πολλαὶ καὶ κατὰ πολλὰ φθοραὶ γεγόνασιν ἀνθρώπων, καὶ ἔσονται, πυρὶ μὲν καὶ ὕδατι μέγισται: "There has been great destruction made of mankind, many times and in many places, and will be so again; the greatest of them have been by fire and water." (Plato, *Timaeus*.) ↩

235. Τοὺς ἀγραμμάτους καὶ ἀμούσους: "Such as could not tell their letters, or distinguish one sound from another," as Plato speaks. (*Timaeus*.) ↩

236. For what has been said only in general, and presumptively, to serve a cause, signifies nothing: no more than that testimony in Arnobius, where he seems to allow that there have been universal conflagrations. *Quando mundus incensus in favillas et cineres dissolutus est? Non ante nos?* "When, says he, was the world so burned as to be reduced to dust and ashes? Has it not been so formerly?" (*Adversus Nationes*.) ↩

237. Propositions V and VI. ↵

238. If that, in Terence, had been (not a question, as it is in *The Eunuch*, but) an affirmation, *Ego homuncio hoc non facerem*, "I, poor mortal, would not have done such a thing," what a bitter reflection had it been upon the heathen deity? ↵

239. Λέγομεν ὃ μὴ ἔστιν· ὃ δέ ἐστιν, οὐ λέγομεν: "We affirm what He is not, but we do not affirm what He is." (Plotinus, *Enneads*.) ↵

240. אין דרך להשיגו אלא ממעשיו: "There is no way to know what sort of being He is, but by his works." (Maimonides, *The Guide for the Perplexed* III, 17.) ↵

241. Ungoverned. (Editor's note.) ↵

242. מקרני ראמים עד ביצי כנים: "From the horns of the unicorns to the feet of the lice," as the Jews speak. (*The Guide for the Perplexed*.) ↵

243. I shall not pretend here to meddle with particular cases relating to inanimate or irrational beings, such as are mentioned in *The Guide for the Perplexed* (a leaf's falling from a tree, a spider's catching a fly, etc.) and which are there said to be במקרה גמור, "by mere accident." Though it is hard to separate these, many times, from the cases of rational beings; as also to comprehend what מקרה גמור, "perfect accident," is. ↵

244. Hermaphroditic. (Editor's note.) ↵

245. Pliny in his chapter *De ordine naturæ in satis, etc.*, "concerning the course and order of nature in the growth of corn, etc." treats of trees in terms taken from animals. (*Natural History*.) ↵

246. Therefore if those Essenes in Josephus, who are said ἐπὶ μὲν Θεῷ καταλιπεῖν τὰ πάντα, "to leave all things to God," excluded human endeavors, they must be much in the wrong. ↵

247. *Ut siquis in domum aliquam, aut in gymnasium, aut in forum venerit, cùm videat omnium rerum rationem, modum, disciplinam, non possit ea sine causa fieri judicare, sed esse aliquem intelligat, qui præsit, et cui pareatur, etc.*: "In the same manner as if anyone should come into a house or place of public exercise, or into any court of justice, and *see* everything in exact order and according to strict discipline; such a one could not think that all those things were done without a cause, but he would immediately apprehend that there was somebody at the head, whose commands were obeyed, etc." (Cicero, *De Natura Deorum*.) ↵

248. Little things have, many times, unforeseen and great effects: et contra. The bare sight of a fig, shown in the senate-house at Rome, occasioned Carthage to be destroyed: *quod*

non Trebia, aut Trasymenus, non Cannæ busto insignes Romani nominis perficere potuere; non castra Punica ad tertium lapidem vallata, portæque Collinæ adequitans ipse Hannibal: "Which neither the river Po, nor the lake Trasymenus, nor the city of Canna, famous for the overthrow of almost the whole Roman nation, could do; no, nor the African camp intrenched for three miles round, nor Hannibal himself who ventured to the very gates of Rome." (Pliny the Elder, *Natural History*.) The whole story is thus related by the same author: Cato, being very solicitous that Carthage should be utterly destroyed, produced one day in the senate-house a ripe fig, which was brought from thence, and, showing it to the senators, asked them how long they thought it was since that fig was plucked off the tree? They all agreed that it was very fresh; upon which he told them that it was plucked at Carthage but three days before; so near, says he, is the enemy to our walls. And this was the occasion of the third Punic war, in which Carthage was utterly destroyed. ↩

249. While everyone pushes his own designs, they must interfere, and hinder one another. *Ad summum succedere honorem Certantes, iter infestum fecere viai*: "By striving to get to the highest dignity, they render the way very dangerous." (Lucretius, *De Rerum Natura*.) ↩

250. Or is it not more likely, πιπτούσης οἰκοδομίας, τὸν ὑποπεσόντα ἀποθανεῖν, ὁ ποιὸς ποτ᾽ ἂν ᾖ: "that when a house falls, he that it falls upon should be killed, what sort of a man soever he be (good or bad)," in Plotinus's words (*Enneads*)? ↩

251. Something more than this we meet with in *Targum Onkelos*'s paraphrase, where it is said that, upon Moses's prayer, (Exodus 9:33), מטרא דחוה נחית לא מטא על ארעא: "the rain, that was falling, did not reach to the earth." Which same place, Rashi eplains after the same manner; /מטר לא הגיע /ארצה. ואף אותן שהיו באויר לא הגיעו לארץ: "The rain came not to the earth, and also that of it, which was in the air, did not fall to the ground." (*Commentary on the Torah*.) ↩

252. In Lucian, τῶν πλεόντων ὁ μὲν βορέαν ηὔχετο ἐπιπνεῦσαι· ὁ δὲ, νότον· ὁ δὲ γεωργὸς ᾔτει ὑετόν· ὁ δὲ κναφεὺς, ἥλιον: "Some of the sailors pray for a north-wind, and some for a south-wind; the countryman wishes for wet weather, and the fuller for sun-shiny." (*Icaromenippus*.) ↩

253. Some have talked to this purpose. So Rabbi Albo says of some prophets and *hasidim*, "holy men," שישנו הטבע או ישתנה בעבורם: "that they can alter the course of nature, or it will be altered for them." (*Sefer ha-Ikkarim*.) So Rabbi Israel Aboab, that the good or evil which happens to a man in this world, by way of reward or punishment, אין זה רק במעשה הנם והוא נס נסתר יחשוב בו הרואה שהוא של עולם: "is not only by plain miracles, but also by obscure marks; as anyone may imagine, who sees the manner of the world." (*Menorat Ha-Maor* III.) So Abravanel היכולת האלהי הוא משנה הטבעים

בהשגחתו וכו׳: "It is that power of God which changes nature by his providence." And accordingly in *Seder Tefillah* we find this thanksgiving: מודים אנחנו... על נסיך שבכל יום עמנו: "praise thee... for thy wonders which we behold every day." ↩

254. What Seneca says of the Gods (in the heathen style), may be said of the true God. *Nota est illi operis sui series: omniumque illi rerum per manus suas iturarum scientia in aperto semper est; nobis ex abdito subit, etc.*: "Known unto him is the whole course of his works; the knowledge, of all those things which are to pass through his hands, is clear to him but obscure to us, etc." (*De Beneficiis.*) ↩

255. Ὁ γὰρ ζωοπλάστης θεὸς ἐπίσταται τὰ ἑαυτοῦ καλῶς δημιουργήματα: "God, who formed all living creatures, understands his own works thoroughly." (Philo Judaeus, *Legum Allegoriæ.*) ↩

256. *Ipsæ nostræ voluntates in causarum ordine sunt, qui certus est Deo, ejusque præscientia continetur, etc.*: "Our wills themselves may be looked upon as causes, the manner of which God certainly knows, and it is contained in his foreknowledge, etc." (St. Augustine, *The City of God.*) ↩

257. *Etsi quem exitum acies habitura sit, divinare nemo potest; tamen belli exitum video, etc.*: "Though nobody can tell what may happen to the army, yet I see what the event of the war will be, etc." And after, *quem ego tam video animo, quam ea, qua oculis cernimus*: "I see it as plainly, in my mind, as I can see anything with my eyes." (Cicero, *Letters to Friends.*) ↩

258. אין זה ידיעה ממין ידיעתנו: "His knowledge is not such a sort of a knowledge as ours is." It differs not ברב ובמעט לבד אבל במין הסציאה: "only in degree, but in kind." (Maimonides, *The Guide for the Perplexed* III, 20.) ↩

259. *Ignari, quid queat esse, Quid nequeat*: "Who are ignorant of what can be, and what cannot be," to use Lucretius's words more properly. (*De Rerum Natura.*) ↩

260. To attempt to comprehend the manner of God's knowing is the same as to endeavor שנהיה אנחנו הוא: "to become what He is." (Maimonides, *The Guide for the Perplexed* III, 21.) ↩

261. ידיעתה במה שיהיה לא יוציא הדבר האפשר מטבעו: "His knowledge of anything that is future does not produce the thing that is possible in nature." (Maimonides, *The Guide for the Perplexed* III, 20.) Much might be inserted upon this subject (out of Abravanel particularly) which I shall omit. ↩

262. *Sicut enim tu memoriâ tuâ non cogis facta esse quæ præterierunt; sic Deus præscientiâ suâ non cogit facienda quæ futura sunt*: "As we do not force the things that are past to

have been done, by our remembering them; so God does not force the things that are future to be done, by his foreknowing them." (St. Augustine, *De Libero Arbitrio*.) ↩

263. Things come to pass καὶ κατὰ φυσικὰς ἀκολουθίας καὶ κατὰ λόγον: "according to their natural course, and according to reason;" and even τὰ σμικρότερα δεῖ συντετάχθαι καὶ συνυφάνθαι νομίζειν: "the most minute things, we ought to think, are duly regulated and connected with each other." (Plotinus, *Enneads*.) That in Seneca looks something like this: *Hoc dico, fulmina non mitti a Jove, sed sic omnia disposita, ut ea etiam, quæ ab illo non fiunt, tamen sine ratione non fiant: qua illius est.… Nam etsi Jupiter illa nunc non facit, fecit ut fierent*: "I affirm this: that lightning does not come immediately from Jupiter himself, but everything is so ordered that even those things which are not done by Him are notwithstanding not done without reason, which reason is his.… For though Jupiter does not do these things at this time, yet He was the cause of their being done." (*Naturales Quaestiones*.) ↩

264. This seems to be what Eusebius means, when he says that Divine providence does (among other things) τοῖς εκτὸς συμβαίνουσι τὴν δέουσαν τάξιν ἀπονέμειν: "appoint a proper course even to those things which we call accidental." (*Church History*.) ↩

265. Τὴν γὰρ οὐδένειαν τὴν ἐμαυτοῦ μετρεῖν ἔμαθον: "For I have learned what a mere nothing I am," in Philo's words. (*Quis Rerum Divinarum Heres Sit*.) ↩

266. The case here put may perhaps supply an answer to that which is said in *Mishnah*, Berakhot IX, צועק לשעבר הרי זו תפלת שוא וכו׳: "It is a vain prayer, to cry out for what is already past." ↩

267. If Plato had not been born in the time of Socrates, in all probability he had not been what he was. And therefore, with Lactantius's favor, he might have reason to thank God, *quòd Atheniensis [natus esset], et quòd temporibus Socratis*: "that He was born at Athens, and in the days of Socrates." (*Divine Institutes*.) Just as Marcus Aurelius ascribes, gratefully, to the Gods τὸ γνῶναι· Ἀπολλώνιον, Ῥούστικον, Μάξιμον: "that he was acquainted with Apollonius Maximus (his tutor), Apollonius, and Rusticus." (*Meditations*.) ↩

268. Plato and the Stoics, in Pseudo-Plutarch, make fate to be συμπλοκὴν αἰτιῶν τεταγμένην, ἐν συμπλοκῇ καὶ τὸ παρ᾽ ἡμᾶς · ὥστε τὰ μὲν εἱμάρθαι, τὰ δ᾽ ἀνειμάρθαι: "a regular connection of causes, and those things which are in our power to belong to this connection. So that some things are decreed, and some things not." (*Placita Philosophorum*.) ↩

269. The Heathen were of this opinion, otherwise Homer could have had no opportunity of introducing their Deities as he does, Τῷ δ᾽ ἂρ ἐπὶ φρεσὶ θῆκε θεὰ γλαυκῶπις Ἀθήνη · Ἄλλά τις ἀθανάτων τρέψε φρένας: "Minerva put it into their minds. But some God

altered their minds" (Homer, *Iliad*), and the like often. Plutarch explains these passages thus: Οὐκ ἀναιροῦντα ποιεῖ [Ὅμηρος] τὸν θεόν, ἀλλὰ κινοῦντα τὴν προαίρεσιν · οὐδ' ὁρμὰς ἐνεργαζόμενον, ἀλλὰ φαντασίας ὁρμῶν ἀγωγούς: "[Homer] does not make God to destroy the will of man, but only to move him to will; nor does he produce the appetites themselves in men, but only causes such imaginations as are capable of producing them." And afterwards, the Gods are said to help men, τῆς ψυχῆς τὸ πρακτικὸν καὶ προαιρετικὸν ἀρχαῖς τισι καὶ φαντασίαις καὶ ἐπινοίαις ἐγείροντες ἢ τοὐναντίον ἀποστρέφοντες καὶ ἱστάντες: "by exciting the powers and faculties of the soul by some secret principles, or imaginations, or thoughts, or, on the contrary, by diverting or stopping them." (*Life of Coriolanus.*) ↩

270. Σφαλεὶς [ὁ μειρακίσκος] οὐκ οἶδ' ὅπως, ἐμοὶ μὲν τὸ φάρμακον, Πτοιοδώρῳ δὲ ἀφάρμακτον [κύλικα] ἐπέδωκα, says Callidemidas, who designed the poison for Ptœodorus, in Lucian of Samosata. (*Dialogues of the Dead.*) ↩

271. When Hannibal was in sight of Rome, *non ausus est obsidere*: "he dared not besiege it." *Sed religione quadam abstinuit, quod diceret, capienda urbis modo non dari voluntatem, modo non dari facultatem, ut testatur et Orosius*: "But forbore upon some religious scruple, because he said that sometimes he had no mind, and at other times no power, to take the city, as is related also by Orofius." (St. Jerome, *Epistles.*) ↩

272. *Non enim cuiquam in potestate est quid veniat in mentem*: "For it is not in any man's power, what shall come into his mind." (St. Augustine, *On Order.*) ↩

273. They, who called Simonides of Ceos out from Scopas and his company, as if it were to speak with him, saved his life. The story known (Cicero, *De Oratore*; Quintilian, *Institutio Oratoria*). ↩

274. They who believe there is nothing but what they can handle or see, οἱ οὐδὲν ἄλλο οἰόμενοι εἶναι ἢ οὗ ἂν δύνωνται ἀπρὶξ τοῖν χεροῖν λαβέσθαι... πᾶν δὲ τὸ ἀόρατον οὐκ ἀποδεχόμενοι ὡς ἐν οὐσίας μέρει: "and do not allow anything that is invisible to have any real existence," are by Plato reckoned to be void of all philosophy, ἀμύητοι, σκληροί, ἀντίτυποι, μάλ' εὖ ἄμουσοι, "not so much as initiated, stupid, obstinate, and entirely illiterate." (Plato, *Theaetetus.*) ↩

275. Οὐχ ὁμοίως ἄνθρωπος ἀμύνεται καὶ θεός: "God does not afford assistance in the same manner as man does." (Philo Judaeus, *Life of Moses.*) ↩

276. *Si curent [Dij] homines, benè bonis sit, malè malis: quod nunc abest*: "If they [the Gods] had any regard for men, things would go well with good men, and ill with bad men; but it is otherwise now." (Cicero, *De Natura Deorum.*) The Jews, who call this case צדיק ורע לו רשע וטוב לו: "evil to the righteous, and good to the wicked," have written many things about it, to be seen in their books: *The Guide for the Perplexed, Sefer ha-*

Ikkarim, Menorat Ha-Maor, Nahalot Abot, etc. So have the Heathen philosophers too: Seneca, Plutarch, Plotinus, Simplicius, others. But the answers of neither are always just. God forbid that should be thought true, which is asserted by Glaucon in Plato (*Republic*), that the just, if they had Gyges's ring, would do as the unjust, and ὅτι οὐδεὶς ἑκὼν δίκαιος ἀλλ' ἀναγκαζόμενος, κτλ.: "that no man is just voluntarily, but is forced to be so." Or that in *Sefer Hasidim* and *Menorath Hammaor* צדיק ורע לו צדוק בן רשע: "Evil befalls the righteous, and the unrighteous inherit good." The reason assigned for this case, in another place, is something better: כדי שלא יאמרו אם לא היה בטובה לא היה צדיק: "Wherefore let them not say that if good does not befall such a one, then he is a wicked man." But the way of solving it in *Sefer Nishmat Hayyim* by גלגול הנשמות, "a revolution of souls," or what the Kabbalists call עיבור, "transmigration," is worst of all (Manasseh ben Israel). ↩

277. *Cadit et Ripheus, justissimus unus Qui fuit in Teucris, et servantissimus æqui. Dis aliter visum*: "Ripheus also was slain, who was one of the most just men amongst the Trojans, and a very strict preserver of equity; but the Gods must be submitted to." (Virgil, *Aeneid*.) ↩

278. *Virtutes ipsas invertimus*: "We turn even virtues into vices." (Horace, *Satires*.) ↩

279. Οὐδὲν γὰρ οὕτως ἡδὺ τοῖς ἀνθρώποις, ὡς τὸ λαλεῖν τὰ ἀλλότρια · καὶ μάλιστα ἐὰν τύχωσιν ὑπ' εὐνοίας τινὸς ἢ μίσους ἑλκόμενοι, ὑφ' ὧν καὶ φιλεῖ κλέπτεσθαι ὡς τὰ πολλὰ ἡ ἀλήθεια: "There is nothing so delightful to men, as prating about things that don't belong to them, especially if they are drawn into it by love or hatred, and they are apt to conceal truth as they do most other things." (Gregory Nazianzen, *The Second Oration*.) ↩

280. Therefore, with Socrates in Plato, we ought not much to care what the multitude /οἱ πολλοὶ/ say of us, ἀλλ' ὅ, τι ὁ ἐπαΐων περὶ τῶν δικαίων, καὶ ἀδίκων, ὁ εἷς, καὶ αὐτὴ ἡ ἀλήθεια: "but what he says who can distinguish betwixt the just and the unjust, the only one who is truth itself." (*Crito*.) ↩

281. Or, vice-versa, he may judge that to be right, which is wrong. This seemss to be pretty much the case in that enumeration of good men who suffered, in Cicero: *Cur duo Scipiones, fortissimos et oprimos viros, in Hispania Pœnus oppressit? Cur Maximus extulit filium consularem? Cur Marcellum Annibal interemit, etc.*: "How did it come to pass, that the Carthaginians overthrew the two Scipios in Spain, those brave and excellent men? How came Maximus to bury his son, when he was fit to be a consul? How came Hannibal to kill Marcellus? etc." (*De Natura Deorum*.) For here they are reckoned *boni*, "good," only because they were *fortes*, "valiant;" that is, because they had been zealous and successful instruments in conquering and destroying them who happened to be so unfortunate as to be neighbors to the Romans, upon various

pretences indeed, but in truth only to enlarge their own territories. Is this to be good? Does it deserve such a particular observation that Fabius Maximus buried a son, after he had been Consul too? How does it appear that Marcellus was a better man than Hannibal? Is it such a wonder if they, who spend their lives in slaughter, should at length be slain themselves? If the margin permitted, more remarks might be made upon this catalogue: as also some upon that which follows in the same place, of others, *quibus improbis optime evênit*: "who, though they were very bad men, yet had very good fortune." ↩

282. *Vitæ postscenia celant*, "that part of life which they keep secret from the world" (in Lucretius, *De Rerum Natura*), may be aptly applied to the wicked. *Multi famam, conscientiam pauci verentur*: "Many are afraid of common report, but few stand in awe of their own consciences." (Pliny the Younger, *Epistles*.) ↩

283. *Neque; mala vel bona, quæ vulgus putat: multi, qui conflictari adversis videntur, beati; ac plerique; quanquam magnas per opes, miserrimi, etc.*: "We are not to judge things to be good or bad, from the opinion which the vulgar have of them; for abundance of people are happy, who have many difficulties to struggle with; and a great many men are very miserable, though they be very rich." (Tacitus, *Annals*.) ↩

284. *Feliciorem tu Mecænatem putas, cui amoribus anxio, et morosæ uxoris quotidiana repudia deflenti, somnus per symphoniarum cantum, ex longinquo bene resonantium, quæritur? Mero se licet spoiat,…; tam vigilabit in plumâ, quàm ille [Regulus] in cruce.… ut dubium [non] sit, an electione fati datâ, plures Reguli nasci, quàm Mecænates velint*: "Do you think Mecænas was very happy, who was always solicitious about intrigues, and complaining of the refusals of an ill-natured wife, insomuch that he could have no other sleep but what was procured by the agreeable sound of soft music at a distance. Though he dozes himself with wine,… he will be as restless in a bed of down, as [Regulus] upon a gibbet.… So that there is no doubt, but if fate would put it to men's choice, there would more men choose to be born Regulus's than Mecænas's." (Seneca, *De Providentia*.) *Isti, quos prop felicibus aspicitis, si non qua occurrunt, sed qua latent, videritis, miseri sunt*: "Those men which you look upon to be happy, if you were to see how different they are in private from what they are in public, you would think miserable." (Tacitus, *Annals*.) ↩

285. Archimedes, having found the way of solving a problem (*examinandi, an corona aurea prorsus esset*: "viz. whether a crown was made of pure gold or no") ran in an ecstasy out of the bath, crying Εὕρηκα: "I have found out a solution;" but who ever heard of a man, that after a luxurious meal, or the enjoyment of a woman, ran out thus, crying out Βέβρωκα or Πεφίληκα: "I have glutted myself; I have enjoyed her"? (Plutarch, *Moralia*.) ↩

286. *Fatis contraria fata rependens*: "Balancing the loss determined by one fate, with the prospect of good determined by another." (Virgil, *Aeneid*.) See what Pliny writes of Agrippa, the other great favorite and minister of Augustus, whom he reckons to be the only instance of felicity among them who were called Agrippæ. *Is quoque adversa pedum valetudine, misera juventa, exercito ævo inter arma mortesque, ... infelici terris stirpe omni, ... præterea brevitate ævi, ... in tormentis adulteriorum conjugis, socerique prægravi servitio, luisse augurium præposteri natalis existimatur*: "He also, by a disease in his feet, by a miserable young time, having spent his years among arms and death, ... all his relations miserable upon earth, ... besides, his life very short, ... it was the general opinion, that what his unnatural birth foreboded was fulfilled in the torments he endured by his wife's adulteries, and the cruel bondage of his father-in-law." (Pliny the Elder, *Natural History*.) ↩

287. Ὀφθαλμῶν μὲν ἄμερσε, δίδου δ' ἡδεῖαν ἀοιδήν: "The loss of his (Homer's) eyes was compensated by the gift of sweet harmony." (Homer, *Odyssey*.) ↩

288. Zeno reckoned he made a good voyage, when he was shipwrecked. (Diogenes Laërtius, *Life of Zeno*.) ↩

289. If a good man labors under poverty, sickness, or the like, εἰς ἀγαθόν τι τελευτήσει ζῶντι ἢ καὶ ἀποθανόντι: "it must end in something that is good, either in his lifetime or after death," for how can he be neglected of God, who studies according to his poor abilities to be like Him? (Plato, *Republic*.) ↩

290. Who blames a drama, because all the persons are not heroes? (Plotinus, *Enneads*.) ↩

291. העולם נידון אחר רובו: "We must judge of the world, according to what it is as to the greatest part." (Abravanel, and what follows.) ↩

292. Μέρος μὲν ἕνεκα ὅλου καὶ οὐχ ὅλον μέρους ἕνεκα ἀπεργάζεται, κτλ.: "The part is made for the sake of the whole, and not the whole for the sake of the part." (Plato, *Laws*.) ↩

293. Divine providence and the immortality of the soul must stand and fall together. Θάτερον οὐκ ἔστιν ἀπολιπεῖν ἀναιροῦντα θάτερον: "If you take away the one, the other will follow." (Plutarch, *Moralia*.) ↩

294. Τοῦτο ταυτόν ἐστι τὸ μὴ οἴεσθαι εἶναι Θεον · ἢ ὄντα μὴ προνοεῖν · ἢ προνοοῦντα μὴ ἀγαθὸν εἶναι καὶ δίκαιον: "It is the same thing to think there is no God; or if there be one, that he does not govern the world; or if he does govern it, he is not a good and just governor." (Hierocles, *Commentary on the Carmen Aureum*.) ↩

295. Sure nobody ever did, in reality, pretend to do this. According to Diogenes Laërtius, the

Egyptians set up ἀγάλματα, "some ornaments," in their temples, τῷ μὴ εἰδέναι τὴν τοῦ θεοῦ μορφήν: for that very reason, because they did not know his shape; or, how to represent Him. Their images seem to have been symbols, or hieroglyphics, expressing something of their sense or opinion concerning Him (*Lives of Eminent Philosophers*). For, as Maimonides observes, no man ever did or ever will worship an idol made of metal, stone, or wood, as that Being who made heaven and earth (*The Guide for the Perplexed* I, 36.) ↵

296. *Non est dubium, quin religio nulla sit, ubicunque simulachrum est*: "Without doubt, there can be no true religion where there are any images." (Lactantius, *Divine Institutes*.) ↵

297. Ὡς γὰρ ἔργον σώματος τὸ σωματικῶς τι ἐπιτελέσαι, οὕτω καὶ ψυχῆς ἔργον τὸ ταῖς ἐννοίαις τὰς ἀρεσκούσας φαντασίας τελεσιουργῆσαι ὡς θέλει, διὸ καὶ τὰς ἐννοίᾳ ἁμαρτίας μὴ ὡ; φαντασίας ἁπλῶς, ἀλλ᾽ ὡς ἔργα ἐν ψυχῇ γινόμενα δίκαιον κρίνεσθαι: "For as, when anything is done by the body, it is done grossly, so, when anything is done by the soul, it is done according to its own will, and by such representations as are agreeable to its thoughts; wherefore, it is but reasonable to think that sins in our thoughts are not mere imaginations only, but works really done in the soul." (St. Basil, *De Vera Integritate Virginitatis*.) ↵

298. Θεοπρεπῶς ἅπαντα νοοῦντες: "To think nothing but what is worthy of God." (St. Chrysostom, *Homilies on Genesis*.) ↵

299. We use them (and speak as the Jews everywhere inculcate, בני אדם כלשון: "according to the language of men") only ἀπορίαι οἰκείας προσηγορίας… τὰ ὀνόματα παρ᾽ ἡμῖν ἀγαπώμεναι μεταφέροντες: "for want of proper words… we convert our favorite words into metaphors." (Plotinus, *Enneads*.) ↵

300. *Mollissima corda Humano generi dare se natura fatetur, Quæ lachrymas dedit, hæc nostri pars optima sensûs.… separat hoc nos à grege mutorum, etc.*: "Nature confesses that she has given to mankind hearts that are very soft (and easy to be affected). She has given them tears, which are the best part of our senses… for these distinguish us from brute creatures." (Juvenal, *Satires*.) ↵

301. The ratio of G to M + q is different from that of G to M − q: and yet G remains unaltered. ↵

302. Πῶς ἂν… δοίη τῷ πρὸς τὰς ὁρμὰς αὐτεξουσίῳ μὴ αἰτοῦντι ὁ διδόναι πεφυκὼς θεός: "Why should God, who is in his own nature beneficent, give anything to a being whose appetites are in his own power, if he does not ask it?" (Hierocles, *Commentary on the Carmen Aureum*.) ↵

303. *Τῶν ἀρίστων οὐκ ἔστιν ἔπαινος, ἀλλὰ μεῖζόν τι καὶ βέλτιον*: "Something, greater and better than praise, belongs to that which is perfectly good." (Aristotle, *Nicomachean Ethics*.) Therefore ὁ Θεὸς καὶ τἀγαθὸν: "God and perfect goodness" are above praise. *Οἱ τοὺς θεοὺς ἐπαινοῦντες γελοῖοί εἰσιν αὐτοὺς ἐξισοῦντες*: "They who praise the Gods make themselves ridiculous, for that is to equal them with ourselves." (Andronicus of Rhodes [from a commentary on Aristotle's *Nicomachean Ethics* sometimes attributed to Andronicus —Editor].) ↩

304. Cleon, only a songster [ἀιδὸς], had a statue at Thebes, kept as sacred, when Pindar himself had none. See the story in Athenæus. (*Deipnosophistae*.) ↩

305. What Seneca says, of Alexander, is true of many another hero: *pro virtute erat felix temeritas*: "that his successful rashness was esteemed virtue." (*De Beneficiis*.) ↩

306. *Tumes alto Druforum sanguine, tanquam Feceris ipse aliquid, etc.*: "You puff yourself up because you are of the noble blood of the Drusi, as if you had done some (great) thing yourself." (Juvenal, *Satires*.) ↩

307. *Gloria quantalibet quid erit, si gloria tantum est?* "What signifies the highest degree of glory, if it be only mere glory?" (Juvenal, *Satires*.) ↩

308. היום כאן ומחר בקבר היום חי ומחר רימה: "Today here, and tomorrow in the grave; now a man, and then a worm." (Judah ben Samuel, *Sefer Hasidim*.) ↩

309. *Κτῆμα σφαλερώτατον*: "A very uncertain possession." (Philo Judaeus, *On Abraham*.) ↩

310. Even the great pyramid in Egypt, though it still remains, has not been able to preserve the true name of its builder, which is lost; one may justly wonder how. ↩

311. *Τὰ ὀνόματα τῶν πάλαι πολυυμνήτων νῦν τρόπον τινὰ γλωσσήματά ἐστι*: "The names of those, who in former times were very much celebrated, are now some way or other become quite obsolete." (Marcus Aurelius, *Meditations*.) ↩

312. *Μικρὸν ἡ μηκίστη ὑστεροφημία, καὶ αὐτὴ δὲ κατὰ διαδοχὴν ἀνθρωπαρίων τάχιστα τεθνηξομένων, καὶ οὐκ εἰδότων οὐδὲ ἑαυτούς, οὔτιγε τὸν πρόπαλαι τεθνηκότα*: "The longest fame amongst posterity is but short, by reason of the quick succession by poor mortals dying, who know neither themselves, nor any that died some time ago." (Marcus Aurelius, *Meditations*.) ↩

313. *Expende Hannibalem: quot libras in duce summo Invenies?* "Weigh Hannibal in the scales, and see how many pounds there remain of that great commander." (Juvenal, *Satires*.) ↩

314. *Μέχρι τοῦδε οἱ ἔπαινοι ἀνεκτοί εἰσιν, εἰς ὅσον ἂν ὁ ἐπαινούμενος γνωρίζῃ ἕκαστον τῶν*

λεγομένων προσὸν ἑαυτῷ · τὸ δὲ ὑπὲρ τοῦτο ἀλλότριον, κτλ.: "Praises may be borne, so long as the person praised knows that all the things which are said belong to him, but all that is beyond this is nothing to the purpose." (Lucian, *Pro Imaginibus*.) ↵

315. Μακαρίσας αὐτὸν [Ἀχιλλέα] ὅτι καὶ ζῶν φίλου πιστοῦ, καὶ τελευτήσας μεγάλου κήρυκος ἔτυχεν: "He esteemed him [Achilles] happy, because he had a faithful friend while living, and one that celebrated him highly after he was dead." (Plutarch, *Life of Alexander*.) ↵

316. As Psaphon was celebrated by the birds, singing Μέγας θεὸς ψάφων: "Psaphon is a great God." (Maximus Tyrius, *Dissertations*.) ↵

317. *Honoribus aucti… cùm diis gratias agimus, tum nihil nostræ laudi assumptum arbitramur*: "When honors are heaped upon us… and we return thanks to the Gods, we do not then take any of the merit to ourselves." (Cicero, *De Natura Deorum*.) Ὅ τι ἂν ἀγαθὸν πράττῃς εἰς θεὸν ἀνάπεμπε: "When you do any good thing, ascribe it to God." (A saying of Bias in Diogenes Laërtius's *Life of Bias*.) ↵

318. Εἰ γὰρ καὶ μὴ δυνάμεθα κατ ἀξίαν ποτὲ τοῦτο ποιῆσαι, … ἀλλ᾽ ὅμως τὴν κατὰ δύναμιν ἀνενεγκεῖν εὐχαριστίαν δίκαιον ἂν εἴη ·: "For though we cannot do the thing as it ought to be done… yet it is but just and fit that we offer up our thanksgiving, so far as is in our power." (Johannes Chrysostom, *Homilies on Genesis*.) ↵

319. כל עובדי פסל׃ את פסיליהם היו עובדים: "all they who serve images, are worshippers of images," and similar passages (e.g. 2 Kings 17:41, Psalms 97:7). Deuteronomy 12:2 mention is made of the places, אשר עבדו שם הגוים וכו׳ "where the nations served their images, etc." in the Chaldee paraphrase it is said פלחו, "worshipped them" (*Targum Onkelos*); and in the Septuagint it is said ἐλάτρευσαν, "worshipped them" (in the ecclesiastical sense) and the same in the vulgar Latin. ↵

320. עבדו אב סלך בבל: "Serve the king of Babylon." (Jeremiah 27:17.) ↵

321. Plato applies the word "serve" even to the laws themselves, in that phrase, viz. δουλεύειν τοῖς νόμοις: "to serve the laws." (*Laws*.) ↵

322. Ἐκείνῳ … οὐδὲν ἔξω φιλοδεσπότου γνώμης παρέξουσι: "We give no more to Him, than to one whom we freely acknowledge to have the dominion over us." (Philo Judaeus, *The Worse Attacks the Better*.) ↵

323. משכיל יבין: "The wise will understand." ↵

324. Care must be taken how we pray, lest we should ask what may be hurtful to us. Οὐκοῦν δοκεῖ πολλῆς προμηθείας γε προσδεῖσθαι, ὅπως μὴ λήσῃ τις αὑτὸν εὐχόμενος μεγάλα κακά, δοκῶν δ᾽ ἀγαθά: "for there seems to be need of great prudence, lest a

man, by not rightly understanding himself, should ask for such things as he imagines to be good for him, but which are indeed great evils." (Plato, *Alcibiades.*) *Evertere domos totas, optantibus ipsis, Di faciles, etc.*: "the Gods who are ready (to grant men's petitions) have overthrown whole houses, at the request of the owners, etc." is a Poet's observation (Juvenal, *Satires*). The author of *Sefer Hasidim* adds that we should not pray for that שאיגו ראוי, or שאין נעשה כפי הפי הטבע, or שאי אפשר לעשות, or שיעשה הקב"ה נס בשנוי עולם: "which is not possible to be done, or which cannot be done according to the course of nature, or which is not fit to be done, or that the holy Being (God) should work a miracle and alter the world." (Judah ben Samuel.) ↵

325. עיגי למטה לבי למעלה: "With my eyes downward, and my heart lifted up." (*Yevamot.*) ↵

326. התפלה... ענף מסתעף מן ההשגחה: "Prayer... is a branch of providence shading us." (Joseph Albo, *Sefer ha-Ikkarim* IV, 1.) בהשגחה יאמין שהתפלה מועיל לו וכו' "He that believes in providence, must believe that prayer is profitable to him." (Joseph Albo, *Sefer ha-Ikkarim.*) ↵

327. Like those Ἀκοιμηταὶ, "wakeful people," at Constantinople, particularly, who continued divine service night and day without intermission. Or the Messalians, perhaps; מצלין, Εὐχῖται: "praying people") who placed (or pretended to place) all religion in prayer, μόνῃ σχολάζειν τῇ προσευχῇ προσποιούμενοι: "and so managed themselves, as never to be at leisure for anything else but prayer." (Cyril of Alexandria, *Epistola ad Calosyrium.*) ↵

328. כל תפלה שאינה בכוונה אינה תפלה: "If a prayer is not performed with earnestness, it is no prayer." (Maimonides, *Mishneh Torah*, Hilkot Tefillah, IV, 15.) התפלה תלויה בלב: "A prayer suspended in the mind." (*Sefer Hasidim* and the like everywhere.) ↵

329. This in general is true: notwithstanding which, I do not deny but there may be occasions when οὐδὲν κωλύει τόπος, οὐδὲ ἐμποδίζει καιρός, ἀλλὰ κἂν γόνατα μὴ κλίνῃς, ... διάνοιαν δὲ μόνον ἐπιδείξῃ θερμὴν, τὸ πᾶν ἀπήρτισας τῆς εὐχῆς · Ἔξεστι καὶ γυναῖκα ἠλακάτην κατέχουσαν καὶ ἱστουργοῦσαν ἀναβλέψαι εἰς τὸν οὐρανὸν τῇ διανοίᾳ, καὶ καλέσαι μετὰ θερμότητος τὸν Θεόν · ἔξεστι καὶ ἄνθρωπον εἰς ἀγορὰν ἐμβάλλοντα καὶ καθ' ἑαυτὸν βαδίζοντα εὐχὰς ποιεῖσθαι ἐκτενεῖς, κτλ.: "the place is no hindrance, nor the time any interruption.... let him show a fervent affection of mind, for this is the perfection of prayer; and a woman, even while she is spinning or weaving, may in her thoughts look up to heaven and call upon God with fervency; and a man as he is going to market, and walking by himself, may pray very intentively." (St. Chrysostom, *De Anna.*) ↵

330. Ὁ μὲν λόγος ἑρμηνεὺς διανοίας πρὸς ἀνθρώπους · ἡ δὲ διάνοια γίνεται τῷ λόγῳ τὰ

πρὸς τὸν θεόν: "Words are the interpreters of our thoughts to men, and we also make known our thoughts to God by words." (Philo Judaeus, *On the Migration of Abraham*.) ↵

331. Cogitation itself, according to Plato, is a kind of speech of the mind. For he calls τὸ διανοεῖσθαι (cogitation) "or thinking," λόγον, ὃν αὐτὴ πρὸς αὑτὴν ἡ ψυχὴ διεξέρχεται, περὶ ὧν ἂν σκοπῇ: "the language by which the soul explains itself to itself, when it considers anything." (*Theaetetus*.) And so Plotinus, Ὁ ἐν φωνῇ λόγος μίμημα τοῦ ἐν ψυχῇ: "the vocal words are an imitation of those of the soul." (*Enneads*.) ↵

332. *Multa sunt verba, quæ, quasi articuli, connectunt membra orationis, quæ formari similitudine nulla possunt*: "There are many words (particles) which are like small joints, to connect the several sentences, which cannot be exhibited by any images." (Cicero, *De Oratore*.) ↵

333. תפלה בלא כונה כגוף בלא נשמה: "A prayer, without the intention of the mind, is like a body without a soul." (Isaac Abravanel, *Nahalot Abot*.) ↵

334. *Second Alcibiades*. The words of the Poet in Plato are these: "O Jupiter, our king, give us those things that are good for us, whether we ask for them or no; and command those things that are hurtful to be kept from us, though we pray for them." ↵

335. דבור אדם הוא בכונה וכו׳: "When a man speaks distinctly, it is always with intenseness." (Isaac Abravanel.) That in *Sefer Haredim*, quoted out of סמ"ק *Sefer Mizwot Katan*, "the lesser book of precepts," explains this thus: ידקדק בכל מלה ומלה כאלו מונה זהובים: "He will consider every word exactly, as if he was looking over his debts." (Eliezer Azkari.) ↵

336. ... *Ut eos [deos,] semper pura... mente et voce veneremur*: "... That we may always worship them [the Gods, in the style of the Heathens] with a pure... mind, and with pure words." (Cicero, *De Natura Deorum*.) Ὢ τῶν ἄλλων ζῴων ὑπὸ σοῦ, Δέσποτα κρείττονες γεγόναμεν, τούτῳ τὴν σὴν εὐλογεῖν μεγαλειότητα πρέπει: "That as thou, O Lord, hast made us better than other creatures, so it becomes us the more to praise thy greatness," says Solomon in his prayer (in Josephus, *Antiquities of the Jews*). ↵

337. This we find often among the Dinim ("orders") of the Jews. הברכות כולן צריך שישמיע לאזנו מה שהוא אומר: "It is necessary, in all our prayers, that we so speak as to be heard by ourselves." (Maimonides, *Mishneh Torah*, Hilkot Berakhot I, 7.) And Rabbi Eliezer Azkari, having cited this passage, adds הסכימו רוב הפוסקים שאם לא השמיע לאזניו לא יצא וכו׳: "In general the judges agree in this, that if he does not hear his own self, he is guilty (of a crime)." (*Sefer Haredim*.) Maimonides, in another place, expresses himself thus: לא יתפלל בלבו [לבד] אלא מחתך הדברים בשפתיו ומשמיע לאזניו בלחש: "A man should not [only] pray in his mind, but pronounce the words distinctly with his

lips, and whisper so as to hear himself" (*Mishneh Torah*, Hilkot Tefillah V, 9; that word לבד, "only," I inserted from Joseph Caro's *Shulhan Aruk*). The same occurs in *Or Hadash*, and other places. ↵

338. המתפלל... יחשיב כאילו שכינה כנגדו וכו': "He that prays... should think about it as much as if the divine presence could appear to him." (Joseph Caro, *Orah Hayyim*.) ↵

339. Ἐν τῷ εἴσω οἷον νεῷ: "In a private retirement, as in a temple." (Plotinus, *Enneads*.) ↵

340. St. Chrysostom says some are so unmindful of what they are about, that they know not so much as what they say themselves. Εἰσέρχονται πολλοὶ ἐν τῇ ἐκκλησίᾳ, ... καὶ ἐξέρχονται, καὶ οὐκ οἴδασι τί εἶπον · τὰ χείλη κινεῖται, ἡ δὲ ἀκοὴ οὐκ ἀκούει: "A great many come to church, ... and go home again, without so much as knowing what they have said. Their lips moved, but their words were not heard." (*De Chananaea*.) ↵

341. The very Heathens thought that the Gods would not hear the prayers of wicked men. Bias, happening to be with some such, in the same ship, when a great storm arose and they (being now frighted) began to invoke their deities, cries out, Σιγᾶτε, μὴ ἄισθωνται ὑμᾶς ἐνθάδε πλέοντας: "Hold your tongues, they'll take no notice of us while we sail here." (Diogenes Laërtius, *Life of Bias*.) ↵

342. Caius Cestius, in Tacitus, says *principes quidem instar deorum esse: sed neque a diis nisi justas supplicum preces audiri*: "Princes indeed are like Gods, but the Gods themselves will not hear the prayers of the supplicant, unless they be just." (*Annals*.) ↵

343. Sometimes πλέον ἥμισυ παντός: "half is better than the whole"; that is, as Plato paraphrases those words of Hesiod, Τὸ ἥμισυ τοῦ παντὸς πολλάκις ἐστὶ πλέον, ὁπόταν ᾖ τὸ μὲν ὅλον λαμβάνειν ζημιῶδες, κτλ.: "Many times half is better than the whole, and when it is so, to receive the whole is an injury to us." (*Laws*.) ↵

344. *Quid quod iste calculi candore laudatus dies originem mali habuit? Quam multos accepta afflixere imperia? quam multos bona perdidere, et ultimis mersere suppliciis?* "What if that day, which came up lucky, should be the beginning of evil? How many, in great power, have been ruined by it? How many has prosperity destroyed, and subjected them to the greatest punishments?" (Pliny the Elder, *Natural History*.) ↵

345. *Religion deorum cultu pio continetur*: "Religion consists in a devout worshipping of the Gods." *Qui omnia, quæ ad cultum deorum pertinerent, diligenter retractarent, et tanquam religerent, sunt dicti religiosi, etc.*: "They are called religious persons, because they are continually revolving, and repeating over and over again the things that belong to the worship of the Gods." (Cicero, *De Natura Deorum*.) ↵

346. Particularly with respect to customary swearing, which, besides the ill consequences it

has in making oaths cheap, etc., is a great instance of disregard and irreverence. For they, who use themselves to it, do, at least, make the tremendous name of God to serve for an expletive only; and commonly to rude, passionate, or debauched discourse (λόγων ἀναπλήρωμα ποιούμενοι τὸ ἁγιώτατον καὶ θεῖον ὄνομα: "making use of the most holy name of God, only to fill up the sentence with" —Philo Judaeus, *Life of Moses*). ↵

347. Οὐδὲν οὕτως ἡμέτερόν ἐστιν, ὡς ἡμεῖς ἡμῖν αὐτοῖς: "so much our own, as we ourselves are." (Xenophon, *Cyropaedia*.) ↵

348. And therefore the produce of a man's labor is often still called his "labor." So יבזו זרים יגיעו: "strangers devour his labor," and יגיע כפיך תאכל: "thou shalt eat the labor of thine hands;" in Psalms (109:11, 128:2) and other places. … *Iliadumque labor vestes*: "… Garments which were the labor of the Trojan women." (Virgil, *Aeneid*.) ↵

349. If B works for another man, who pays him for his work, or labor, that alters not the case. He may commute them for money, because they are *his*. ↵

350. *Tanquam Sparti illi poetarum, sic se invicem jugulant, ut nemo ex omnibus restet*: "Like those Spartans mentioned by the Poets, who cut one another's throats, so that not one of them all remained," as Lactantius says in another case. (*Divine Institutes*.) ↵

351. Ἀνθρωπόμορφον θηρίον: "A wild beast in the shape of a man." (Philo Judaeus.) ↵

352. *Nec enim æquus judex aliam de suâ, aliam de alienâ causâ, sententiam fert*: "A fair judge will not give a different sentence in his own cause, from that which he gives in the cause of another." (Seneca, *De Ira*.) ↵

353. Ἀεὶ ταὐτὰ περί γε τῶν αὐτῶν γίνωσκε: "We must always understand the same things relating to the same things." (Isocrates, *Oratio ad Nicoclem*.) ↵

354. אל תדון חברך עד שתגיע למקומו: "You must not judge your companion, till you have put yourself in his place." (*Mishnah*, Abot II, 5.) *Eo loco nos constituamus, quo ille est, cui irascimur*: "We ought to put ourselves in the place of him we are angry with." (Seneca, *De Ira*.) ↵

355. He was a mere flatterer, who told Cyrus, Βασιλεὺς μὲν ἔμοιγε δοκεῖς σὺ φύσει πεφυκέναι οὐδὲν ἧττον ἢ ὁ ἐν τῷ σμήνει φυόμενος τῶν μελιττῶν ἡγεμών: "You seem to me to be born a king as much by nature, as he who is born in the hive is the king of the bees." (Xenophon, *Cyropaedia*.) ↵

356. *Nihil est unum uni tam simile, tam par, quàm omnes inter nosmet ipsos sumus.… Quæcunque est hominis definitio, una in omnes valet*: "There is no one thing more like or equal to another, than we all are among ourselves.… Whatever definition we give of a man, the same will hold good of us all." (Cicero, *De Legibus*.) ↵

357. When the Romans, in Livy, asked the Galls, *Quodnam id jus esset, agrum à possessoribus petere, aut minari arma*: "Where is the justice of demanding the lands of the owners, or else threatening them with the sword;" they answered, *se in armis jus ferre, et omnia fortium virorum esse*: "that their swords were their law, and that valiant men had a right to everything." (*History of Rome.*) Like barbarians indeed! ↩

358. Josephus, when he says νόμον γε μὴν ὡρίσθαι, καὶ παρὰ θηρσὶν ἰσχυρότατον, καὶ ἀνθρώποις, εἴκειν τοῖς δυνατωτέροις: "that it is an established law, and it is the strongest amongst both beasts and amongst men, viz.: to submit to them that have the most power," can only mean that necessity, or perhaps prudence, obliges to do this; not any law in the stricter sense of that word. (*The Jewish War.*) ↩

359. *Societatis [inter homines] arctissimum vinculum est magis arbitrari esse contra naturam, hominem homini detrahere, sui commodi causa, quàm omnia incommoda subire, etc.*: "The strongest bond of society, among men, is to think that it is more contrary to nature for one man to take away that which belongs to another, to advantage himself, than it is to undergo all the inconveniences that can be, etc." (Cicero, *De Officiis.*) ↩

360. All this is supposed to be in a state of nature and the absence of human laws. ↩

361. For εἰ ὁ ἀδικῶν κακῶς, ὁ ἀντιποιῶν κακῶς οὐδὲν ἧττον ποιεῖ κακῶς, κἂν ἀμύνηται: "if he who does an act of injustice does an ill thing, he that returns the injustice does a thing equally ill, though it be by way of retaliation." (Maximus Tyrius, *Dissertations.*) ↩

362. *Nam propriæ telluris herum natura neque illum, Nec me, nec quenquam statuit*: "For nature did not make him, nor me, nor anyone else, the owner of any particular piece of land." (Horace, *Satires.*) ↩

363. Τὰς κτήσεις, καὶ τὰς ἰδίας καὶ τὰς κοινάς, ἢν ἐπινένηται πολὺς χρόνος, κυρίας καὶ πατρῴας ἅπαντες εἶναι νομίζουσιν: "They think that possessions, whether private or public, after they have continued for a long time, are secure, and belong to the family." (Isocrates, *Archidamus.*) ↩

364. To this may be reduced that title to things which Cicero mentions as conferred by some law (*lege*); and even those which accrue *conditione*: "by covenant," or *forte*: "by lot." For I suppose the government to have a right of giving them thus. ↩

365. Which must not give way to the opinions of *fitness*, etc. The master was in the right, who corrected Cyrus for adjudging the great coat to the great boy, and the little one to the little. He was not τοῦ ἁρμόττοντος κριτής: "a judge of the fitness," but of *the*

property (Xenophon, *Cyropaedia*). *Omnium, quæ in hominum doctorum disputatione versantur, nihil est profecto præstabilius, quàm planè intelligi nos ad justitiam esse natos, neque opinione, sed naturâ constitutum esse just*: "Of all the things that learned men dispute about, there is none better than this: that we should be thoroughly convinced that we were born to do what is right, and that right is not made by opinion but by nature." (Cicero, *De Legibus*.) ↵

366. There is another way of acquiring a title mentioned: which is, by the right of war, as it is called. *Sunt privata nulla naturâ: sed aut veteri occupatione, ut qui quondam in vacua venerunt; aut victoriâ, ut qui bello potiti sunt, etc.*: "Nothing belongs to particular persons by nature: but either by long possession, as when men, a long while since, came into lands which had no owners; or else by victory, as they who enjoy them from war, etc." (Cicero, *De Officiis*.) And so, in Xenophon, it is said to be an eternal law among men that if a city be taken in war, the bodies and goods of the people in it are the conqueror's; and they may possess them as their own, not ἀλλότρια: "as belonging to others." But sure this wants limitations. ↵

367. *Allodium*, "Freehold." ↵

368. Πολλάκις ἐγέλασα διαθήκας ἀναγινώσκων λεγούσας ὁ δεῖνα μὲν ἐχέτω τὴν δεσποτείαν τῶν ἀγρῶν, ἢ τῆς οἰκίας, τὴν δὲ χρῆσιν ἄλλος · Πάντες γὰρ τὴν χρῆσιν ἔχομεν, τὴν δεσποτείαν δὲ οὐδείς. … καὶ ἑκόντες, καὶ ἄκοντες ἐν τῇ τελευτῇ παραχωρήσομεν ἑτέροις, τὴν χρῆσιν καρπωσάμενοι μόνον: "I have oftentimes laughed when I read any of those wills in which it is said, 'let such or such a one be the real owner of the lands or houses, and let another person have the use of them,' for the use is all that belongs to any of us; we are not the real owners.… After death they go to others, whether we will or no, when we have enjoyed the use only." (St. Chrysostom, *On Wealth and Poverty*.) Τούτων μὲν φύσει οὐδενός ἐσμεν κύριοι, νόμῳ δὲ καὶ διαδοχῇ τὴν χρῆσιν αὐτῶν εἰς ἀόριστον παραλαμβάνοντες, ὀλιγοχρόνιοι δεσπόται νομιζόμεθα κἀπειδὰν ἡ προθεσμία παρέλθῃ τηνικαῦτα παραλαβὼν ἄλλος ἀπολαύει τοῦ ὀνόματος: "We are not by nature the real owners of any of these things, but are invested by law or by succession with the use of them for an uncertain time, and are therefore called temporary tenants; and when the time prescribed is past, then they go to another, and he enjoys the same title." (Lucian, *Letter to Nigrinus*.) ↵

369. *Qui te pascit ager, tuus est*: "The field that maintains you is your field, etc." (Horace, alluding to this truth, *Epistles*.) Περὶ παντὸς: "As to the matter of injuries," says Plato, ἓν εἰρήσθω τοιόνδε δέ τι νόμιμον βιαίων περί · τῶν ἀλλοτρίων μηδένα μηδὲν φέρειν μηδὲ ἄγειν · : "there is only some such general law as this for every man, viz.: that no man should plunder, or by violence take anything that belongs to another," and then proceeds, μηδ᾽ αὖ χρῆσθαι μηδενὶ τῶν τοῦ πέλας, ἐὰν μὴ πείσῃ τὸν κεκτημένον, κτλ.: "nor make any use of anything that comes in their way, without the leave of the

owner." (*Laws.*) In Plutarch the thing is carried farther, where it is said that a man passing by another man's door μὴ βλέπειν ἔισω, κτλ.: "ought not to look in" (*De Curiositate.*); according to a saying of Xenocrates, μηδὲν διαφέρειν ἢ τοὺς πόδας ἢ τοὺς ὀφθαλμοὺς εἰς ἀλλοτρίαν οἰκίαν τιθέναι: "there is no difference between looking in and going into another man's house." (quoted in *De Curiositate.*) ↩

370. *Furtum fit,... cum quis alienam rem invito domino contrectat*: "It is real theft... to meddle with anything that belongs to another against his will." (Justinian, *Institutes.*) ↩

371. On the contrary נעשה דין—נעשה אמת: "We shall make justice, we shall make truth." A saying of ריב״ל, Rabbi Joshua ben Levi. And Cicero more than once uses the word *verum*, "true" for *justum*, "just," and *veritas*, "truth" for *bonitas*, "goodness" or *probitas*, "probity." ↩

372. Account τὸ σὸν μόνον σὸν εἶναι, τὸ δὲ ἀλλότριον, ὥσπερ ἐστίν, ἀλλότριον: "that only your own which really is so, and look upon that as another's which really is so." (Epictetus's words, *Enchiridion.*) *Justitiæ primum munus est, ut ne cui quis noceat, nisi lacessitus injuria; deinde, ut communibus pro communibus utatur, privatis ut suis*: "The first property of justice is that no man should do any hurt to another, unless provoked by some injury; after this, he is to make use of those things that are common, in common with others, and use the things that belong to himself as his own." (Cicero, *De Officiis.*) This is to use things as being what they are. ↩

373. Blepsias ὁ δανειστής, "the usurer," in Lucian, dies of hunger (λιμῷ ἄθλιος ἐλέγετο ἀπεσκληκέναι: "the miserable wretch is reported to have pined away till he died." —*Dialogues of the Dead*). Ridiculous enough. ↩

374. Or only πρὸς τὸ ἀριθμεῖν: "to be perpetually telling it over," as Anacharsis said of some Greeks. (Athenæus, *Deipnosophistae.*) ↩

375. As that man, in Athenæus's *Deipnosophistae*, endeavored literally to do; of whom it is reported, that, being much in love with his money, before he died he swallowed as much of it as he could (καταπιόντα οὐκ ὀλίγους χρυσοῦς ἀποθανεῖν: "he swallowed a great many pieces of gold and then died"). ↩

376. Of such it is, that Diogenes used to say, Ὁμοίους τοὺς φιλαργύρους τοῖς ὑδρωπικοῖς, κτλ.: "That covetous men were like men that had the dropsy." (Stobaeus, *On Injustice.*) The Mamshilim, that is, "the writers of proverbs," mentioned in *Nahalot Abot*, compare them צמא יוסיף שישתה כל עוד כי המלוחים מהמים שישתה לצמא: "to thirsty people drinking saltwater: the more they drink, the drier they are." (Isaac Abravanel.) ↩

377. Properly called "humanity," because nothing of it appears in brutes. בהמה אינה מקפדתו חוששת בצער חברתה: "for brutes have no concern or uneasiness at their

companions being in pain." (Judah ben Samuel, *Sefer Hasidim*.) ↩

378. When Seneca says, *Clementiam… omnes boni præstabunt, misericordiam autem vitabunt*, "all good men should show mildness, but avoid showing pity," he seems only to quibble (*De Clementia*). He has many other weak things upon this subject. That (sentence) *succurret [sapiens] alienis lachrymis, non accedet*, "a wise man will relieve a person in tears, but not cry himself," owns one use of tears: they obtain succor even from a Stoic. (Ibid.) ↩

379. Ἀγαθοὶ ἀριδάκρυες ἄνδρες: "Good men are very apt to shed tears." They who, of all writers, undertake to imitate nature most, oft introduce even their heroes weeping. (See how Homer represents Ulysses: *Odyssey* ε. 151–2–7–8.) The tears of men are in truth very different from the cries and ejulations of children. They are silent streams, and flow from other causes: commonly some tender, or perhaps philosophical, reflection. It is easy to see how hard hearts and dry eyes come to be fashionable. But for all that, it is certain the *glandulæ lacrymales*, "the glands we use when we cry," are not made for nothing. ↩

380. Plutarch, *Life of Pelopidas*. ↩

381. A generous nature pities even an enemy in distress. Ἐποικτείρω δέ νιν δύστηνον ἔμπας, καίπερ ὄντα δυσμενῆ: "I always pity a man in misery, although he be my enemy." (Sophocles, *Ajax*.) ↩

382. *Est hominum naturæ, quam sequi debemus, maximè inimica crudelitas*: "Cruelty is the most contrary that can be to human nature, which we ought to follow." (Cicero, *De Officiis*.) ↩

383. Δεινὸν μὲν ὁ κλέπτης, ἀλλ᾽ οὐχ οὕτω ὡς ὁ μοιχός: "A thief is a horrid creature, but not so bad as an adulterer." (Johannes Chrysostom, *Ad Populum Antiochenum*.) ↩

384. One of the *Subsessores alienorum matrimoniorum*: "them that lie in wait for other men's wives," as they are called in Valerius Maximus. (*Facta et dicta memorabilia*.) ↩

385. *Palam apparet, adhuc ætate Divi Hieronymi adulterium capite solere puniri: nunc magnatum lusus est*: "It is very manifest that, in the time of St. Jerome, adultery was punished with death: but now it is the sport of great men." (Erasmus, scholiast on St. Jerome.) ↩

386. For hence follows impunity, etc. משרבו מנאפים פסקו מים המרים: "From the overflowing of it, the adulterous derive bitter waters." (*Mishnah*, Sotah IX, 9.) ↩

387. *Is, qui nullius non uxorem concupiscit,… idem uxorem suam aspici non vult: et fidea acerrimus exactor, est perfidus: et mendacia persequitur, ipse perjurus*: "He who desires

every other man's wife... will not have his own looked upon, and is very strict with other men to keep their word, but breaks his own; prosecutes others for lying and is perjured himself." (Seneca, *De Ira*.) ↩

388. אשתו, τὴν ἑαυτοῦ γυναῖκα: "His own wife." ↩

389. What a monster in nature must he be, who, as if it was meritorious to dare to act against all these, (to use Seneca's words again, from *De Ira*) *satis justam causam putat amandi, quod aliena est [uxor]?* "Who thinks it a sufficient reason to be in love with her, because she is another man's wife." ↩

390. Οὐδὲ γὰρ τοῦτ' ἔνεστιν εἰπεῖν, ὡς τὸ σῶμα μόνον διαφθείρεται τῆς μοιχευομένης γυναικός, ἀλλ' εἰ δεῖ τἀληθὲς εἰπεῖν, ἡ ψυχὴ πρὸ τοῦ σώματος εἰς ἀλλοτρίωσιν ἐθίζεται, διδασκομένη πάντα τρόπον ἀποστρέφεσθαι, καὶ μισεῖν τὸν ἄνδρα, καὶ ἧττον ἂν ἦν δεινόν, εἰ τὸ μῖσος ἐπεδείκνυτο ἐμφανές, κτλ.: "For we may not only affirm that the body of an adulterous woman is not all that is corrupted; but if we would speak the truth, that her mind is more habitually alienated (from her husband) than her body; for she is taught to have an utter aversion and hatred to him, and it is no wonder if she shows her hatred in public." (Philo Judaeus, *De Decalogo*.) ↩

391. Marriage is κοινωνία παντὸς τοῦ βίου, ... οἰκειοτέρα καὶ μείζων τῶν ἄλλων [κοινωνιῶν]: "the partaking equally of everything in life... more freely and familiarly, than in any other [society]." (Isocrates, *Nicocles*.) ↩

392. Ἁπαλὸν ζῶον: "The soft creature," St. Basil. (*Homilia dicta in Lacisis*.) ↩

393. Ἔπεισας, ἐξέθωψας: "over-persuaded and enticed," says the penitent woman in Sophocles (according to Plutarch, *Moralia*). ↩

394. Ψυχρὸν παραγκάλισμα... Γυνὴ κακὴ ξύνευνος: "A cold embrace... to have a lewd woman for a wife." (Sophocles, *Antigone*.) ↩

395. *Quid enim salvi est mulieri, amissa pudicitia?* "What else can be safe, when the woman has lost her modesty?" (Livy, *History of Rome*.) ↩

396. Οἱ μηδὲν ἠδικηκότες ἄθλιοι παῖδες μηδ' ἑτέρῳ γένει προσνεμηθῆναι δυνάμενοι, μή τε τῷ τοῦ γήμαντος, μή τε τῷ τοῦ μοιχοῦ: "The miserable children, who have done nobody any injury, will not be owned by any relations, either of the married person or of the adulterer." (Philo Judaeus, *De Decalogo*.) ↩

397. Such as Aristippus uses to Diogenes, in Athenæus: Ἆρά γε μή τι σοι ἄτοπον δοκεῖ εἶναι Διογενὲς οἰκίαν οἰκεῖν, ἐν ᾗ πρότερον ᾤκησαν ἄλλοι; οὐ γὰρ ἔφη. τί δὲ ναῦν, ἐν ᾗ πολλοὶ πεπλεύκασιν; οὐδὲ τοῦτο ἔφη. οὕτως...: "Do you see any absurdity, Diogenes, in living in a house that another person has lived in before? No, says he; or in sailing in a

ship where a great many have sailed? No, nor in that neither, says he. No more is there in…" (*Deipnosophistae*.) Senseless stuff. Nor is that of the adulterous woman in Proverbs 30:18–20 better: where דרך גבר בעלמה: "the way of a man with a maid," is placed with the way of an eagle in the air, of a serpent upon a rock, and of a ship in the sea, שלא יעשה בה רושם יוכר אחר שעה: "which leave no track to be seen after them;" and therefore she מקנחת פיה של מטה: "wipes her mouth," and then thinks that אחר זה תוכל לא פעלתי און: "she may say afterwards, 'What have I done amiss?'" (see *Kab we-Naki*.) ↩

398. *Nemo malus felix: minimè corruptor, etc.*: "No bad man can be happy; to be sure no debauchee can, etc." (Juvenal, *Satires*.) ↩

399. Ἀναπόδραστος γὰρ ὁ θεῖος νόμος: "There is no escaping the divine law." (Plotinus, *Enneads*.) ↩

400. Καὶ γὰρ ἂν παραντίκα κρύψῃ, ὕστερον ὀφθήσῃ: "For, if you are hid for the present, you will be found out afterwards." (Isocrates, *Demonicus*.) Μαρτυρήσουσιν… ἡ κλίνη καὶ ὁ λύχνος ὁ Μεγαπένθους: "The bed, the lamp, will bear testimony, O Megapenthus." (Lucian, *Cataplus*.) ↩

401. Ἡδονὴ μὲν γὰρ ἁπάντων ἀλαζονέστατον: "Pleasure is the aptest of anything to boast." (Plato, *Philebus*.) ↩

402. *Quid non sentit amor?* "What is it that love can't see?" (Ovid, *Metamorphoses*.) ↩

403. Ἀγαθὸν οὐ τὸ μὴ ἀδικεῖν, ἀλλὰ τὸ μηδὲ ἐθέλειν: "To be good is not only not to do an injury, but not so much as to desire to do one." A *gnome*, "saying," of Democrates. (*Ethica*.) ↩

404. אבק לשון הרע: "The dust of an ill tongue." (*Bava Batra*.) ↩

405. המלבין פני חבירו ברבים אין לו חלק לעה"ב: "He that puts his companion to shame in public, shall have no portion in the next life." (Maimonides, *Mishneh Torah*, Hilkot Deot VI, 8, and similar passages.) For, according to the Jewish doctors, he who does this breaks the sixth commandment. (Isaac Abravanel.) ↩

406. See how chaste the Romans were once. *Quo matronale decus verecundiæ munimento tutius esset, in jus vocanti matronam corpus ejus attingere non permiserunt, ut inviolata manûs alienæ tactu stola relinqueretur*: "That the decent modesty of a matron might the more securely be preserved, if any man sued her, he was not allowed so much as to touch her, that her garment might remain undefiled by the hands of any stranger." (Valerius Maximus, *De Matrimoniorum Ritu, et Necessitudinum Officiis*.) And it is told of Publius Mænius, that *tristi exemplo præcepit [filiæ fuæ], ut non solum*

virginitatem illibatam, sed etiam oscula ad virum sincera perferret: "He gave it in charge to his daughter, with a severe threat, that she should carry to her husband not only her virginity untouched, but her kisses chaste." (Valerius Maximus, *Facta et dicta memorabilia*.) ↵

407. *Quanto autem præstantior est animus corpore, tanto sceleratiùs corrumpitur*: "By how much the mind is more excellent than the body, by so much is the corrupting of it a greater wickedness." (St. Augustine, *De Mendacio*.) ↵

408. Meddlers. (Editor's note.) ↵

409. Οὗτοί εἰσιν οἱ λοιμοὶ οἱ τὸ ἴδιον κακὸν ἐπὶ πάντας ἄγειν φιλονεικοῦντες, κτλ.: "These are the pestilent fellows, who labor to persuade everybody to be guilty of the same crimes with themselves." (St. Basil, *Homily on Psalm 1*.) ↵

410. *Omnes enim immemorem beneficii oderunt*: "For everybody hates a man that forgets the kindnesses that have been done to him." (Cicero, *De Officiis*.) And the same may be said of the unfaithful, perjured, etc. ↵

411. *Quid ergo, anima… nullane habet alimenta propria? an ejus esca scientia vobis videtur?* "What then, is there no proper nourishment for the mind? does not knowledge seem to be the food of it?" (St. Augustine, *De Beata Vita*.) ↵

412. *Alter in alterius exitium levi compendio ducitur*: "They destroy one another in the shortest way that they can." (Seneca, *De Ira*.) ↵

413. Aristotle says a good man would be neither ἄφιλος, "without a friend," nor πολύφιλος, "have a great number of friends." (*Nicomachean Ethics*.) This is just. Therefore Seneca seems to go a little too far, when he writes, *Omnes amicos habere operosum esse, satis esse inimicos non habere*: "It requires great pains to make all men our friends, it is sufficient to have no enemies." (*Epistles*.) ↵

414. Ζῶον συναγελαστικὸν ὁ ἄνθρωπος: "Man is a sociable creature." (St. Basil, *Homily on Psalm 14*.) ↵

415. Man is, in Gregory Nazianzen's words, τὸ πολυτροπώτατον τῶν ζώων, καὶ ποικιλώτατον: "a creature who loves to turn his thoughts to variety of things, and to employ himself in different ways." (*The Second Oration*.) ↵

416. Πᾶς ἐστι νόμος… πόλεως συνθήκη κοινή: "Every law… is the general compact of the city." (Demosthenes, *Against Aristogeiton*.) ↵

417. Νόμος ἐστὶ τοῦ ὄντος εὕρεσις: "The law is the finding out and specifying that which really is." (Stobaeus on Plato's *Minos*.) ↵

418. Δίκαιον φύσει, ἀκίνητον, καὶ πανταχοῦ τὴν αὐτὴν ἔχει δύναμιν, ὥσπερ τὸ πῦρ καὶ ἐνθάδε καὶ ἐν *Πέρσαις* καίει: "Justice is founded in nature, is unalterable, and is equally in force everywhere; in the same manner as the fire burns here and in Persia." (Aristotle, *Nicomachean Ethics*.) ↵

419. Even the Heathens believed that above all human κηρύγματα: "edicts" there were ἄγραπτα κἀσφαλῆ θεῶν νόμιμα: "unwritten and unalterable laws of the Gods," which mortals ought not to transgress: οὐ γὰρ τι νῦν γε κἀχθὲς ἀλλ᾽ ἀεί ποτε ζῇ ταῦτα: "because these are in force, not only for a day or two, but forever." (Sophocles, *Oedipus Rex*.) *Nec si regnante Tarquinio nulla erat Romæ scripta lex de stupris, idcirco non contra... legem sempiternam Sex. Tarquinius vim Lucretiæ... attulit. Erat enim ratio profecta à rerum natura, et ad rectè faciendum impellens, et à delicto avocans: quæ non cum denique incipit lex esse, cùm scripta est, sed tum cùm orta est. Orta autem simul est cum mente divina*: "Wherefore if, in the reign of Tarquin, there were no written laws at Rome against whoredom, yet nevertheless Sextus Tarquinius acted contrary to an eternal law when he ravishd Lucretia; for there is such a thing as reason, which proceeds from the nature of things, and which urges us to do that which is right, and forbids us to commit any crimes; which (reason) does not then begin to be a law when it is written down, but was from the beginning; that is, it began when the divine mind began." (Cicero, *De Legibus*.) ↵

420. *Si tanta potestas est stultorum sententiis atque jussis, ut eorum suffragiis rerum natura vertatur; cur non sanciunt, ut, quæ mala perniciosaque sunt, habeantur pro bonis, ac salutaribus? aut cùr, cum jus ex injuria lex facere possit, bonum eadem facere non possit ex malo?* "If the opinions or commands of weak and foolish men are of so great force as to overturn the nature of things by their majority; why do they not establish it by a law, that those things which are evil and pernicious shall become good and advantageous? And why cannot the same law make the things that are good evil, as well as make an injury a lawful thing?" (Cicero, *De Legibus*.) ↵

421. In person, or by proxy. ↵

422. Plato says when any man has seen our form of government, etc., and remains under it, ἤδη φαμὲν τοῦτον ὡμολογηκέναι ἔργῳ ἡμῖν: "that then we say, such a one does indeed agree with us." (*Crito*.) ↵

423. *Illud stultissimum, existimare omnia justa esse, quæ scita sint in populorum institutis, aut legibus. ... Si populorum jussis, si principum decretis, si sententiis judicum, jurà constituerentur, jus esset latrocinari: jus, adulterare: jus, testamenta falsa supponere, si hæc suffragiis aut scitis multitudinis probarentur*: "That's very foolish indeed, to imagine that all those things are just which are establishd by the decrees and laws of the people.... If right were made by the ordinances of the people, by the decrees of

princes, or by the sentences of judges, it would be right to rob on the highway; it would be right to commit adultery; it would be right to forge wills; supposing all these were allowed by the majority and by the decrees of the populacy." (Cicero, *De Legibus*.) ↩

424. Manicheans of old, and some moderns. ↩

425. Like those particularly of Julius Cæsar, of whom it is reported that *anamadversâ apud Herculis templum magni Alexandri imagine, ingemuit; quasi pertæsus ignaviam suam, quod nihil dum à se memorabile actum esset in ætate quâ jam Alexander orbem terrarum subegisset*: "upon viewing the statue of Alexader the Great in the temple of Hercules, he gave a sigh, as it were, to reproach his own sluggishness that he had done no memorable thing, at an age when Alexander had conquered the whole world." (Suetonius, *Lives of the Caesars*.) ↩

426. Some go to war ὥσπερ ἐπὶ θήραν καὶ κυνηγέσιον ἀνθρώπων: "in order to hunt down and worry men." (Plutarch, *Life of Alexander*.) Not out of necessity, and in order to peace; which is the true end of war, Πολεοῦμεν, ἵνα εἰρήνην ἄγωμεν: "We go to war, that we may procure peace." (Aristotle, *Nicomachean Ethics*.) *Ita bellum suscipiatur, ut nihil aliud quàm pax quæsita videatur*: "War should be undertaken in such a manner that nothing else but peace may be seen to be aimed at by it." (Cicero, *De Officiis*.) ↩

427. Οἱ ἄνθρωποι οὐ μόνον τῆς τεκνοποιίας χάριν συνοικοῦσιν, ἀλλὰ καὶ τῶν εἰς τὸν βίον, κτλ.: "Men do not marry for the sake of having children only, but for all the other purposes of life." (Aristotle, *Nicomachean Ethics*.) ↩

428. Ἀνδρὶ καὶ γυναικὶ φιλία δοκεῖ κατὰ φύσιν ὑπάρχειν · ἄνθρωπος γὰρ τῇ φύσει συνδυαστικὸν μᾶλλον ἢ πολιτικόν: "It is natural for a man to love a woman; for man is as much made for the society of a woman, as for the society of each other." (Aristotle, *Nicomachean Ethics*.) Ὡς γὰρ ἡ μαγνῆτις λίθος... πρὸς ἑαυτὴν τὸν σίδηρον ἕλκει · οὕτω τὸ τοῦ θήλεος σῶμα... τὸ τοῦ ἄρρενος σῶμα πρὸς τὴν μίξιν ἕλκει: "For as the lodestone draws iron, so the woman attracts the man to unite with her." (St. Basil.) ↩

429. That sure is a hard law in Plato, which enjoins ἀπέχεσθαι ἀρούρας θηλείας πάσης, ἐν ᾗ μὴ βούλοιο ἄν σοι φύεσθαι τὸ σπαρέν: "men to have no familiarity with a woman, without wishing for the success of it." (*Laws*.) That mentioned in *Sefer Haredim* says otherwise; מ"ע לק"ם אדם עונתו ואף כשאשתי מעוברה וכו: "It is an affirmative precept, that a man should act the part of a husband, though his wife is incapable of having any children." (Eliezer Azkari.) Many opinions are taken up upon slight reasons. When Ocellus Lucianus says, Αὐτὰς τὰς δυνάμεις, καὶ τὰ ὄργανα, καὶ τὰς ὀρέξεις τὰς πρὸς τὴν μίξιν ὑπὸ θεοῦ δεδομένας ἀνθρώποις, οὐχ ἡδονῆς ἕνεκα δεδόσθαι συμβέβηκεν, ἀλλὰ τῆς εἰς τὸν ἀεὶ χρόνον διαμονῆς τοῦ γένους: "that the powers, the organs, and the desire of procreation, were given men by God, not for the sake of

pleasure, but for the perpetual continuation of mankind," how does he know that they were not given for both these ends, in a regular way (*On the Nature of the Whole*)? And so when Clement of Alexandria shows his zeal against τὰς ἀκάρπους σποράς, τὴν πρὸς τὰς ἐγκύους ὁμιλίαν: "such familiarities as produce no effect, meddling with pregnant women," etc., adding, ψιλὴ γὰρ ἡδονή, κἂν ἐν γάμῳ παραληφθῇ, παράνομός ἐςι, κτλ.: "that such mean pleasure is unlawful, even in married persons" (*Paedagogus*), he does this because ὁ Μωσῆς ἀπάγει τῶν ἐγκύων τοὺς ἄνδρας: "Moses forbids a man coming near a pregnant woman," and then cites a text to prove this which is nothing to the purpose, nor I believe anywhere to be found: Οὐκ ἔδεσαι τὸν λαγῶν, οὐδὲ τὴν ὕαιναν: "Thou shalt not eat a hare or a hyaena" (*Quem interpretem secutus sit Clemens nescio*: "What commentator Clement followed, I know not." —Gentian Hervetus). Certainly the Jews understand their lawgiver otherwise. See how that עונה, "conjugal due," mentioned in the law is explained by Maimonides in *Mishneh Torah* (Hilkot Ishut XIV). Nor are the suffrages of Christians wanting, *Deus, cum cæteras animantes, suscepto fœtu, maribus repugnare voluisset, solam omnium mulierem patientem viri fecit;... ne feminis repugnantibus, libido cogeret viros aliud appetere, etc.*: "When God made all other female animals, so as to refuse the males when they are pregnant, he made women only capable of men;... lest, upon their refusal, men's violent passions should force them to go after others, etc.," that is, that the man and wife might be kept inseparably together. (Lactantius, *Divine Institutes*.) ↩

430. Καὶ τὸ χρήσιμον εἶναι δοκεῖ, καὶ τὸ ἡδὺ ἐν ταύτῃ τῇ φιλίᾳ: "There seems to be both profit and pleasure in this sort of friendship." (Aristotle, *Nicomachean Ethics*.) כשאיש ואשה נוהגים כראוי שכינה ביניהם: "When the man and the wife behave themselves towards each other as they ought, they are then most intimately united." (*Reshit Hokmah*.) ↩

431. Ἔρως... καθάπερ ἑνὸς ζώου διττὰ τμήματα... εἰς ταὐτὸν ἁρμόττεται: "Love... is like two parts of the same living creature... united into one." (Philo Judaeus, *On The Creation*.) ↩

432. True love is to be found in marriage, or nowhere. Πόρνη γὰρ φιλεῖν οὐκ ἐπίσταται, ἀλλ' ἐπιβουλεύει μόνον: "For there is no real love in whoring; nothing but ensnaring one another." (St. Chrysostom, *Ad Populum Antiochenum*.) ערותה מגולה והלב מכוסה: "They discover their nakedness, but hide their real sentiments," a homely but true saying of a Jewish commentator (Levi ben Gershom). ↩

433. *Quod facere turpe non est modò occultè; id dicere obscœnum est*: "That which has no evil in it when it is done in private, may be obscene when spoke publicly." (Cicero, *De Officiis*.) ↩

434. Ἐὰν γὰρ ᾖ κοσμία καὶ ἐπιεικής, οὐ μόνον τὴν ἀπὸ τῆς κοινωνίας παραμυθίαν παρέξει

τῷ ἀνδρὶ, ἀλλὰ καὶ ἐν τοῖς ἄλλοις ἅπασι πολλὴν τῆς ἑαυτῆς χρείαν ἐπιδείξεται, κτλ.: "For, if she be neat and good-natured, she will not only in general be a comfort to her husband, but will be very useful to him in every particular." (St. Chrysostom, *Homily on Genesis* 16.) ↩

435. Διῄρηται τὰ ἔργα, καὶ ἔστιν ἕτερα ἀνδρὸς, καὶ γυναικός · ἐπαρκοῦσιν οὖν ἀλλήλοις εἰς τὸ κοινὸν τιθέντες τὰ ἴδια: "Their business is different, there is one sort of employment for the man, and another for the woman; so that they are assistant to each other, by joining their forces together." (Aristotle, *Nicomachean Ethics.*) ↩

436. See the conversation between Ischomachus and his wife in Xenophon. (*Oeconomicus.*) ↩

437. Though Plato (like most of the old Greeks and Romans) among many very fine things has now and then some that are weak, and even absurd; yet I cannot think that by his community of women he meant anything like that which is said in Athenæus to have been practiced παρὰ Τυρρηνοῖς ἐκτόπως τρυφήσασιν: "among the Tyrrhenians, who were exceedingly debauched" (*Deipnosophistae*), or that his thought could be so gross as Lactantius represents it: *Scilicet ut ad eandem mulierem multi viri, tanquam canes, confluerent*: "namely, that several men, like so many dogs, should run after one woman." (*Divine Institutes.*) For thus, property being taken out of the world, a great part of virtue is extinguished, and all industry and improvements are at an end. And besides that, many of the most substantial comforts and innocent delights of this life are destroyed at once. *Si omnes omnium fuerint et mariti, et patres, et uxores, et liberi, quæ ista confusio generis humani est?... Quis aut vir mulierem, aut mulier virum diligit, nisi habitaverint semper unà? nisi devota mens, et servata invicem fides individuam fecerit caritatem, etc.*: "If all were the husbands and fathers, and wives and children, of all, what a confusion would there be among mankind?... for how can the man love the woman, and the woman the man, unless they live always together? unless their minds be devoted to each, and their fidelity mutual, which will make their affections inseparable, etc." (Lactantius, *Divine Institutes.*) However it must be confessed that Plato has advanced more than was consistent with his own gravity, or with nature. The best excuse to be made for him, that I know of, is that in Athenæus, Ἔοικεν ὁ Πλάτων μὴ τοῖς οὖσιν ἀνθρώποις γράψαι τοὺς νόμους, ἀλλὰ τοῖς ὑπ' αὐτοῦ διαπλαττομένοις: "That Plato seems to have made his laws not for such as men now are, but for men of his own imagination" (*Deipnosophistae*): or perhaps to say, that he was so intent upon strengthening and defending his commonwealth, that he forgot, if men must live after his manner, there would be little in it worth defending. After all, his meaning to me is not perfectly clear. ↩

438. Everyone knows how marriages were made among the Romans, *confarreatione*, "by offering up of burnt cakes," *coemptione*, "by the man and his wife, as it were, buying one another, by giving and taking a piece of money," *usu*, "or by use, when the woman

had lived with the man a whole year:" of which ways the two former were attended with many ceremonies: and the *legitimæ tabellæ*, "writings appointed by law," or at least consent of friends (which could not be given without some solemnity) preceded all, *auspicia*, "omens," were usually taken, public notaries and witnesses assisted, etc. Among the Greeks, men and women were espoused by mutual promises of fidelity: besides which there were witnesses, and dotal writings (προικῷα); at the wedding, sacrifices to Diana and other deities, and the γαμήλιοι ἐυχαὶ, "nuptial prayers;" and after that, perhaps the being shut up together, eating the κυδώνιον, "quince, together," a formal λύσις ζώνης, "untying of the bride's girdle," etc. The קדושין, "nuptials," of the Jews have been performed בכסף, "by money," or בשטר, "by writings of contract," or ביאה, "by going into the house:" the ceremonies accompanying which may be seen particularly in *Shulhan Aruk* with the additions of Rabbi Moses Isserles (*Eben Ha-Ezer*). And (to pass by other nations) the form of solemnization of matrimony, and the manner in which persons married give their troth each to other among us, are extant in our public offices: where they may be seen by such as seem to have forgot what they are. ↩

439. *Connubio stabili*: "By a lasting marriage." (Virgil, *Aeneid*.) ↩

440. והיו לבשר אחד דכך דרכה לאתייחדא דכר ונוקבא. בקירוב בשר ... דלא יהא דבר חוצץ וכו׳: "And they became one flesh, for it is the custom for men and women to come together, ... and that they be no more divided." (Elijah ben Moses de Vidas, *Reshit Hokmah*.) ↩

441. Αὕτη χρημάτων κοινωνία προσήκει μάλιστα τοῖς γαμοῦσιν, εἰς μίαν οὐσίαν πάντα καταχεαμένοις καὶ ἀναμίξασι, μὴ τὸ μέρος ἴδιον, καὶ τὸ μέρος ἀλλότριον, ἀλλὰ πᾶν ἴδιον ἡγεῖσθαι, καὶ μηδὲν ἀλλότριον: "It belongs chiefly to married persons to mix their fortunes together, so as to have but one common stock; and not for them to think that part of it belongs particularly to one and part to the other, but the whole is their own jointly." (Plutarch, *Moralia*.) ↩

442. Σύνδεσμος τὰ τέκνα δοκεῖ εἶναι: "Children seem to be the bond (of matrimony)." (Aristotle, *Nicomachean Ethics*.) ↩

443. In respect of which, that in Plutarch particularly is true, Ἡ φύσις μάγνυσι διὰ τῶν σωμάτων ἡμᾶς, ἵν᾽ ἐξ ἑκατέρων μέρος λαβοῦσα, καὶ τυγχέασα, κοινὸν ἀμφοτέροις ἀποδῷ τὸ γενόμενον: "Nature, by means of our bodies, so intermixes us, that what is produced becomes common to both, being a part of each, when united together." (*Advice to Bride and Groom*.) ↩

444. *Socrates ab adolescentulo quodam consultus, uxorem duceret, an se omni matrimonio abstineret, respondit, Utrum eorum fecisset, acturum pœnitentiam. Hîc te, inquit, solitudo, hîc orbitas, hîc generis interitus, hîc hæres alienus excipiet: illic perpetua*

solicitudo, contextus querelarum, ... incertus liberorum eventus: "Socrates being consulted by a young man, whether he should take a wife or abstain wholly from matrimony, answered that which of them so ever he did, he would repent of it. On the one hand, says he, solitariness, want of children, the death of relations, want of an heir, will attend you; on the other hand (you will find) perpetual anxiety, uninterrupted complaints,... and the uncertain event of children." (Valerius Maximus, *Facta et dicta memorabilia*.) ↩

445. Χρόνῳ συνηθείας ἐντεκούσης πάθος αἰσθάνεται τῷ λογισμῷ τὸ φίλειν καὶ τὸ ἀγαπᾶν ἐπιτεινόμενον: "When, by living a long time together, their mutual affection is eslablished, we find that, which was at first passion, is by reason become true friendship and love." (Plutarch, *Moralia*.) ↩

446. It is visible that polygamy, pellicate [keeping a mistress], etc. must be included here. They are not only inconsistent with our forms, and the very letter of the marriage contract, but with the essence of marriage, which lies in such a union and love as can only be between two. Aristotle does not allow there can be even perfect friendship between more than two: much less therefore, perfect love: Πολλοῖς εἶναι φίλον, κατὰ τὴν τελείαν φιλίαν, οὐκ ἐνδέχεται, ὥσπερ οὐδ' ἐρᾶν πολλῶν ἅμα: "It is impossible to be a friend to a great many, I mean, to be in perfect friendship with them, as it is impossible to have a love for a great many at the same time." (*Nicomachean Ethics*.) Ἔστι γὰρ φίλος ἄλλος αὑτός: "For a friend is a second self." (Plutarch, *Moralia*.) ↩

447. *Fœcunda culpæ sæcula nuptias Primàm inquinavere, et genus, et domos. Hôc fonte derivata clades In patriam, populumque fluxit*: "The ages that were fruitful in vice first defiled marriages, corrupted relations and families. From this fountain flowed that destruction which overwhelmed the country and its inhabitants." (Horace, *Odes*.) ↩

448. Κρατεῖν δεῖ τὸν ἄνδρα τῆς γυναικός οὐχ ὡς δεσπότην κτήματος, ἀλλ' ὡς ψυχὴν σώματος, συμπαθοῦντα καὶ συμπεφυκότα τῇ εὐνοίᾳ: "The husband ought to have a power over the wife, not such as a man has over his goods, but such as the soul has over the body, sympathizing and becoming one in benevolence." (Plutarch, *Advice to Bride and Groom*.) (A sentence which deserves to be written in letters of gold.) Ὅπου σὺ Γάϊος, ἐγὼ Γαΐα · ... ὅπου σὺ κύριος καὶ οἰκοδεσπότης, καὶ ἐγὼ κυρία καὶ οἰκοδέσποινα: "Where you are the man Gaias, I am the woman Gaia; where you are master and governor, I am mistress and governess." (Also in Plutarch, *Roman Questions*.) ↩

449. Κατὰ φύσιν οἱ ἄρρενες οὐ μόνον ἐν τοῖς ἀνθρώποις, ἀλλὰ καὶ ἐν τοῖς ἄλλοις ζώοις ἄρχουι: "Nature has appointed the males to govern, not only among mankind, but among all other living creatures." (Plato, according to Diogenes Laërtius, *Lives and Opinions of Eminent Philosophers*.) ↩

450. Πολυπλέθρους δέ σοι γυίας Λείψω. πατρὸς γὰρ ταῦτ᾽ ἐδεξάμην πάρα: "I shall leave you a very good estate. For I had such a one from my father." (Euripides, *Alcestis*.) *Parentes vos alendo nepotum nutriendorum debito (si quis est pudor) alligaverunt*: "Your parents, in maintaining you, made it a debt upon you (if you have any sense of shame) to maintain your children." (Valerius Maximus, *Facta et dicta memorabilia*.) ↩

451. *Incertus quò fata ferant, ubi sistere detur*: "it is uncertain which way fate will carry me, or where I shall settle," in the poet's language. (Virgil, *Aeneid*.) ↩

452. See that moving description of the Ἦμαρ ὀρφανικὸν: "an orphan" in Homer's *Iliad*. ↩

453. I could never think of that Arabic saying without pity, "The barber [אלחגאם] learns to shave upon the head of an orphan." ↩

454. For certainly, when it can be, *Hoc patrium est, potius consuefacere filium sua sponte recte facere, quàm alieno metu*: "It is the duty of a father to accustom his son to do right from his own good will, rather than from the fear of others." (Terence, *The Brothers*.) ↩

455. Πρὸς ταῦτα μόνον ἀπειθοῦντες γονεῦσι, πρὸς ἃ καὶ αὐτοὶ τοῖς θείοις νόμοις οὐ πείθονται: "We should refuse obedience to parents, only in such things as are contrary to the laws of God." (Hierocles, *Commentary on the Carmen Aureum*.) ↩

456. The barbarity of the thing at length put a stop to the custom of exposing children: but it had been practised by the Persians, Greeks, etc. Romulus's law only restrained it, but did not abolish it. For it enjoined his citizens only, ἅπασαν ἄρρενα γενεὰν ἐκτρέφειν, καὶ θυγατέρων τὰς πρωτογόνους · ἀποκτιννύναι δὲ μηδὲν τῶν γεννωμένων νεώτερον τριετοῦς, πλὴν εἴ τι γένοιτο παιδίον ἀνάπηρον, κτλ.: "to bring up all the males, and the firstborn of the daughters; and not to destroy any of them after they were three years old, unless they were maimed." (Dionysius of Halicarnassus, *Roman Antiquities*.) And besides, ἅπασαν, ὡς εἰπεῖν, ἔδωκεν ἐξουσίαν πατρὶ καθ᾽ υἱοῦ, καὶ παρὰ πάντα τὸν τοῦ βίου χρόνον, κτλ.: "the father had absolute power over the son given him, and that during his whole life." (Hierocles, *Commentary on the Carmen Aureum*.) ↩

457. Ῥωμαίοις οὐθὲν ἴδιόν ἐστι κτῆμα ζώντων ἔτι τῶν πατέρων, ἀλλὰ καὶ τὰ χρήματα καὶ τὰ σώματα τῶν παίδων ὅ, τι βούλονται διατιθέναι τοῖς πατράσιν ἀποδέδοται: "Among the Romans, children had nothing of their own, while their fathers were alive; but the goods and the bodies of the children were entirely at the disposal of the fathers, to do what they would with them." (Dionysius of Halicarnassus, *Roman Antiquities*.) These are instances of such laws as should not be, by proposition IV, section VII. ↩

458. *Roma patrem patriæ Ciceronem libera dixit*: "When Rome had liberty to speak, she called Cicero the father of his country." (Juvenal, *Satires*.) ↩

459. Ὡς λογικῶν ἡμῶν ἄρξον: "That should govern us as rational creatures." (Arrian, *Discourses of Epictetus.*) ↵

460. שללתך שותפין ביצירתם: "All the three had a share in the formation of them." (Eliezer Azkari, *Sefer Haredim.*) ↵

461. *Utinam oculos in pectora possent Inserere, et patrias intus deprendere curas*: "I wish they could look into their breasts, and see what the inward cares of parents are." (Ovid, *Metamorphoses.*) ↵

462. I confess in Seneca's words, *minimum esse beneficium patris matrisque concubitum, nisi accesserint alia, quæ prosequerentur hoc initium muneris, et aliis oficiis hoc ratum facerent*: "that parents merely begetting of their children is the smallest kindness, if there were nothing else which followed this first office, and confirmed it by other duties." (*De Beneficiis.*) ↵

463. *Τὸ αἰσθάνεσθαι ὅτι ζῇ τῶν ἡδέων καθ' αὑτό · φύσει γὰρ ἀγαθὸν ἡ ζωή ·*: "To feel that we are alive is a real pleasure of itself; for life is naturally a good thing." (Aristotle, *Nicomachean Ethics.*) The sense of life (of being alive) seems to be something more than what Seneca calls *muscarum ac vermium bonum*: "the good of flies and worms." (*De Beneficiis.*) ↵

464. Οἱ παλαιοὶ τῶν Ῥωμαίων νόμοι, κτλ. ... οἱ δὲ ἔτι παλαιότεροι τοσοῦτο τοὺς γονέας ἐσέφθησαν, ὡς καὶ θεοὺς αὐτοὺς ὁρμῆσκι: "The ancient laws of the Romans,... and they that are older yet, paid so much reverence to parents as to oblige us to call them Gods." (Simplicius, *Commentary on the Enchiridion.*) ↵

465. *Meo judicio pietas fundamentum est omnium virtutum*: "In my opinion, piety is the foundation of all virtues." (Cicero, *Oration for Plancius.*) The same author reckons, among those things that are laudable, *parentem vereri ut deum (neque enim multo secus parens liberis)*: "to reverence a parent as a God (for the relation of a parent to his children is pretty much the same)." (Ibid.) Οὐδ' αὖ πάλιν μείζων ἐπίδειξις ἀθέου γέγονε τῆς περὶ γονεῖς ὀλιγωρίας καὶ πλημμελείας: "There is no greater demonstration of an atheist, than is shown in the contemning or abusing parents." (Plutarch, *Concerning Brotherly Love.*) ↵

466. Πάντες... λέγουσι καὶ ᾄδουσιν, ὡς γονεῦσι τιμὴν μετὰ θεοὺς πρώτην καὶ μεγίστην ἥ τε φύσις, ὅ, τε τὴν φύσιν σῴζων νόμος ἀπέδωκε: "All writers in prose or poetry affirm that nature, and the laws that are agreeable to nature, command the first and greatest reverence to be paid to parents next to the Gods." (Plutarch, *Concerning Brotherly Love.*) Γονέων τιμὴν μετὰ τὴν πρὸς θεὸν δευτέραν ἔταξεν *[Μωυσῆς]*: "[Moses] commanded that honor should be paid to parents next to God." (Josephus, *Against Apion.*) We indeed usually divide the two tables of Moses's law so that the fifth

commandment (Honor thy father and thy mother) falls in the second, but the Jews themselves divide them otherwise, ὡς εἶναι τῆς μὲν μιᾶς γραφῆς τὴν ἀρχὴν Θεὸν καὶ πατέρα... τοῦ παντός, τὸ δὲ στέλος γονεῖς, κτλ.: "so that the first table begins with (the duty to) the God and father... of all, and ends with (the duty to) parents." (Philo Judaeus, *De Decalogo*.) Agreeably to this, Josephus says that οἱ δέκα λόγοι: "the ten commandments" were written upon two tables, ἀνὰ πέντε μὲν εἰς ἑκατέραν [πλάκα]: "five upon each [table]." (*Antiquities of the Jews*.) Abravanel reckons the fifth commandment the last of the first table, and says their *Hhakamim*: "wise men" do so; and in the offices of that nation these commandments are mentioned as written על הלוחות חמשה חמשה: "five upon each table." (*Commentary on the Torah*.) ↩

467. *Prima igitur et optima rerum natura pietatis est magistra, etc.*: "The nature of things, which is the first and best rule of all, teaches us what piety is, etc." (Valerius Maximus, *Facta et dicta memorabilia*.) ↩

468. Ὁ χρόνος, τἄλλα πάντ᾽ ἀφαιρῶν, τῷ γήρᾳ προστίθησι τὴν ἐπιστήμην: "Time, which takes away everything else from us, adds knowledge to old age." (Plutarch, *The Education of Children*.) ↩

469. שאל אביך ויגדך: "ask thy father, and he will show thee." (Deuteronomy 32:7.) ↩

470. Δόξειε δ᾽ ἂν τροφῆς γονεῦσι δεῖν μάλιστ᾽ ἐπαρκεῖν, ὡς ὀφείλοντας, καὶ τοῖς αἰτίοις τοῦ εἶναι... καὶ τιμὴν δὲ καθάπερ θεοῖς: "We ought, in the first place, to supply the necessities of our parents, as a debt due to them who are the authors of our being... and to reference them as Gods." (Aristotle, *Nicomachean Ethics*.) Among the ancients θρεπτήρια, "the rewards of education," and τροφεῖα, "maintenance of parents," were reckoned *due*. And he, who does not requite to his parents הטובה שגמלוהו, "the good which they have bestowed on him," is called κατ᾽ ἐξοχην, רשע: "in an eminent sense *wicked*." (Eliezer Azkari, *Sefer Haredim*.) ↩

471. Τοιοῦτος γίνου περὶ τοὺς γονεῖς, οἵους ἂν εὔξαιο περὶ σεαυτὸν γενέσθαι τοὺς σαυτοῦ παῖδας: "Do you behave yourself, to your parents, as you would wish your children to behave themselves towards you." (Isocrates.) ↩

472. That epithet *pius* (*pius Æneas*) shines in Virgil's *Aeneid*. ↩

473. *Posita est inter parentes ac liberos honesta contentio, dederint majora, an receperint*: "There is a very laudable contest betwixt parents and children, viz.: whether they have given or received most." (Seneca, *De Beneficiis*.) ↩

474. That is, methinks, a moving description in St. Basil (Περὶ πλεονεξ) a conflict which a poor man had within himself, when he had no other way left to preserve life but by selling one of his children. (*Homilia in illud Lucæ, destruam horrea mea*.) ↩

475. *Prima societas in ipso conjugio est: proxima in liberis, etc.*: "The strongest alliance is in marriage itself, the next in children, etc." (Cicero, *De Officiis*.) ↵

476. *Mulier conjuncta viro concessit in unum*: "After the man and woman are joined together, they become one." (Lucretius, *De Rerum Natura*.) כגוף אחד חשיבי: "They are looked upon as one body," (according to Rabbi Eliezer Azkari and others). ↵

477. Ἡ συγγενικὴ [φιλία] φαίνεται πολυειδὴς εἶναι, καὶ ἠρτῆσθαι πᾶσα ἐκ τῆς πατρικῆς · οἱ γονεῖς μὲν γὰρ στέργουσι τὰ τέκνα, ὡς ἑαυτῶν τι ὄντα · τὰ δὲ τέκνα τοὺς γονεῖς, ὡς ἀπ' ἐκείνων τι ὄντα… Ἀδελφοὶ δ' ἀλλήλους [φιλοῦσι] τῷ ἐκ τῶν αὐτῶν πεφυκέναι… Ἀνεψιοὶ δὲ καὶ οἱ λοιποὶ συγγενεῖς… τῷ ἀπὸ τῶν αὐτῶν εἶναι · γίνονται δ' οἳ μὲν οἰκειότεροι οἳ δ' ἀλλοτριώτεροι, κτλ.: "There are a great many sorts of friendship among relations, all of them depending upon the parents. For parents have a tender affection for their children because they are part of themselves; and so have the children for the parents, because they are derived from them.… Brothers also (love) one another, because they are born of the same parents.… cousins also and other relations,… because they proceed from the same parents also.… And there are some nearer related, and some further off." (Aristotle, *Nicomachean Ethics*.) ↵

478. *Quàm copiosæ suavitatis illa recordatio est? In eodem domicilio, antequam nascerer, habitavi: in iisdem incunabulis infantiæ tempora peregi: eosdem appellavi parentes, etc.*: "How very pleasant is the remembrance of these things? I dwelt in the same dwelling (with such a one) before I was born; I passed my infancy in the same cradle; I called the same persons my parents, etc." (Valerius Maximus, *Facta et dicta memorabilia*.) ↵

479. There is no name for any descendent who is more than *trinepos*: "three degrees removed from us." ↵

480. It becomes ἀμυδρά: "very obscure." (Andronicus of Rhodes.) ↵

481. Man and Wife are supposed to be one, and therefore have no place here, any more than a man and his self. Otherwise considered distinctly, the one of them ought always to be the first care of the other. ↵

482. Μηδὲ κασιγνήτῳ ἶσον ποιεῖσθαι ἑταῖρον: "We must not treat a friend equally with a relation." (Hesiod, *Works and Days*.) ↵

483. For many I acknowledge there are, who seem to be without reflection, and almost thought. Τίς ἀγνοεῖ τὴν οἰκείαν φύσιν; πολλοί · τάχα δὲ πάντες πλὴν ὀλίγων: "Who is there that does not understand what he himself is? A great many truly; nay, all but a very few." (St. Chrysostom, *Homily on Acts of the Apostles*.) ↵

484. *Nec se quæsiverit extra*: "Let him not seek for himself out of himself." (Plotinus,

Enneads.) ↩

485. *Illud* γνῶθι σεαυτὸν *noli putare ad arrogantiam minuendam solùm esse dictum, verùm etiam ut bona nostra norimus*: "Do not imagine that that (precept) 'understand yourself thoroughly,' was said only to lessen men's pride, but further that they might know all the good things which belong to them." (Cicero, in his letters to his brother Quintus.) ↩

486. *Non sentire mala sua non est hominis: et non ferre non est viri*: "Not to be sensible of the evils we lie under is not to be a man, and not to be able to bear them is to want the courage of a man" (Seneca, who condescends here, in *De Consolatione ad Polybium*, to be something like other men). As also when he says, *Alia sunt, quæ sapientem feriunt, etiamsi non pervertunt; ut dolor capitis, etc. Hæt non nego sentire sapientem, etc.*: "There are some things which strongly affect a wise man, though they don't quite overpower him, as the headache, etc.; I do not deny but that a wise man feels such things," etc. (*De Constantia Sapientis.*) ↩

487. *Qui se ipse norit, aliquid sentiet se babere divinum, etc.*: "He that understands what sort of a being he himself is, will perceive that he has something that is divine in him." (Cicero, *De Legibus.*) ↩

488. טבע החומר ויצר הרע: "nature which is backward, and a will corrupted," are (in Jewish language, see *Berakhot*) שאור בעיסה: "the leaven in the lump." ↩

489. Ἀμήχανον εἶναι ἄνθρωπόν τινα ἀναμάρτητον: "It is next to impossible for a man to be free from all sin." (Johannes Chrysostom, *De Lazaro.*) ↩

490. The author of *Sefer Haredim* reckons eight, the right use of which comprehends all practical religion: the heart, the eye, the mouth, nose, ear, hand, foot, and ראש הגויה: "the principal member." The duties respecting these are the subject of that (not bad) book. ↩

491. *Cùm tria sint hæc, esse, vivere, intelligere: et lapis est, et pecus vivit, nec tamen lapidem puto vivere, aut pecus intelligere: qui autem intelligit, eum et esse et vivere certissimum est. Quare non dubito id excellentius judicare, cui omnia tria insunt, quàm id cui duo vel unum desit*: "Since there are these three things: to exist, to live, and to have understanding; and a stone exists, beasts live, for I cannot think that a stone lives, or a beast has understanding; it is most certain, that the being which has understanding, both exists and lives. Wherefore I don't at all scruple to declare him, that has in him all these three, to be a superior being to him who wants one or two of them." (St. Augustine, , *De Libero Arbitrio.*) Thus reason sets man above the other visible orders of beings, etc. ↩

492. *Præsto est domina omnium et regina ratio... Hæc ut imperet illi parti animi, quæ*

obedire debet, id videndum est viro: "Reason, the governor and ruler of all things, is ready...; every man therefore is to see that she governs that part of the soul which ought to be obedient to her." (Cicero, *Tusculan Disputations*.) ↩

493. *Abjecto homine in sylvestre animal transire*: "To cast off the man, and become a wild creature." (Seneca, *De Clementia*.) Ἐν τῷ λογικῷ τίνων χωριζόμεθα; τῶν θηρίων… Ὅρα οὖν μὴ τί πως ὡς θηρίον ποιήσῃς: "Whom are we distinguished from by our reason?... from the beasts; take care then that you do not imitate the beasts in anything." (Arrian, *Discourses of Epictetus*.) *Pertinet ad omnem officii quæstionem semper in promptu habere, quantum natura hominis pecudibus reliquisque belluis antecedat*: "In all inquiries concerning our duty we ought always to have this uppermost, viz.: how much the nature of man is superior to that of cattle or any other beasts." (Cicero, *De Officiis*.) ↩

494. Πρὸς τὴν τῶν θηρίων ἀλογίαν ἐκπεσών: "To sink into as little reason as a beast has." (Johannes Chrysostom, *Homily on Genesis 6.*) ↩

495. A thing too often done. *Quæ enim libido, quæ avaritia, quod facinus aut suscipitur nisi consilio capto, aut sine... ratione perficitur?* "For what sensual pleasure, what avaricious thing is undertaken, without first advising about it; or completed... without making use of reason?" (Cotta, in Cicero, *De Natura Deorum*.) ↩

496. Something like him, who in Chrysostom's words, διὰ τῶν οἰάκων καταδύει τὸ σκάφος: "made use of the rudder to sink the ship." (*Commentary on the Psalms*.) ↩

497. This makes Cotta say, *Satius fuit nullam omnino nobis à diis immortalibus datam esse rationem, quàm tanta cum pernicie datam*: "That it had been better that the immortal Gods had never given us any reason at all, than to have given it us in so destructive a manner," with other bitter things. Though an answer to this may be given in the words which follow afterward: *A deo tantùm rationem habemus, si modò habemus: bonam autem rationem, aut non bonam, à nobis*: "The reason which we have (the faculty) is given us by God, but whether it be good or bad, that is from ourselves." (Cicero, *De Natura Deorum*.) ↩

498. This certainly excludes all that talk which familiarizes vice, takes off those restraints which men have from nature or a modest education, and is so utterly destructive of virtue that Aristotle banishes it out of the commonwealth. Ὅλως μὲν αἰσχρολογίαν ἐκ τῆς πόλεως, ὥσπερ ἄλλο τι, δεῖ τὸν νομοθέτην ἐξορίζειν · ἐκ τοῦ γὰρ εὐχερῶς λέγειν ὁτιοῦν τῶν αἰσχρῶν καὶ τὸ ποιεῖν σύνεγγυς: "A lawgiver ought above all things entirely to banish all filthy discourse out of a city, for men easily go from saying filthy things to doing them." (*Politics*.) ↩

499. True, manly reason, which is a very different thing from that superstitious preciseness

which carries things too far. As e.g. when the Jews, not contented to condemn דבור נבלה, "obscene discourse," or נבלות הפה, "filthy talk," and everywhere to express גודל האסור, "the heinousness of the thing forbidden," go so far as to comprehend under it אפי׳שיחה קלה שאדם ססיח עם אשתו, "that trifling discourse which passes betwixt a man and his wife;" and to add מוציא מלה לבטלה כמוציא זרע עבטלה וכו׳, "that bringing forth an idle word is like bringing forth idle seed." There are other sayings of this kind to be seen, many of them, among those which Rabbi Elijah ben Moses de Vidas has collected: as that particularly, כז ענין ראות צריך שלא להיציאו לבטלה וכו׳, "that a man should not make an idle use of his eyes." What Ælian reports of Anaxagoras and others, belongs to this place: *that they never laughed* (*Various Histories*), with many other unnecessary austerities which might be added. ↵

500. אם אין אני לי מי לי: "If I don't take care of myself, who will take care of me." (*Mishnah, Abot* I, 14.) ↵

501. *Προσδεῖται τούτων [τῶν ἐκτὸς ἀγαθῶν] ὁ ἀνθρώπινος βίος · κύριαι δ᾽ εἰσὶν αἱ κατ᾽ ἀρετὴν ἐνέργειαι τῆς εὐδαιμονίας* · : "These [external goods] are necessary to the life of man, but virtuous actions are necessary to his happiness." (Aristotle, *Nicomachean Ethics*.) They, who treated the body and things pertaining to it as merely ἀλλότρια, "things that did not belong to them;" distinguishing between τὰ ἡμέτερα, "such things as are our own," and τὰ τοῦ σώματος, "such as belong to the body;" making the latter to be οὐδὲν πρὸς ἡμᾶς, "nothing to us," and leaving the body as it were to itself (αὐτὸ [σωμάτιον] μεριμνάτω, ... εἴ τι πάσχει: "to be solicitous for itself,... if it suffers anything." —Marcus Aurelius, *Meditations*): they, I say, might enjoy their own philosophy, but they would scarce gain many proselytes nowadays, or ever persuade people that the pains they feel are not theirs or anything to them. Nor indeed do I much credit many stories that are told of some old philosophers: as that of Anaxarchus, when he was put to a most cruel death by Nicocreon (viz. pounded in a mortar) οὐ φροντίσαντα τῆς τιμωρίας, εἰπεῖν... Πτίσσε τὸν Ἀναξάρχου θύλακον, Ἀνάξαρχον δὲ οὐ πτίσσεις: "not valuing the punishment, cried out;... You may beat the bag of Anaxarchus, but you cannot strike Anaxarchus himself." (Diogenes Laërtius, *Life of Anaxarchus*.) See Epictitus, Arrian, Simplicius, Marcus Aurelius, Diogenes Laërtius, and others. ↵

502. *Ne offeramus nos periculis sine causa; quo nihil potest esse stultius. ... In tranquillo tempestatem adversam optare dementis est*: "Nothing can be more foolish than to run ourselves into dangers without any reason.... He is a mad man that wishes for a storm when the weather is good." (Cicero, *De Officiis*.) ↵

503. *Levius fit patientia, Quicquid corrigere est nefas*: "What cannot be quite cured, is made easier by patience." (Horace, *Odes*.) ↵

504. Μελέτη θανάτου: "a meditation upon death," was a great man's definition of

philosophy. (Plato, *Phaedo*.) ↩

505. Ἡ ὀργή... ὑπνηλὸν ἡμῶν διεγείρει: "Anger... is to excite the drowsy." (Johannes Chrysostom.) ↩

506. When the Stoics say that a wise man may relieve one who wants his help, without pitying him, I own indeed he *may*, but I very much doubt whether he would. If he had not some compassion, and in some measure felt the ails or wants of the other, I scarce know how he should come to take him for an object of his charity. ↩

507. Ὁ μὲν ἐφ' οἷς δεῖ, καὶ οἷς δεῖ ὀργιζόμενος, ἔτι δὲ καὶ ὡς δεῖ, καὶ ὅτε, καὶ ὅσον χρόνον, ἐπαινεῖται: "He is to be commended, who is angry with those persons that he ought to be angry with, and for such things as he ought to be angry for, and in such a manner, and in the proper time, and only for so long, as he ought." (Aristotle, *Nicomachean Ethics*.) To be angry under these conditions is a different thing from rage, and those transports which perhaps scarce comply with any one of them: such as that of Alexander, who, because his ἐρώμενος, "beloved friend," died, commanded the Ἀσκληπεῖα, "temples of Æsculapius," to be all burnt. (Arrian, *Anabasis of Alexander*.) ↩

508. There is, according to Cicero, *Civile odium, quo omnes improbos odimus*: "a public hatred, by which we hate all wicked persons in general." (*Pro Milone*.) ↩

509. Φοβούμεθα δηλονότι τὰ φοβερά... φοβούμεθα οὖν πάντα τὰ κακά · οἷον ἀδοξίαν, πενίαν, νόσον, ἀφιλίαν, θάνατον... ἔνια γὰρ καὶ δεῖ φοβεῖσθαι, καὶ καλόν · τὸ δὲ μή, αἰσχρόν, κτλ.: "We are afraid, indeed, of such things as are really dreadful;... and therefore we are afraid of all real evils, such as disgrace, poverty, diseases, want of friends, and death... It is right to be afraid of some things, and wicked not to be afraid of them." (Aristotle, *Nicomachean Ethics*.) When one called Xenophanes coward, because he would not play at dice with him, ὁμολογεῖ πάνυ δειλὸς εἶναι πρὸς τὰ αἰσχρὰ καὶ ἄτολμος: "he owned that he was a coward, and had no courage with regard to things that are wicked." (Plutarch, *Moralia*.) ↩

510. A wise man is not ἀπαθής, "entirely without passions," but μετριοπαθής, "has them in a moderate degree." (Aristotle, in Diogenes Laërtius.) ↩

511. Δεῖ τὸν στοχαζόμενον τοῦ μέσου ἀποχωρεῖν τοῦ μᾶλλον ἐναντίου... τῶν γὰρ ἄκρων, τὸ μέν ἐστιν ἁμαρτωλότερον · τὸ δ' ἧττον: "He who aims at a medium should depart from that (extreme) which is most contrary;... for one of the two extremes has more of vice in it than the other." (Aristotle, *Nicomachean Ethics*.) In the same chapter he gives two other excellent rules, which I cannot but set down here: Σκοπεῖν δεῖ πρὸς ἃ αὐτοὶ εὐκατάφοροί ἐσμεν... εἰς τοὐναντίον δ' ἑαυτοὺς ἀφέλκειν·... ὅπερ οἱ τὰ διεστραμμένα τῶν ξύλων ὀρθοῦντες ποιοῦσιν: "We ought to consider what (vices) we are most inclined to,... and to bend ourselves to the contrary;... as they do, who endeavor to make

crooked sticks straight." And after, **Ἐν παντὶ δὲ μάλιστα φυλακτέον τὸ ἡδὺ καὶ τὴν ἡδονήν· οὐ γὰρ ἀδέκαστοι κρίνομεν αὐτήν**: "In everything, we should take great care as to the pleasure of it; for we are very apt to have our judgment corrupted by pleasure." ↩

512. **Ἀγεσιλάῳ μέχρι τῶν ὀφθαλμῶν ὁ ἔρως, ἐνταῦθα ἔστη ἐπὶ θύραις τῆς ψυχῆς**: "When love was got to the eyes of Agesilaus, it stood then at the door of his mind." (Maximus Tyrius, *De Eodem Amore*.) To appoint things, as the Jewish doctors have done, to be סייג לתורה, "a fence for the law," or כדי להרחיק את האדם מן העבירה, "to remove men as far as can be from sin," would be right, if they were judiciously chosen, and not so very particular and trifling (*Mishnah*, Abot I, 1). Some of their cautions are certainly just, as that לא יסתכל אדם באשת איש ובשאר עריות פן ינקש גם: "A man should not trifle with another man's wife, nor with nakedness, lest he be ensnared by them." (*Mishnah* Berakhot I, 1.) ↩

513. What should a man do to live? ימית עצמו: "Should he destroy himself?" (*Mishnah*, Tamid.) ↩

514. No monkery, no superstitious or phantastical mortifications, are here recommended. ↩

515. חסיד עושה טובה לפנים משורה הדין: "the merciful man does good according to the best of his judgment," (which words I understand in the sense that Rashi seems to put upon them, in his commentary on Genesis 44:10). ↩

516. **Πῇ παρέβην; τι δ᾽ ἔρεξα; τί μοι δέον οὐκ ἐτελέσθη**: "have I transgressed? and what have I done? wherein have I failed in what was my duty?" (*Pythagoreorum Aureum Carmen*.) ↩

517. **Τίς γὰρ εἰς τὸν ἀγῶνα τοῦ βίου παρ παρελθὼν ἄπτωτος ἔμεινε; τίς δ᾽ οὐχ ὑπεσκελίσθη; εὐδαίμων ὁ μὴ πολλάκις.**: "For who has gone through the circuit of life and kept his legs? nay, who is there that has not fallen quite down? He is a happy man if if he has not done so a great many times." (Philo Judaeus, *De Somniis*.) ↩

518. *Quem pœnitet peccasse, penè est innocens*: "He that repents of his crime is almost innocent." (Seneca, *Agamemnon*.) ↩

519. Even a Jew says, תשובה/ שקולה כנגד כל הקרבנות: "that repentance may be weighed against any sacrifice." (Judah ben Samuel, *Sefer Hasidim*.) ↩

520. **Ἐλοιδόρησας; εὐλόγησον· ἐπλεονέκτησας; ἀπόδος· ἐμεθύσθης; νήστευσον**: "Have you spoke evil of any man? speak well of him for the future. Have you overreached any man? make him satisfaction. Have you been drunk? then fast." (St. Basil, *Homilae super Psalmos*.) ↩

521. Ἔστι γὰρ τῷ ὄντι φιλοσοφία μέγιστον κτῆμα: "For philosophy is really the best of all possessions." (Justin Martyr, *Dialogus cum Tryphone Judaeo*.) ↩

522. And perhaps as if our own minds were not what they are. For πάντες ἄνθρωποι τοῦ εἰδέναι ὀρέγονται φύσει: "all men have naturally a thirst after knowledge." (Aristotle, *Metaphysics*.) ↩

523. Aristotle, being asked "what he got by philosophy," answered, Τὸ ἀνεπιτάκτως ποιεῖν ἅ τινες διὰ τὸν ἀπὸ τῶν νόμων φόβον ποιοῦσιν: "To do that without being commanded, which other people do out of fear of the laws." And another time, "how the learned differed from the unlearned," said Ὅσῳ οἱ ζῶντες τῶν τηθνηκότων · τὴν παιδείαν ἔλεγεν ἐν μὲν εὐτυχίαις εἶναι κόσμον, ἐν μὲν ταῖς ἀτυχίαις καταφυγήν: "As much as the living do from the dead. Learning, he said, was an ornament to men when they were in prosperity, and a refuge for them to flee to when they were in adversity." (Diogenes Laërtius, *Life of Aristotle*.) ↩

524. Ἀδύνατον γὰρ, ἢ οὐ ῥᾴδιον, τὰ καλὰ πράττειν ἀχορήγητον ὄντα. πολλὰ μὲν γὰρ πράττεται καθάπερ δι' ὀργάνων, κτλ.: "It is impossible, at least it is very difficult, for a man to do much good if he want the necessaries of life; for many things are done as it were by instruments." (Aristotle, *Nicomachean Ethics*.) ↩

525. *Nam fuit quoddam tempus, cum in agris himines passime bestiarum modo vagabantur, etc.*: "For there was a time when men wandered about the fields, just as the beasts do now, etc." (Cicero, *De Inventione*.) ↩

526. The effect which Xenocrates's lecture had upon Polemo is remarkable: *unius orationis saluberrima medicina sanatus, ex infami ganeone maximus philosophus evasit*: "He was restored by the most wholesome physic of one oration, and from an infamous debauchee became a very great philosopher." (Valerius Maximus, *Facta et dicta memorabilia*.) ↩

527. Like them, who submit to their *Hhakamim*, "wise men," אפילו יאמרו על ימין שהוא שמאל וכו׳: "though they should affirm a man's right hand to be his left." (In Joseph Albo, *Sefer ha-Ikkarim*.) Many more instances might easily be given. ↩

528. Not only we. Τῆς ῥινὸς ἕλκεσθαι: "To lead a man by the nose," was used in the same sense by the Greeks. ↩

529. *Nihil magis præstandum est, quàm ne, pecorum ritu, sequamur antecedentium gregem, pergentes non qua eundem est, sed qua itur*: "We ought to take the greatest care, not like cattle to follow the crowd that go before, and so go where others go, and not where we should go." (Seneca, *De Vita Beata*.) Something may perhaps be expected in this place concerning vogue and fashion, which seem to be public declarations of some general opinion; showing how far they ought to sway with us. I think: so far as to keep

us from being contemned, derided, or marked, where that may lawfully and conveniently be done; especially in respect of trifling and little matters. But further, a wise man will scarce mind them. That is a good sentence in Demophilus, Ποίει ἃ κρίνεις εἶναι καλὰ, κἂν ποιῶν μέλλης ἀδοξήσειν · φαῦλος γὰρ κριτὴς καλοῦ πράγματος ὄχλος: "Do those things that you yourself judge to be right, though men may have an ill opinion of you for so doing; for the multitude are very ill judges of what is right." (*Carmen Aureum.*) ↩

530. *Ipsa virtus brevissimè recta ratio dici potest*: "Virtue may briefly be called right reason." (Cicero, *Tusculan Disputations.*) *Quæ non aliud est quàm recta ratio*: "It is nothing else but right reason." (Seneca, *Epistles.*) ↩

531. *Idem esse dicebat Socrates veritatem et virtutem*: "Socrates said that virtue and truth were the same thing." (Seneca, *Epistles.*) ↩

532. Viz. That a man cannot practice reason without practicing them. ↩

533. Τά τ᾽ ἐόντα, τά τ᾽ ἐσσόμενα, πρό τ᾽ ἐόντα: "The things that are, the things that will be, and the things that have been." (Homer, *Iliad.*) ↩

534. That saying of Timotheus to Plato, with whom he had supped the night before in the Academy, should be remembered: Ὑμεῖς εὖ δειπνεῖτε... εἰς τὴν ὑστεραῖαν... ἡμέραν: "This supper will be of great use to us tomorrow (from the conversation we have had)." (In Athenæus, *Deipnosophistae.*) ↩

535. *Corpus onustum Hesternis vitiis animum quoque prægravat unà, etc.*: "A body overcharged with yesterday's vices is a load upon the mind also, etc." (Horace, *Satires.*) ↩

536. *Quibus in solo vivendi causa palato est*: "Who live only to please their palates." (Juvenal, *Satires.*) *Sic prandete commilitones tanquam apud inferos cœnaturi*: "Come, fellow-soldiers, let us dine today in such a manner as if we expected to sup amongst the dead," (Leonidas, according to Valerius Maximus, *Facta et dicta memorabilia*) may be turned to a general memento, no man knowing how near his death may be. ↩

537. Τί εἶδες;... καλήν; Ἔπαγε τὸν κανόνα: "What is it you look upon?... a beautiful woman. Observe the rule (of right)." (Arrian, *Discourses of Epictetus.*) ↩

538. *Venerem incertam rapientes, more ferarum*: "Laying hold of any women they meet, like beasts." (Horace, *Satires.*) ↩

539. In which words are comprehended naturally (Τὸ μὴ τὰς παρὰ φύσιν ἡδονὰς διώκειν: "not to pursue pleasures in an unnatural way"). ↩

540. Not as Crates and Hipparchia (of whom see Diogenes Laërtius, Sextus Empiricus, et al.), and indeed the Cynics in general are said to have done: *quibus in propatulo coire cum conjugibus mos fuit*: "who used to lie with their wives in public." (Lactantius, *De Falsa Sapientia*.) Of whom, therefore, Cicero says with good reason, *Cynicorum ratio [al. natio] tota est ejicienda. Est enim inimica verecundiæ, sine qua nihil rectum esse potest, nihil honestum*: "The method [some copies have it, 'the nation'] of the Cynics ought entirely to be rejected; for they are enemies to modesty, without which nothing can be right, nothing virtuous." (*De Officiis*.) אל אשתו יבא [איש] בצנעא: "A man should go in unto his wife in private." (Judah ben Samuel, *Sefer Hasidim*.) That in Herodotus, Ἅμα κιθῶνι ἐκδυομένῳ συνεεδυεται τὴν αἰδὼ γυνήν: "that a woman should put off her modesty with her clothes," ought not to be true (*Histories*). *Verecundiâ naturali habent provifum lupanaria ipsa secretum*: "Even public stews have a private place provided, out of natural modesty." (St. Augustine, *City of God*.) ↩

541. Εἰς τὸ τῆς τύχης ἀτεκμαρτον ἀφορῶσα: "Providing for contingencies that we cannot so much as guess at." (Philo Judaeus, *De Humanitate*.) ↩

542. Simonides was wont to say, Βουλοιμην ἂν ἀποθανῶν τοῖς ἐχθροῖς μᾶλλον ἀπολιπεῖν, ἢ ζᾶν δεῖσθαι τῶν φίλων: "I had rather leave something to my enemies when I die, than want friends while I am alive." (Joannes Stobaeus, *On Injustice*.) ↩

543. *Non intelligunt homines quàm magnum vectigal sit parsimonia*: "Men don't understand how great a revenue sparingness is." (Cicero, *Paradoxa Stoicorum*.) ↩

544. Like them, who ἐν τῇ νεότητι τὰ τοῦ γήρως ἐφόδια, προκαταναλίσκουσιν: "in their youth, devoured the provision that should have supported them in their old age," as in Athenæus. (*Deipnosophistae*.) ↩

545. *Ea liberalitate utamur, quæ prosit amicis, noceat nemini*: "We should use such liberality as may be of advantage to our friends, but not to the hurt of anybody else." (Cicero, *De Officiis*.) ↩

546. *Non est incommodum, quale quodque... sit, ex aliis judicare: ut si quid dedeceat in aliis, vitemus et ipsi. Fit enim nescio quo modo, ut magis in aliis cernamus, quàm in nobismet ipsis, si quid delinquitur*: "It is by no means an ill way of judging of anything, by seeing how it looks in others; so that if anything is unbecoming them, we may avoid it ourselves. For I don't know how it is, but we are apt to see faults in others more than in ourselves." (Cicero, *De Officiis*.) ↩

547. Οἷον, ἐν δείπνῳ προπίνει τις ἀδηνέχοντι; μὴ δυσωπηθῇς, μηδὲ προσβιάσῃ σεαυτὸν, ἀλλὰ κατάθου τὸ ποτήριον, κτλ.: "As if, at an entertainment, anyone drinks to another that has drank enough, he ought not to be out of countenance, nor force himself, but refuse the cup." (Plutarch, *Moralia*.) ↩

548. Even Epicurus himself ἀχώριστον φησὶ τῆς ἡδονῆς τὴν ἀρετὴν μόνην: "says that it is virtue, only, that is necessarily attended with pleasure;" and διὰ τὴν ἡδονὴν τὰς ἀρετὰς δεῖν αἱρεῖσθαι: "that we ought to choose virtue for the sake of such pleasure." (Diogenes Laërtius, *Life of Epicurus*.) ↩

549. Isocrates gives one reason for this, where he compares vicious pleasures with virtue. Ἐκεῖ μὲν πρῶτον ἡσθέντες, ὕστερον ἐλυπήθημεν · ἐντᾶυθα δὲ μετὰ τὰς λύπας τὰς ἡδονὰς ἔχομεν: "In the one case, we have the pleasure first and the uneasiness afterwards; in the other case (that of virtue) we have the uneasiness first, and the pleasure afterwards." (*Discourse to Demonicus*.) ↩

550. Whereas virtue is ἐφόδιον πρὸς γῆρας: "like provision which will maintain us till we are old." (Bias, in Basil's *On Greek Literature*.) ↩

551. For who can bear such rants as that, *Epicurus ait, sapientem, si in Phalaridis tauro peruratur, exclamaturum, Dulce est, et ad me nihil pertinet?* "Epicurus says that if a wise man were burnt alive in Phalaris's bull, he would cry out, 'How agreeable a thing is this, and it does not affect me at all'" (Seneca, *Epistles*)? Cicero reports the same. ↩

552. It is in the power of very few to act like him, *qui dum varices exsecandas præberet, legere librum perseveravit:* "who continued reading in a book while they were cutting swellings out of his legs," or him, *qui non desiit ridere, dum ob hoc ipsum irati tortores omnia instrumenta crudelitatis experirentur:* "who continued laughing, though his tormentors, who were enraged at him for it, tried all their instruments of cruelty upon that very account." (Seneca, *Epistles*.) ↩

553. Εἰ μάλα καρτερός ἐσσι, θεός που σοὶ τόγ' ἔδωκεν: "If you are a very valiant man, yet it is the gift of God that you are so." (Homer, *Iliad*.) ↩

554. *Propter virtutem jure laudamur, et in virtute recte gloriamur. Quod non contingeret, si id donum à Deo, non à nobis haberemus*: "We are justly commended upon the account of our virtue, and it is right in us to boast of our virtue; which it would not be, if it were the gift of God, and we had it not from ourselves." (Cicero, *De Natura Deorum*.) ↩

555. As that word is used here. For when it is used as in that in Lucian, Ἀρετὴ μὲν σώματος ἰσχὺς: "virtue is the strength of the body," and the like passages, it has another meaning. (*The Cynic*.) ↩

556. Καπνοῦ καὶ κύματος ἐκτὸς ἔεργε Νῆα: "Guide the ship on the outside of the smoke and waves." (Homer, *Odyssey*.) ↩

557. Εἰσὶ δ' οἳ καὶ ἐν οἰκίᾳ διατρίβοντες, τῶν σωμάτων αὐτοῖς ἢ μακραῖς νόσοις ἢ ἐπιπόνῳ γήρᾳ κατεσκελετευμένων... τὴν ἀληθῆ διαπονοῦσιν ἀνδρίαν, ἀσκηταὶ σοφίας ὄντες:

"There are some that live retired in their own houses, who have their bodies reduced to mere skeletons, either by wasting diseases or laborious old age;... they, who labor for true courage, are such as exercise themselves in true wisdom." (Philo Judaeus, *De Virtutibus.*) *Non in viribus corporis et lacertis tantummodo fortitudinis gloria est, sed magis in virtute animi.... Jure ea fortitudo vocatur, quando unusquisque seipsum vincit, iram continet, nullis illecebris emollitur atque inflectitur, non adversis perturbatur, non extollitur secundis, etc.*: "The true excellency of courage does not consist so much in the strength of the body and arms, as in the virtue of the mind;... that is truly called courage when a man subdues himself, keeps under his passions, is not weakened or drawn aside by any temptations, is not depressed in adversity nor puffed up in prosperity, etc." (St. Ambrose, *De Officiis Ministrorum.*) ↩

558. *Qui se ipse norit, primùm aliquid sentiet se habere divinum, etc.*: "He that understands what sort of a being he himself is, will find that he has something divine in him, etc." (Cicero, *De Legibus.*) ↩

559. Εἰ μήτε ἔξωθεν κινεῖται [τὸ σῶμα] ὡς τὰ ἄψυχα, μήτε φυσικῶς ὡς τὸ πῦρ, δῆλον ὅτι ὑπὸ ψυχῆς κινεῖται, κτλ.: "If [the body] be not moved by something external, as things inanimate are; or if it has not a natural motion, as fire has; it is manifest that it must then be moved by the soul." (Gregory Thaumaturgus, *Ad Tatianum de anima per capita disputatio.*) ↩

560. Which is, ὡς εἰπεῖν, οἶκός ἐστι τῶν αἰσθήσεων: "as it were, the seat of sensation." (Artemidorus Daldianus, *Oneirocritica.*) ↩

561. Ὅπου ὁ βασιλεύς, ἐκεῖ καὶ οἱ δορυφόροι · δορυφόροι δὲ αἰσθήσεις τοῦ νοῦ, περὶ κεφαλὴν οὖσαι: "Where the king is, there are his guards also; now the senses are the guards of the mind, and these are about the head." (Philo Judaeus, *Legum Allegoriarum.*) ↩

562. Τὰ μέρη τοῦ σώματος ἄλογά ἐστιν, ἀλλ' ὅταν ὁρμὴ γένηται, σείσαντος ὥσπερ ἡνίας τοῦ λογισμοῦ, πάντα τέτακται καὶ συνῆκται καὶ ὑπακούει: "The members of the body are not endowed with reason, but as soon as any appetites arise, the reason directs them as a bridle, and all things are regulated, adjusted, and submit to it." (Plutarch, *Moralia.*) ↩

563. *Nos ne nunc quidem oculis cernimus ea, quæ videmus: neque enim est ullus sensus in corpore, sed... viæ quasi quædam sunt ad oculos, ad aures, ad nares à sede animi perforatæ. Itaque sæpe aut cogitatione aut aliqua vi morbi impediti, apertis atque integris et oculis et auribus, nec videmus, nec audimus: ut facilè intelligi possit, animum et videre, et audire, non eas partes, quæ quasi fenestræ sunt animi: quibus tamen sentire nihil queat mens, nisi id agat, et adsit*: "We do not now see objects with our

eyes; for there is no perception in the body,... but there are particular passages which go from the seat of the soul to the eyes, the ears, and the nose. Wherefore when we are very thoughtful, or when we are hindered by any violent disease, we neither see nor hear, though our eyes and ears be open and sound; whence we may easily apprehend, that it is the soul that sees and hears, and not those parts which are, as it were, the windows of the soul, and which it cannot make use of unless it be present and attends to it." (Cicero, *Epistles*.) ↵

564. Or even *detracto corpore multo*: "if a great part of the body were pulled off," as Lucretius speaks. (*De Rerum Natura*.) ↵

565. Πολλάκις καὶ τῶν χειρῶν καὶ τῶν ποδῶν ἐκκεκομμένων, ὁλόκληρος ἐκείνη [ἡ ψυχὴ] μένει: "Very often when the hands and legs are cut off, yet the soul remains entire." (Johannes Chrysostom, *De incomprehensibili dei natura*.) ↵

566. Therefore Aristotle says, if an old man had a young man's eye βλέποι ἂν ὥσπερ καὶ ὁ νέος. Ὥστε τὸ γῆρας, οὐ τῷ τὴν ψυχὴν πεπονθέναι τι, ἀλλ᾽ ἐν ᾧ καθάπερ ἐν μέθαις καὶ νόσοις, κτλ.: "He would see like a young man. So that, in old age, the soul is not affected; but is in the same state, as when a man is in drink, or in any distemper." (*De Anima*.) ↵

567. Hierocles (with others) accounts the soul to be the true man. Σὺ γὰρ εἶ ἡ ψυχή · τὸ δὲ σῶμα σόν: "It is the soul that is you, and the body that is yours." (*Commentary on the Carmen Aureum*.) ↵

568. So Plato uses the word Αὐτὸς, "Self," for the whole of the man; by which the soul, as one part of it, is called κτῆμα, "a possession." ↵

569. Φαίνεται ἐν αὐτοῖς καὶ ἄλλό τι παρὰ τὸν λόγον πεφυκός, ὃ μάχεται καὶ ἀντιτείνει τῷ λόγῳ: "It is evident that there is something else in us, beside reason, which wars against and contradicts reason." (Aristotle, *Nicomachean Ethics*.) ↵

570. Whether any form, modification, or motion of matter can be a human soul, seems to be much such another question as that in one of Seneca's epistles, *An justitia, an fortitudo, prudentia, ceteræque virtutes, animalia sint*: "Whether justice, or fortitude, or prudence, and the rest of the virtues, be living creatures." (*Epistle to Lucilius*.) ↵

571. Νοῦν οὐδὲν σῶμα γεννᾷ · πῶς γὰρ ἂν τὰ ἀνόητα νοῦν γεννήσοι: "Nobody can produce a mind, for how can understanding come out of that which has no understanding." (Sallustius, *On the Gods and the Cosmos*.) ↵

572. That the soul is the principle of motion, or that which begins it in us, is (though it wants no testimony) often said by the ancients. Φασὶ γὰρ ἔνιοι, καὶ μάλιστα, καὶ

πρώτως ψυχὴν εἶναι τὸ κινοῦν: "Some affirm that the soul is the chief and the First mover." (Aristotle, *De Anima*.) Ἡ ψυχὴ τὸ ἔνδοθε, κινοῦν τὰ σώματα, καὶ αὐτοκίνητον: "It is the soul that moves the body from within, and is a self-moving being." (Simplicius.) Ἀρχὴ κινήσεως: "The principle of motion." (Plotinus, *Enneads*.) ↩

573. Ἡ ψυχὴ περίεισι πᾶσαν γῆν, ἐῃ γῆς ἐπ' οὔρανον, κτλ.: "The soul can take a view over the whole earth, and ascend from thence into heaven." (Maximus Tyrius, *Dissertations*.) ↩

574. What a ridiculous argument for the materiality of the soul is that in Lucretius (*De Rerum Natura*)? *Ubi propellere membra, Conripere ex somno corpus, etc. videtur (Quorum nil fieri sine tactu posse videmus, Nec tactum porro sine corpore); nonne fatendum est Corporeâ naturâ animum constare, animamque?* "For do we not see that the mind moves the several members, wakes the body out of sleep, etc. (none of which can be done without touching it, and there can be no such thing as touching, without matter) must not we own then, that the soul and mind are material?" If nothing can move the body but another body, what moves this? The body might as well move itself, as be moved by one that does. ↩

575. Τάχιστον νοῦς· διὰ παντὸς γὰρ τρέχει: "The soul is very quick, for it runs everywhere." (Thales, in Diogenes Laërtius's *Life of Thales*.) ↩

576. Diogenes, though he could see the table and the pot, could not by his eyes see Plato's τραπεβότης, καὶ κυαθότης: "tableity or potteity;" that is, he could not see what it was that constituted them a table or a pot. (Diogenes Laërtius, *Life of Diogenes*.) ↩

577. Plato, and οἱ σοφοὶ, "the wise men," (more generally) say that the soul indeed perceives objects of sense by the mediation of the body, but there are νοητὰ, "intellectual things," which it does καθ' αὑτὴν ἐνθυμεῖσθαι, "meditate upon by itself." (in Diogenes Laërtius, *Life of Plato*.) ↩

578. Such a soul must be indeed as Gregory Thaumaturgus has it, σῶμα ἔμψυχον. Ἄτοπον δὲ ψυχῆς ψυχὴν λέγειν: "an animated body. For it is absurd to speak of the soul of a soul." ↩

579. This is worse than ψυχὴ ψυχῆς, "the soul of a soul," in Maximus Tyrius and the place just before cited. The author of the *Essay concerning Human Understanding* [John Locke] has himself exploded it, or what is very like it. "To ask," says he, "whether the will has freedom, is to ask whether one power has another power, one ability another ability; a question at first sight too grossly absurd to make a dispute or need an answer. For who is it that sees not, that powers belong only to agents, and are attributes only of substances, and not of powers themselves?" There is, if my memory does not deceive me, another passage somewhere in the same book as much (or more) to my purpose, but

at present I cannot find it. ↩

580. If the soul is only an accident (or attribute) of the body, how comes this accident to have (or be the support of) other accidents, contrary ones too? As when we say, נפש חכמה ונפש סכלה וכו׳: "a wise soul, or a foolish soul." (*Emunoth ve-Deoth.*) ↩

581. Ἕτερον δη τότε χρώμενον καὶ ᾧ χρῆται: "For that which uses, and that which is used, are two different things." (Plato, *Alcibiades*.) ↩

582. Or, "if to a thinking substance can be superadded the modification of solidity." Which way of speaking, though I do not remember to have met with it anywhere, nor does it seem to differ much from the other, yet would please me better. ↩

583. "It is worth our consideration, whether active power be not the proper attribute of spirit, and passive power of matter. Hence may be conjectured that created spirits are not totally separate from matter, because they are both active and passive. Pure spirit, viz. God, is only active; pure matter is only passive; those Beings, that are both active and passive, we may judge to partake of both." (John Locke, *An Essay Concerning Human Understanding*.) ↩

584. This is Socrates's argument in Plato. The soul is altogether ἀδιάλυτος, "indissolvible," and therefore ἀνώλεθρος, "cannot be destroyed." (*Phaedo*.) Which Cicero interprets thus: *nec discerpi, nec distrahi potest; nec interire igitur*: "it can neither be divided nor separated into parts, and consequently cannot be destroyed." (*Tusculan Disputations*.) ↩

585. Lucretius seems to be aware of this. *Jam triplex animi est natura reperta: Nec tamen hæc sat sunt ad sensum cuncta creandum, etc. Quarta quoque his igitur quædam natura necesse est Atribuatur: ea est omnino nominis expers*: "The soul is found to be made up of three parts, nor are all these sufficient to produce understanding, etc. It is necessary therefore that some other particular fourth nature should be added to these: and this we have no name at all for." (*De Rerum Natura*.) ↩

586. If Lucan, by *sensus*, "sense," means all manner of apprehension and knowledge, there is no room for that disjunction: *Aut nihil est sensûs animis à morte relictum, Aut mors ipsa nihil*: "Either there remains no sense at all in the soul after death, or death itself is nothing." (*Pharsalia*.) For if the former part be true, the other will follow. ↩

587. *Velut è diutino carcere emissus [animus]*: "[The soul] is, as it were, let out of a prison, in which it has been a long while." (Seneca, *De Consolatione ad Polybium*.) ↩

588. Those kinds of animals which do not speak, do not reason: but those which do the one, do the other. Therefore, הי מדבר, "a living," (or Arabic ناطق, "a speaking animal") is

a *rational animal*: and λόγος signifies both "speech" and "reason," as going together. ↩

589. Θυρίδες γὰρ ὄντως τῆς ψυχῆς ἀι αἰσθήσεις: "The senses are the windows of the soul." (Basil, *De Virginitate*.) ↩

590. Ἄσαρκος καὶ ἀσώματος ἐν τῷ τοῦ παντὸς θεάτρῳ διημερεύουσα: "When it shall dwell upon the stage of the universe, without flesh and without a body." (Philo Judaeus, *De Gigantibus*.) ↩

591. So Hierocles distinguishes τὸ αὐγοειδὲς ἡμῶν σῶμα, ὁ καὶ ψυχῆς λεπτὸν ὄχημα: "our glorious body, and the thin vehicle of the soul," from that which he calls τὸ θνητὸν ἡμῶν σῶμα, "our mortal body," and to which the former communicates life. Τῷ αὐγοειδεῖ ἡμῶν σώματι προσέφυ σῶμα θνητὸν ὄν: "The mortal and the glorious body adhere to, and grow up with, each other." (Hierocles, *Commentary on the Carmen Aureum*.) This fine body he calls also ψυχικὸν σῶμα, "a living body," and πνευματικὸν ὄχημα, "a spiritual vehicle." In *Nishmat Hayyim*, there is much concerning that "fine body" in which the soul is clothed, and from which it is never to be separated, according to an old tradition. Menasseh Ben Israel gives the sum of it in such words as these: יש גוף דק עד מאד בו מתלבש הנשמה טרם ביאה לעולם: "There is a very thin, fine body, with which the soul is clothed before it comes into the world," and afterward, הנשמות המה בבריאתם הראשונה נקשרות עם גשמים דקים רוחניים מהטבע השמימי בלתי מושגים לחוש הראות. והנשמות לא יתפרדו מאותם הגשמים הדקים הרוחניים כל ימי עולם אם קודם בואם לגוף ואם בהיותם עמו וגם אחרר הפרדם ממנו: "These souls, at their first creation, were joined with some thin, spiritual, and celestial bodies, which cannot be perceived by our eyes. Neither can these thin, spiritual bodies be separated from those souls so long as the world lasts, neither before they came into this (gross) body, nor while they remain in it, nor after they are separated from it." Saadya long before him joins to the soul עצם דק, "a thin substance," which he says is דק/יותר זך מן הגלגלים: "thinner than the ether in the skies," etc. ↩

592. *Cùm corpora quotidie nostra fluant, et aut crescant aut descrescant, ergo tot erimus homines, quot quotidie commutamur? qut alius fui, cùm decem annorum essem; alius, cùm triginta; alius cùm quinquaginta, alius, cùm jam toto cano capite sum?* "Because our bodies are continually altering, and either increasing or diminishing, shall we therefore be as many different men, as we undergo perpetual changes? Or was I one person when I was ten years old, another when I was thirty, another when I was fifty, and another now I am grey-headed." (St. Jerome, *Epistles*.) So it must be, if our souls are nothing different from our bodies. ↩

593. I would say the egoity remains, that is, that by which I am the same as I was; Cicero has his *Lentulitas*, "Lentulity," and *Appietas*, "Appiety," that is, that by which Lentulus remained Lentulus and Appius remained Appius in the same form, though not

just the like sense. (*Letters to Friends.*) ↩

594. That passage in *Sefer ha-Ikkarim* imports much the same thing that has been said here: הוא מבואר שהדבר שמציאותו טוב ראוי שימצא והדבר שמציאותו רע אין ראוי שימצא ומה שמציאותו מעורב מן הטוב והרע אם הטוב הוא הגובר ראוי שימצא ואם הרע הוא הגובר אין ראוי שימצא: "This is manifest, that that thing whose existence is good, ought to exist; and that thing whose existence is evil, ought not to exist; and if the existence of anything is made up of a mixture of good and evil, if the good prevail, it ought to exist, and if the evil prevail, it ought not to exist." ↩

595. *C. Cæsar... Senatores et Equites... cecidit, torsit, non quæstionis, sed animi causâ. Deinde quosdam ex illis... ad lucernam decollabat.... Torserat per omnia, quæ in rerum natura tristissima sunt, fidiculis, etc.*: "Gaius Cæsar... the Senators and the Knights... killed and put to the rack (a great many), not in order to find out the truth, but for their own pleasure only. Afterwards, he cut off the heads of some... by candlelight... tormented others, by all the most cruel tortures that could be thought of in nature; stretched them with cords, etc." (Seneca, *De Ira.*) *Homo, sacra res, jam per lusum et jocum occiditur*: "A man, who is a divine creature, is slain out of sport and jest." (Ibid.) ↩

596. Slaves were reckoned among beasts of old: Οὔτε γὰρ γυνὴ ἠέφυκας, οὔτ ἐν ἀνδράσι σύγ εἶ: "For you are not really a woman, nor are you to be reckoned of human race." (Euripides, *Orestes.*) And sometimes as mere instruments and tools: Ὁ γὰρ δοῦλος ἔμψυχον · τὸ δ' ὄργανον ἄψυχος δοῦλος: "For a slave is a living instrument, and an instrument is a lifeless slave." (Aristotle, *Nicomachean Ethics.*) Their sad condition I will set down in Plato's words: Οὐκ ἀνδρὸς τοῦτό γ' ἐστὶ τὸ πάθημα, τὸ ἀδικεῖσθαι ἀλλὰ ἀνδραπόδου τινός, ᾧ κρεῖττόν τεθνάναι ἐστὶν ἢ ζῆν · ὅστις ἀδικούμενος καὶ προπηλακιζόμενος, μὴ οἷός ἐστιν αὐτὸς αὑτῷ βοηθεῖν μηδὲ ἄλλῳ οὗ ἂν κήδηται: "To be injured is not the suffering of a man but of a slave, to whom death is better than life: who, if he be unjustly treated and abused, is wholly unable to help himself, and nobody else has any concern for him." (*Gorgias.*) ↩

597. Those ἄρρητοι καὶ ἄπιστοι δυστυχίαι, "unspeakable and incredible calamities," which the τελῶναι, "collectors of the taxes," had brought upon the cities of Asia, are too many to be transcribed: but some account of them is to be seen in Plutarch's *Life of Lucullus* which may serve for one instance out of thousands. It may be reckoned madness, indeed, *maximas virtutes, quasi gravissima delicta, punire*: "to punish the greatest virtues as if they were the greatest crimes," as Valerius Maximus says, speaking of Phocion's case (*Facta et dicta memorabilia*): but such madness has been very common, and men have suffered even for their virtue. Ochus cruelly put to death, *Ocham sororem..., et patruum cum centum ampliùs filiis ac nepotibus..., nulla injuria lacessitus, sed quòd in his maximam apud Persas probitatis et fortitudinis laudem*

consistere videbat: "his sister Ocha..., and his uncle with a hundred of his sons and grandsons..., without being provoked by any injury, but only because he saw that they were in great reputation amongst the Persians for probity and valor." (Ibid.) And Seneca, having recommended the example of Græcinus Julius (Julius Græcinus, according to Tacitus, the father of Julius Agricola), adds *quem C. Cæsar occidit ob hoc unum, quòd melior vir erat, quàm esse quemquam tyranno expediret*: "whom Gaius Cæsar killed for this reason only: because he was a better man than it was expedient for a tyrant that any man should be." (*De Beneficiis*.) ↩

598. Οἱ ἀδίκοις διαβολαῖς περιπεσόντας, καὶ διὰ θυμὸν εἰς φυλακὰς παραδεδομένοι, ποτὲ μὲν αὐτοὶ, ποτὲ δὲ καὶ μετὰ πάσης συγγενείας: "Some fell, either by false accusations, or they were arbitrarily delivered up to prison, sometimes themselves only, and sometimes all their relations with them." (Diodorus Siculus, *Bibliotheca Historica*.) ↩

599. Mentioned by Cicero with Phalaris. He was tyrant of Cassandria, and is represented (out of Polyænus, *Stratagems in War*) as φονικώτατος καὶ ὠμότατος πάντων, ὅσοι παρ᾽ Ἕλλησιν ἢ παρὰ βαρβάροις ἐτυράννησαν: "the bloodiest and most cruel of all the tyrants that ever reigned in Greece, or amongst the Barbarians." Yet Ælian says, Ἐκ τοῦ οἴνου ὑπαναφλεγόμεεος καὶ ὁπεξαπτόμενος, ἐγίνετο φονικώτερος, κτλ.: "That, when he was heated and inflamed with wine, then he was still more bloody." (*Varia Historia*.) ↩

600. It is said of Sylla's peace, after Marius's party were broken, *Pax cum bello de crudelitate certavit, et vicit*: "That the peace rivalled the war in cruelty, and overcame it." (St. Augustine, *The City of God*.) ↩

601. *Qui ita evisceratus, ut cruciatibus membra deessent, implorans cœlo justitiam, torvùm renidens fundato pectore mansit immobilis, etc.*: "Whose bowels were torn out, in such a manner that they wanted members to torment; he called upon heaven for justice, and looking sternly with a calm countenance, he continued unmoved by his firm resolution, etc." (Ammianus Marcellinus, *Res Gestae*.) In the reign of Constantius. ↩

602. *Mœrebantque docti quidam, quòd apud Atlanteos nati non essent, ubi memorantur somnia non videri*: "Some learned men were very sorry that they were not born amongst the Atlantes, of whom it is reported that they never dream." (Ammianus Marcellinus, *Res Gestae*.) ↩

603. See Plutarch in *The Life of Artaxerxes*. ↩

604. *Ob noxam unius omnis propinquitas perit*: "All the whole neighborhood perished for the fault of one single person." (Ammianus Marcellinus, *Res Gestae*.) ↩

605. Scaphism (Editor's note.) ↩

606. *Dies deficiet, si velim numerare, quibus bonis malè evenerit: nec minùs, si commemorem, quibus improbis optimè*: "The day would not hold out, if I should undertake to enumerate all the good men whom evil befell; nor would it, if I should reckon up all the wicked men that have fared best of all." (Cicero, *De Natura Deorum*.) This is justly said; though I account his instances not the most apposite. ↩

607. Yet, according to Aristotle, he cannot be happy for all that. His opinion Diogenes Laërtius represents thus: τὴν ἀρετὴν μὴ εἶναι αὐτάρκη πρὸς εὐδαιμονίαν · προσδεῖσθαι γὰρ τῶν τε περὶ σῶμα καὶ τῶν ἐκτὸς ἀγαθῶν... τὴν μέν τοι κακίαν αὐτάρκη πρὸς κακοδαιμονίαν, κἂν ὅτι μάλιστα παρῇ αὐτῇ τὰ ἐκτὸς ἀγαθὰ καὶ τὰ περὶ σῶμα: "Virtue is not alone sufficient to produce happiness, because external good things and things relating to the body are also necessary... but vice is of itself sufficient to produce misery, and especially if external good things and the things relating to the body are joined with it." (*Life of Aristotle*.) ↩

608. *Et vacet annales nostrorum audire laborum*: "And it may be of use to hear a catalogue of our misfortunes." (Virgil, *Aeneid*.) For, as Seneca says, *Nulli contigit impunè nasci*: "No man is born free of them." (*De Consolatione ad Marciam*.) ↩

609. Οἵηπερ φύλλων γενεή, τοιήδε καὶ ἀνδρῶν... ἡ μὲν φύει, ἡ δ' ἀπολήγει: "The life of man is like the leaves of trees;... some spring forth, and others wither." (Homer, *Iliad*.) This is true not only of single men, but even of cities (famous ones), kingdoms, empires. One may say the same concerning many of them, that Florus says of Veii: *Laborat annalium fides, ut Veios fuisse credamus*: "The credit of history is not quite sufficient to convince us that there ever was any such city as Veii." (*Epitome Rerum Romanarum*.) ↩

610. *Labor voluptasque; dissimillima naturâ, societate quadam inter se naturali sunt juncta*: "Pain and pleasure, though in the nature of things the most unlike each other, yet are united by some natural bond." (Livy, *Ab Urbe Condita Libri*.) ↩

611. Sensible of this, Socrates used to say, δεῖν τὰς ἡδονὰς, μὴ παρ' ἄλλων, ἀλλὰ παρ' ἡμῶν θηρᾶσθαι: "We ought to seek pleasures from ourselves, and not from others." (Joannes Stobaeus, *On Education*.) ↩

612. *Senex, et levissimis quoque; curis impar*: "I am an old man, and unequal to the smallest cares:" as Seneca, of himself, in Tacitus. (*Annals*.) ↩

613. *Rogus aspiciendus amatæ Conjugis, etc.*: "You must see the funeral pile of your beloved Wife." (Juvenal, *Satires*.) ↩

614. Σμίκρα παλαιὰ σώματ' εὐνάζει ῥοπή: "A small matter will push an old man into his grave." (Sophocles, *Oedipus Tyrannus*.) ↩

615. Πάντες ἐσμὶν ἐν ὁδῷ... ἴδες ἐπὶ τῆς ὁδοῦ φυτὸν ἢ πόαν ἢ ὕδωρ ἢ ὅ, τι ἂν τύχῃ τῶν ἀξίων θεάματος· μικρὸν ἐτέρφθης; εἶτα παρέδραμες· πάλιν ἐνέτυχες λίθοις καὶ φάραγξι καὶ κρημνοῖς καὶ σκοπέλοις, ἤ που καὶ θηρίοις, κτλ.: "We are all upon a road. ... When you see upon the road plants, and herbs, and water, and whatever else happens to be worth seeing there, are you not a little delighted with it? Then you go on, and meet with stones, and valleys, and precipices, and rocks, and sometimes with wild beasts. Life is very like this." (Basil, *Homilae super Psalmos*.) ↩

616. *Non mehercule quisquam accepisset [vitiam], nisi daretur insciis*: "Truly nobody would accept of [life], if it was not given them when they did not know it." (Seneca, *De Consolatione ad Marciam*.) ↩

617. *Paulisper te crede subduci in montis ardui verticem celsiorem; speculare inde rerum infra te jacentium facies; et oculis in diversa porrectis, fluctuantis munti turbines intuere. Jam seculi et ipse misereberis, etc.*: "Imagine yourself to be removed to the top of some very high mountain, and see how the things that are below you look; and turning your eyes every way, behold the trouble of a stormy world. And then you will take pity on the inhabitants, etc." (St. Cyprian, *Ad Donatum*.) ↩

618. העולם הזה דומה לפרוזדור בפני: "This world is only like a porch to the world to come." (*Mishnah*, Abot IV, 21.) ↩

619. *O si possis in illa sublimi specula constitutus oculos tuos inserere secretis, revludere cubiculorum obductas fores, et ad conscientiam luminum penetralia occulta reserare, etc.*: "O that, when you are placed upon the top of that high tower, you could cast your eyes into the secret places, and unbar the doors of bedchambers, and lay open their secret recesses to the discovery of the light, etc." (St. Cyprian, *Ad Donatum*.) ↩

620. By any means, proper or improper. (Editor's note.) ↩

621. Besides, there being no satiety of knowledge in this life, we may hope for future opportunities when our faculties shall be exalted, etc. *Τῆς ἀληθείας καὶ θέας τοῦ ὄντος οὐδεὶς ἐνταῦθα τῶν ἐρώντων ἐνέπλησεν ἑαυτὸν ἱκανῶς, κτλ.*: "They who are desirous of truth, and of seeing things as they really are, can never be fully satisfied here." (Plutarch, *Moralia*.) ↩

622. In *Tusculan Disputations*. ("Pherecydes the Syrian is the first on record who said that the souls of men were immortal.") ↩

623. "Nature silently asserts the truth of the immortality of the soul," "there is, I know not how, deeply rooted in the minds of men the premonition of a future state," and "the consent of all nations induces us to believe that our souls survive." (Editor's note.) ↩

624. Methinks those philosophers make but an odd appearance in story, who, looking big and fastuous, at the same time professed that their own souls were not superior to those of gnats, etc. οἱ τὰς ὀφρῦς ἀνεσπακότες μηδὲν κατὰ τὴν οὐσίαν διαφέρειν ἀπεφήναντο ἐμπίδος τε καὶ εὐλῆς, καὶ μυίας, ... καὶ συὸς ψυχῆς... τὴν σφῶν αὐτῶν φιλοσοφωτάτων ψυχήν: "These men, who are so swelled with pride, affirm that, as to the substance, there is no difference betwixt the soul of a philosopher, and that of a gnat, or a worm, or a fly, ... or the soul of a hog." (As Eusebius, *Demonstratio Evangelica*.) ↩

625. Alexander, after death, might be in the same state with his muletier (Marcus Aurelius, *Meditations*), but sure not with his mule. ↩

626. *Brevis est hic fructus homullis*: "this is the short-lived pleasure of frail man." (*De Rerum Natura*), may be justly said for all Lucretius. ↩

627. Ὁ κόσμος σκηνή, ὁ βίος πάροδος ἦλθες, εἶδες, ἀπῆλθες: "This world is a stage, life is the play; we come on, look about us, and go off again." (Democritus, *Fragments*.) ↩

628. את צנועים חכמה: "Wisdom is in modest men." (Proverbs 11:2.) ↩

629. *Hic pietatis honos?* "Is this reward of piety?" (Virgil, *Aeneid*.) ↩

630. *Feræ pericula, quæ vident, fugiunt: cum effugere, secura sunt, etc.*: "Wild beasts, when they see any dangers, avoid them; and, after they have avoided them, they look no further, etc." (Seneca, *Epistles*.) ↩

631. לא יצטערו בהיוום משערים שסופם למות כאדם וכו׳: "They are not uneasy, as men are, while they are alive, imagining that the end of them is to die." (Joseph Albo, *Sefer ha-Ikkarim*.) ↩

632. *Sic mihi persuasi, sic sentio, cùm... semper agitetur animus, nec principium motus habeat, quia se ipse moveat; ne finem quidem habiturum esse motus, quia nunquam se ipse sit relicturus*: "I do verily believe, it is my real opinion, that because... the soul is always in action, and has not any (external) cause of its motion, because it moves itself, therefore neither will it ever have any end of its motion, because it will never desert itself." (Cicero, *Cato Maior de Senectute*.) That in Gregory Thaumaturgus is like this thought of Cicero: Ἡ ψυχή, αὐτοκίνητος οὖσα, οὐδέποτε τοῦ εἶναι διαλείπει · ἀκολουθεῖ γὰρ τῷ αὐτοκινήτῳ τὸ ἀεὶ κινητὸν εἶναι · Τὸ δὲ ἀεὶ κινητὸν ἄπαυστόν ἐστι, κτλ.: "The soul, because it is able to move itself, can never cease to be; for it is a necessary consequence of self-motion to be always in motion, and what is always in motion cannot cease to move." (*Ad Tatianum de anima per capita disputatio*.) But that in St. Augustine comes something nearer to my meaning: *Est animus vita quædam, unde omne quod animatum est vivit... Non ergo potest animus mori. Nam si carere poterit vita, non animus sed animatum aliquid est*: "The soul is a sort of life, whence it

follows that everything which has a soul is alive;... wherefore the soul cannot die, for, if it could be without life, it would not be a soul but something with a soul." (*De Immortalitate Animæ*.) ↩

633. "Self-taught." (Editor's note.) ↩

634. The transmigration of souls has been much talked of, but *ea sententia,... quoniam ridicula et mimo dignior quàm scholâ, ne refelli quidem feriò debet; quod qui facit, videtur vereri, ne quis id credat*: "that opinion... is so ridiculous, that it is fitter for the stage than the schools, and therefore ought not seriously to be confuted; and he who attempts it, seems to be afraid that nobody should believe it." So Lactantius (*Divine Institutes*). Indeed, who can but laugh when he reads in Lucian of Homer's having been a camel in Bactria, etc. (*Gallus*.) ↩

635. Χωρεῖν γὰρ ἀνάγκη τὸ ὅμοιον πρὸς τὸ ὅμοιον: "For, of necessity, like things must go to each other." (Hierocles, *Commentary on the Carmen Aureum*.) ↩

636. *Ex humili atque depresso in eum emicabit locum, quisquis ille est, qui solutas vinculis animas beato recipit sinu*: "It will mount up, from this low mean place into that, whatever it be, which receives those souls that are freed from their imprisonment into its happy bosom." (Seneca, *De Consolatione ad Polybium*.) Ἡ τῆς θνητῆς προσπαθειας ἀπιβολὴ, καὶ ἡ τῶν ἀρετῶν, οἷον πτερῶν τινων, ἔκφυσις πρὸς τὸν τῶν καλῶν καθαρὸν τόπον, εἰς τὴν θείαν εὐζωΐαν ἡμᾶς ἀνάξει: "The putting off these human affections, and putting on virtues as so many wings, will carry us to that pure region of virtue where we shall live a divine life." (Hierocles, *Commentary on the Carmen Aureum*.) ↩

637. *Depositâ sarcinâ, levior volavit ad cœlum*: "Having laid down our burden, we shall fly the lighter to heaven." (St. Jerome, *Epistles*.) ↩

638. The Jews, who generally say that by the practice of religion the soul acquires perfection and life eternal, lay such a stress upon *habits* of piety, that Rabbi Albo makes the effect of giving 1,000 *zuzin*, "pence" in charity at once by no means equal to that of giving one *zuz*, "penny," and repeating it 1,000 times, התמדת עשיית פעל אחד בעצמו יקנה מדרגה יותר גדולה מעשיית הפעל ההוא פעם אחת: "The continuing to repeat the doing of a thing will procure a higher degree (of reward) than the doing the whole at once." (*Sefer ha-Ikkarim*.) ↩

639. כל עושה מצות הבורא יתברך ימצא שכל טוב.... והגמול הנמשך אחר השכל האמיתי הוא השארת הנפש אחר כלות הגוף והדבקו בשכל הפועל והיותו קים לעד: "He that does the commandment of the Creator shall be blessed; he shall find good understanding... and that reward which follows good understanding, is that the soul shall continue after the body is consumed, and shall be united to the understanding of its Maker, and be established to eternity." (Is. Levi.) ↩

640. Τόπους προσήκοντας τῇ ἀρετῇ: "Places fitted for virtue." (Plato, *Epinomis*.) ↵

641. With an equal or impartial regard to every man's deserts: equitably. ↵

642. "Spiritual body." (Editor's note.) ↵

643. Ἀγαθῶν ἐπὶ δαῖτας ἴασιν Αὐτόματοι ἀγαθοί: "Good men, when left to their own liberty, go to those entertainments where good men are." (Plato, *Symposium*.) ↵

644. Οἱ πεφιλοσοφηκότες ὀρθῶς or οἱ ἀληθῶς φιλόσοφοι: "they who rightly philosophize," or, "they who are truly philosophers," in Plato's style. (*Phaedo*.) ↵

645. Τελευτήσαντας αὐτοὺς ἐκεῖνος μὲν ὁ τῶν κακῶν καθαρὸς τόπος οὐ δέξεται, ἐνθάδε δὲ τὴν αὐτοῖς ὁμοιότητα τῆς διαγωγῆς ἀεὶ ἕξουσι, κακοὶ κακοῖς συνόντες: "That place, in which there are no evils, will not receive them (the wicked) but they shall be with one another, and continue forever to lead the same sort of life that they led here." (Plato, *Theaetetus*.) ↵

646. Εἰ πλέον τῶν ἁμαρτημάτων κολάβεται *[ὁ δίκαιος]*, προθήκη δικαιοσύνης αὐτῷ λογίβεται: "If [a good man] be punished [here] beyond what his sins deserve, all that is above what he justly deserves shall be accounted for to him." (Johannes Chrysostom.) ↵

647. Sure those arguments in Lucretius can convince nobody, *Nunc quoniam, quassatis undique vasis, Diffluere humorem, et laticem discedere cernis… Crede animam quoque diffundi, etc.*: "For we see that as soon as the vessel is broken in pieces, the liquor runs all about; so the soul likewise will be dissipated, etc." And *Præterea gigni pariter cum corpore et unà Crescere sentimus, pariterque senescere mentem, etc. Quare animum quoque dissolvi fateare necesse est; Quandoquidem penetrant in eum contagia morbi*: "Further we see that the soul and the body are produced together, and increase and grow old together also, etc. Wherefore we cannot but own that the soul must be dissolved, for the contagion of the disease reaches to it." (*De Rerum Natura*.) Nor those in Pliny (*Naturalis Historia* 6. 55): if there really are any at all. For to plead the *antegenitale experimentum* ("argument drawn from what we were before we were born"), is to beg the question, which may be put thus: Whether we shall after death be more conscious of our existence than we were before we were born. And if Dicæarchus's *Lesbiaci* were extant, I believe we should find nothing stranger in them. The truth seems to be Οὐ βούλεται ὁ κακὸς ἀθάνατον εἶναι τὴν αὐτοῦ ψυχήν: "That a wicked man does not desire that his soul should be immortal," but he comforts himself with this thought, that ἡ μετὰ θάνατον οὐδένεια ἑαυτοῦ: "the being nothing after death" will prevent future sufferings. This is εἰς τὸ μὴ εἶναι καταφυγή: "to have recourse to nonexistence." (Hierocles, *Commentary on the Carmen Aureum*.) ↵

648. Nor that the soul still exists ἔρημον καταλιποῦσα ζωῆς τὸν ἡμέτερον οἶκον: "having left

the house, in which it lived, desolate." (Philo Judaeus, *De cherubim.*) *Domus ab habitatore deserta dilabitur:... et corpus, relictum ab anima, defluit*: "A house that is forsaken by the inhabitants becomes ruinous:... and a body, after it is forsaken by the soul, decays." (Lactantius, *Divine Institutes.*) ↩

649. Μακρὸς δὲ καὶ ὄρθιος οἶμος ἐς αὐτὴν [ἀρετήν], καὶ τρηχὺς τὸ πρῶτον · ἐπὴν δ᾽ εἰς ἄκρον ἵκηαι, Ῥηιδίη δ᾽ ἤπειτα πέλει: "The way to virtue is long and steep, and very rugged at first; but, after you are come at the top, it then becomes easy." (Hesiod, *Works and Days.*) ↩

650. *Cœlo præfertur Adonis*: "Adonis is preferred to heaven." (Ovid, *Metamorphoses.*) ↩

651. Ὁ ἀρετῇ διαπρέπων καὶ ἡδονὰς ἀμεταμελήτους καρποῦται: "He who excels in virtue, reaps pleasures that can never be repented of." (Hierocles, *Commentary on the Carmen Aureum.*) ↩

652. If the soul was mortal, yet the virtuous man τὴν ἑαυτοῦ τελειότητα ἀπολαμβάνων, τὸ οἰκεῖον καρπούμενος ἀγαθὸν, εὐδαίμων ὄντως ἐστὶ καὶ μακάριος καὶ γὰρ καὶ τὸ σῶμα, κτλ.: "becomes as perfect as he can be, reaps his own proper good, being truly blessed and happy: and the body also, etc." (Simplicius, *Commentary on the Enchiridion.*) ↩

653. Ὥστε μὴ μόνον τῷ καλῷ περιεῖναι τὸν σπουδαῖον τοῦ φαύλου, ἀλλὰ καὶ αὐτῇ τῇ ἡδονῇ νικᾶν, δι᾽ ἣν μόνην δοκεῖ εἰς κακίαν ὁ φαῦλος ὑπάγεσθαι: "So that a good man excels a bad man not only in goodness, but he exceeds him in pleasure also, by which alone the bad man was led to be wicked." (Hierocles, *Commentary on the Carmen Aureum.*) ↩

654. Οἱ γὰρ δίκαιοι τῶν ἀδίκων, εἰ μηδὲν ἄλλο πλεονεκτοῦσιν, ἀλλ᾽ οὖν ἐλπίσι γε σπουδαίαις ὑπερέχουσιν: "If the righteous do not excel the wicked in anything else, yet they do in their expectations of happiness." (Isocrates, *Demonicus.*) ↩

655. Τρόπος γὰρ θεοῦ θεραπείας ὗτος ὁσιώτατος [ἀσκεῖν ἀρετήν]: "For [to practice virtue] is the most sacred manner of worshipping God." (Josephus, *Against Apion.*) ↩

656. Some more were added in the second impression. ↩

657. Nothing more was intended at first. ↩

658. However, "W. B." in *Notes and Queries* (#61, 27 February 1875) writes: "Though obliged to grope in the dark, through not having the works of Maimonides at hand, I venture to dissent from the interpretation given by Dr. Clarke... Instead of supposing, as he seems to have done, that the right-hand group of letters are the initials of the word *Mi cha el*, which compose the name *Michael* and signify 'Who [is] like God?' I take them to represent *Mah cha emeth*, substituting *emeth* for *el*, and to mean 'What [is] like

truth?' In the left-hand group I take the first two characters (from right to left) to be an abbreviation for the personal pronoun *othah*... and the remaining letter to represent the verb *lachad*, to seize, lay hold of. The two mysterious Hebrew words would thus mean, 'What is like truth? On her fix thy hold'..." (Editor's note.) ↵